Macroeconomic Modeling

Bridging the gap between undergraduate and graduate macroeconomics, this book approaches DSGE models from a unified perspective based on the concept of competitive equilibrium (CE) and the equivalent social planner problem (SPP). Equilibrium conditions derived from a CE are used to motivate the methods that solve the models. A guided focus on Dynare enables students to solve problems while avoiding the typical pitfalls associated with the software. The approach is "we have a need and here's a tool that solves it," instead of "here's a tool and let's look for an application." It is consistent with current practices: define an equilibrium, characterize its solution, find its steady state, approximate the equilibrium conditions, and solve for its policy functions. This book is for the student who wants to follow current macroeconomic research and build on that to gain a competitive edge in creating and solving empirical models with real-world applicability.

Mario Solis-Garcia is Professor of Economics at Macalester College in Saint Paul, Minnesota, where he teaches courses in macroeconomics. He holds a PhD in Economics from the University of Minnesota and an MA in Economics from El Colegio de Mexico. Professor Solis-Garcia worked for the Mexican government in the Secretariat of Trade and Industry, the Secretariat of the Economy, and the Secretariat of the Treasury and Public Credit. He has authored several academic publications that center around computational macroeconomics and the pedagogy of teaching macroeconomics at the undergraduate level.

Macroeconomic Modeling

A Gentle Introduction to DSGE Models

MARIO SOLIS-GARCIA
Macalester College, Minnesota

CAMBRIDGE
UNIVERSITY PRESS

CAMBRIDGE
UNIVERSITY PRESS

Shaftesbury Road, Cambridge CB2 8EA, United Kingdom

One Liberty Plaza, 20th Floor, New York, NY 10006, USA

477 Williamstown Road, Port Melbourne, VIC 3207, Australia

314–321, 3rd Floor, Plot 3, Splendor Forum, Jasola District Centre,
New Delhi – 110025, India

Cambridge University Press is part of Cambridge University Press & Assessment,
a department of the University of Cambridge.

We share the University's mission to contribute to society through the pursuit of
education, learning and research at the highest international levels of excellence.

www.cambridge.org
Information on this title: www.cambridge.org/highereducation/isbn/9781009612906

DOI: 10.1017/9781009612913

When citing this work, please include a reference to the DOI 10.1017/9781009612913

First published 2027

Cover image: Sean Gladwell / Moment / Getty Images.

A catalogue record for this publication is available from the British Library

A Cataloging-in-Publication data record for this book is available from the Library of Congress

ISBN 978-1-009-61290-6 Hardback
ISBN 978-1-009-61289-0 Paperback

Additional resources for this publication at www.cambridge.org/solis-garcia

Contents

Figures

Preface

Why Do We Need DSGE Models?

The answer is: because **dynamic stochastic general equilibrium** (DSGE) models have become the workhorse of modern macroeconomics and the standard way to communicate ideas among applied macroeconomists. (Also, borrowing a line from Galí 2018, because macroeconomists would be rightfully criticized if we only relied on static, deterministic, and partial equilibrium models!)

Designed to rival structural macroeconometric models – and to stay clear of the Lucas critique (Lucas 1976) – DSGE models have multiplied in the profession, serving as laboratories for testing theories, inputs for policymakers (e.g., Del Negro et al. 2013), and even tools for forecasting the business cycle (e.g., Del Negro & Schorfheide 2013).

Yet the ethos of quantitative macroeconomics is put forward by Lucas (1980):

> One of the functions of theoretical economics is to provide fully articulated, artificial economic systems that can serve as laboratories in which policies that would be prohibitively expensive to experiment with in actual economies can be tested out at much lower cost . . . Our task as I see it . . . is to write a FORTRAN program that will accept specific economic policy rules as "input" and will generate as "output" statistics describing the operating characteristics of time series we care about, which are predicted to result from these policies.

Put differently, our aim is to create models that can replicate the real world along some key dimensions (to be decided by the modeler) and then, once we have a reasonable degree of trust in the model, run experiments (what Lucas calls "policies") and see what our artificial model of the economy predicts as outcomes.

But what are these key dimensions? How can we be sure that our model is "replicating" the real world? Answering this question is a bit trickier, but in that same paper, Lucas offers a hint:

> At the same time, not all well-articulated models will be equally useful. Though we are interested in models because we believe they may help us to understand matters about which we are currently ignorant, we need to test them as useful imitations of reality by subjecting them to shocks for which we are fairly certain how actual economies, or parts of economies, would react. The more dimensions on which the model mimics the answers actual economies give to simple questions, the more we trust its answers to harder questions. This is the sense in which more "realism" in a model is clearly preferred to less.
>
> On this general view of the nature of economic theory then, a "theory" is not a collection of assertions about the behavior of the actual economy but rather an explicit set of instructions for building a parallel or analogue system – a mechanical, imitation economy. A "good" model, from this point of view, will not be exactly more "real" than a poor one, but will provide better imitations. Of course, what one means by a "better imitation" will depend on the particular questions to which one wishes answers.

The guidelines for said realism come, again, from an earlier paper (Lucas, 1977, emphasis in original):

> Let me begin to sharpen the discussion by reviewing the main qualitative features of economic time series which we call "the business cycle." Technically, movements about trend in gross [domestic] product . . . do not exhibit uniformity of either period or amplitude, which is to say, they do not resemble the deterministic wave motions which sometimes arise in the natural sciences. Those regularities which are observed are in the *co-movements* among different aggregative time series.

What are these **co-movements** that Lucas talks about? In a nutshell, these correspond to the idea that economic variables move together *in predictable ways*. For example, the deviations from trend in consumption are positively correlated with those of output, and the deviations from trend in investment are much more volatile than those of output (and in turn, those of consumption). Moreover, most macroeconomic variables are highly **persistent**, meaning that if a variable is currently above its trend, it will tend to stay above trend – unlike, say, the time series implied by the flips of a fair coin.

What is remarkable about these co-movements is that we observe them regardless of the state of the economy or the world: for example, these patterns are clearly observed in the United States across time, no matter if the country has a Democrat or Republican president, if there is a war going on, or if the economy is booming or in the middle of a recession. Thus, the real world tells us that we should expect these patterns – and that's what our models will try to imitate before we set them up as artificial labs to test out some policies.

As with most things in life, a picture is worth a thousand words. Chapter 1 begins by showing a set of graphs – and some handy tables – that illustrate these co-movements using US data. (To be fair, I use the United States as an example due to the rich datasets that are available to the public. Most countries, if not all, will exhibit these co-movements as well.)

What This Book Is About

As its name suggests, this book offers a gentle yet rigorous introduction to DSGE modeling. It links theory and practice and is aided by companion codes in Dynare (available for MATLAB and Julia).

But why is a book of this nature needed in the first place? Fernández-Villaverde, Rubio-Ramírez, and Schorfheide (2016, p. 530) share that: "Unfortunately for [economics] PhD students and fortunately for those who have worked with DSGE models for a long time, the barriers to entry into the DSGE literature are quite high." These words apply to PhD-level students, yet if these barriers are in place for graduate students, common sense suggests that undergraduate students do not stand a chance, and the divergence between graduate and undergraduate macroeconomics will go on forever.

Can we make these barriers go away? I say yes. If I've piqued your interest, read on. (But before that, a fair warning.)

What This Book Is *Not* About

Despite my best intentions, this is not a book on macroeconomic theory. Rather, it is a book that explains how to use – and the logic behind – the tools, methods, and "tricks" that applied macroeconomists use when building models.

To use an analogy, suppose the reader wants to learn Spanish literature from the late twentieth century. This book would then cover modern Spanish grammar and offer one or two relevant essays written by Spanish authors to clarify the relevant ideas. Working through the book would offer the tools to better understand the literature, but not provide a definitive source to everything there is to it.

The same situation applies in this case. I do my best to cite references when they are closely linked to the tools at hand, but I generally stay clear of deep discussions regarding macroeconomic theory. As a somewhat crude approximation, the *Handbooks of Macroeconomics* (1999 and 2016) and *Monetary Economics* (1990 and 2010) add up to over 7,200 pages, and they still don't cover every single aspect of modern macro theory. Trying to achieve this feat in this book would be a foolish (and perhaps irresponsible) task.

Book Features

The book is as self-contained as can be, and it assumes little beyond (a) intermediate macroeconomics, (b) some basic familiarity with coding, and (c) calculus and optimization before moving forward with the material. (Of course, the more mathematical maturity, the better. There is no such thing as having taken "too many math courses.")

Overall, two goals drive this book. First, I want to help students get as close as possible to the macroeconomics research frontier: I believe students should be able to access and understand the top journals and papers in the field (and alas, as we know, this task is far from trivial). Second, I want to increase students' human capital and make them attractive candidates in the labor market or graduate school applications. Far too many undergraduates have felt intimidated by the sheer amount of material and new ideas found in first-year PhD macroeconomics. Mastering the tools found in this book should make them feel less overwhelmed.

Maybe you, dear reader, are wondering "*But why not just aim for the big ideas found in the abstract/introduction/conclusion of DSGE papers? Isn't that enough?*" As the quote from Fernández-Villaverde et al. suggests, there is a "secret handshake" that makes reading (and understanding) papers at the research frontier rather hard for an uninitiated undergraduate. The average DSGE paper contains many insights that go beyond talking points drilled during class; these insights are important *because of the underlying economic mechanisms*, and it's hard to appreciate these mechanisms without a clear understanding of DSGE models.

Here's my attempt to say the same idea using econometrics lingo: I want students to understand how ordinary least-square regression coefficients can be derived with linear algebra and why the equation $\beta = \left(X^{\mathrm{T}}X\right)^{-1}X^{\mathrm{T}}Y$ makes sense. I don't want them to just know that said coefficients characterize the "best fit" line and can be obtained in Stata after typing "`regress y x`."

This book is unique in that it approaches DSGE models from a unified perspective based on the concept of **competitive equilibrium** (CE). (No, I don't forget about the concept of the social planner problem. But the fact that not every DSGE model can be tackled with a planner problem closes the deal for me.) As such, equilibrium theory takes center stage and is a building block of everything that we do in the text. Moreover, equilibrium conditions derived from a CE (or a social planner problem) are then used to motivate the methods that solve the models; put differently, the approach in the book is "we have a need and here's a tool that solves it" instead of "here's a tool and let's look for an application." In this sense, the book's approach is consistent with current practice in macroeconomics: we define an equilibrium, characterize its solution, find its steady state, approximate the equilibrium conditions, and solve for its policy functions.

I emphasize first-order linearization methods and intentionally avoid more complicated solution techniques (e.g., value function iteration, higher-order linearization, etc.). The reason behind this choice is simple: first-order approximations (log-linearization in particular) allow students to "see" how the equilibrium conditions become inputs to the solution method; moreover, the procedure for log-linearizing equations is simple enough to be done with pen and paper, which aids with intuition and understanding. (Some of my fellow macroeconomists may disagree on the choice to *avoid* dynamic programming tools, yet I've found that undergraduates have a really hard time understanding the foundations of this topic up to a point that allows them to internalize, say, what value function iteration is about. As time is precious during a 14-week semester, the tradeoff is not worth it for me.)

Target Audience

This book is a natural fit for an advanced undergraduate or graduate-level course in macroeconomics. Indeed, there is a large gap between undergraduate and graduate macroeconomics. This gap is a consequence of the traditional approach to college-level education, where the emphasis is placed on "getting the intuition right" as opposed to putting the technical aspects in place. This textbook aims to bridge the gap between what students cover in intermediate macroeconomics and what they will likely face in their first year of graduate school.

In this sense, I see three potential audiences for this book. First, advanced undergraduates and their professors, who might be itching to teach their students the same concepts that they learned in their PhD training. Second, MA or incoming first-year PhD students in economics (or even pre-docs!) who want to build bridges between what they learned in college and what they are currently facing in their coursework. Finally, PhD economists who have specialized in a different field, but want to get into macroeconomics in a fairly painless way.

Pedagogical Approach

Most resources aiming to teach DSGE macroeconomics decide to skip one step – or maybe all of them! My journey was one of frequent starts and stops: when learning how to use or apply a tool (or a model), oftentimes I couldn't find an example or blueprint to follow. These frustrations led me to become a firm believer in learning by doing (and Lucas 1993 would agree): there is value in *replicating* a simple model if said model can be used as a template for richer exercises. Throughout the book I offer many opportunities to interact with the material – from verifying a simple calculation to full-blown replication exercises – and this design choice allows students to get comfortable with the ideas surrounding DSGE models. If you like getting your hands dirty, this is the book for you.

Computational Approach

When this project started, my goal was to offer a triple-language approach: all the concepts in the book would be thoroughly explained and, at the end of the day, the reader would have the tools to replicate these in Dynare (using either Matlab or Julia) or Python. Alas, I was unsuccessful in meeting this goal.

On one hand, it is true that Matlab and Julia are fairly similar, with the advantage going to Julia as it is open source and, consequently, free. Python, however, has a completely different syntax and internal logic, which would imply writing long appendices to account for how programming languages differ and their own characteristics. Since Brian Jenkins already offers a suite of Python-based DSGE tools, I found that trying to replicate his work would provide little value added – far better to explain the logic behind the models and then let Python users rely on his existing code to solve DSGE models.

On the other hand, while Dynare's implementation of Julia does exist at the time of writing, it only contains a small subset of the full suite of tools that are available to Matlab users. Dynare, however, is its own programming language and the same file (say, `test_run.mod`) can be used in both languages; for Matlab, just write

```
>> dynare test_run
```

whereas for Julia, the syntax is slightly more complicated:

```
julia> context = @dynare test_run.mod;
```

What matters for this book is that the file itself, `test_run.mod`, is identical in both cases. I can thus make an argument that Matlab and Julia are the engines that drive Dynare, but the instructions that allow me to go from point A to point B are the same no matter which engine I choose (with the caveat that the set of instructions supported by Julia is, at the time of writing, smaller relative to Matlab).

Given these details, I've decided to port the book's material to Dynare directly, bypassing the main engine, which, I assume, will be whatever the reader feels more comfortable with. (For what it's worth, throughout the book I add snippets of Matlab code; Julia users should feel right at home.)

A Suggested Roadmap

When designing the book, I had two goals in mind. First, the book should be as self-contained as possible. Second, the chapters ought to be modular, minimizing the dependency among them.

I believe that the first goal has been (mostly) accomplished. The book contains plenty of examples, end-of-chapter problems, and actual code to allow readers to learn by doing. There are appendices on linear algebra basics (Appendix A) and models with trend growth (Appendix B) at the end of the book, followed by Appendices C–H giving details relevant to specific chapters. Three additional appendices on calculus and basic optimization (Online Appendix 1), solving nonlinear systems of equations (Online Appendix 2), and an introduction to the Solow growth model (Online Appendix 3) are offered online, together with solutions to selected problems and additional codes.

Regarding the second goal, I also believe I have succeeded in creating a "choose your own adventure" book. Students who have used equilibrium-based tools in their intermediate macroeconomics courses – say, after using Williamson (2017) – could skim the components of Part I and start on Part II by reviewing the notion of a steady state (Chapter 5) and stochastic shocks (Chapter 6). That said, Part II is integral and should be covered by all students regardless of their background.

At this point the book opens up two possibilities. Instructors who wish to focus on real business cycle (RBC) models can spend time in Part III and, time permitting, spend some time in Part V for a brief coverage of macroeconometrics (Chapter 16). Alternatively, instructors who want to emphasize nominal frictions (and the New Keynesian model) may want to cover the canonical RBC model (Chapter 10 and one or two of the real frictions contained in Part III) before moving along to Part IV.

New Keynesian models are a completely different animal relative to RBC models, but Part IV provides a thorough exposition that clarifies how they work and all the "tricks" needed to go from the definition of equilibrium to the usual three-equation system of an IS curve, a Phillips curve, and a Taylor rule. For space considerations I have omitted many interesting variations on this class of models (e.g., sticky wages or TANK models), but it is my hope that the foundations contained in Chapters 14 and 15 are a good starting point for covering these (slightly more advanced) topics.

Finally, the last chapter in the book deals with Bayesian estimation with Dynare. As Part II includes a primer on parametrization using calibration, learning Bayesian methods is not really critical for getting the models to work. That said, instructors who are keen to get their students closer to the frontier can use the contents of Chapter 16 to motivate the use of econometrics in DSGE models.

To summarize, a 10-week undergraduate course could take Parts I and II (possibly omitting the former) and specialize on either Part III or IV depending on the interests of the instructor and students. A 14-week undergraduate course (like the one I teach at Macalester College) has a bit more room to include chapters; I have successfully covered Parts I through IV (to be fair, not all chapters are covered at a deep level) and, when the students are strong, some bits of Part V. Of course, at an advanced level, the instructor will know how much to push the students – who should be able to handle most of what's contained in the book on their own.

Some Words of Wisdom to Instructors (and Students)

To All Readers of This Book All computer programs have bugs – and books are no different. Even though I've tried my best to eliminate all mistakes that could embarrass me, errors may still (and will) be around, and no one is to blame but me. Should you happen to find one such error or typo, please tell me about it, so I can fix it and add it to the inevitable Errata document. (Also, you never know when a second edition might pop up.)

To Instructors of This Book I hope you enjoy reading this book – and incorporating it in your courses (or research). If you're skimming through these pages, there's a chance that you started from the same place as me: you wanted to teach a course on DSGE macroeconomics but couldn't find a reasonable resource to help you out. Perhaps you thought this feat wasn't possible and left the idea on the side. Maybe you thought it was possible but the target audience was limited to graduate students, who were supposed to learn these methods on their own anyway, so the project was self-defeating. Or maybe you tried to write a book like this one, but came face to face with the tenure clock (and then remembered that the name of the game rhymes with "published papers" and not "textbooks").

If some (or all) of these origin stories fit you, then this book will help you to share your knowledge of modern macroeconomics with your students. At this time I do not think that you will face any challenges when doing this, for the simple reason that I expect that you are already familiar with the "secret handshake." All that remains to say is: Godspeed.

To Students Using This Book I hope you enjoy working through this book – and learning what modern macroeconomics is all about. Maybe you've been told that the undergraduate macroeconomic curriculum consists of IS–LM–AS models (e.g., De Araujo, O'Sullivan & Simpson 2013) paired with some version of the Solow growth model and you don't know what the DSGE fuss is all about. This conception is mostly correct, but you'll be in for a surprise if you decide to go to graduate school in economics. Alas, there won't be any trace of IS–LM–AS anymore; instead, everything will look like a Solow growth model on steroids (more precisely, a *neoclassical growth model*) – or worse. You'll feel like you're learning another language, because that's exactly what you'll be doing.

Of course, maybe you have no intention of going to graduate school. You might be taking this course because you appreciate the professor, need the credits for your major, or because it's the only option that fits your schedule – and you need to graduate. If some (or all) of these origin stories fit you, just know that I've spent a lot of time thinking about how to teach you the secret handshake. You'll learn some neat tools, understand the concepts behind really cool papers, and add one or two computing tools to your kit. If this is the last time you deal with macroeconomics and have no plan to return, at the very least I hope that this book increases your human capital to some degree.

But at the same time, you can't fall in love with something you don't know exists. Who knows? Maybe you will.

Acknowledgments

No project of this nature is created in a vacuum, and there is a long list of people who have influenced and motivated this work. The genesis of this book goes all the way back to the University of Minnesota, where I learned the ropes of applied theory from Ellen McGrattan. (Or at least, I tried to. Strictly speaking, I never submitted the last problem set!) Simran Sahi, in her position as Director of Undergraduate Students, also deserves a lot of credit for allowing me to teach a course whose last instructor had been, of all people, Ed Prescott. Finally, V. V. Chari, as my dissertation advisor, helped me focus on the task at hand and navigate the last years of the program until I managed to defend my thesis. To all of you, my most heartfelt thanks.

Of course, being an instructor necessarily requires students, and I have been fortunate enough to have taught quite a few (more than I anticipated) over my teaching life at the University of Minnesota and Macalester College. Every student who had to endure me for 14 weeks deserves a big "thank you," as they went above and beyond and pointed out several obvious (and not-so-obvious) typos and errors in the notes that eventually became this book – and for teaching me how to think about the material in order to make it clear.

That said, I'd be remiss not to give special thanks to a handful of them who are making (or will make) their way to become stars in the profession. Sasha Indarte, Hossein Alidaee, Yingtong Xie, and Stefan Faridani have already started their academic careers, while Valeska Kohan, Cheikh Fall, Paige Stevenson, Grace Ellsworth, Anna Durall, Gavin Engelstad, Samina Stack, and Zak Yudhishthu are, at the time of writing, starting their graduate programs – or getting ready for them while working on their pre-docs.

I also want to express my gratitude to Melanie McFadyen and Wendy Ashenberg from Cambridge University Press. To Melanie, for taking a chance on this project; to Wendy, for keeping me on track and giving me the necessary encouragement to complete a project like this one.

Finally, I thank my wife Blanca for being an awesome team player, standing by me from year one in grad school up to being promoted to full professor – and also for being polite enough not to question why typing up my notes (or preparing for class) took so much time, which could obviously have been distributed in a different fashion.

To everyone in this list – and to everyone I forgot to mention but who still managed to help me be who I am today – thank you.

1 Macroeconomic Variable Co-Movements

This chapter starts by studying what the real world looks like. Building models *for the sake of building models* has never been a good idea; rather, we want to understand the properties and dynamics of real-world data before we get to work on the modeling piece.

The material that follows aims to show the regularities and co-movements that Lucas (1980) tells us about. (See the Preface for details.) Section 1.1 starts at the foundation of everything, by discussing GDP and the transformations that macroeconomists use before working with this variable. Section 1.2 takes this discussion a step further by decomposing real GDP into trend and cycle via the Hodrick–Prescott filter. Section 1.3 talks about the "big ratios" and Section 1.4 wraps up by showing (both graphically and in tables) how Lucas's co-movements look in practice.

1.1 Gross Domestic Product

I begin this book by exploring the *main* macroeconomic variable, namely, **gross domestic product** (GDP). As a refresher, remember that the **expenditure approach** to measuring GDP defines this measure as

$$Y \equiv C + X + G + NX,$$

where C denotes consumption, X is investment, G equals government expenditure, and NX represents net exports. On its own, GDP provides quite a bit of information, but macroeconomists often perform some transformations before putting it to use. Typically, a macroeconomist will

1. Divide the value of nominal GDP by the GDP deflator (a price index measure) in order to get real GDP.
2. Divide real GDP by population in order to get real GDP per capita.
3. Apply the natural log function to real GDP per capita in order to remove the exponential trend that is present in the data.
4. Apply the Hodrick–Prescott (HP) filter (Hodrick and Prescott 1997) in order to obtain percent deviations from trend in real GDP.

What about the last two steps, you ask? Well, before moving on, I should probably share more details about them.

Notation 1.1 To keep notation light, I will take "GDP" and "real GDP" to denote the same macroeconomic variable unless there is risk of confusion.

1.1.1 Intermezzo I: The Usefulness of the Natural Logarithm

While the log transformation might seem exotic, it is a very useful change of variable – especially when plotting a time series. As it turns out, the slope of the logged time series equals the growth rate of the variable. Formally,

Proposition 1.2 *Given a variable x_t, the slope of the graph of its logarithm approximates the growth rate of x_t.*

Proof. The growth rate γ of a macro variable x_t is defined by

$$\begin{aligned}\gamma_t &\equiv \frac{x_t - x_{t-1}}{x_{t-1}}\\ &= \frac{x_t}{x_{t-1}} - 1.\end{aligned}$$

I rearrange this expression as

$$\frac{x_t}{x_{t-1}} = 1 + \gamma_t \tag{1.1}$$

and apply the natural logarithm function to both sides

$$\log\left(\frac{x_t}{x_{t-1}}\right) = \log\left(1 + \gamma_t\right).$$

The laws of logarithms allow me to rewrite the left-hand side as

$$\log\left(\frac{x_t}{x_{t-1}}\right) = \log x_t - \log x_{t-1}.$$

Now I use this result: if γ_t is small (which it is, because it's a growth rate), then the right-hand side of equation (1.1) can be approximated as

$$\log(1 + \gamma_t) \approx \gamma_t.$$

(I provide a proof of this step in Appendix C.) Getting both sides together, I have

$$\log x_t - \log x_{t-1} \approx \gamma_t.$$

Since $\log x_t - \log x_{t-1}$ is the slope of the time-series graph between periods $t-1$ and t, the result follows. *Hint*: Remember rise over run. □

1.1.2 Intermezzo II: The Hodrick–Prescott Filter

Hodrick and Prescott (1997) develop what is likely the most often-used filtering procedure in macroeconomics. As to why it is useful, remember that real GDP per capita is a variable that grows most of the time; hence, if I use this measure to think about business cycles, I won't be able to say much since the inherent exponential growth in GDP will dwarf all other components. However, the fact that GDP grows means I can build a trend and then derive the business cycle residually, by subtracting observed GDP from trend. If I cast the series in logarithms, then I immediately obtain percent deviations from trend.

To set ideas, let a time series y_t (where $t = 1, 2, \ldots, T$) equal the sum of a *trend component* g_t and a *cyclical component* c_t, so that

$$y_t = g_t + c_t. \tag{1.2}$$

Hodrick and Prescott tell us that the (time-varying) trend g_t is obtained by solving

$$\min_{\{g_t\}_{t=-1}^{T}} \left\{ \sum_{t=1}^{T} (y_t - g_t)^2 + \lambda \sum_{t=1}^{T} \left[(g_t - g_{t-1}) - (g_{t-1} - g_{t-2}) \right]^2 \right\} \tag{1.3}$$

and, in a second step, c_t is obtained residually from (1.2). The solution to the minimization problem found in (1.3) yields the desired cycle and trend series. Note, importantly, that the "trend" varies over time – and depends on the time series under analysis.

Remark 1.3 The HP filter says nothing about the underlying economics of the series itself (in this case, real GDP) as the filter is a statistical tool only. So, if there's no economic meaning attached to the filter, why do macroeconomists use it? Because the cycles generated by the filter are consistent with business cycle fluctuations. Now for some context: in the United States, the start and end dates of expansions and recessions are determined by the Business Cycle Dating Committee at the National Bureau of Economic Research (NBER). Since the HP cycle of real GDP falls below trend at the same time the NBER declares a recession hits the United States, this tool becomes a useful shortcut to determine when fluctuations begin and end.

1.2 Real GDP: Trend and Cycle

Armed with these ideas, I now move on to analyze the behavior of (logged) real GDP. I center my attention over the period 1985Q1 to 2019Q4 (see the Bibliographic Notes to this chapter for details regarding this choice). Figure 1.1 presents two graphs. In part (a), I plot both the logarithm of GDP and its associated HP trend. Part (b) plots the HP cycle, calculated as the difference between the logarithm of GDP and its HP trend.

Figure 1.1(a) shows how the logarithm of GDP per capita has grown for most of the quarters in the sample. The obvious exceptions are periods next to recessions, which are indicated in the diagram with gray bars. (Also called *NBER recession dates.*) During this sample, the United States experienced two short recessions in 1991 and 2001, and a longer (and deeper) one in 2007–9, namely, the **Great Recession**. The dashed line in the figure shows the HP trend of real GDP; note how the series closely follows observed GDP and slows down considerably during the Great Recession.

Subtracting the HP trend from observed GDP yields the HP cycle. This series is shown in Figure 1.1(b). While GDP moves from being above trend to below trend – and vice versa – over time, there is **persistence** in this pattern. For example, look at the trough

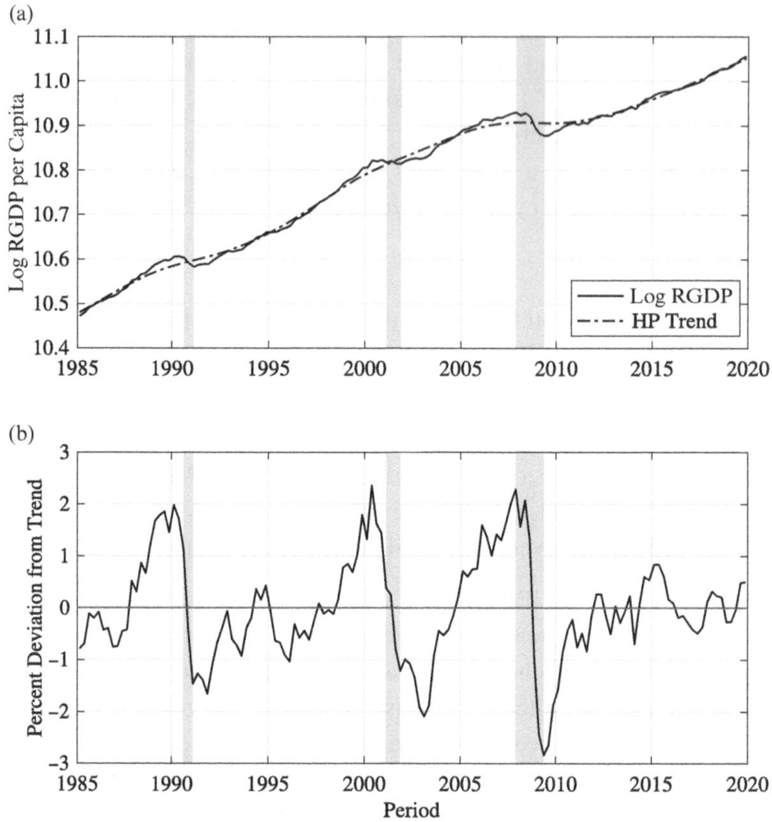

Figure 1.1 (a) United States, log real GDP per capita and Hodrick–Prescott trend. (b) Percent deviation from real GDP trend according to the Hodrick–Prescott cycle. Gray bars denote NBER recession dates.

immediately following the 2001 recession. Since GDP is below trend, it tends to stay below trend – and it is not until 2005 that the series crosses over the zero line. Conversely, if GDP is above trend, it tends to stay above trend – but not forever. Moreover, it is clear that HP-cycle "recessions" are consistent with the ones identified by the NBER (as shown by the gray bars).

1.3 The "Big Ratios"

Another stylized feature of macroeconomic data is the fact that the *ratios* of the expenditure components (consumption, net exports, etc.) relative to GDP are surprisingly constant over time. When referring to this feature, macroeconomists often talk about the **big ratios**.

It's easy to see how these ratios get their name. Figure 1.2 shows the evolution of these variables over 1985Q1 to 2019Q4; for example, the C/Y ratio average equals 66.1% while

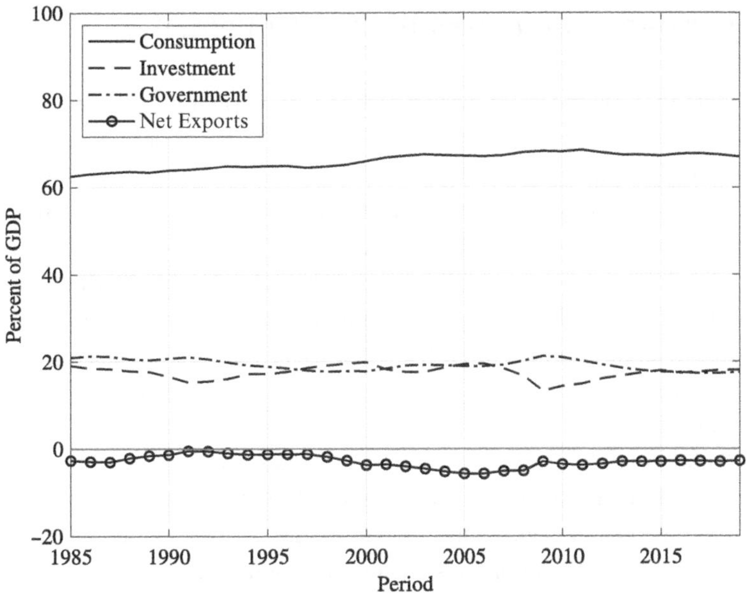

Figure 1.2 The big (expenditure) ratios: consumption, investment, government expenditure, and net exports as a fraction of GDP.

the G/Y ratio is 19.3%. The fact that these values remain steady over time is another feature of the business cycle, and I will rely on these ratios later in the book.

Similarly, the capital-to-output ratio also remains fairly constant over time. Throughout the sample, the ratio averages 2.91. Figure 1.3 presents the evolution of this variable over time.

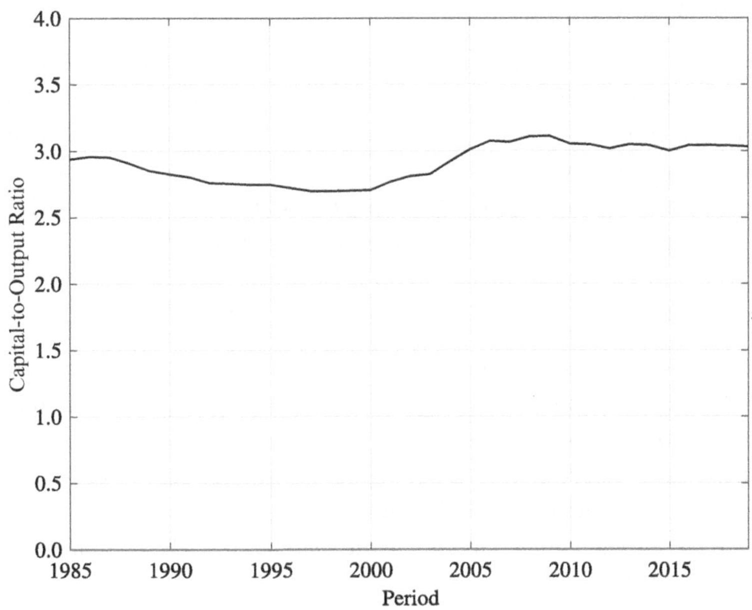

Figure 1.3 The capital-to-output ratio.

1.4 Macroeconomic Variable Co-Movements

I now look at the co-movements between economic variables. Traditionally, macroeconomists compare the percent deviations from trend in a given variable (say, investment) with those of real GDP. An economic variable is **procyclical** if its deviations from trend are positively correlated with those of real GDP, **countercyclical** if negatively correlated, and **acyclical** if the correlation is zero or very small in absolute value.

Similarly, macroeconomists look at the volatility of a variable *relative* to that of real GDP. Variables like investment or imports are much more volatile than real GDP, while hours worked or employment are just as volatile (and consumption is much less volatile). These stylized features of the data are the co-movements that Lucas (1977) talks about.

While I could present a battery of graphs showing how every possible economic variable is related to real GDP, in the interest of space I restrict my analysis to a select few series and then present a summary of statistics below. (King & Rebelo 1999 provide such a battery of graphs.) For consistency, all graphs use the sample 1985Q1–2019Q4.

Notation 1.4 To avoid repetition, I will no longer write "the log of real GDP per capita" and use the much lighter "GDP" or "output" label instead. The same applies to all other economic variables (e.g., "durable consumption" stands for "the log of real durable consumption per capita"). Since all the variables in this chapter are transformed in the same way, there is no room for confusion.

1.4.1 Graphical Analysis

Consumption

Figure 1.4 presents the co-movement between GDP (thick line) and aggregate consumption (thin line), defined as the sum of durable, nondurable, and services consumption. This graph clearly shows the co-movement between both series: the deviations from trend of consumption move alongside those of GDP, and it is clear from the diagram that aggregate consumption is a procyclical variable. While it is a bit hard to discern from the graph, consumption is slightly less volatile than output, but not much so.

Investment

Aggregate investment equals the sum of residential and nonresidential investment (the former corresponds to housing while the latter is what firms purchase in order to produce goods), plus change in firms' inventories. Figure 1.5 presents the co-movement of investment with respect to GDP. Aggregate investment is procyclical – though this is not immediately obvious given the difference in scales between both series. Indeed, aggregate investment is much more volatile than GDP – which is another of the stylized facts from the data.

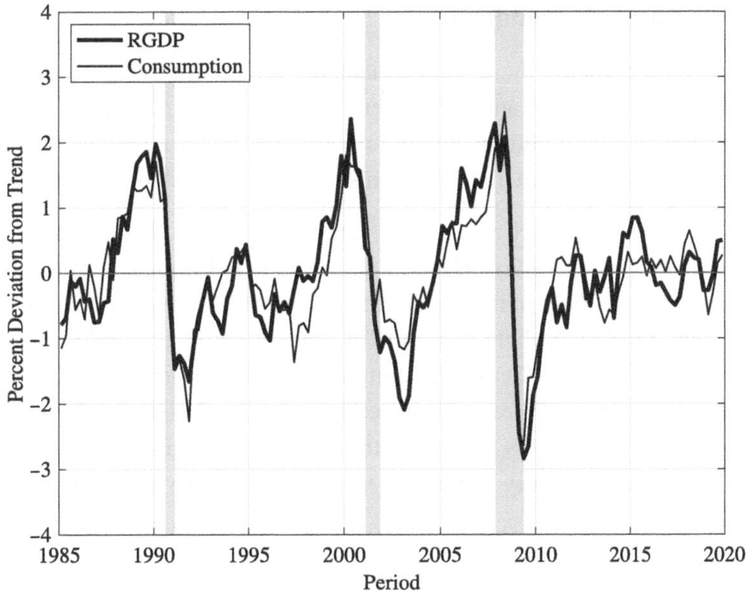

Figure 1.4 Co-movement: GDP (thick line) and aggregate consumption (thin line). Gray bars denote NBER recession dates.

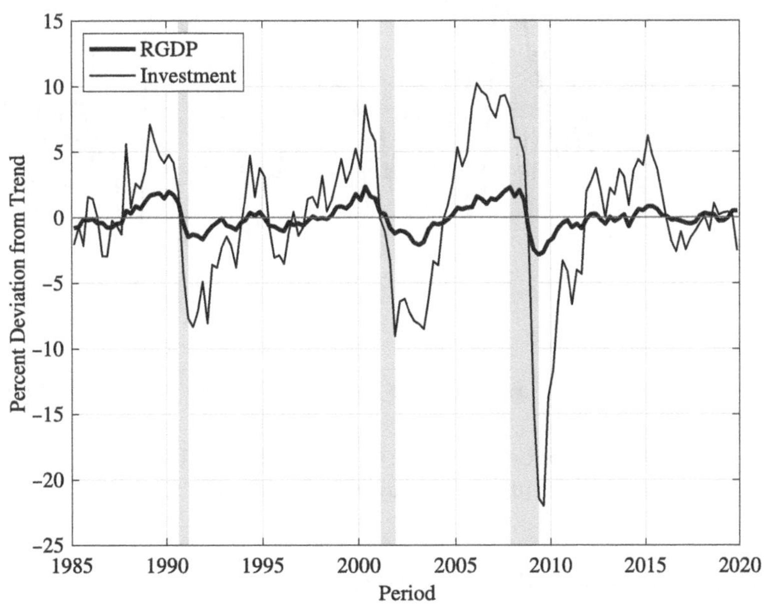

Figure 1.5 Co-movement: GDP (thick line) and aggregate investment (thin line). Gray bars denote NBER recession dates.

Government Expenditure

Figure 1.6 presents the co-movement of GDP and total government expenditure (the sum of federal, state, and local spending). A surprising feature about this graph is that government expenditure is countercyclical – just as traditional Keynesian theory says it ought to be. Note the volatility of this series is comparable to that of output.

Remark 1.5 The cyclicality and volatility of government expenditure should be taken with a grain of salt. Why? Because in the models I'll present in the book, this variable is taken as exogenous (unlike most other ones, which are endogenously determined within the model). Hence, there is room for feedback effects: while government expenditure mechanically affects GDP (since output is defined as the sum of consumption, investment, government expenditure, and net exports), it is also likely that policymakers respond to the state of GDP by changing the level of government expenditure – just as traditional Keynesian theory suggests. Disentangling these feedback effects is hard to say the least.

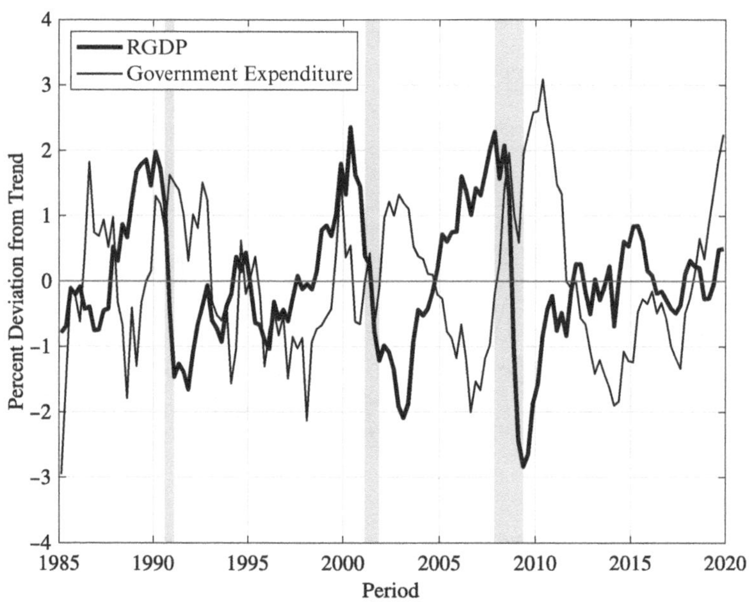

Figure 1.6 Co-movement: GDP (thick line) and total government expenditure (thin line). Gray bars denote NBER recession dates.

Hours Worked and Productivity

In theory, hours worked and GDP should track each other very closely. Since output requires labor as an input, periods with high output require a large number of hours, and vice versa. Figure 1.7 confirms this theory. Hours worked are procyclical and slightly more volatile than output.

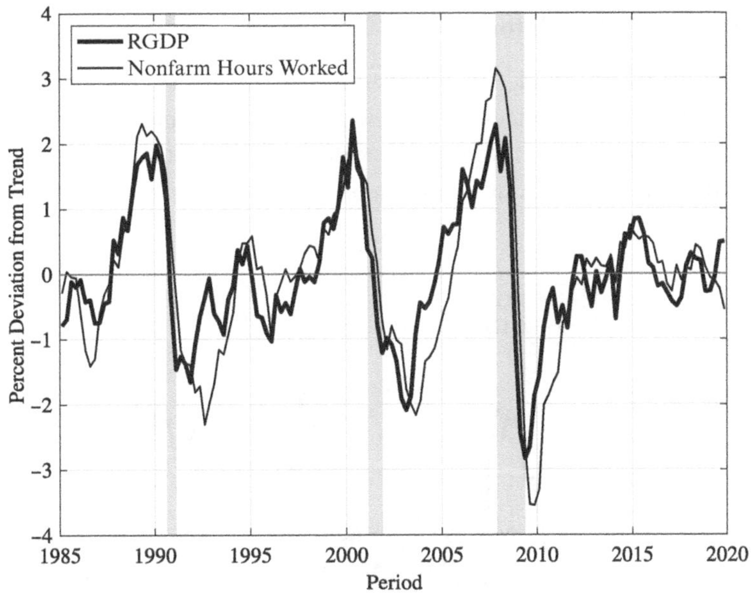

Figure 1.7 Co-movement: GDP (thick line) and nonfarm hours worked (thin line). Gray bars denote NBER recession dates.

Similarly, productivity is defined as the amount of output produced per hour worked. Perhaps surprisingly, per Figure 1.8, productivity seems to be slightly countercyclical – and much less volatile than output.

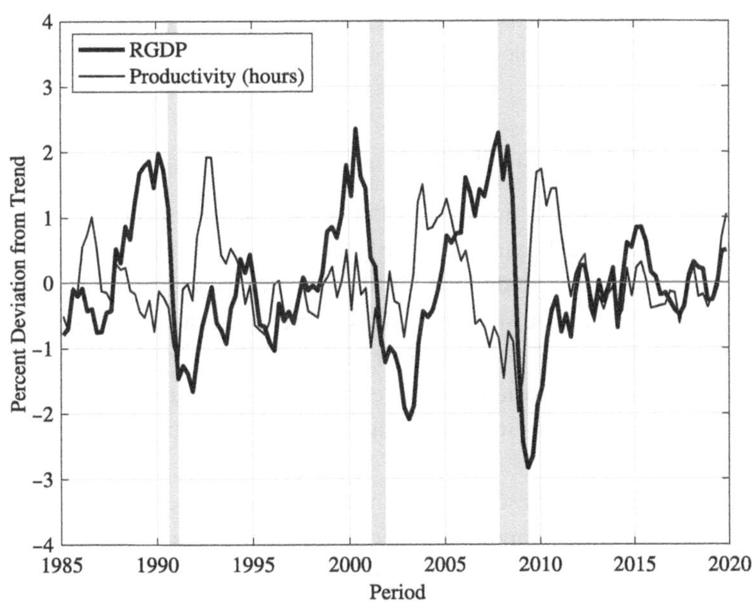

Figure 1.8 Co-movement: GDP (thick line) and output per hour worked (thin line). Gray bars denote NBER recession dates.

Prices (GDP Deflator)

The final variable under analysis is prices (more precisely, the GDP deflator index). Figure 1.9 shows that prices are somewhat procyclical and much less volatile than output. The fact that prices move together with GDP suggests that most economic fluctuations are demand-based. (A quick sketch of a demand–supply diagram helps here.)

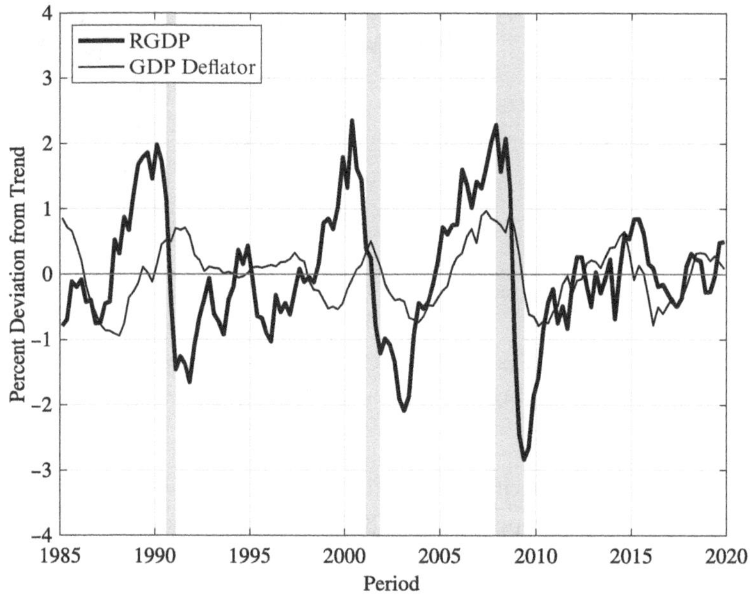

Figure 1.9 Co-movement: GDP (thick line) and GDP deflator (thin line). Gray bars denote NBER recession dates.

1.4.2 Business Cycle Statistics

The previous graphs are useful, but sometimes these connections are hard to figure out. For example, Figure 1.6 clearly displays a countercyclical pattern, yet relying on Figure 1.8 to claim productivity is also countercyclical could be a hard sell.

In these situations, statistical measurements are useful. Key to the analyses that will follow later in the book are determining (i) the correlation and (ii) standard deviations of any given variable relative to GDP. Fortunately, once the cyclical series have been calculated, deriving these statistics is a straightforward task. This is what I do below.

Table 1.1 shows these statistics in detail, where I include some variables not discussed above – like exports and nonfarm employment. Note it's much easier to determine the statistical properties of each series (cyclicality and volatility) from the table than from a time-series plot.

Table 1.1 US business cycle statistics, 1985Q1 to 2019Q4. Column (a) presents the standard deviation of the variable, column (b) reports the *relative* standard deviation (with respect to output), and column (c) shows the correlation of the variable with respect to GDP.

Variable	(a)	(b)	(c)
Output	1.0294	1.0000	1.0000
Consumption	0.8847	0.8594	0.8869
Investment	5.4849	5.3284	0.8961
Government expenditure	1.1461	1.1134	−0.2881
Exports	4.6290	4.4969	0.6887
Imports	5.3172	5.1654	0.7532
Nonfarm payroll employment	1.0758	1.0451	0.8019
Hours worked	1.3041	1.2669	0.8496
Output per hour	0.6923	0.6725	−0.1136
GDP deflator	0.4589	0.4458	0.2455

1.5 Up Next

This book had to start somewhere, and there's no better place to do so than the real world. After all, if we cannot make sense of what the data tell us, the likelihood of building useful economic theory is nil. And economic theory is where I go next.

As discussed in the Preface, the modern approach to macroeconomics uses models grounded in general equilibrium theory to make sense of what we measure in the data. To the uninitiated, the theory that follows seems closer to *microeconomics* than macroeconomics. But this is a feature, not a bug, as the microeconomics allow us to think in general equilibrium terms.

Chapter 2 starts our discussion of economic theory with the simplest possible model, that of a static general equilibrium economy. While not very realistic (after all, real-world economies last for more than one period!), it trades realism for pedagogical convenience. From there on I add another period (to get a two-period economy), and then an arbitrary number of them. As we get closer to "solving" for *realistic* economies, the features learned in this chapter will prove useful in order to determine which models fit the data (and which ones don't).

1.6 Bibliographic Notes

It goes without saying, but the groundbreaking contributions by Lucas (1977, 1980) remain fundamental readings for understanding the approach I'll follow in the book. Williamson (2017, chapter 3) also provides an introductory-level discussion regarding co-movement among macroeconomic variables.

Kaldor (1961) is the first researcher to put forward the relative stability of the capital-to-output ratio. The set of features he discusses in the paper are now known as the **Kaldor facts**.

There's a reason why I chose 1985Q1 to 2019Q4 as the sample period for this chapter. It encompasses what's known in the literature as the **Great Moderation**, a period in which the volatility of all macroeconomic variables decreased relative to the postwar period that preceded it. (In addition, I don't want to deal with the chaos brought by COVID-19.) Good sources regarding the Great Moderation include Stock and Watson (2002), Arias, Hansen, and Ohanian (2007), Clark (2009), and Galí and Gambetti (2009).

As mentioned earlier, I purposefully refrain from discussing the co-movements associated with many economic variables. King and Rebelo (1999, Section 2) offer a complementary set of graphs and statistics. While their analysis begins at an earlier date (1947Q1), it stops in 1996Q4; their exposition shows how the co-movements discussed in this chapter are not a consequence of cherry-picking sample periods.

A final note: while the HP filter is widely used among macroeconomists, it is not the only available tool to uncouple trend from cycle in an economic variable. The band-pass filter (Baxter and King 1999) is one such alternative, as are linear/quadratic/cubic detrending techniques. Hamilton (2018) critiques the HP filter and offers an alternative detrending tool. Notwithstanding this critique, the HP filter continues to be widely used by the profession in applied work.

1.7 Problems

1.7.1 Disaggregating the Expenditure Components

In Section 1.4 I showed the co-movements between *aggregate* consumption and investment with respect to GDP. But are the individual components of consumption (or investment) the same? Put differently, does consumption of durable goods share the same properties as, say, services consumption? Here I ask you to disaggregate Figures 1.4 and 1.5 as follows:

1. Redo Figure 1.4 for each of the individual expenditure components that form aggregate consumption (durables, nondurables, and services).
2. Do the same for Figure 1.5, but only use residential and nonresidential investment.

(You should have five time-series plots in total.) Based on your plots, are all consumption and investment components the same? Discuss. *Note*: If you can't find a working code that implements the HP filter, approximate the trend with a simple linear/quadratic regression. That is, after logging each series, calculate

$$\log x_t = a + bt + ct^2 + e_t,$$

where t is a time trend. Then use the coefficients $\{a, b, c\}$ and the time trend to predict the log of the series ($\log x_t^{\text{trend}} = a + bt + ct^2$). Finally, the cyclical component follows

$$x_t^{\text{cycle}} = \log x_t - \log x_t^{\text{trend}}.$$

1.7.2 Business Cycles in Other Countries

Replicate Table 1.1 (or do your best at it) for a country that is not the United States. The Penn World Tables and the St. Louis Fed's FRED database are good places to look for data.

Part I

Equilibrium Theory

2 A One-Period GE Model

The building block of dynamic macroeconomic models is the notion of a **competitive equilibrium** (CE). This chapter will teach you how to work with CEs by using a one-period (static) economy model as an example. As will become apparent in Chapter 3, the structure of a multi-period (dynamic) economy is very similar to that of a static one. (If it helps, think that I begin by laying out the "GE" part in DSGE. The "D" part will show up in Chapter 3, but I'll wait until Chapter 6 to find out how the "S" part works.)

More precisely, this chapter builds a one-period environment with two agents: a representative household and a representative firm. My immediate goal is to develop a framework that puts order into what can (and cannot) happen in this model economy. In this framework, each agent behaves according to its best interest, which allows me to use standard optimization techniques to characterize their behavior. However, the "competitive" part of any CE means that both the household and the firm are price takers; neither agent believes its behavior can change the market price.

The chapter is structured as follows. Section 2.1 discusses the representative household's utility maximization problem, while Section 2.2 lays out the representative firm's profit maximization problem. Armed with these concepts, Section 2.3 puts forward the difference between partial and general equilibrium and, once this difference is well established, Section 2.4 proceeds to define, characterize, and solve a competitive equilibrium. Finally, Section 2.5 expands the horizon by adding a government sector to our one-period economy.

2.1 The Representative Household's Problem

The representative household derives utility out of a composite consumption good C – which I also set as the **numeraire good** – and leisure time ℓ.

Remark 2.1 Setting consumption as the numeraire good means that I normalize the price of consumption to unity (i.e., $P_C = 1$) and quote all other prices in terms of consumption goods. In the real world, currency plays the role of the numeraire; for example, the dollar is the numeraire good in the United States. Moreover, the price of one dollar is \$1 and the prices of all goods are quoted in terms of dollars.

The household owns (strictly positive and finite) endowments of time h and capital K, both of which are traded for units of the consumption good. In addition, the household is the sole owner of the firm, so it receives its profits in the form of a dividend payment D. (Throughout the book, "dividend" and "profit" are equivalent.)

The goal of the household is to choose the values of consumption and leisure that maximize the value of its utility function

$$u(C, \ell)$$

subject to the budget constraint

$$C \leq r_k K_H + w(h - \ell) + D.$$

In the expression above, r_k is the real rental rate of capital, K_H represents the amount of capital that the household rents to the representative firm, and w is the real wage per unit of time worked (here the household's labor supply is $h - \ell$). From the household's perspective, the triple $\{r_k, w, D\}$ is taken as given.

I restrict the household's choices in three ways. First, consumption and leisure must be non-negative. Second, leisure time cannot exceed h. Finally, the household cannot rent more capital than its initial endowment K.

2.1.1 Setting Up the Problem

Formally, the utility maximization problem (UMP) of the household is the following: choose the values $\{C^*, \ell^*, K_H^*\}$ that solve

$$\begin{aligned} \max \quad & u(C, \ell) \\ \text{subject to} \quad & C \leq r_k K_H + w(h - \ell) + D, \\ & C \geq 0,\ \ell \in [0, h],\ K_H \in [0, K]. \end{aligned} \tag{2.1}$$

UMP (2.1) is a fairly standard optimization problem. I assume households have a *well-behaved* utility function: strictly increasing in both arguments, strictly concave, and twice continuously differentiable. To avoid corner solutions, I also assume the utility function satisfies the **Inada conditions** (Inada 1963):

$$\lim_{C \to 0} u_C(C, \ell^\star) = \infty, \quad \lim_{C \to \infty} u_C(C, \ell^\star) = 0$$

and

$$\lim_{\ell \to 0} u_\ell(C^\star, \ell) = \infty, \quad \lim_{\ell \to \infty} u_\ell(C^\star, \ell) = 0,$$

where $C^\star, \ell^\star \in \mathbb{R}_{++}$ represent arbitrary values of consumption and leisure and u_j denotes the marginal utility with respect to good $j = C, \ell$. (**Quasilinear utility functions** are well behaved but may still generate corner solutions. Problem 2.8.1 asks you to verify whether some well-known utility functions satisfy the Inada conditions.)

2.1.2 Characterizing the Solution

Graphically, the household's optimal consumption–leisure choice is found at the point where the indifference curve is tangent to the budget constraint, and Figure 2.1 offers a graphical representation of what I'm talking about. Two things are happening here. First, the **marginal rate of substitution** (MRS) of leisure for consumption equals the price ratio. Second, the optimal consumption–leisure choice is consistent with the household's resources, as indicated by the budget constraint.

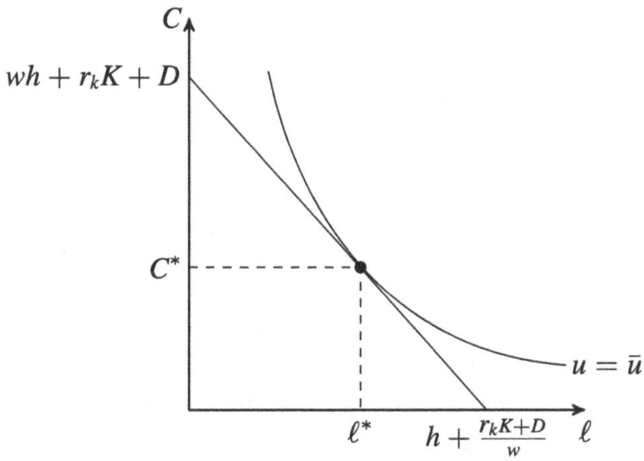

Figure 2.1 The household's optimal consumption–leisure choice is the point at which the budget constraint and the indifference curves are tangent.

Let's work these details further. The "MRS equal to price ratio" condition is given by

$$\text{MRS}_{\ell,C} = \frac{w}{1} \iff \frac{u_\ell(C,\ell)}{u_C(C,\ell)} = w,$$

where I use that the MRS equals the ratio of the marginal utilities. Rearranging this expression yields the first equilibrium condition for the household, namely,

$$u_\ell(C,\ell) = w u_C(C,\ell). \tag{2.2}$$

Equation (2.2) doesn't provide any information regarding the optimal choice of K_H; moreover, the inequality in the budget constraint still needs to be dealt with.

I proceed as follows. First, recall that the utility function does not depend on capital; therefore, the household is willing to rent its entire capital endowment to the firm as long as $r_k \geq 0$, since this choice maximizes its rental income without making the household worse off. This discussion implies $K_H^* = K$ and an updated budget constraint:

$$C \leq r_k K + w(h - \ell) + D.$$

Second, as u is strictly increasing, income will be fully exhausted when purchasing both goods. Thus, the budget constraint holds with equality and is given by

$$C = r_k K + w(h - \ell) + D. \tag{2.3}$$

Equations (2.2) and (2.3) characterize the solution to the household's problem. However, finding a closed-form solution for the pair $\{C^*, \ell^*\}$ requires values for parameters and exogenous variables and a functional form for the utility function. Example 2.1 shows how to do this.

Example 2.1 Let $u(C,\ell) = C^{1/2}\ell^{1/2}$, $w = 7$, $h = 14$, $r_k = 4/7$, $K = 7$, and $D = 14$. To find the optimal consumption bundle $\{C^*, \ell^*\}$, all that's needed is to "plug and play" the right expressions and values into (2.2) and then combine with (2.3). Looking at (2.2), the first step is to calculate the marginal utilities $u_\ell(C,\ell)$ and $u_C(C,\ell)$, given by

$$u_\ell(C,\ell) = \frac{1}{2}C^{1/2}\ell^{-1/2},$$
$$u_C(C,\ell) = \frac{1}{2}C^{-1/2}\ell^{1/2}.$$

Substitute these expressions in (2.2) and use that $w = 7$ to get

$$\frac{1}{2}C^{1/2}\ell^{-1/2} = 7\frac{1}{2}C^{-1/2}\ell^{1/2}.$$

Cross-multiplying by $2C^{1/2}\ell^{1/2}$ yields $C = 7\ell$, which is the "MRS equals price ratio" condition. Now use this condition to replace for consumption in the budget constraint, equation (2.3). After substituting values for w, h, r_k, K, and D, solve for leisure:

$$7\ell = (4/7)(7) + 7(14 - \ell) + 14,$$
$$14\ell = 4 + 98 + 14,$$
$$14\ell = 116,$$

so that $\ell^* = 8.2857$. Since $C = 7\ell$, $C^* = 58$ units of the consumption good. These results imply a household labor supply of $14 - \ell^* = 5.7143$ units of time.

2.2 The Representative Firm's Problem

The representative firm operates the production technology

$$Y = AF(K_F, N_F),$$

where Y denotes the firm's output, A represents total factor productivity (TFP), and F is a function that combines the firm's capital input K_F and the firm's labor input N_F. The firm does not own any of the production inputs: it merely rents capital and hires labor from the household at rates r_k and w. From the firm's perspective, the pair $\{r_k, w\}$ is taken as given.

I assume the production function F is well behaved: the marginal products of capital and labor (denoted by MP_K and MP_N) are strictly positive and decreasing in their own inputs but increasing in the other input. Formally:

$$\text{MP}_K, \text{MP}_N > 0; \quad \frac{\partial \text{MP}_K}{\partial K_F}, \frac{\partial \text{MP}_N}{\partial N_F} < 0; \quad \frac{\partial \text{MP}_K}{\partial N_F}, \frac{\partial \text{MP}_N}{\partial K_F} > 0. \tag{2.4}$$

I also assume the production function satisfies a version of the Inada conditions:

$$\lim_{K_F \to 0} F_K(K_F, N^*) = \infty, \quad \lim_{K_F \to \infty} F_K(K_F, N^*) = 0 \tag{2.5}$$

and

$$\lim_{N_F \to 0} F_K(K^\star, N_F) = \infty, \quad \lim_{N_F \to \infty} F_N(K^\star, N_F) = 0, \tag{2.6}$$

where $K^\star, N^\star \in \mathbb{R}_{++}$ are arbitrary values of capital and labor input. Lastly, I require that F exhibits constant returns to scale (CRS; see Section 2.2.3).

2.2.1 Setting Up the Problem

Formally, the firm's profit maximization problem (PMP) requires choosing the pair $\{K_F^*, N_F^*\}$ that maximizes household dividends D (remember the firm is owned by the household), defined as total revenue (price times output, where the price of the final good has been normalized to 1) minus total costs (capital and labor rental):

$$\begin{aligned} \max \quad & D \equiv Y - r_k K_F - w N_F \\ \text{subject to} \quad & Y = AF(K_F, N_F), \\ & K_F, N_F \geq 0, \end{aligned} \tag{2.7}$$

where the value of A is known by the firm before production takes place. For simplicity, I assume the entire capital stock rented by the firm (i.e., K_F) is destroyed after it is used. I will modify this assumption in Chapter 3.

2.2.2 Characterizing the Solution

The first-order conditions that solve problem (2.7) are

$$r_k = AF_K(K_F, N_F), \tag{2.8}$$

$$w = AF_N(K_F, N_F). \tag{2.9}$$

Equations (2.8) and (2.9) imply that the factors of production are paid the value of their marginal products.

2.2.3 Intermezzo III: Constant Returns to Scale Imply Zero Profits

I now take a detour to highlight the role of CRS. If a production function exhibits CRS, scaling all inputs by a positive factor changes the firm's output by the same factor. More formally,

Definition 2.2 The production function $F(K_F, N_F)$ exhibits **constant returns to scale** if, for any $\upsilon > 0$,

$$F(\upsilon K_F, \upsilon N_F) = \upsilon F(K_F, N_F).$$

Why do I care about having a production function with CRS? Because it allows me to make a sharp prediction about profits, as shown in the proposition below (the proof can be found in Appendix D):

Proposition 2.3 *Let $F(K_F, N_F)$ be a CRS production function. Then equilibrium profits are zero.*

As a consequence of Proposition 2.3, I will no longer report dividend income in the household's UMP (2.1).

Remark 2.4 The ownership arrangement described in this section casts the firm as a black box that transforms capital and labor services into output. (The "black box" monicker follows as the firm doesn't own productive resources – it merely rents them from the household.) This arrangement is often used in research papers, which is why I take it as a starting point. However, in the real world, *firms* (and not households) own the capital stock. Does this feature imply that the modeling I just laid out is wrong? The short answer is "no." As long as firms are owned by households, firms will aim toward maximizing dividend payments, which implies that they will make the same decisions on capital utilization (and, in Chapter 3, investment) as if the households were the owners of capital. Problem 2.8.4 asks to verify this claim.

2.3 General vs. Partial Equilibrium

At this time, it may be convenient to lay out why I emphasize the "(general) equilibrium" part in the book. Thus, I ask the question: How does GE differ from partial equilibrium (PE)? To answer this, let's bring forth some examples that make use of the modeling framework I've built so far.

2.3.1 Solving the Profit Maximization Problem

Let's start on the representative firm's side. To keep things simple – and because it doesn't change the point I'm trying to make – I assume the production function depends on labor only, so $Y = AF(N)$ with $F'(N) > 0$.

Example 2.2 Suppose the representative firm's production function is $F(N) = N^{2/3}$. The firm hires labor from the household, which it pays at a rate of $w = 2$ goods per hour worked. In order to avoid working with fractions, I set $A = 6$.
It follows that the firm's output is given by $Y = 6N^{2/3}$. In turn, the solution to the firm's PMP satisfies

$$\frac{4}{N^{1/3}} = 2, \tag{2.10}$$

which is nothing more than equating the marginal product of labor with the wage rate. A bit of algebra shows that $N = 8$ solves the expression; moreover, the firm's output is

$$Y = 6N^{2/3} = 6(8)^{2/3} = 24 \tag{2.11}$$

goods, and the associated value of dividends D equals

$$D = 6(N)^{2/3} - 2N = 6(8)^{2/3} - 2(8) = 8. \tag{2.12}$$

Hence, at a given wage of $w = 2$, the firm's optimal labor demand is $N = 8$ hours; the firm produces $Y = 24$ goods and generates $D = 8$ goods in dividend payments. (Why is it that $D > 0$? See Problem 2.8.5.)

2.3.2 Solving the Utility Maximization Problem

Now let's add the household to the mix. Note I use the same wage rate ($w = 2$) and optimal dividends ($D = 8$) following Example 2.2.

Example 2.3 Suppose utility takes the logarithmic form $U(C, \ell) = \log C + \log \ell$. The household has $h = 14$ hours of available time in the period, gets $w = 2$ goods per hour worked, and receives $D = 8$ goods as a dividend payment from the firm. (These last two values follow Example 2.2.) The solution to the household's UMP requires two conditions: first, the "MRS equals price ratio" equation, given by

$$\frac{1}{\ell} = 2\frac{1}{C},$$

which I simplify to

$$C = 2\ell. \tag{2.13}$$

Plugging this expression in the second condition, the household's budget constraint $C = w(14 - \ell) + D$ results in

$$2\ell = 2(14 - \ell) + 8.$$

Solving for ℓ is easy; I get

$$2\ell = 28 - 2\ell + 8 \implies 4\ell = 36,$$

so that optimal leisure is $\ell = 9$ hours, which implies that the household's optimal labor supply is $14 - \ell = 5$ hours. Since $C = 2l$, it follows that the household sets C equal to 18 goods.

2.3.3 Taking Stock

The examples above are straightforward, but something doesn't look right. While the answers are correct, not everything fits together. How so? Well, consider Figure 2.2 in what follows (supply and demand curves are not drawn to scale, but the main idea should still make sense).

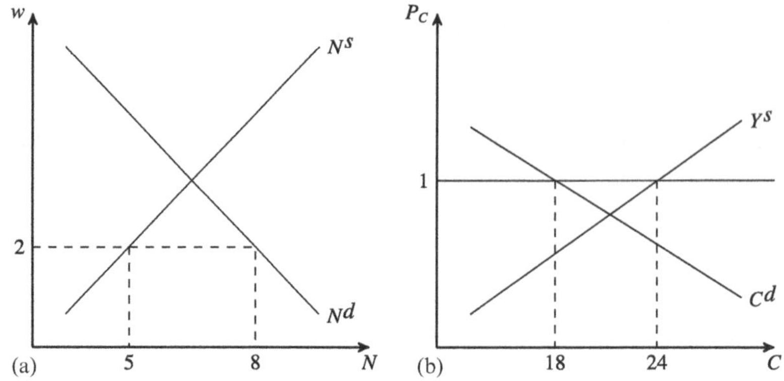

Figure 2.2 As shown, labor and goods markets are in partial equilibrium but not in general equilibrium. (a) The labor market given a wage rate that's different from the market clearing level. (b) The goods market given the (normalized) price $P_C = 1$.

To start, there are two markets in operation, namely, goods and labor. Intuitively, **market clearing** occurs when the quantity demanded is equal to the quantity supplied; the difference is that now there are *two* markets (goods and labor) to deal with at the same time.

Consider the labor market. Given a wage rate of $w = 2$ goods per hour worked, the firm looks at its labor demand curve N^d and is happy to hire $N = 8$ hours of the household's time. However, given that same wage rate of $w = 2$ goods per hour worked, the household looks at its labor supply curve N^s, which tells it to put $14 - \ell = 5$ hours on the market. Clearly, the labor market is not in equilibrium, as quantity demanded (8 hours) is not the same as quantity supplied (5 hours).

The problem doesn't end here, though: given a price of consumption $P_C = 1$, the household looks at its consumption demand curve C^d, which tells it to purchase $C = 18$ units of the final good. However, given $P_C = 1$, the firm looks at its output supply curve Y^s, which tells it that the optimal production plan requires $Y = 24$ goods. Clearly, the goods market isn't clearing either, since quantity demanded (18 goods) is not the same as quantity supplied (24 goods).

What's the problem here? It all boils down to PE vs. GE. Under partial equilibrium, the UMP and PMP are considered in isolation and everything makes sense. But under general equilibrium, both markets fail to clear because the wage rate is too low. What do I mean? Read on.

Example 2.4 In macroeconomic lingo, "$w = 2$ *is not a market clearing value*." The discussion above shows that $w = 2$ is too low, but which wage rate passes the Goldilocks test? Let's try $w^* = 2.2525$. (No, I haven't told you how to find this value. For the time being, it suffices to show that such a magical wage rate exists.) Starting from what I've derived so far, let's solve for the GE values. On the firm side, equilibrium labor should satisfy equation (2.10), namely,

$$\frac{4}{N^{1/3}} = 2.2525,$$

where I've already substituted for the equilibrium wage w^*. Solving, I get $N^* = 5.6$. Similarly, the firm's output follows (2.11):

$$Y^* = 6(5.6)^{2/3} = 18.9210$$

and the associated value of profits, given equation (2.12), is

$$D^* = 6(5.6)^{2/3} - 2.2525(5.6) = 6.3070.$$

On the consumer side, the updated "MRS equals price ratio" condition, equation (2.13), is now

$$C = 2.2525l.$$

Plugging in the updated budget constraint yields

$$2.2525\ell = 2.2525(14 - \ell) + 6.3070.$$

Solving for ℓ, I find that equilibrium leisure is now $\ell^* = 8.4$ hours, implying an equilibrium labor supply of $14 - \ell^* = 5.6$ hours – the same amount demanded by the firm. Also, equilibrium consumption is $C^* = 2.2525\ell^* = 18.9210$ – the same amount supplied by the firm. As labor supply equals labor demand *and* consumption demand equals the firm's supply, both markets clear at the equilibrium wage $w^* = 2.2525$. The economy is in general equilibrium.

Now that it's clear why I need general equilibrium theory, let's move along and explain how to find the magical value $w^* = 2.2525$.

Notation 2.5 Unless I say otherwise or it is clear from the context, I use asterisks (e.g., w^* or C^*) to denote equilibrium values.

2.4 Competitive Equilibrium

The main idea is this: I want to determine what happens to the set of *endogenous* model variables $\{r_k, w, C, \ell, K_F, N_F, Y\}$ when there are changes in the set of *exogenous* variables $\{A, K\}$. At the same time, the actions of all agents in the model must be consistent: given market prices, demand should equal supply in all markets (i.e., markets clear).

There are three markets in this static model: goods, labor, and capital. In addition, there are two prices: the real rental rate of capital r_k and the real wage w. (Strictly speaking there are three prices, but I've normalized the price of the consumption good to 1 since it is the numeraire.) A CE occurs when the real rental rate and the real wage are such that (i) the quantity of capital the household wishes to supply equals the amount of capital the firm wants to rent, (ii) the quantity of labor the household wishes to supply equals the amount of labor the firm wishes to rent, (iii) the firm produces the same output the household is willing to consume, and (iv) all agents solve their optimization problems.

The next definition formalizes all these ideas.

Definition 2.6 A competitive equilibrium consists of market prices $\mathcal{P} \equiv \{r_k^*, w^*\}$ and allocations for the household $\mathcal{A}_H \equiv \{C^*, \ell^*\}$ and the firm $\mathcal{A}_F \equiv \{K_F^*, N_F^*\}$ such that, given the set of exogenous variables $\mathcal{Z} \equiv \{A, K\}$,

1. The representative household chooses the elements in $\mathcal{A}_H$ to solve

$$\begin{aligned} \max \quad & u(C, \ell) \\ \text{subject to} \quad & C = r_k^* K + w^* (h - \ell), \\ & C \geq 0,\ \ell \in [0, h]. \end{aligned}$$

2. The representative firm chooses the elements in $\mathcal{A}_F$ to solve

$$\begin{aligned} \max \quad & D \equiv Y - r_k^* K_F - w^* N_F \\ \text{subject to} \quad & Y = AF(K_F, N_F), \\ & K_F, N_F \geq 0. \end{aligned}$$

3. All markets clear:

$$\begin{aligned} K_F^* &= K, \\ N_F^* &= h - \ell^*, \\ C^* &= AF(K, h - \ell^*). \end{aligned}$$

Remark 2.7 I can simplify Definition 2.6 by invoking **Walras's Law**, which states that in an environment with $N \geq 2$ markets, if $N - 1$ markets clear, then the remaining one clears as well. Walras's Law implies that I can focus on clearing two (out of the three) markets since the third one will clear too. (Usually, the goods market is omitted from the market clearing part of the CE definition.)

Notation 2.8 This is a good place to clarify three key terms that will be used throughout the book: *defining*, *characterizing*, and *solving* a competitive equilibrium.

- *Defining* a competitive equilibrium requires a list of the relevant prices and markets within the economy, and also the agents within (including their objective functions and what actions they choose in order to reach their goals). This is what Definition 2.6 is about.
- *Characterizing* a competitive equilibrium asks for deriving the first-order conditions that need to hold (for all agents) if an equilibrium is to exist. Section 2.4.1 shows how to accomplish this step.
- Finally, *solving* a competitive equilibrium involves combining the results of the characterization step with exogenous variable and parameter values, in order to find a numerical solution for the economy's endogenous variables. This is the topic of Section 2.4.2.

2.4.1 Characterizing a Competitive Equilibrium

To characterize a CE, I make a list of the first-order conditions that arise from the household and firm's optimization problems and then reduce the dimension of the system. For the model economy at hand, the result is a 2×2 system of nonlinear equations that must hold in a CE.

The general idea behind this procedure is to eliminate the equilibrium prices r_k^* and w^* and set the system of equations in terms of the elements in $\mathcal{A}_H$ and $\mathcal{A}_F$. Once these expressions have been derived, it's easy to back out the relevant prices (and other endogenous variables) that hold in the CE.

Let's start from the household's UMP. From Section 2.1.2, the two optimality conditions are

$$u_\ell(C^*, \ell^*) = w^* u_C(C^*, \ell^*), \tag{2.14}$$
$$C^* = r_k^* K + w^*(h - \ell^*), \tag{2.15}$$

where asterisks tell me I'm dealing with equilibrium values (see Notation 2.5). Also, the firm's optimality conditions (Section 2.2.2) are

$$r_k^* = AF_K(K_F^*, N_F^*), \tag{2.16}$$
$$w^* = AF_N(K_F^*, N_F^*). \tag{2.17}$$

Finally, I add the capital and labor market clearing conditions:

$$K_F^* = K, \tag{2.18}$$
$$N_F^* = h - \ell^*. \tag{2.19}$$

Equations (2.14)–(2.19) form a 6×6 system of equations; my goal is to reduce its dimension until I have two equations in two unknowns.

The first step in this process is to impose market clearing: take equations (2.18) and (2.19) and substitute in (2.16) and (2.17):

$$r_k^* = AF_K(K, h - \ell^*), \tag{2.20}$$
$$w^* = AF_N(K, h - \ell^*). \tag{2.21}$$

Next, I eliminate the wage rate: combining (2.14) and (2.21) gives

$$u_\ell(C^*, \ell^*) = AF_N(K, h - \ell^*) u_C(C^*, \ell^*).$$

As equilibrium profits are zero (Proposition 2.3), $AF(K, h - \ell^*) = r_k^* K + w^*(h - \ell^*)$; plug this expression into (2.15) to get the goods market clearing condition

$$C^* = AF(K, h - \ell^*).$$

(This is Walras's Law in action.) Hence, the CE is characterized by

$$u_\ell(C^*, \ell^*) = AF_N(K, h - \ell^*) u_C(C^*, \ell^*), \tag{2.22}$$
$$C^* = AF(K, h - \ell^*). \tag{2.23}$$

Equations (2.22) and (2.23) form a system of two equations in $\{C^*, \ell^*\}$; given (i) values for parameters and exogenous variables and (ii) functional forms for u and F, I solve the system and obtain equilibrium consumption and leisure. The equilibrium prices $\{r_k^*, w^*\}$ are obtained from equations (2.20) and (2.21) and the rest of the equilibrium values are trivially derived from the results above.

2.4.2 Solving a Competitive Equilibrium

Most of the time, characterizing the CE is not enough: *quantitative* measures of the model's equilibrium values are far more useful than qualitative statements (e.g., "consumption increases"). Example 2.5 shows how to use the characterization step to calculate the solution of the one-period model under analysis.

Example 2.5 Let $u(C,\ell) = C^{1/2}\ell^{1/2}$; $h = 14$; $F(K_F, N_F) = K_F^{1/2}N_F^{1/2}$; $A = 1$; and $K = 1{,}225$. I now find the equilibrium values $\{r_k^*, w^*, C^*, \ell^*, K_F^*, N_F^*, Y^*\}$.
As a first step, plug the value $A = 1$ into the production function; note capital and labor market clearing imply $K_F = K = 1{,}225$ and $N_F = 14 - \ell$. Substituting these terms, output is then given by

$$\begin{aligned} Y &= AK_F^{1/2}N_F^{1/2} \\ &= (1)(1{,}225)^{1/2}(14-\ell)^{1/2} \\ &= 35(14-\ell)^{1/2}, \end{aligned}$$

with marginal products

$$\mathrm{MP}_K = \frac{1}{70}(14-\ell)^{1/2}, \ \mathrm{MP}_N = \frac{35}{2}(14-\ell)^{-1/2}.$$

I've already calculated the marginal utilities in Example 2.1, so it's a matter of substituting the right expressions in equation (2.22):

$$\frac{1}{2}C^{1/2}\ell^{-1/2} = \frac{35}{2}(14-\ell)^{-1/2}\frac{1}{2}C^{-1/2}\ell^{1/2}.$$

Cross-multiplying by $2C^{1/2}\ell^{1/2}$ and canceling some terms yields

$$C = \frac{35}{2}(14-\ell)^{-1/2}\ell.$$

Equation (2.23) is simply

$$C = 35(14-\ell)^{1/2}$$

and I equate both expressions to get

$$\begin{aligned} \frac{35}{2}(14-\ell)^{-1/2}\ell &= 35(14-\ell)^{1/2}, \\ \ell &= 2(14-\ell), \\ \ell &= 28 - 2\ell, \end{aligned}$$

so $\ell^* = 28/3 = 9.3334$ and $N_F^* = 14 - 28/3 = 14/3 = 4.6667$. Since I already know N_F^*, the remaining equilibrium values are calculated directly: $C^* = 35(14/3)^{1/2} = 75.6086$, $w^* = (35/2)(14/3)^{-1/2} = 8.1009$, and $r_k^* = (1/70)(14/3)^{1/2} = 0.0309$. Finally, $K_F^* = K = 1{,}225$ and $Y^* = C^* = 75.6086$.

2.5 Adding a Government Sector

I now modify the baseline environment by adding a *government sector*. I assume the government levies a **lump-sum tax** T on the household and spends an exogenous amount $G \geq 0$.

Remark 2.9 Unlike a **distortionary tax** that is proportional to, say, income or consumption, a lump-sum tax doesn't change with the characteristics of the household.

For now I assume G is wasteful – it doesn't increase the household's utility nor the firm's productivity. In order to define an equilibrium, I need to modify the household's budget constraint and the aggregate feasibility constraint; I also need to model the government's behavior. These changes are incorporated into the CE definition below.

Definition 2.10 A CE consists of market prices $\mathcal{P} \equiv \{r_k^*, w^*\}$, allocations for the household $\mathcal{A}_H \equiv \{C^*, \ell^*\}$ and the firm $\mathcal{A}_F \equiv \{K_F^*, N_F^*\}$, and government policy T^* such that, given the set of exogenous variables $\mathcal{Z} \equiv \{A, K, G\}$,

1. The representative household chooses the elements in $\mathcal{A}_H$ to solve

$$\begin{aligned} \max \quad & u(C, \ell) \\ \text{subject to} \quad & C = r_k^* K + w^*(h - \ell) - T^*, \\ & C \geq 0,\ \ell \in [0, h]. \end{aligned}$$

2. The representative firm chooses the elements in $\mathcal{A}_F$ to solve

$$\begin{aligned} \max \quad & D \equiv Y - r_k^* K_F - w^* N_F \\ \text{subject to} \quad & Y = AF(K_F, N_F), \\ & K_F, N_F \geq 0. \end{aligned}$$

3. The government chooses T^* so that its budget constraint holds:

$$G = T.$$

4. All markets clear:

$$\begin{aligned} K_F^* &= K, \\ N_F^* &= h - \ell^*. \end{aligned}$$

Remark 2.11 It may seem silly to require that $G = T$ in any equilibrium. However, two points deserve attention:

- Under the current assumptions, the value of G is exogenously given to the government. As such, the government's problem is to collect enough tax revenue T to finance the amount G. (Here's a real-world way to think about this idea: Congress sets a spending goal G and then the Treasury arranges the tax code to obtain tax revenue $T = G$.)
- There's nothing in the government's problem that prevents it from raising revenue above G. But would it be reasonable (in an "equilibrium" way) for the government to set $T^* > G$?

2.6 Up Next

I've done a lot of modeling, yet I'm only getting started. I still need to figure out how to build an economy that lasts for two periods (more realistic than the one discussed here, but still a stretch) or for an arbitrary (but finite) number of periods. As it turns out, a two-period economy is fairly similar to a one-period economy, and a multi-period economy is fairly similar to a two-period one. We're building the underlying structure of our models, so hang on tight.

2.7 Bibliographic Notes

The model in this chapter is meant to build intuition and therefore aims for pedagogical soundness rather than realism. Readers who wish to get another look at the material may benefit from the intermediate-level textbooks by Barro (1997) or Williamson (2017, see chapters 4 and 5). The paper by Christiano, Eichenbaum, and Trabandt (2018) also offers valuable context on what DSGE models are and why they work the way they do.

Some readers might wonder why we need to go over the hassle of getting *quantitative* answers to questions that are just as well served by qualitative ones. If you're in this category, I suggest skimming the paper by Judd (1997).

Finally, the monograph by Athreya (2013) offers what its name promises: a nontechnical introduction to modern macroeconomics under general equilibrium. The exposition assumes basic knowledge at the level of intermediate macroeconomics and then builds up from this intuition.

2.8 Problems

2.8.1 Verifying the Inada Conditions

Consider the following utility functions:

$$u(C, l) = C + \ell, \tag{2.24}$$

$$v(C, l) = \log C + a \log \ell, \tag{2.25}$$

where $a > 0$.

1. Show that equation (2.25) satisfies the Inada conditions but equation (2.24) does not.
2. Draw the indifference set generated by each of the utility functions above. Is it possible to get corner solutions in (2.24)? In (2.25)?
3. What role do the Inada conditions play in the results you found in part 2? Explain.

2.8.2 Well-Behaved Production Functions

Prove that the Cobb–Douglas production function

$$F(K_F, N_F) = K_F^{\alpha} N_F^{1-\alpha}, \ \alpha \in (0,1),$$

satisfies conditions (2.4), (2.5), and (2.6).

2.8.3 Changing the Depreciation Rate

In the firm's PMP (2.7), I assume the capital stock rented by the firm is destroyed after production takes place. This is equivalent to a 100% depreciation rate. In the real world, however, this value is an order of magnitude smaller, approximately 10%.

This problem asks you to calculate how, if at all, the profit maximization conditions (2.8) and (2.9) change when I modify this assumption. Thus, assume the firm uses the entire capital stock K_F to produce output, and a fraction $\delta \in (0,1)$ gets destroyed during this process. After production, the firm now returns the remaining capital to the household, which converts it one-to-one into consumption goods. The firm's PMP is then

$$\begin{aligned} \max \quad & D \equiv Y - r_k K_F - w N_F + (1-\delta) K_F \\ \text{subject to} \quad & Y = AF(K_F, N_F), \\ & K_F, N_F \geq 0. \end{aligned}$$

With this new problem at hand, how do the firm's profit maximization conditions (2.8) and (2.9) change? If they change, interpret what the equations are saying. If they stay the same, explain why this is the case.

2.8.4 Changing Ownership of the Capital Stock

Following on Remark 2.4, consider an alternative environment in which the firm owns the capital stock. In this new environment, the representative household chooses the pair $\{C^*, \ell^*\}$ that solves the UMP

$$\begin{aligned} \max \quad & u(C, \ell) \\ \text{subject to} \quad & C = w(h - \ell) + D, \\ & C \geq 0, \ \ell \in [0, h]. \end{aligned}$$

As the firm now owns the strictly positive capital endowment K, the firm's PMP is to choose values for the pair $\{K_F^*, N_F^*\}$ to solve

$$\begin{aligned}\max \quad & D \equiv Y - w^* N_F \\ \text{subject to} \quad & Y = AF(K_F, N_F), \\ & K_F \in [0, K],\ N_F \geq 0.\end{aligned}$$

For this new environment,

1. Define a competitive equilibrium.
2. Show that the firm will always use all its available capital, so that $K_F^* = K$.
3. Use the same parameter values as in Example 2.5 to solve for the competitive equilibrium values. Show that (i) equilibrium profits are nonzero and (ii) equilibrium household and firm allocations are identical to those in Example 2.5.

2.8.5 Nonzero Profits?

Why does the firm in Example 2.2 have nonzero profits?

2.8.6 Equilibrium Wages

Use the methodology from Section 2.4.2 to verify that $w^* = 2.2525$ is indeed the market-clearing wage rate.

2.8.7 Distortionary Taxes

Suppose the government levies a tax on the household's (capital and labor) income at rate $\tau \in (0, 1)$ and is required to spend an exogenous amount $G > 0$ (still wasteful).

1. Assume the government uses lump-sum taxes or transfers T to balance the budget. Modify Definition 2.10 to incorporate this tax instrument.
2. Do I need to include lump-sum taxes in the definition? Why or why not?

2.8.8 Government Expenditure as a Public Good

Suppose government expenditure G provides a public good that increases the household's utility; in particular, let the utility function take the form $u(C, \ell, G)$, where $u_G > 0$. Modify Definition 2.10 to incorporate this new functional form.

2.8.9 Solving a CE with Positive Government Expenditure

Solve for the CE values from the model economy in Example 2.5 (which implicitly sets $G = 0$) but now assume $G = 10$. If you find the equilibrium values, comment on what happens to the equilibrium allocations $\mathcal{A}_H$ and $\mathcal{A}_F$ as government expenditure increases from $G_1 = 0$ to $G_2 = 10$. If you cannot get the equilibrium values, comment on why you're unable to do so.

3 A Multi-Period GE Model

This chapter expands on the previous one by presenting and characterizing CEs in dynamic environments. In Section 3.1, I first describe an environment with two periods, which is the simplest version of a dynamic economy. This change allows me to introduce an *intertemporal* dimension to the household's and firm's choices: the actions these agents take today will have an impact tomorrow, and vice versa. When this logic is settled, I follow Chapter 2 and include a government sector in this environment; this is shown in Section 3.2.

As it turns out, the structure of a two-period economy is very similar to that of a one-period economy, and that of a multi-period economy is (almost) the same as that of a two-period economy. Section 3.3 provides arguments to convince you this is true, and keeping this fact in mind while working through the chapter will be helpful. (What happens when I bump into an infinite-horizon problem? Even though it doesn't seem likely, the material in this chapter will prove very useful to get this more complicated problem under control.)

3.1 A Two-Period Model

The model economy has two agents: a representative household and a representative firm. As in Chapter 2, I wait until this easier model is solved to introduce a government sector.

3.1.1 The Representative Household's Problem

The representative household enjoys consumption C_t and leisure time ℓ_t in periods $t = 0, 1$. (To avoid repetition, I will sometimes call period 0 "today" and period 1 "tomorrow.") The household has no exogenous income, but has a fixed time endowment h in each period, as well as an initial capital endowment K_0. Both h and K_0 take on strictly positive values.

I assume that the household's lifetime utility function U is **time separable** and takes the form

$$U = u\big(C_0, \ell_0\big) + \beta u\big(C_1, \ell_1\big),$$

where u is a (well-behaved) instantaneous utility function with the same properties as the one in Chapter 2 and $\beta \in \big(0, 1\big)$ denotes the household's **discount factor**. Parameter β accounts for household impatience: other things the same, a unit of consumption enjoyed in period 0 (today) is more valuable – that is, yields more utility – than a unit of consumption enjoyed in period 1 (tomorrow).

The Household's Investment Decision

Before discussing the household's budget constraint, I take a detour to explain how investment decisions are made. In this environment, without money or a banking sector, the household saves by accumulating capital and renting it to the firm; thus, the household purchases investment goods to accumulate assets. The dynamics of the capital stock obey the laws of motion

$$K_1 = (1-\delta)K_0 + X_0$$

and

$$K_2 = (1-\delta)K_1 + X_1,$$

where $\delta \in (0,1)$ is the depreciation rate of physical capital and X_t denotes the household's investment in period $t=0,1$.

I already explained how the firm and the household interact in period 0, so let's discuss what happens in period 1. (Before moving on, it may be useful to review Problem 2.8.3.) At the start of the period, the household owns capital K_1 and rents it to the firm at rate r_{k1}. Once the firm uses the capital, it returns the net-of-depreciation stock $(1-\delta)K_1$ to the household. However, the household has no further need for this asset as the economy ends in period 1; moreover, as capital does not enter the utility function, it makes no sense to end the period with a positive capital stock. I assume the household is able to transform capital to consumption in a one-to-one ratio: $(1-\delta)K_1$ units of capital are converted to $(1-\delta)K_1$ units of consumption. Hence, $K_2 = 0$.

As expected, the household has two budget constraints (in addition to the laws of motion for capital). The first one concerns period 0, which is

$$C_0 + X_0 = r_{k0}K_0 + w_0(h-\ell_0).$$

The one for period 1 is given by

$$C_1 + X_1 = r_{k1}K_1 + w_1(h-\ell_1).$$

Following Problem 3.6.1, I don't need to report firm dividends in the budget constraints.

Summing Up

The household's UMP requires choosing $\{C_0, C_1, \ell_0, \ell_1, X_0, X_1\}$ to solve

$$\max \quad u(C_0,\ell_0) + \beta u(C_1,\ell_1)$$

$$\text{subject to} \quad C_0 + X_0 = r_{k0}K_0 + w_0(h-\ell_0), \tag{3.1}$$

$$K_1 = (1-\delta)K_0 + X_0, \tag{3.2}$$

$$C_1 + X_1 = r_{k1}K_1 + w_1(h-\ell_1), \tag{3.3}$$

$$K_2 = (1-\delta)K_1 + X_1, \tag{3.4}$$

$$C_0, C_1 \geq 0; \; \ell_0, \ell_1 \in [0,h],$$

$$K_2 = 0.$$

The problem simplifies quite a bit once I substitute the laws of motion for capital, equations (3.2) and (3.4), into the corresponding budget constraints, (3.1) and (3.3). The UMP now looks slightly different: the household chooses $\{C_0, \ell_0, K_1, C_1, \ell_1, K_2\}$ to solve

$$\begin{aligned} \max \quad & u(C_0,\ell_0) + \beta u(C_1,\ell_1) \\ \text{subject to} \quad & C_0 + K_1 = (r_{k0} + 1 - \delta)K_0 + w_0(h - \ell_0), \\ & C_1 + K_2 = (r_{k1} + 1 - \delta)K_1 + w_1(h - \ell_1), \\ & C_0, C_1 \geq 0;\ \ell_0, \ell_1 \in [0,h], \\ & K_2 = 0. \end{aligned} \tag{3.5}$$

This is the UMP I will use when characterizing the solution of the household's problem.

Characterizing the Solution

UMP (3.5) is more complicated than the one in Chapter 2 but still fairly manageable. The best way to characterize its solution is to form the Lagrangian function

$$\begin{aligned} \mathscr{L} = {} & u(C_0,\ell_0) + \beta u(C_1,\ell_1) \\ & + \lambda_0 \left[r_{k0}K_0 + w_0(h-\ell_0) - C_0 - K_1 + (1-\delta)K_0\right] \\ & + \beta\lambda_1\left[r_{k1}K_1 + w_1(h-\ell_1) - C_1 - K_2 + (1-\delta)K_1\right] + \zeta K_2, \end{aligned}$$

where λ_0, $\beta\lambda_1$, and ζ are Lagrange multipliers. (The last term in the Lagrangian function, ζK_2, takes care of the constraint $K_2 = 0$.)

Remark 3.1 I use $\beta\lambda_1$ as the Lagrange multiplier for the period-1 budget constraint; this is without loss of generality and it simplifies the algebra that follows.

Remark 3.2 Note the Lagrangian function for this two-period economy can be cast as

$$\mathscr{L} = \sum_{t=0}^{1} \beta^t \left\{u(C_t,\ell_t) + \lambda_t\left[r_{kt}K_t + w_t(h-\ell_t) - C_t - K_{t+1} + (1-\delta)K_t\right]\right\} + \zeta K_2. \tag{3.6}$$

Equation (3.6) will prove useful below.

First-order conditions with respect to $\{C_0, \ell_0, K_1, C_1, \ell_1, K_2\}$ and the multipliers are

$$\begin{aligned} C_0 : \quad & u_C(C_0,\ell_0) - \lambda_0 = 0, & (3.7) \\ \ell_0 : \quad & u_\ell(C_0,\ell_0) + \lambda_0 w_0(-1) = 0, \\ K_1 : \quad & -\lambda_0 + \beta\lambda_1(r_{k1} + 1 - \delta) = 0, \\ C_1 : \quad & \beta u_C(C_1,\ell_1) - \beta\lambda_1 = 0, & (3.8) \\ \ell_1 : \quad & \beta u_\ell(C_1,\ell_1) + \beta\lambda_1 w_1(-1) = 0, \\ K_2 : \quad & -\beta\lambda_1 + \zeta = 0, \\ \lambda_0 : \quad & r_{k0}K_0 + w_0(h-\ell_0) - C_0 - K_1 + (1-\delta)K_0 = 0, \\ \beta\lambda_1 : \quad & r_{k1}K_1 + w_1(h-\ell_1) - C_1 - K_2 + (1-\delta)K_1 = 0, \\ \zeta : \quad & K_2 = 0. \end{aligned}$$

Equations (3.7) and (3.8) tell me that the multipliers λ_0 and λ_1 equal the marginal utility of consumption for that period, and I substitute where needed. This step reduces the dimension of the system by two equations and I no longer have to worry about these multipliers (though ζ is still around). The system now looks like this:

$$\begin{aligned}
u_\ell(C_0,\ell_0) &= u_C(C_0,\ell_0)w_0,\\
u_C(C_0,\ell_0) &= \beta u_C(C_1,\ell_1)(r_{k1}+1-\delta),\\
u_\ell(C_1,\ell_1) &= u_C(C_1,\ell_1)w_1,\\
\zeta &= \beta u_C(C_1,\ell_1),\\
C_0+K_1 &= (r_{k0}+1-\delta)K_0+w_0(h-\ell_0),\\
C_1+K_2 &= (r_{k1}+1-\delta)K_1+w_1(h-\ell_1), \qquad (3.9)\\
K_2 &= 0. \qquad (3.10)
\end{aligned}$$

I'm almost done – just one more substitution to go. Equation (3.10) is a natural candidate to use and so I plug it into (3.9); after some algebra, I obtain the final version of the system, given by

$$\begin{aligned}
u_\ell(C_0,\ell_0) &= u_C(C_0,\ell_0),w_0, \qquad (3.11)\\
u_C(C_0,\ell_0) &= \beta u_C(C_1,\ell_1)(r_{k1}+1-\delta), \qquad (3.12)\\
u_\ell(C_1,\ell_1) &= u_C(C_1,\ell_1)w_1, \qquad (3.13)\\
C_0+K_1 &= (r_{k0}+1-\delta)K_0+w_0(h-\ell_0), \qquad (3.14)\\
C_1 &= (r_{k1}+1-\delta)K_1+w_1(h-\ell_1), \qquad (3.15)
\end{aligned}$$

which is a 5×5 system in $\{C_0, \ell_0, K_1, C_1, \ell_1\}$, together with the multiplier equation

$$\zeta = \beta u_C(C_1,\ell_1).$$

Note, however, that the value of ζ is not a system variable; rather, it is the marginal utility gained by relaxing the $K_2 = 0$ constraint (also known as a *shadow price*).

Equations (3.11)–(3.15) characterize the solution to the household's UMP. These expressions will prove useful later on. For now, it's time to offer an example and then move on to the representative firm's problem.

Example 3.1 Suppose consumer preferences are represented by the utility function

$$u(C_0,\ell_0)+\beta u(C_1,\ell_1) = \log C_0 + \log \ell_0 + \beta(\log C_1 + \log \ell_1).$$

Given this utility function, equations (3.11)–(3.15) are given by

$$\begin{aligned}
\frac{1}{\ell_0} &= \frac{1}{C_0}w_0, \qquad (3.16)\\
\frac{1}{C_0} &= \beta\frac{1}{C_1}(r_{k1}+1-\delta), \qquad (3.17)\\
\frac{1}{\ell_1} &= \frac{1}{C_1}w_1, \qquad (3.18)
\end{aligned}$$

$$C_0 + K_1 = \left(r_{k0} + 1 - \delta\right)K_0 + w_0\left(h - \ell_0\right), \tag{3.19}$$
$$C_1 = \left(r_{k1} + 1 - \delta\right)K_1 + w_1\left(h - \ell_1\right). \tag{3.20}$$

Suppose further that $\beta = 0.95$, $w_0 = 5$, $w_1 = 8$, $r_{k0} = r_{k1} = 0.05$, $K_0 = 100$, $h = 16$, and $\delta = 0$. Substituting these values, equations (3.16)–(3.20) become

$$C_0 = 5\ell_0, \tag{3.21}$$
$$C_1 = 8\ell_1, \tag{3.22}$$
$$C_1 = 0.9975C_0, \tag{3.23}$$
$$C_0 + K_1 = 185 - 5\ell_0, \tag{3.24}$$
$$C_1 = 128 + 1.05K_1 - 8\ell_1, \tag{3.25}$$

where I've used a bit of algebra to simplify the expressions. To solve the system, start by plugging (3.21) and (3.22) in (3.23)–(3.25); this results in

$$8\ell_1 = 4.9875\ell_0, \tag{3.26}$$
$$5\ell_0 + K_1 = 185 - 5\ell_0, \tag{3.27}$$
$$8\ell_1 = 128 + 1.05K_1 - 8\ell_1, \tag{3.28}$$

which is a system of three equations in $\left\{\ell_0, \ell_1, K_1\right\}$. There are several ways to attack this 3×3 system; I choose to solve for ℓ_0 from (3.27),

$$10\ell_0 + K_1 = 185 \implies \ell_0 = \frac{185 - K_1}{10}, \tag{3.29}$$

for ℓ_1 from (3.28),

$$16\ell_1 = 128 + 1.05K_1 \implies \ell_1 = \frac{128 + 1.05K_1}{16}, \tag{3.30}$$

and then substitute the resulting expressions into (3.26):

$$8\left(\frac{128 + 1.05K_1}{16}\right) = 4.9875\left(\frac{185 - K_1}{10}\right). \tag{3.31}$$

Some tedious algebra later, equation (3.31) can be solved to get $K_1^* = 27.6129$. Using (3.29) and (3.30), $\ell_0^* = 15.7387$ and $\ell_1^* = 9.8121$. Finally, from (3.21) and (3.22), $C_0^* = 78.6935$ and $C_1^* = 78.4968$.

Remark 3.3 Strictly speaking, the calculations in Example 3.1 do not give me all the equilibrium values that solve the UMP; I am still missing the values X_0^*, X_1^*, and K_2^*. Fortunately, the hard work done in Example 3.1 allows me to get these immediately. First, I know that $K_2^* = 0$. Second, equation (3.2) says $X_0^* = K_1^* - \left(1 - \delta\right)K_0$; since $\delta = 0$, it follows that $X_0^* = -72.3871$. Finally, equation (3.4) shows $X_1^* = -\left(1 - \delta\right)K_1^*$; by the same logic, $X_1^* = -27.6129$.

3.1.2 The Representative Firm's Problem

For $t = 0, 1$, the representative firm operates the production technology

$$Y_t = A_t F(K_{Ft}, N_{Ft}),$$

where Y_t denotes the firm's output, A_t represents TFP (which is known by the firm before production takes place), and F is a CRS function that combines the firm's capital input K_{Ft} and labor input N_{Ft} to produce the output. As in Chapter 2, the firm does not own any of the production inputs and only rents capital and labor from the household.

Given this structure, the firm's PMP relies on period-by-period optimization (there is no intertemporal link between them). More precisely, for $t = 0, 1$, the firm chooses values for its capital and labor inputs to solve the PMP

$$\begin{aligned} \max \quad & \Pi_t \equiv Y_t - r_{kt}K_{Ft} - w_t N_{Ft} \\ \text{subject to} \quad & Y_t = A_t F(K_{Ft}, N_{Ft}), \\ & K_{Ft}, N_{Ft} \geq 0. \end{aligned} \tag{3.32}$$

The first-order conditions that solve problem (3.32) are

$$\begin{aligned} r_{k0} &= A_0 F_K(K_{F0}, N_{F0}), \\ w_0 &= A_0 F_N(K_{F0}, N_{F0}), \\ r_{k1} &= A_1 F_K(K_{F1}, N_{F1}), \\ w_1 &= A_1 F_N(K_{F1}, N_{F1}). \end{aligned}$$

In words: the factors of production are paid the value of their marginal products. I'll use these equations, together with (3.11)–(3.15), to characterize the CE.

3.1.3 Competitive Equilibrium

Here I provide the appropriate definition of a CE.

Definition 3.4 A competitive equilibrium consists of prices $\mathcal{P} \equiv \{r_{k0}^*, w_0^*, r_{k1}^*, w_1^*\}$ and allocations for the household $\mathcal{A}_H \equiv \{C_0^*, \ell_0^*, K_1^*, C_1^*, \ell_1^*, K_2^*\}$ and the firm $\mathcal{A}_F \equiv \{K_{F0}^*, N_{F0}^*, K_{F1}^*, N_{F1}^*\}$ such that, given the set of exogenous variables $\mathcal{Z} \equiv \{A_0, K_0, A_1\}$,

1. The representative household chooses the elements in $\mathcal{A}_H$ to solve

$$\begin{aligned} \max \quad & u(C_0, \ell_0) + \beta u(C_1, \ell_1) \\ \text{subject to} \quad & C_0 + K_1 = (r_{k0}^* + 1 - \delta)K_0 + w_0^*(h - \ell_0), \\ & C_1 + K_2 = (r_{k1}^* + 1 - \delta)K_1 + w_1^*(h - \ell_1), \\ & C_0, C_1 \geq 0;\ \ell_0, \ell_1 \in [0, h], \\ & K_2 = 0. \end{aligned}$$

2. For each $t = 0, 1$, the representative firm chooses the elements in $\mathcal{A}_F$ to solve

$$\begin{aligned} \max \quad & \Pi_t \equiv Y_t - r_{kt}^* K_{Ft} - w_t^* N_{Ft} \\ \text{subject to} \quad & Y_t = A_t F(K_{Ft}, N_{Ft}), \\ & K_{Ft}, N_{Ft} \geq 0. \end{aligned}$$

3. All markets clear:

$$\begin{aligned} K_{F0}^* &= K_0, \\ N_{F0}^* &= h - \ell_0^*, \\ K_{F1}^* &= K_1^*, \\ N_{F1}^* &= h - \ell_1^*. \end{aligned}$$

Remark 3.5 In this two-period environment, Walras's Law allows me to look at markets within each period: as long as two markets clear (say) today, the third one clears too. As I will show below, I get the goods market clearing conditions for free – see equations (3.55) and (3.56) later.

Armed with a definition, the next step is to characterize the equilibrium.

Characterizing the Competitive Equilibrium

The household's equilibrium conditions are

$$u_\ell(C_0^*, \ell_0^*) = u_C(C_0^*, \ell_0^*) w_0^*, \tag{3.33}$$

$$u_C(C_0^*, \ell_0^*) = \beta u_C(C_1^*, \ell_1^*)(r_{k1}^* + 1 - \delta), \tag{3.34}$$

$$u_\ell(C_1^*, \ell_1^*) = u_C(C_1^*, \ell_1^*) w_1^*, \tag{3.35}$$

$$C_0^* + K_1^* = (r_{k0}^* + 1 - \delta) K_0 + w_0^*(h - \ell_0^*), \tag{3.36}$$

$$C_1^* = (r_{k1}^* + 1 - \delta) K_1^* + w_1^*(h - \ell_1^*). \tag{3.37}$$

From the firm's problem

$$r_{k0}^* = A_0 F_K(K_{F0}^*, N_{F0}^*), \tag{3.38}$$

$$w_0^* = A_0 F_N(K_{F0}^*, N_{F0}^*), \tag{3.39}$$

$$r_{k1}^* = A_1 F_K(K_{F1}^*, N_{F1}^*), \tag{3.40}$$

$$w_1^* = A_1 F_N(K_{F1}^*, N_{F1}^*), \tag{3.41}$$

and finally, I add the market clearing conditions

$$K_{F0}^* = K_0, \tag{3.42}$$

$$N_{F0}^* = h - \ell_0^*, \tag{3.43}$$

$$K_{F1}^* = K_1^*, \tag{3.44}$$

$$N_{F1}^* = h - \ell_1^*. \tag{3.45}$$

Although it seems intimidating, the system (3.33)–(3.45) is simplified by following the same ideas as in Chapter 2. First, impose market clearing: from (3.42)–(3.45) substitute in (3.36)–(3.41) to get

$$C_0^* + K_1^* = (r_{k0}^* + 1 - \delta) K_0 + w_0^*(h - \ell_0^*), \tag{3.46}$$

$$C_1^* = (r_{k1}^* + 1 - \delta) K_1^* + w_1^*(h - \ell_1^*), \tag{3.47}$$

$$r_{k0}^* = A_0 F_K(K_0, h - \ell_0^*), \tag{3.48}$$

$$w_0^* = A_0 F_N(K_0, h - \ell_0^*), \tag{3.49}$$

$$r_{k1}^* = A_1 F_K\big(K_1^*, h - \ell_1^*\big), \tag{3.50}$$
$$w_1^* = A_1 F_N\big(K_1^*, h - \ell_1^*\big). \tag{3.51}$$

Now get rid of prices: for wages, take (3.49) and (3.51) and substitute in (3.33) and (3.35),

$$u_\ell\big(C_0^*, \ell_0^*\big) = u_C\big(C_0^*, \ell_0^*\big) A_0 F_N\big(K_0, h - \ell_0^*\big),$$
$$u_\ell\big(C_1^*, \ell_1^*\big) = u_C\big(C_1^*, \ell_1^*\big) A_1 F_N\big(K_1^*, h - \ell_1^*\big).$$

Similarly, substitute (3.50) in (3.34) to get rid of the interest rate,

$$u_C\big(C_0^*, \ell_0^*\big) = \beta u_C\big(C_1^*, \ell_1^*\big)\big[A_1 F_K\big(K_1^*, h - l_1^*\big) + 1 - \delta\big].$$

As optimal profits are zero (Problem 3.6.1), I use this fact in equations (3.46) and (3.47) to get

$$C_0^* + K_1^* = A_0 F\big(K_0, h - \ell_0^*\big) + \big(1 - \delta\big) K_0,$$
$$C_1^* = A_1 F\big(K_1^*, h - \ell_1^*\big) + \big(1 - \delta\big) K_1^*.$$

Thus, the CE is characterized by

$$u_\ell\big(C_0^*, \ell_0^*\big) = u_C\big(C_0^*, \ell_0^*\big) A_0 F_N\big(K_0, h - \ell_0^*\big), \tag{3.52}$$
$$u_C\big(C_0^*, \ell_0^*\big) = \beta u_C\big(C_1^*, \ell_1^*\big)\big[A_1 F_K\big(K_1^*, h - \ell_1^*\big) + 1 - \delta\big], \tag{3.53}$$
$$u_\ell\big(C_1^*, \ell_1^*\big) = u_C\big(C_1^*, \ell_1^*\big) A_1 F_N\big(K_1^*, h - \ell_1^*\big), \tag{3.54}$$
$$C_0^* + K_1^* = A_0 F\big(K_0, h - \ell_0^*\big) + \big(1 - \delta\big) K_0, \tag{3.55}$$
$$C_1^* = A_1 F\big(K_1^*, h - \ell_1^*\big) + \big(1 - \delta\big) K_1^*. \tag{3.56}$$

Here, (3.52)–(3.56) form a system of five equations in five variables. Note, however, that there are three groups of equations: (3.52) and (3.54) look alike, and so do (3.55) and (3.56). The only different expression is (3.53). (This result is not a coincidence, as I explain in Section 3.3.3.)

Solving this system yields values for $\{C_0^*, \ell_0^*, C_1^*, \ell_1^*, K_1^*\}$; the equilibrium prices follow equations (3.48)–(3.51) and the rest of the equilibrium values are trivially derived from the results above.

At this time, an example helps summarize what I've shown so far.

Example 3.2 Suppose consumer preferences are represented by the utility function

$$u(C_0, \ell_0) + \beta u(C_1, \ell_1) = \log C_0 + \log \ell_0 + \log C_1 + \log \ell_1$$

and technology is given by the Cobb–Douglas production function $F\big(K_t, N_t\big) = K_t^\alpha N_t^{1-\alpha}$ for $t = 0, 1$. Also let $A_0 = A_1 = 1$; $K_0 =$ 1,000; $h = 16$; $\alpha = 1/3$; and $\delta = 1$. Under these assumptions, equations (3.52)–(3.56) become

$$C_0 = \frac{20}{3} \frac{\ell_0}{\big(16 - \ell_0\big)^{1/3}}, \tag{3.57}$$

$$C_1 = \frac{2}{3} \frac{K_1^{1/3} \ell_1}{\big(16 - \ell_1\big)^{1/3}}, \tag{3.58}$$

$$C_1 = \frac{1}{3}\frac{\left(16-\ell_1\right)^{2/3}}{K_1^{2/3}}C_0, \tag{3.59}$$

$$C_0 = 10\left(16-\ell_0\right)^{2/3} - K_1, \tag{3.60}$$

$$C_1 = K_1^{1/3}\left(16-\ell_1\right)^{2/3}. \tag{3.61}$$

To solve the system, take (3.57) and (3.58) and substitute in (3.59)–(3.61). These operations result in a 3×3 system in $\{\ell_0, K_1, \ell_1\}$, namely,

$$\frac{2}{3}\frac{K_1^{1/3}\ell_1}{\left(16-\ell_1\right)^{1/3}} = \left[\frac{1}{3}\frac{\left(16-\ell_1\right)^{2/3}}{K_1^{2/3}}\right]\left[\frac{20}{3}\frac{\ell_0}{\left(16-\ell_0\right)^{1/3}}\right], \tag{3.62}$$

$$\frac{20}{3}\frac{\ell_0}{\left(16-\ell_0\right)^{1/3}} = 10\left(16-\ell_0\right)^{2/3} - K_1, \tag{3.63}$$

$$\frac{2}{3}\frac{K_1^{1/3}\ell_1}{\left(16-\ell_1\right)^{1/3}} = K_1^{1/3}\left(16-\ell_1\right)^{2/3}. \tag{3.64}$$

Next, take (3.64) and note some algebra allows me to write this equation as

$$\frac{2}{3}\ell_1 = 16 - \ell_1. \tag{3.65}$$

Since this is one equation in ℓ_1, its solution is immediate: $\ell_1^* = 9.6$. I use this value and some algebra to rewrite (3.62) as

$$\frac{10}{3}\frac{\ell_0}{\ell_1} = \frac{K_1}{16-\ell_1}\left(16-\ell_0\right)^{1/3}.$$

Plugging (3.65) in the equation above and simplifying yields

$$K_1 = \frac{20}{9}\frac{\ell_0}{\left(16-\ell_0\right)^{1/3}}. \tag{3.66}$$

Armed with an expression for K_1, put (3.66) in (3.63):

$$\frac{20}{3}\frac{\ell_0}{\left(16-\ell_0\right)^{1/3}} = 10\left(16-\ell_0\right)^{2/3} - \frac{20}{9}\frac{\ell_0}{\left(16-\ell_0\right)^{1/3}}$$

and, after some algebra, I get one equation in ℓ_0:

$$16 - \ell_0 = \frac{8}{9}\ell_0.$$

The expression above is solved to $\ell_0^* = 8.4706$. Now go back to (3.66) and solve for K_1:

$$K_1 = \frac{20}{9}\frac{8.4706}{7.5294^{1/3}},$$

or $K_1^* = 9.6039$. With this value, C_0 and C_1 are obtained from equations (3.60) and (3.61):

$$C_0 = 10\left(7.5294\right)^{2/3} - 9.6039,$$

$$C_1 = \left(9.6039\right)^{1/3}\left(6.4\right)^{2/3},$$

which results in $C_0^* = 28.8117$ and $C_1^* = 7.3272$. Formally, the solution to the CE is $\{C_0^*, \ell_0^*, C_1^*, \ell_1^*, K_1^*\} = \{28.8117, 8.4706, 7.3272, 9.6, 9.6039\}$.

3.2 A Two-Period Model with a Government Sector

Now that I've shown how a two-period model economy with a representative household and representative firm works, I expand the horizon and add a government sector. Relative to what I presented in Chapter 2, the government now has the option to borrow from the household in order to fund its expenditure (on top of levying taxes), and I use this modeling choice below.

In order to arrive at a definition of competitive equilibrium, I need to describe the government's problem and list the changes on the household side. (By construction, the firm does not pay taxes, so its PMP remains the same.) This is what I do next.

3.2.1 The Government Sector

The government levies lump-sum taxes T_t and spends an exogenous amount $G_t \geq 0$ in $t = 0, 1$. In addition, it can borrow from the household by issuing bonds (i.e., debt) with the following characteristics: a bond sold in period t, denoted B_{t+1},

1. Has a period-t price of $q_{t+1} \leq 1$ goods, and
2. Is repaid in period $t+1$ at a rate of one good per bond.

Note that the timing convention for the bond and its price corresponds to the period in which the bond matures, not the time at which it was purchased by the household. In addition, the fact that $q \leq 1$ means that bonds are sold "at a discount." Of course, the value of q implicitly determines the real net interest rate paid by government bonds, denoted by r.

Remark 3.6 A *net* growth rate is just what one typically understands as a growth rate, like 0.03 or −0.05. A *gross* growth rate just adds 1 to this value, like 1.03 or 0.95.

Some examples can come in handy, and that's what I share next.

Example 3.3 Consider a bond that is purchased for price q today and that promises to pay one good tomorrow. Let's look at some scenarios. Suppose first that $q = 0.9$. What's the interest rate associated with this bond? An intuitive answer would be "around 10%," and this result is easily confirmed via the formula $r = (1-q)/q$: the answer is $r = 0.1111$. Now suppose that $q = 0.99$; what's the interest rate associated with this bond? If you say "about 1%" you would be almost right, since the exact value is $r = 0.0101$.

Example 3.4 This information also allows me to calculate the real *gross* interest rate R^r; this value equals $R^r = 1/q = 1.1111$ for $q = 0.9$ and $R^r = 1.0101$ for $q = 0.99$.

Example 3.3 provides the intuition behind the following result:

Proposition 3.7 *There is an inverse relationship between the price of the bond and its return rate.*

Under these assumptions, the government has two budget constraints. The period-0 constraint is given by

$$G_0 = T_0 + q_1 B_1, \tag{3.67}$$

while the one for period 1 reads

$$G_1 + B_1 = T_1 + q_2 B_2. \tag{3.68}$$

However, as the economy ends in period 1, it must be that $B_2 = 0$. Put differently, why would the household lend to the government, knowing that those resources will never be paid back?

3.2.2 The Representative Household, Revisited

UMP (3.5) remains very similar except for the parts where fiscal policy comes into play. These changes, however, are straightforward: I subtract lump-sum taxes from the budget constraint and add a formal saving channel (besides capital accumulation), denoted S_{t+1}, which represents the amount of bonds (savings) purchased from the government in period t that will be repaid in period $(t+1)$.

Formally, the household's UMP requires choosing $\{C_0, \ell_0, K_1, S_1, C_1, \ell_1, K_2, S_2\}$ that solve problem (3.69):

$$\begin{aligned}
\max \quad & u(C_0, \ell_0) + \beta u(C_1, \ell_1) \\
\text{subject to} \quad & C_0 + K_1 + q_1 S_1 = (r_{k0} + 1 - \delta) K_0 + w_0 (h - \ell_0) - T_0, \\
& C_1 + K_2 + q_2 S_2 = (r_{k1} + 1 - \delta) K_1 + w_1 (h - \ell_1) - T_1 + S_1, \\
& C_0, C_1, S_1 \geq 0; \; \ell_0, \ell_1 \in [0, h], \\
& K_2 = S_2 = 0.
\end{aligned} \tag{3.69}$$

Here the household takes prices $\{r_{k0}, w_0, q_1, r_{k1}, w_1, q_2\}$ as given.

3.2.3 Competitive Equilibrium

Here's the definition:

Definition 3.8 A CE consists of prices $\mathcal{P} \equiv \{r_{k0}^*, w_0^*, q_0^*, r_{k1}^*, w_1^*, q_1^*\}$, allocations for the household $\mathcal{A}_H \equiv \{C_0^*, \ell_0^*, K_1^*, S_1^*, C_1^*, \ell_1^*, K_2^*, S_2^*\}$ and the firm $\mathcal{A}_F \equiv \{K_{F0}^*, N_{F0}^*, K_{F1}^*, N_{F1}^*\}$, and government policy $\{T_0^*, T_1^*, B_1^*, B_2^*\}$ such that, given the set of exogenous variables $\mathcal{Z} \equiv \{A_0, K_0, G_0, A_1, G_1\}$,

1. The representative household chooses the elements in $\mathcal{A}_H$ to solve

$$\begin{aligned} \max \quad & u(C_0, \ell_0) + \beta u(C_1, \ell_1) \\ \text{subject to} \quad & C_0 + K_1 + q_1^* S_1 = (r_{k0}^* + 1 - \delta) K_0 + w_0^* (h - \ell_0) - T_0^*, \\ & C_1 + K_2 + q_2^* S_2 = (r_{k1}^* + 1 - \delta) K_1 + w_1^* (h - \ell_1) - T_1^* + S_1, \\ & C_0, C_1, S_1 \geq 0; \ \ell_0, \ell_1 \in [0, h], \\ & K_2 = S_2 = 0. \end{aligned}$$

2. For each $t = 0, 1$, the representative firm chooses the elements in $\mathcal{A}_F$ to solve

$$\begin{aligned} \max \quad & \Pi_t \equiv Y_t - r_{kt}^* K_{Ft} - w_t^* N_{Ft} \\ \text{subject to} \quad & Y_t = A_t F(K_{Ft}, N_{Ft}), \\ & K_{Ft}, N_{Ft} \geq 0. \end{aligned}$$

3. The government chooses its policy instruments so that its budget constraints hold:

$$\begin{aligned} G_0 &= T_0 + q_1^* B_1, \\ G_1 + B_1 &= T_1 + q_2^* B_2. \end{aligned}$$

4. All markets clear:

$$\begin{aligned} K_{F0}^* &= K_0, \\ N_{F0}^* &= h - \ell_0^*, \\ B_1^* &= S_1^*, \\ K_{F1}^* &= K_1^*, \\ N_{F1}^* &= h - \ell_1^*, \\ B_2^* &= S_2^*. \end{aligned}$$

Note Walras's Law allows me to skip the goods market clearing for $t = 0, 1$.

3.3 A Multi-Period Model

The two-period model is a good stepping stone for more complicated environments. The reason is that the ideas that hold for a two-period model also hold for multi-period ones: just as in (3.52)–(3.56) I had three groups of equations leading to a 5×5 system, multi-period models also generate three groups of equations, though the dimension of the system is now larger.

With this context, I now characterize a full-fledged CE that lasts for any arbitrary (but finite) number of periods; to keep thing simple, I do not include a government sector. With some minor tweaks, this will be the workhorse model for the rest of the book.

3.3.1 The Representative Household's Problem

The representative household enjoys consumption and leisure time in $t = 0, 1, \ldots, T-1$, where T takes an arbitrarily large but finite value. The household has no exogenous income, but it has a fixed time endowment h in each period and an initial capital endowment K_0. I assume both values are strictly positive.

The household's lifetime utility function U is time separable and takes the form

$$U = u(C_0, \ell_0) + \beta u(C_1, \ell_1) + \beta^2 u(C_2, \ell_2) + \cdots + \beta^{T-1} u(C_{T-1}, \ell_{T-1}),$$

where C_t and ℓ_t denote consumption and leisure in period t, u is a (well-behaved) instantaneous utility function with the same properties as the one in Chapter 2, and $\beta \in (0, 1)$ is the household's discount factor.

Notation 3.9 Writing up $\{C_0, C_1, \ldots, C_{T-1}\}$ and $\{\ell_0, \ell_1, \ldots, \ell_{T-1}\}$ (or whatever other sequence of length T) is tedious, so I'll condense these expressions as $\{C_t\}_{t=0}^{T-1}$, $\{\ell_t\}_{t=0}^{T-1}$, and $\{C_t, \ell_t\}_{t=0}^{T-1}$ to save space.

The Household's Investment Decision

Just as in Section 3.1.1, the household has the option to buy investment goods to increase its initial capital stock. The capital accumulation process still obeys

$$K_{t+1} = (1 - \delta) K_t + X_t, \; t = 0, 1, \ldots, T - 1,$$

where $\delta \in (0, 1)$ is the depreciation rate and X_t denotes the household's investment in period t. In all periods, the household rents its capital stock K_t to the firm at a rental rate r_{kt}. After the firm uses the capital, it returns the remaining stock $(1 - \delta) K_t$ to the household.

Following the same logic as in Section 3.1.1, the household has no further need for capital once period-T output has been produced. I assume that the household transforms capital to consumption on a one-to-one ratio: $(1 - \delta) K_{T-1}$ units of capital are exchanged for $(1 - \delta) K_{T-1}$ units of consumption. Hence, $K_T = 0$.

Summing Up

In this case, the household has T budget constraints, given by

$$C_t + X_t = r_{kt} K_t + w_t (h - \ell_t), \; t = 0, 1, \ldots, T - 1,$$

together with the T laws of motion for capital from above. After substituting the laws of motion for capital into the budget constraints, the household's UMP is given by problem (3.70):

$$\begin{aligned}
\max_{\{C_t, \ell_t, K_{t+1}\}_{t=0}^{T-1}} \quad & \sum_{t=0}^{T-1} \beta^t u(C_t, \ell_t) && (3.70) \\
\text{subject to} \quad & C_t + K_{t+1} = (r_{kt} + 1 - \delta) K_t + w_t (h - \ell_t), \; t = 0, 1, \ldots, T - 1, \\
& C_t \geq 0, \; \ell_t \in [0, h], \; t = 0, 1, \ldots, T - 1, \\
& K_T = 0.
\end{aligned}$$

Characterizing the Solution

Once again, a Lagrangian function is useful to characterize the solution. Following Remark 3.2, the Lagrangian function is given by

$$\mathscr{L} = \sum_{t=0}^{T-1} \beta^t \{u(C_t, \ell_t) + \lambda_t [(r_{kt} + 1 - \delta)K_t + w_t(h - \ell_t) - C_t - K_{t+1}]\} + \zeta K_T.$$

I next calculate the first-order conditions with respect to the decision variables and the multipliers. (Note I take the derivative with respect to K_T too.) These are:

$$\begin{aligned}
C_t :& \quad \beta^t u_C(C_t, \ell_t) - \beta^t \lambda_t = 0, && (3.71)\\
\ell_t :& \quad \beta^t u_\ell(C_t, \ell_t) - \beta^t \lambda_t w_t = 0, && (3.72)\\
K_{t+1} :& \quad -\beta^t \lambda_t + \beta^{t+1} \lambda_{t+1}(r_{k,t+1} + 1 - \delta) = 0, && (3.73)\\
K_T :& \quad -\beta^{T-1} \lambda_{T-1} + \zeta = 0, && (3.74)\\
\beta^t \lambda_t :& \quad (r_{kt} + 1 - \delta)K_t + w_t(h - \ell_t) - C_t - K_{t+1} = 0, && (3.75)\\
\zeta_t :& \quad K_T = 0, && (3.76)
\end{aligned}$$

where all but equations (3.74) and (3.76) run from $t = 0$ to $t = T - 1$. Combine (3.71) with (3.72) to get

$$u_\ell(C_t, \ell_t) = u_C(C_t, \ell_t) w_t, \; t = 0, 1, \ldots, T - 1$$

and do the same with (3.71) and (3.73):

$$u_C(C_t, \ell_t) = \beta u_C(C_{t+1}, \ell_{t+1})(r_{k,t+1} + 1 - \delta), \; t = 0, 1, \ldots, T - 1.$$

I now move on to the budget constraints. From equation (3.76), I know $K_T = 0$. Plugging into the budget constraint for period $T - 1$, which can be obtained from (3.75), I find that the system that characterizes the equilibrium in this economy is given by

$$\begin{aligned}
u_\ell(C_t, \ell_t) &= u_C(C_t, \ell_t) w_t, \; t = 0, 1, \ldots, T - 1, && (3.77)\\
u_C(C_t, \ell_t) &= \beta u_C(C_{t+1}, \ell_{t+1})(r_{k,t+1} + 1 - \delta), \; t = 0, 1, \ldots, T - 2, && (3.78)\\
C_t + K_{t+1} &= (r_{kt} + 1 - \delta)K_t + w_t(h - \ell_t), \; t = 0, 1, \ldots, T - 2, && (3.79)\\
C_{T-1} &= (r_{k,T-1} + 1 - \delta)K_{T-1} + w_{T-1}(h - \ell_{T-1}), && (3.80)
\end{aligned}$$

which is a system of $3T - 1$ variables in $3T - 1$ equations. Of course, equation (3.74) must hold too:

$$\zeta = \beta^{T-1} \lambda_{T-1} = \beta^{T-1} u_C(C_{T-1}, \ell_{T-1}),$$

though it doesn't affect the values of the endogenous variables along the equilibrium path. Thus, equations (3.77)–(3.80) characterize the solution to the household's UMP.

3.3.2 The Representative Firm's Problem

For $t = 0, 1, \ldots, T - 1$, the representative firm operates the production technology

$$Y_t = A_t F(K_{Ft}, N_{Ft}),$$

where Y_t denotes the firm's output, A_t represents TFP (again, known by the firm before production takes place), and F is a CRS function that combines the firm's capital input K_{Ft} and the firm's labor input N_{Ft}. The firm does not own any of the production inputs and only rents capital and labor inputs from the household.

As in Section 3.1.2, the firm's PMP simply requires period-by-period optimization: for each $t = 0, 1, \ldots, T-1$, the firm chooses the pair $\{K_{Ft}, N_{Ft}\}$ to solve

$$\begin{aligned} \max \quad & \Pi_t \equiv Y_t - r_{kt}K_{Ft} - w_t N_{Ft} \\ \text{subject to} \quad & Y_t = A_t F\big(K_{Ft}, N_{Ft}\big), \\ & K_{Ft}, N_{Ft} \geq 0. \end{aligned} \tag{3.81}$$

Equilibrium requires that factors of production are paid the value of their marginal products for each $t = 0, 1, \ldots, T-1$:

$$\begin{aligned} r_{kt} &= A_t F_K\big(K_{Ft}, N_{Ft}\big), \\ w_t &= A_t F_N\big(K_{Ft}, N_{Ft}\big). \end{aligned}$$

3.3.3 Competitive Equilibrium

I now define an equilibrium for this multi-period economy. The following structure should be familiar by now:

Definition 3.10 A CE consists of prices $\mathcal{P} \equiv \{r_{kt}^*, w_t^*\}_{t=0}^{T-1}$ and allocations for the household $\mathcal{A}_H \equiv \{C_t^*, \ell_t^*, K_{t+1}^*\}_{t=0}^{T-1}$ and the firm $\mathcal{A}_F \equiv \{K_{Ft}^*, N_{Ft}^*\}_{t=0}^{T-1}$ such that, given the set of exogenous variables $\mathcal{Z} \equiv \{\{A_t\}_{t=0}^{T-1}, K_0\}$,

1. The representative household chooses the elements in $\mathcal{A}_H$ to solve

$$\begin{aligned} \max_{\{C_t, \ell_t, K_{t+1}\}_{t=0}^{T-1}} \quad & \sum_{t=0}^{T-1} \beta^t u\big(C_t, \ell_t\big) \\ \text{subject to} \quad & C_t + K_{t+1} = \big(r_{kt}^* + 1 - \delta\big)K_t + w_t^*\left(h - \ell_t\right),\ t = 0, 1, \ldots, T-1, \\ & C_t \geq 0,\ \ell_t \in \big[0, h\big],\ t = 0, 1, \ldots, T-1, \\ & K_T = 0. \end{aligned}$$

2. For each $t = 0, 1, \ldots, T-1$, the representative firm chooses the elements in $\mathcal{A}_F$ to solve

$$\begin{aligned} \max \quad & \Pi_t \equiv Y_t - r_{kt}^* K_{Ft} - w_t^* N_{Ft} \\ \text{subject to} \quad & Y_t = A_t F\big(K_{Ft}, N_{Ft}\big), \\ & K_{Ft}, N_{Ft} \geq 0. \end{aligned}$$

3. For each $t = 0, 1, \ldots, T-1$, all markets clear:

$$\begin{aligned} K_{Ft}^* &= K_t^*, \\ N_{Ft}^* &= h - \ell_t^*. \end{aligned}$$

Note the slight abuse of notation: the period-0 capital market clearing condition requires $K^*_{F0} = K_0$, where K_0 is exogenously given, not an equilibrium value.

Characterizing the Competitive Equilibrium

From the household's problem I get the conditions

$$u_\ell(C^*_t, \ell^*_t) = u_C(C^*_t, \ell^*_t) w^*_t, \tag{3.82}$$
$$u_C(C^*_t, \ell^*_t) = \beta u_C(C^*_{t+1}, \ell^*_{t+1})(r^*_{k,t+1} + 1 - \delta), \tag{3.83}$$
$$C^*_t + K^*_{t+1} = (r^*_{kt} + 1 - \delta)K^*_t + w^*_t(h - \ell^*_t), \tag{3.84}$$
$$C^*_{T-1} = (r^*_{k,T-1} + 1 - \delta)K^*_{T-1} + w^*_{T-1}(h - \ell^*_{T-1}). \tag{3.85}$$

(As it's clear from the context, I'm no longer listing the range that time runs from.) From the firm's problem,

$$r^*_{kt} = A_t F_K(K^*_{Ft}, N^*_{Ft}), \tag{3.86}$$
$$w^*_t = A_t F_N(K^*_{Ft}, N^*_{Ft}), \tag{3.87}$$

and finally, I add the market clearing conditions:

$$K^*_{Ft} = K^*_t, \tag{3.88}$$
$$N^*_{Ft} = h - \ell^*_t. \tag{3.89}$$

To characterize the equilibrium, first impose market clearing: use (3.88) and (3.89) in (3.86) and (3.87) to get

$$r^*_{kt} = A_t F_K(K^*_t, h - \ell^*_t), \tag{3.90}$$
$$w^*_t = A_t F_N(K^*_t, h - \ell^*_t). \tag{3.91}$$

Now get rid of wages: substituting (3.91) in (3.82) yields

$$u_\ell(C^*_t, \ell^*_t) = u_C(C^*_t, \ell^*_t) A_t F_N(K^*_t, h - \ell^*_t),$$

and get rid of interest rates by plugging (3.90) in (3.83):

$$u_C(C^*_t, \ell^*_t) = \beta u_C(C^*_{t+1}, \ell^*_{t+1}) \left[A_{t+1} F_K(K^*_{t+1}, h - \ell^*_{t+1}) + 1 - \delta\right].$$

Since $A_t F(K^*_t, h - \ell^*_t) = r^*_{kt} K^*_t + w^*_t(h - \ell^*_t)$ for $t = 0, 1, \ldots, T-1$ (profits are zero), substitute in (3.84) and (3.85) to get

$$C^*_t + K^*_{t+1} = A_t F(K^*_t, h - \ell^*_t) + (1 - \delta)K^*_t$$

and

$$C^*_{T-1} = A_{T-1} F(K^*_{T-1}, h - \ell^*_{T-1}) + (1 - \delta)K^*_{T-1}.$$

Three (Groups of) Key Equations

Gathering these results, the CE is uniquely characterized by a set of **intratemporal conditions**

$$u_\ell(C^*_t, \ell^*_t) = u_C(C^*_t, \ell^*_t) A_t F_N(K^*_t, h - \ell^*_t), \tag{3.92}$$

for $t = 0, 1, \ldots, T-1$; a set of **intertemporal conditions**

$$u_C\left(C_t^*, \ell_t^*\right) = \beta u_C\left(C_{t+1}^*, \ell_{t+1}^*\right)\left[A_{t+1}F_K\left(K_{t+1}^*, h - \ell_{t+1}^*\right) + 1 - \delta\right], \tag{3.93}$$

for $t = 0, 1, \ldots, T-2$, and a set of **aggregate feasibility constraints**, given by

$$C_t^* + K_{t+1}^* = A_t F\left(K_t^*, h - \ell_t^*\right) + \left(1 - \delta\right)K_t^*, \tag{3.94}$$

for $t = 0, 1, \ldots, T-2$, and

$$C_{T-1}^* = A_{T-1}F\left(K_{T-1}^*, h - \ell_{T-1}^*\right) + \left(1 - \delta\right)K_{T-1}^*, \tag{3.95}$$

for the last period, $T-1$. By inspection, (3.92)–(3.95) is a system of $3T-1$ variables in $3T-1$ equations; its solution yields the equilibrium sequences $\left\{C_t^*, \ell_t^*, K_{t+1}^*\right\}_{t=0}^{T-1}$. (Note I'm abusing notation once again, since $K_T^* = 0$ does not come out of this system of equations.) The equilibrium prices are backed out from equations (3.86) and (3.87), while the rest of the equilibrium values follow from the results above.

3.4 Up Next

In Section 3.1.3 I characterized a two-period economy and showed that solving for the equilibrium values requires working with a 5×5 system of nonlinear equations. While solving a 5×5 system is doable by hand, increasing the number of periods is not as easy as it seems.

To see why, consider a $T = 10$ economy: this requires me to solve a 29×29 system, which is far beyond the limit of what I can achieve with pencil and paper. Even worse, a $T=35$ economy (one generation) calls for the solution to a 104×104 system, and a $T=100$ economy (a century) demands that I make sense of a 299×299 system. (These calculations assume an annual frequency. What if I want to think in quarters instead?) If I want to tackle these problems, I *definitely* need a computer to do the heavy lifting.

Moreover, there's still one big issue waiting. If I want to think about an economy that goes on forever, I need something more technical than "an $\infty \times \infty$ system of equations"; I need to work around this problem if I want to analyze economies that are reasonable approximations to the real world. For the time being, I'll throw this issue under the rug and come back to attack it later, once we have the appropriate tools to handle infinite-horizon problems.

3.5 Bibliographic Notes

Just as in Chapter 2, the material in these last pages is geared toward pedagogy, not realism. (I'll change this tune pretty soon.) Readers who want to look for applications of a two-period model should look at Williamson (2017, see chapters 9–11).

3.6 Problems

3.6.1 Firm Profits in the Two-Period Model

Prove that optimal profits in (3.32) are zero for each $t = 0, 1$.

3.6.2 Interpreting Equilibrium Conditions

What is the economic interpretation of equations (3.52)–(3.56)?

3.6.3 Solving a CE in a Two-Period Model, Part I

Suppose that household preferences are represented by the utility function

$$U(C_0, \ell_0, C_1, \ell_1) = \log C_0 + \log \ell_0 + \beta (\log C_1 + \log \ell_1)$$

and that technology takes the Cobb–Douglas form $F(K_{Ft}, N_{Ft}) = K_{Ft}^{\alpha} N_{Ft}^{1-\alpha}$, for $t = 0, 1$. To make things tractable, set $\beta = \delta = A_0 = A_1 = 1$; $K_0 = 1{,}000$; $\alpha = 1/3$; and $h = 16$.

1. Write the system of equations that corresponds to (3.52)–(3.56) and verify that its solution is

$$\{C_0^*, \ell_0^*, K_1^*, C_1^*, \ell_1^*\} = \{28.8117, 8.4706, 9.6039, 7.3272, 9.6\}.$$

2. Find all the elements in the equilibrium allocations $\mathcal{A}_H$ and $\mathcal{A}_F$.
3. You know from your intermediate macroeconomics course that the household likes to smooth consumption as much as possible. However, the equilibrium above has $C_0^* = 28.8$ and $C_1^* = 7.3$. Why is this so? Explain.

3.6.4 Solving a CE in a Two-Period Model, Part II

Consider the same environment as in Problem 3.6.3 but now assume $A_1 = 2$. Find all the elements in $\mathcal{A}_H$ and $\mathcal{A}_F$. Are these results consistent with what you know from intermediate macroeconomics? Why or why not?

3.6.5 Solving a CE in a Two-Period Model with a Government Sector

Use Section 3.1.3 as a guideline to characterize the competitive equilibrium of the two-period model with a government sector found in Section 3.2.3. Your solution should include five equations in $\{C_0^*, \ell_0^*, K_1^*, C_1^*, \ell_1^*\}$.

3.6.6 Characterizing a Three-Period Model

Use Section 3.1 as a guideline to build, define, and characterize the competitive equilibrium of a three-period model. Your solution should include eight equations in $\{C_0^*, \ell_0^*, K_1^*, C_1^*, \ell_1^*, C_2^*, \ell_2^*, K_2^*\}$. Then (and only then) use the results from Section 3.3.3 to verify your results are correct.

3.6.7 Characterizing a Multi-Period Model with Logarithmic Preferences

Suppose household preferences are represented by the utility function

$$U = \sum_{t=0}^{T-1} \beta^t \left(\log C_t + \phi \log \ell_t\right),$$

where $\phi > 0$ represents the relative weight of leisure. Suppose also that technology takes the Cobb–Douglas form $F\left(K_{Ft}, N_{Ft}\right) = K_{Ft}^{\alpha} N_{Ft}^{1-\alpha}$, with $\alpha \in \left(0, 1\right)$. Find the equivalent expressions for equations (3.92)–(3.95).

3.6.8 Characterizing a Multi-Period Model with GHH Preferences

Suppose household preferences are represented by a Greenwood, Hercowitz, and Huffman (1988) utility function (hereafter GHH utility function)

$$U = \sum_{t=0}^{T-1} \beta^t \left[\frac{1}{1-\eta}\left(C_t - \frac{\left(h - \ell_t\right)^{1+\chi}}{1+\chi}\right)^{1-\eta} - 1\right],$$

where $1/\eta > 0$ denotes the **elasticity of intertemporal substitution** and $1/\chi > 0$ is the **Frisch elasticity of labor supply**. (Note that $h - \ell_t$ equals labor supply.) The production function is still a Cobb–Douglas functional form as in Problem 3.6.7. Find the equivalent expressions for equations (3.92)–(3.95).

3.6.9 Comparing Equilibrium Conditions

Compare the intratemporal, intertemporal, and feasibility conditions (3.92)–(3.95) derived from the logarithmic and GHH utility functions found in Problems 3.6.7 and 3.6.8. In particular, comment on how parameters η and χ affect the equilibrium conditions.

4 The Social Planner Problem

In Chapters 2 and 3, you learned how to define, characterize, and solve a competitive equilibrium (CE). However, you may also agree that defining an equilibrium is burdensome and, in addition, characterizing and solving a CE is a time-consuming process. The **social planner problem** (SPP) offers an alternative approach.

The SPP sets up the problem faced by a hypothetical *social planner*: a benevolent dictator who cares about the welfare of the representative household and wants to make it as well off as possible given the feasibility constraints of the economy. Since the planner doesn't need to worry about prices, the complexity of the SPP is much lower relative to the CE.

As you will see, the SPP yields the same equilibrium conditions as the more complicated CE. Understanding how this equivalency works – and the conditions under which it holds – will make our lives easier in the material ahead.

This chapter is short but its contents are important; Section 4.1 begins by explaining who the social planner is and what his contribution to the model economy is. Section 4.2 takes a detour and introduces the welfare theorems, which establish the conditions under which the solution to the SPP is identical to that of a CE. Finally, Section 4.3 starts laying out the foundations for later chapters by setting up a planner problem that abstracts from leisure and TFP.

4.1 The Social Planner Problem

Consider a benevolent dictator, called the social planner. To keep things simple, and without loss of generality, I assume the planner is in charge of a two-period economy similar to that in Section 3.1. Being a dictator, the planner orders the household to work a given amount of hours – and also orders the firm to hire the household the same amount of hours. If needed, the planner may take a certain amount of output (say, to hand it to the government) and give the remaining goods to the household.

Remark 4.1 Don't fall for the classic SPP pitfall: the social planner is *not* a stand-in for the government. As I use the SPP to solve for the equilibrium of economies with a government, this connection is not quite right.

The planner's goal is to choose values for the economy's endogenous variables in order to make the representative household as well off as possible. In this sense, the solution to the SPP is a **Pareto optimal** outcome: the planner is maximizing the utility of the household without making any other household worse off (it helps that there is only one household in the economy!). In this context, Pareto optimality means that the planner will not leave unused resources when choosing an allocation; put differently, he will not pick a point on the interior of the *production possibilities frontier*.

As the social planner is in charge of everything in the economy, it doesn't make sense to distinguish between household and firm quantities. I just assume the planner sets quantities in a way that markets clear.

4.1.1 The Planner's Restrictions

Even well-behaved dictators can't get free lunches: the planner must comply with the aggregate feasibility constraints, given by

$$\begin{aligned} A_0 F(K_0, h - \ell_0) &= C_0 + X_0, \\ A_1 F(K_1, h - \ell_1) &= C_1 + X_1, \end{aligned}$$

and the laws of motion for capital,

$$\begin{aligned} K_1 &= (1-\delta)K_0 + X_0, \\ K_2 &= (1-\delta)K_1 + X_1. \end{aligned}$$

I assume the household has strictly positive and bounded time and capital endowments h and K_0. As in Section 3.1, the household has no further need for capital after period 1; thus, the planner orders the household to transform capital to consumption so that $(1-\delta)K_1$ units of capital are exchanged for $(1-\delta)K_1$ units of consumption. Hence, $K_2 = 0$.

After combining the laws of motion for capital and the feasibility constraints, the SPP requires the planner to choose the elements in the allocation $\mathcal{A}_P = \{C_0^*, \ell_0^*, K_1^*, C_1^*, \ell_1^*, K_2^*\}$ to solve

$$\begin{aligned} \max \quad & u(C_0, \ell_0) + \beta u(C_1, \ell_1) \\ \text{subject to} \quad & A_0 F(K_0, h - \ell_0) = C_0 + K_1 - (1-\delta)K_0, \\ & A_1 F(K_1, h - \ell_1) = C_1 + K_2 - (1-\delta)K_1, \\ & C_0, C_1 \geq 0; \ \ell_0, \ell_1 \in [0, h], \\ & K_2 = 0, \end{aligned} \tag{4.1}$$

where the values $\{A_0, K_0, A_1\}$ are known to the planner.

While similar, the SPP (4.1) is not identical to the representative household's UMP from Definition 3.4. The feasibility constraints replace the household's budget equations, which follows from the fact that the planner doesn't use prices when deciding on the (Pareto) optimal allocations. Note, however, that the statement of an SPP is much shorter than that of the associated CE, Definition 3.4.

4.1.2 Characterizing the Solution

I use a Lagrangian function to characterize the SPP, which takes the form

$$\begin{aligned}\mathscr{L} &= u(C_0, \ell_0) + \beta u(C_1, \ell_1) \\ &\quad + \lambda_0 \left[A_0 F(K_0, h - \ell_0) - C_0 - K_1 + (1-\delta)K_0\right] \\ &\quad + \beta\lambda_1 \left[A_1 F(K_1, h - \ell_1) - C_1 - K_2 + (1-\delta)K_1\right] + \zeta K_2.\end{aligned}$$

First-order conditions with respect to $\{C_0, \ell_0, K_1, C_1, \ell_1, K_2\}$ and the multipliers are

$$C_0: \quad u_C(C_0, \ell_0) - \lambda_0 = 0, \tag{4.2}$$

$$\ell_0: \quad u_\ell(C_0, \ell_0) + \lambda_0 A_0 F_N(K_0, h - \ell_0)(-1) = 0,$$

$$K_1: \quad -\lambda_0 + \beta\lambda_1 \left[A_1 F_K(K_1, h - \ell_1) + 1 - \delta\right] = 0,$$

$$C_1: \quad \beta u_C(C_1, \ell_1) - \beta\lambda_1 = 0, \tag{4.3}$$

$$\ell_1: \quad \beta u_\ell(C_1, \ell_1) + \beta\lambda_1 A_1 F_N(K_1, h - \ell_1)(-1) = 0,$$

$$K_2: \quad -\beta\lambda_1 + \zeta = 0,$$

$$\lambda_0: \quad A_0 F(K_0, h - \ell_0) - C_0 - K_1 + (1-\delta)K_0 = 0,$$

$$\beta\lambda_1: \quad A_1 F(K_1, h - \ell_1) - C_1 - K_2 + (1-\delta)K_1 = 0,$$

$$\zeta: \quad K_2 = 0.$$

Just as in Section 3.1, I substitute equations (4.2) and (4.3) where needed. The reduced system looks like

$$u_\ell(C_0, \ell_0) = u_C(C_0, \ell_0) A_0 F_N(K_0, h - \ell_0),$$

$$u_C(C_0, \ell_0) = \beta u_C(C_1, \ell_1)\left[A_1 F_K(K_1, h - \ell_1) + 1 - \delta\right],$$

$$u_\ell(C_1, \ell_1) = u_C(C_1, \ell_1) A_1 F_N(K_1, h - \ell_1),$$

$$\zeta = \beta u_C(C_1, \ell_1),$$

$$C_0 + K_1 = A_0 F(K_0, h - \ell_0) + (1-\delta)K_0,$$

$$C_1 + K_2 = A_1 F(K_1, h - \ell_1) + (1-\delta)K_1, \tag{4.4}$$

$$K_2 = 0. \tag{4.5}$$

Following on the same script laid out in Section 3.1, I plug equation (4.5) into (4.4); doing so, the system that characterizes the solution to the SPP is given by

$$u_\ell(C_0, \ell_0) = u_C(C_0, \ell_0) A_0 F_N(K_0, h - \ell_0), \tag{4.6}$$

$$u_C(C_0, \ell_0) = \beta u_C(C_1, \ell_1)\left[A_1 F_K(K_1, h - \ell_1) + 1 - \delta\right], \tag{4.7}$$

$$u_\ell(C_1, \ell_1) = u_C(C_1, \ell_1) A_1 F_N(K_1, h - \ell_1), \tag{4.8}$$

$$C_0 + K_1 = A_0 F(K_0, h - \ell_0) + (1-\delta)K_0, \tag{4.9}$$

$$C_1 = A_1 F(K_1, h - \ell_1) + (1-\delta)K_1, \tag{4.10}$$

along with the multiplier equation

$$\zeta = \beta u_C(C_1, \ell_1).$$

Compare the system (4.6)–(4.10) with the set of equations that characterize the competitive equilibrium, namely, (3.52)–(3.56). Other than a minor cosmetic change – the equations above don't have asterisks attached to them – both sets of equations are identical. This is not a coincidence, as the next section shows.

4.2 Intermezzo IV: The Welfare Theorems

The derivations above show that the solutions to the SPP and the CE are the same. This result isn't just luck or a feature of dealing with a two-period economy; rather, it's a consequence of the **welfare theorems**. The first of these theorems tells us about the properties of a CE:

Theorem 4.2 (First Fundamental Theorem of Welfare Economics) *Suppose the set* $\left\{C_t^*, l_t^*, K_{t+1}^*\right\}_{t=0}^{T-1}$ *is a CE allocation. Then, under certain conditions, this allocation is Pareto optimal.*

This theorem shows Adam Smith's *invisible hand*: if some conditions apply, then market allocations are efficient and an almighty planner cannot improve on said market outcomes. The second theorem provides a converse to this result:

Theorem 4.3 (Second Fundamental Theorem of Welfare Economics) *Suppose the set* $\left\{C_t^*, l_t^*, K_{t+1}^*\right\}_{t=0}^{T-1}$ *is the solution to an SPP (and therefore Pareto optimal). Then, under certain conditions, there exist prices* $\left\{r_{kt}^*, w_t^*\right\}_{t=0}^{T-1}$ *that together with the allocation give rise to a CE.*

Arguably, the second theorem is even more interesting than the first: if some conditions apply, then for any Pareto-optimal allocation there exists a price system that supports said allocation as a market equilibrium.

What the Theorems Imply

In plain English: under certain conditions, (i) any CE allocation is Pareto optimal and (ii) any Pareto-optimal allocation can be implemented as a CE. As a consequence, it is convenient to first solve the (simpler) SPP and then use its solution to derive the CE allocation values.

That being said, the equivalency between CE and Pareto-optimal allocations is not guaranteed, and it breaks down when the economy exhibits

- Externalities.
- Asymmetric information.
- Bounded rationality, either on the household or the firm side.
- Market power, either on the household or the firm side.
- Distortionary taxes.

Models with externalities, asymmetric information, or bounded rationality are of no consequence since this book doesn't consider environments that incorporate these frictions. In addition, I've taken care of market power by imposing price-taking behavior by the household and the firm.

However, I *will* be working extensively in environments with market power and distortionary taxes later in the book. More precisely,

1. **New Keynesian models** drop the perfect competition assumption; instead, these models assume a monopolistically competitive market structure and go from there. In this case, an SPP will not allow us to solve for equilibrium quantities – a CE is the way to go.
2. Real-world economies have governments that do not rely on lump-sum taxes to get their tax revenue; they use *distortionary* taxes instead. In this case, I have to work with a CE that includes the effect of these type of taxes, also known as a **tax-distorted competitive equilibrium**, or TDCE.

I'll tackle both of these cases later in the book.

4.3 A Planner Problem without Leisure and TFP

I am now in a position to start thinking deeply about the dynamics (and solution) of multi-period models. To help set ideas, let's build the SPP associated with a multi-period economy with the following simplifying assumptions: (i) the household doesn't care about leisure (and thus supplies its entire time endowment h to the firm) and (ii) TFP is constant and normalized to 1 in all periods ($A_t = 1$). Under these assumptions, the SPP requires the planner to choose elements in $\mathcal{A}_P \equiv \left\{C_t^*, K_{t+1}^*\right\}_{t=0}^{T-1}$ to solve

$$\begin{aligned}
\max \quad & \sum_{t=0}^{T-1} \beta^t u(C_t) \\
\text{subject to} \quad & F(K_t, h) = C_t + K_{t+1} - (1-\delta)K_t,\ t = 0, 1, \ldots, T-1, \\
& C_t \geq 0,\ t = 0, 1, \ldots, T-1, \\
& K_T = 0,
\end{aligned}$$

where K_0 is known to the planner. Without loss of generality, set $h = 1$. Also, to economize on notation, let $f(K_t) \equiv F(K_t, 1)$; after doing this, the SPP now reads

$$\begin{aligned}
\max_{\{C_t, K_{t+1}\}_{t=0}^{T-1}} \quad & \sum_{t=0}^{T-1} \beta^t u(C_t) \\
\text{subject to} \quad & f(K_t) = C_t + K_{t+1} - (1-\delta)K_t,\ t = 0, 1, \ldots, T-1, \\
& C_t \geq 0,\ t = 0, 1, \ldots, T-1, \\
& K_T = 0.
\end{aligned} \tag{4.11}$$

Let's characterize the solution to this particular SPP. I set up the Lagrangian function as

$$\mathcal{L} = \sum_{t=0}^{T-1} \beta^t \left\{u(C_t) + \lambda_t \left[f(K_t) - C_t - K_{t+1} + (1-\delta)K_t\right]\right\} + \zeta K_T.$$

First-order conditions are

$$C_t: \quad \beta^t u'(C_t) - \beta^t \lambda_t = 0, \tag{4.12}$$

$$K_{t+1}: \quad -\beta^t \lambda_t + \beta^{t+1}\lambda_{t+1}\left[f'(K_{t+1}) + 1 - \delta\right] = 0, \tag{4.13}$$

$$K_T: \quad -\beta^{T-1}\lambda_{T-1} + \zeta = 0, \tag{4.14}$$

$$\beta^t \lambda_t: \quad f(K_t) - C_t - K_{t+1} + (1-\delta)K_t = 0, \tag{4.15}$$

$$\zeta: \quad K_T = 0. \tag{4.16}$$

(Note the slight change in notation: as both the utility and production functions now depend on only one variable, I use a prime to denote derivatives.) The intertemporal conditions come from combining (4.12) and (4.13):

$$u'(C_t) = \beta u'(C_{t+1})\left[f'(K_{t+1}) + 1 - \delta\right], \tag{4.17}$$

for $t = 0, 1, \ldots, T-2$. I also add the aggregate feasibility constraints, given by equation (4.15):

$$C_t + K_{t+1} = f(K_t) + (1-\delta)K_t, \tag{4.18}$$

for $t = 0, 1, \ldots, T-2$, and

$$C_{T-1} = f(K_{T-1}) + (1-\delta)K_{T-1}, \tag{4.19}$$

for the last period, $T-1$; remember that K_0 is given and $K_T = 0$ must hold given equation (4.16). Equations (4.16)–(4.19) characterize the solution to the benchmark SPP (and its associated CE, given the welfare theorems); they form a $(2T-1) \times (2T-1)$ system which, given parameter values and functional forms for u and F, yield the equilibrium allocation that I'm looking for. Of course, (4.14) remains an equilibrium condition but it doesn't affect the values of the endogenous variables along the equilibrium path.

Example 4.1 Suppose household preferences are given by the lifetime utility function

$$U = \sum_{t=0}^{T-1} \beta^t \log C_t.$$

Let $F(K_t, N_t) = K_t^{\alpha} N_t^{1-\alpha}$, $\alpha \in (0,1)$, and K_0 be given. I now show how to derive the expressions equivalent to (4.17), (4.18), and (4.19).

To do this, note that (i) $u'(C_t) = 1/C_t$ and (ii) if $h = 1$, then $Y_t = K_t^{\alpha}$. Hence, (4.17) is given by

$$\frac{1}{C_t} = \beta \frac{\alpha K_{t+1}^{\alpha-1} + 1 - \delta}{C_{t+1}}, \quad t = 0, 1, \ldots, T-2.$$

Similarly, (4.18) is given by

$$C_t + K_{t+1} = K_t^{\alpha} + (1-\delta)K_t, \; t = 0, 1, \ldots, T-2$$

and (4.19) equals

$$C_{T-1} = K_{T-1}^{\alpha} + (1-\delta)K_{T-1}.$$

As expected, this is a $(2T-1) \times (2T-1)$ system of equations.

4.4 Up Next

Chapters 2 through 4 have provided the necessary tools to think about equilibrium models under the assumption of a finite time horizon. Basically, "solving for the CE" of these models is equivalent to finding the zeros of a large system of nonlinear equations. Armed only with pencil and paper, this is easier said than done.

This is why familiarizing ourselves with numerical methods and computational algorithms is useful. Finding the zeros of a large system of (linear or nonlinear) equations is a rather trivial task for a computer; we only need to know *how* to do this efficiently so we are able to code it and get to work (and this is the goal of Online Appendix 2).

Of course, I have yet to discuss what happens when I want to tackle economies where $T \to \infty$. Even though it doesn't seem like it, we're making a lot of progress on this front.

4.5 Problems

4.5.1 Solving an SPP in a Two-Period Model

Suppose household preferences are represented by the lifetime utility function

$$U = \log C_0 + \log \ell_0 + \beta\left(\log C_1 + \log \ell_1\right)$$

and that technology takes the Cobb–Douglas form $F\left(K_{Ft}, N_{Ft}\right) = K_{Ft}^{\alpha} N_{Ft}^{1-\alpha}$ for $t = 0, 1$. To make things tractable, set $\beta = \delta = A_0 = A_1 = 1$; $K_0 = 1{,}000$; $\alpha = 1/3$; and $h = 16$. Derive equations (4.6)–(4.10) and make an argument – you don't need to calculate anything – to show that the solution to this problem is exactly the same as the one for Problem 3.6.3.

4.5.2 Characterizing an Equilibrium under GHH Preferences

Set up the associated SPP for the economy described in Problem 3.6.8 in Chapter 3. Once you're done with this, characterize the economy above; that is, derive the equivalent expressions for equations (4.17), (4.18), and (4.19).

4.5.3 A Second Pass at the Welfare Theorems

Take a dive into an advanced macroeconomics book (e.g., Stokey, Lucas & Prescott 1989, Acemoglu 2009) to tackle the questions below:

1. Prove Theorem 4.2 for the one-period case. What explicit assumptions do you need?
2. Prove Theorem 4.3 for the one-period case. Is this as simple as that of Theorem 4.2? What explicit assumptions do you need?

4.5.4 Consequences of Inelastic Labor Supply

Why does the set of equilibrium conditions from problem (4.11) lack *intratemporal* equations?

4.5.5 Characterizing an Equilibrium under CRRA Preferences

Suppose that household preferences are given by the constant relative risk aversion (CRRA) utility form

$$U = \sum_{t=0}^{T-1} \beta^t \left(\frac{C_t^{1-\eta} - 1}{1 - \eta} \right),$$

where $1/\eta > 0$ represents the elasticity of intertemporal substitution. Let $h = 1$, $Y_t = K_t^{\alpha} N_t^{1-\alpha}$ with $\alpha \in (0, 1)$, and K_0 be given. Derive expressions equivalent to (4.17), (4.18), and (4.19).

Part II

Solution Methods

5 Steady States and Finite Horizons

By now you can characterize a competitive equilibrium in a multi-period setting and also use the equivalency between the social planner's problem and the competitive equilibrium. However, we shouldn't lose track of our main goal: modeling dynamic economies that are useful for policy simulation exercises.

This chapter brings us one step closer, as I introduce the concept of the **steady state**. Although fairly straightforward, this concept is critical for the material that follows. I start in Section 5.1, which presents the economic model I'll use as an example throughout this chapter (and the next ones). Section 5.2 introduces – and shows how to find – the steady state in a dynamic model; Section 5.3 then makes an argument that economies with a finite horizon do not have a steady state, and thus we need to drop this assumption.

Of course, "solving" an infinite-horizon economy is far from trivial, which is why Section 5.4 introduces the concept of the policy function. Instead of finding the sequence(s) of equilibrium values that satisfy the first-order conditions, a policy function is a "rule" that determines the model's equilibrium values as a function of the current state of the economy. (This statement will make much more sense below.)

5.1 Revisiting the Social Planner Problem

Let's start from the SPP discussed in Section 4.3. In this simplified environment, the household doesn't care about leisure – it supplies its entire time endowment to the firm – and $A_t = 1$ in all periods. The SPP is given by

$$\begin{aligned} \max_{\{C_t, K_{t+1}\}_{t=0}^{T-1}} \quad & \sum_{t=0}^{T-1} \beta^t u(C_t) \qquad (5.1) \\ \text{subject to} \quad & f(K_t) = C_t + K_{t+1} - (1-\delta)K_t,\ t = 0, 1, \ldots, T-1, \\ & C_t \geq 0,\ t = 0, 1, \ldots, T-1, \\ & K_T = 0. \end{aligned}$$

Back in Chapter 4, I showed that the intertemporal conditions take the form

$$u'(C_t) = \beta u'(C_{t+1})\left[f'(K_{t+1}) + 1 - \delta\right], \qquad (5.2)$$

for $t = 0, 1, \ldots, T-2$; the aggregate feasibility constraints are

$$C_t + K_{t+1} = f(K_t) + (1-\delta)K_t, \qquad (5.3)$$

for $t = 0, 1, \ldots, T-2$; and

$$C_{T-1} = f(K_{T-1}) + (1-\delta)K_{T-1}, \tag{5.4}$$

for period $T-1$, where $K_T = 0$ needs to be satisfied. Equations (5.2)–(5.4) form a $(2T-1) \times (2T-1)$ system that characterizes the equilibrium of the economy. Since I want to arrive at quantitative results, it is useful to review Example 4.1, reproduced below for convenience.

Example 5.1 Suppose household preferences are given by

$$U = \sum_{t=0}^{T-1} \beta^t \log C_t.$$

Let $F(K_t, N_t) = K_t^{\alpha} N_t^{1-\alpha}$, $\alpha \in (0,1)$, and K_0 be given. Example 4.1 shows equation (5.2) is given by

$$\frac{1}{C_t} = \beta \frac{\alpha K_{t+1}^{\alpha-1} + 1 - \delta}{C_{t+1}}, \tag{5.5}$$

for $t = 0, 1, \ldots, T-2$; (5.3) takes the form

$$C_t + K_{t+1} = K_t^{\alpha} + (1-\delta)K_t, \tag{5.6}$$

for $t = 0, 1, \ldots, T-2$; and (5.4) is simply

$$C_{T-1} = K_{T-1}^{\alpha} + (1-\delta)K_{T-1} \tag{5.7}$$

and holds in the last period, $T-1$.

5.2 The Steady State

Loosely speaking, the steady state is a *dynamic equilibrium* of the economy, such that the conditions $C_t = C_{t+1} = C_{ss}$ and $K_t = K_{t+1} = K_{ss}$ are satisfied. (Here the subscript "*ss*" denotes a steady-state value.) Imposing these steady-state conditions, equation (5.2) becomes

$$u'(C_{ss}) = \beta u'(C_{ss})\left[f'(K_{ss}) + 1 - \delta\right],$$

which I simplify to

$$1 = \beta\left[f'(K_{ss}) + 1 - \delta\right]. \tag{5.8}$$

Similarly, equation (5.3) becomes

$$C_{ss} + K_{ss} = K_{ss}^{\alpha} - (1-\delta)K_{ss},$$

and algebra allows me to rewrite the expression as

$$C_{ss} = K_{ss}^{\alpha} + \delta K_{ss}. \tag{5.9}$$

(Yes, I'm purposefully ignoring an equation, but only because I want to make a point. For now, I move along and come back to address this matter in a minute.) Equations (5.8) and (5.9) form a system of two equations in $\{C_{ss}, K_{ss}\}$. Given a functional form for f, equation (5.8) allows me to solve for the value of K_{ss}; with this at hand, I derive steady-state consumption C_{ss} from equation (5.9).

Notation 5.1 If there is no risk of confusion, I use variables without subscripts to denote steady-state values (e.g., "C" instead of "C_{ss}").

Example 5.2 Consider the same setup as Example 5.1. In the steady state, equations (5.5) and (5.6) become

$$\frac{1}{C} = \beta \frac{\alpha K^{\alpha-1} + 1 - \delta}{C}, \tag{5.10}$$

$$K^{\alpha} = C + \delta K. \tag{5.11}$$

Take equation (5.10) and multiply across by C to get

$$1 = \beta\left(\alpha K^{\alpha-1} + 1 - \delta\right).$$

This is one equation in steady-state capital; after some algebra, the solution to K_{ss} is

$$K_{ss} = \left[\frac{\alpha\beta}{1 - \beta(1-\delta)}\right]^{1/(1-\alpha)}.$$

Deriving the value for C is easy: rearrange equation (5.11) to read $C = K^{\alpha} - \delta K$ and then plug and play to get

$$C_{ss} = \left[\frac{\alpha\beta}{1 - \beta(1-\delta)}\right]^{\alpha/(1-\alpha)} - \delta\left[\frac{\alpha\beta}{1 - \beta(1-\delta)}\right]^{1/(1-\alpha)}.$$

One (perhaps not obvious) takeaway from Example 5.2 is this: *all steady-state values are a function of model parameters*. Put differently, the dynamic equilibrium of the model does not depend on initial conditions; rather, it depends on the "deep" characteristics of the economy (i.e., the model parameters).

5.3 The Need for Infinite Horizons

Solving the $(2T-1) \times (2T-1)$ system formed by, say, (5.5)–(5.7) is straightforward: just apply brute force (or the tools from Online Appendix 2) to find the values $\{C_t^*, K_{t+1}^*\}_{t=0}^{T}$. But as long as T is finite, the economy cannot have a steady state.

5.3.1 No Steady States in Finite Time

To show why it's not possible to have steady states when T is finite, let's return to the SPP (5.1), shown below for convenience:

$$\begin{aligned} \max_{\{C_t, K_{t+1}\}_{t=0}^{T-1}} \quad & \sum_{t=0}^{T-1} \beta^t u(C_t) \\ \text{subject to} \quad & f(K_t) = C_t + K_{t+1} - (1-\delta)K_t, \ t = 0, 1, \ldots, T-1, \\ & C_t \geq 0, \ t = 0, 1, \ldots, T-1, \\ & K_T = 0. \end{aligned} \tag{5.12}$$

Does this problem have a steady state to begin with? No. Recall that in any steady state we have $C_t = C_{t+1} = C_{ss}$ and $K_t = K_{t+1} = K_{ss}$; clearly, $K_{ss} > 0$, but one of the equilibrium conditions in this SPP requires $K_T = 0$. It follows that we cannot have a steady state since $K_T \neq K_{ss}$.

5.3.2 The Benchmark Social Planner Problem

The way forward is to drop the finite-horizon assumption. How does this change earlier results? Consider the infinite-horizon counterpart of SPP (5.12), namely,

$$\begin{aligned} \max_{\{C_t, K_{t+1}\}_{t=0}^{\infty}} \quad & \sum_{t=0}^{\infty} \beta^t u(C_t) \\ \text{subject to} \quad & f(K_t) = C_t + K_{t+1} - (1-\delta)K_t, \ t = 0, 1, \ldots, \\ & C_t \geq 0, \ t = 0, 1, \ldots, \end{aligned} \tag{5.13}$$

where K_0 is given. In what follows, I will call problem (5.13) the **benchmark social planner problem**. A Lagrangian function is still useful to characterize the solution to problem (5.13); I get

$$\mathscr{L} = \sum_{t=0}^{\infty} \beta^t \{u(C_t) + \lambda_t [f(K_t) - C_t - K_{t+1} + (1-\delta)K_t]\}.$$

I now take first-order conditions with respect to the two decision variables C_t and K_{t+1} and the multiplier $\beta^t \lambda_t$; as long as I don't pay much attention to the infinity sign on top of the sum operator, this is rather straightforward:

$$\begin{aligned} C_t: \quad & \beta^t u'(C_t) - \beta^t \lambda_t = 0, \\ K_{t+1}: \quad & -\beta^t \lambda_t + \beta^{t+1} \lambda_{t+1} [f'(K_{t+1}) + 1 - \delta] = 0, \\ \beta^t \lambda_t: \quad & f(K_t) - C_t - K_{t+1} + (1-\delta)K_t = 0. \end{aligned}$$

Notation 5.2 To avoid clutter, from now on I won't add the "$t = 0, 1, \ldots$" clarification.

I combine these expressions just as before; not surprisingly, the intertemporal and feasibility conditions look identical to the finite-horizon case, equations (5.2) and (5.3). The equilibrium conditions are now given by

$$u'(C_t) = \beta u'(C_{t+1}) [f'(K_{t+1}) + 1 - \delta], \tag{5.14}$$

$$C_t + K_{t+1} = f(K_t) + (1 - \delta)K_t. \tag{5.15}$$

So, what changes? First, I now have infinitely many equations in infinitely many variables. This last fact is problematic, since I don't know of any way of brute-forcing a solution for a system of this nature. Second, this infinite-horizon economy does not have a terminal condition – I cannot ask for "$K_\infty = 0$." The first issue is a much bigger problem to solve, so I will put it on hold until I get to Section 5.4. In the meantime, I will argue that the lack of a terminal condition is not that much of an issue in the first place.

5.3.3 Finite vs. Infinite: The Transversality Condition

In a finite-period environment, there is a perfectly defined path for capital, as I require $K_T = 0$ to hold as an equilibrium condition – see equation (5.4). Indeed, when I'm dealing with a finite horizon, the economy does not have a steady state: the time path of K_t looks like an inverted U and, as $t \to T$, the capital stock must fall in order to satisfy this terminal condition.

When the economy no longer has a finite horizon, I require a technical condition – the **transversality condition** (TVC) – to hold:

$$\lim_{t \to \infty} \beta^t \lambda_t K_{t+1} = 0. \tag{5.16}$$

Loosely speaking, the TVC prevents the household from accumulating capital at a faster rate than what is optimal. For an infinite-horizon problem like (5.13), equation (5.16) is a necessary condition, as are (5.14) and (5.15).

5.3.4 Characterizing the Infinite Solution

From (5.15) I solve for consumption as a function of output today and capital tomorrow:

$$C_t = f(K_t) - K_{t+1} + (1 - \delta)K_t, \tag{5.17}$$

and then use equation (5.17) to substitute in (5.14). This process yields

$$u'\left[f(K_t) - K_{t+1} + (1-\delta)K_t\right] = \beta u'\left[f(K_{t+1}) - K_{t+2} + (1-\delta)K_{t+1}\right]\left[f'(K_{t+1}) + 1 - \delta\right]. \tag{5.18}$$

Equation (5.18) is a second-order difference equation. Paired with the TVC (5.16), these two equations completely characterize the sequence $\left\{K^*_{t+1}\right\}_{t=0}^{\infty}$ that solves the benchmark SPP (5.13).

5.4 The Policy Function

Dropping the finite-horizon assumption is not innocuous. Why? Well, recall that the techniques covered so far – which assume T is finite – allow me to solve the system of equations that characterizes the equilibrium.

But what happens when the system that characterizes the equilibrium has an infinite number of equations in an infinite number of variables? While I am still able to characterize the solution as a set of intertemporal and aggregate feasibility conditions, I can no longer "solve" for the equilibrium values as I did before.

The way forward, instead, starts by looking at the problem that the planner faces every period. In period 0, the planner needs to decide how much output $f(K_0)$ to assign as next-period capital (K_1) and how much to allocate to the consumer (C_0). However, in period 1, the planner faces the same problem as in period 0, namely, deciding how much output $f(K_1)$ to assign as next-period capital (K_2) and how much to allocate to the consumer (C_1). This process repeats on and on.

Since the planner's problem is the same regardless of the period under consideration (by assumption, functions u and f remain constant over time), it makes sense to approach the problem in a different way: instead of finding the sequence $\left\{K_{t+1}^*\right\}_{t=0}^{\infty}$ that solves the infinite-dimensional system of equilibrium conditions in (5.18), I now look for a function $g : \mathbb{R}_+ \to \mathbb{R}_+$ that satisfies

$$\begin{aligned}
K_1^* &= g\left(K_0\right),\\
K_2^* &= g\left(K_1^*\right),\\
&\vdots\\
K_{t+1}^* &= g\left(K_t^*\right),
\end{aligned}$$

and so on, *such that the sequence* $\left\{K_{t+1}^*\right\}_{t=0}^{\infty}$ *generated by* g *satisfies* (5.18). Function g is called the **policy function**. Once I know what g is, calculating the equilibrium sequence for consumption $\left\{C_t^*\right\}_{t=0}^{\infty}$ is a trivial task since, following (5.17), consumption is a known function of capital:

$$\begin{aligned}
C_1^* &= f\left(K_0\right) - K_1^* + (1-\delta)K_0,\\
C_2^* &= f\left(K_1^*\right) - K_2^* + (1-\delta)K_1^*,\\
&\vdots\\
C_t^* &= f\left(K_t^*\right) - K_{t+1}^* + (1-\delta)K_t^*,
\end{aligned}$$

and so on.

Under fairly mild conditions, the policy function g exists and has nice properties; that being said, proving this fact formally is way beyond the scope of this book. (Chapter 4 in Stokey et al. 1989 is a good place to start.) The bad news is that except for a few select cases, it is impossible to derive the policy function for a problem of this nature using only pencil and paper. Below I present one of these few exceptions, which requires me to take the infinite-horizon benchmark SPP (5.13) and impose full depreciation of the capital stock.

Example 5.3 Consider the same environment as in Example 5.1, but now I assume that (i) $T \to \infty$ and (ii) the capital stock has full depreciation, which requires setting $\delta = 1$. This changes the intertemporal and aggregate feasibility conditions, equations (5.5) and (5.6), to

$$\frac{1}{C_t} = \alpha\beta \frac{K_{t+1}^{\alpha-1}}{C_{t+1}},$$
$$C_t = K_t^{\alpha} - K_{t+1}.$$

I combine both expressions to get the equivalent of equation (5.18), which is

$$\frac{1}{K_t^{\alpha} - K_{t+1}} = \alpha\beta \frac{K_{t+1}^{\alpha-1}}{K_{t+1}^{\alpha} - K_{t+2}}. \tag{5.19}$$

I now use the **method of undetermined coefficients** to derive an expression for the policy function. The procedure works as follows: I guess a particular policy function and then verify whether this conjecture is correct or not. (As you may suspect, the difficulty comes from finding a "correct" guess that allows the model to work.)
To set ideas, I guess that the policy function takes the form

$$K_{t+1} = g(K_t) = bK_t^{\alpha},$$

so that next-period capital is a proportion $b \in (0,1)$ of current-period output K_t^{α}. Substituting bK_t^{α} for K_{t+1} and bK_{t+1}^{α} for K_{t+2} in (5.19) gives

$$\frac{1}{K_t^{\alpha} - bK_t^{\alpha}} = \alpha\beta \frac{K_{t+1}^{\alpha-1}}{K_{t+1}^{\alpha} - bK_{t+1}^{\alpha}},$$

which is a first-order difference equation instead of a second-order one. Now take common factors and simplify:

$$\frac{1}{(1-b)K_t^{\alpha}} = \alpha\beta \frac{K_{t+1}^{\alpha-1}}{(1-b)K_{t+1}^{\alpha}} \implies \frac{1}{K_t^{\alpha}} = \alpha\beta \frac{1}{K_{t+1}}.$$

Solving for K_{t+1}, I get

$$K_{t+1} = \alpha\beta K_t^{\alpha} \tag{5.20}$$

and thus $b = \alpha\beta$, so I've verified my original guess. Equation (5.20) is the policy function of this economy. Given a value for K_0, the sequence $\{K_{t+1}^{*}\}_{t=0}^{\infty}$ is obtained recursively with (5.20): for instance, K_1 is given by

$$K_1^* = g(K_0) = \alpha\beta K_0^\alpha$$

and K_2 is given by

$$K_2^* = g(K_1^*) = \alpha\beta(K_1^*)^\alpha = \alpha\beta(\alpha\beta K_0^\alpha)^\alpha,$$

where the last equality shows the recursive structure of the policy function.

5.4.1 Using the Policy Function

What can I do with a policy function? A lot. To start, set the parameter values to $\alpha = 0.33$ and $\beta = 0.95$. The policy function (5.20) equals

$$K_{t+1} = 0.3135K_t^{0.33}.$$

I next plot the policy function to visualize its properties, as shown in Figure 5.1: note the policy function is strictly increasing and strictly concave. Moreover, the steady state is found at the intersection of the policy function and the 45° line; since the diagonal is mathematically equivalent to the function $y = x$, the point of intersection with the policy function guarantees that $K_{t+1} = K_t$, which is the definition of the steady state.

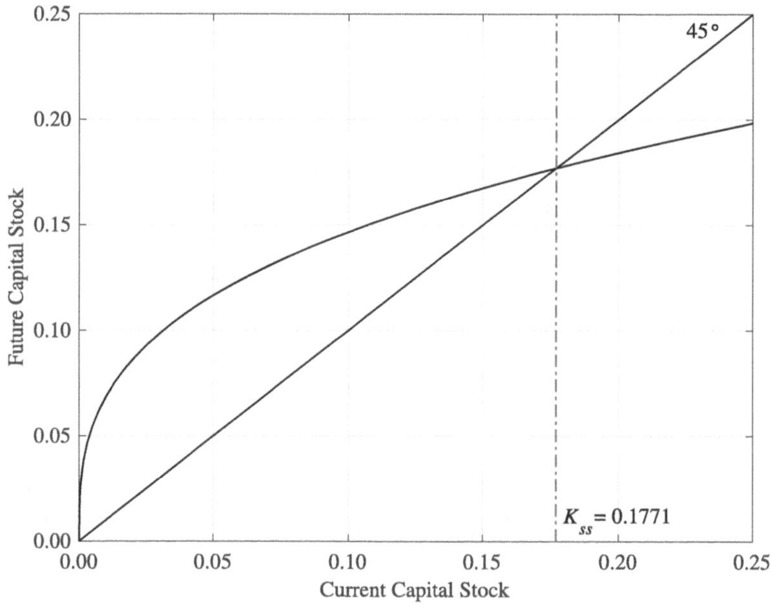

Figure 5.1 Policy function for the economy in Example 5.3. Note how it intersects with the 45° line exactly at the steady-state value $K_{ss} = 0.1771$.

For this particular parametrization, $K_{ss} = 0.1771$. Thus, given any $K_0 \in \mathbb{R}_{++}$, the policy function shows that the economy will converge to K_{ss}. Indeed, given an initial capital stock $K_0 = 0.02$, Figure 5.2 shows that the capital stock monotonically increases to the steady-state value. Moreover, the convergence is fast, as the simulated value is virtually indistinguishable from the steady state by period 7.

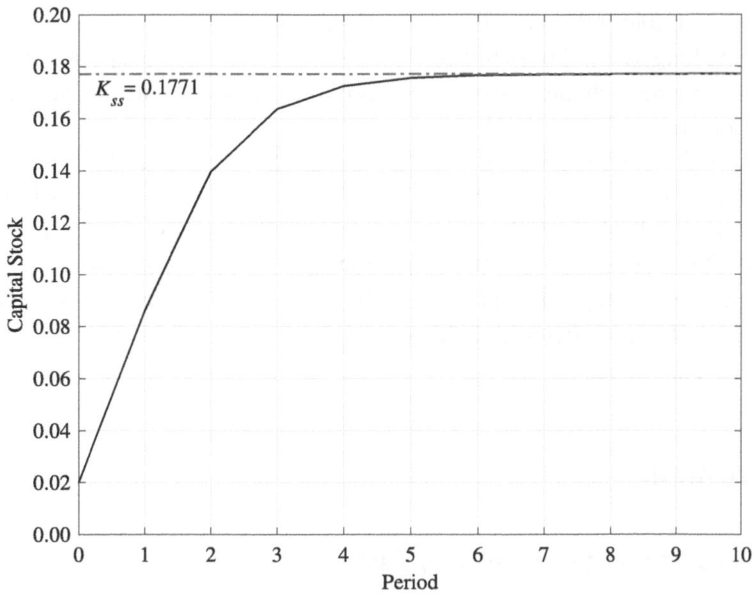

Figure 5.2 Simulated path of capital for the economy in Example 5.3, starting at $K_0 = 0.02$. Note the fast convergence toward the steady-state value $K_{ss} = 0.1771$.

5.5 Up Next

Let's summarize what you've learned in this chapter:

1. Given an initial capital value K_0, the policy function generates the equilibrium sequence $\left\{K_{t+1}^*\right\}_{t=0}^{\infty}$.
2. Once the capital stock reaches its steady-state value (so that $K_t = K_{ss}$), it remains there forever. This is the same notion of convergence that you know from the Solow growth model (see Online Appendix 3).

It is possible to show (but I won't) that under fairly general conditions, an infinite-horizon sequence problem – like the ones we are interested in – has a solution (i.e., a policy function). Proving this fact requires taking a dive into the field of **dynamic programming** (Bellman 1957). The reason behind this choice is that doing so would take us too far from our goal with little return in terms of empirical applications.

What I'll do instead is to build upon the concepts we've developed so far and think about approximations to the equilibrium conditions around the economy's steady state. Put differently, instead of worrying about finding a policy function that works *globally* (like the one in Figure 5.1), my goal is to solve a much simpler problem: finding a policy function that works *locally*; that is, within an interval around the steady state.

Following on Figure 5.1, think of a policy function that is fairly accurate within the $[0.15, 0.20]$ interval but fails miserably outside of this range. Why would I want to do this? I can think of two reasons:

1. It's simpler relative to the alternative, and
2. As long as the shocks hitting the economy are small (this phrase will make more sense in the next chapter), the local approximation works just as well as the global policy function.

In a nutshell, what I want to do is to transform a highly nonlinear system into something that is linear. As I will show, the method of undetermined coefficients (or, for more complicated problems, linear algebra) offers a way to derive policy functions for an infinite-dimensional system of equations, provided said equations are linear. In the meantime, the last step is to add a stochastic component to our economy. By construction, the real world is not deterministic, and we want our models to be as similar as possible to what's out there.

5.6 Problems

5.6.1 Calculating Steady States, Part I

Consider the same setup as Example 5.2. Suppose $\alpha = 1/3$, $\beta = 0.95$, $\delta = 0.05$, and $K_0 = 0.1$. Calculate the steady-state values K_{ss} and C_{ss}.

5.6.2 Calculating Steady States, Part II

In Section 5.4.1, I claimed that the steady-state value of capital was $K_{ss} = 0.1771$. Prove this claim.

5.6.3 Calculating (and Using) a Policy Function

Consider the same environment as in Section 5.4.1. Let $\alpha = 0.25$ and $\beta = 0.85$.

1. Find the value of K_{ss}.
2. Suppose that $K_0 = 5$. Generate a plot similar to Figure 5.2 and provide intuition to explain why your graph looks the way it does.

6 Adding Randomness to the Model

How should we introduce randomness into our benchmark social planner problem? The traditional way of doing so is by augmenting the model with *stochastic* technology shocks. That said, the framework introduced below does not limit the analysis to technology, as the same set of ideas allows me to introduce a suite of **stochastic shocks** (taxes, government expenditure, money supply, taste shocks, markup shocks, etc.). For the task at hand, however, a single shock will suffice.

To motivate the discussion, it is useful to start from ideas we are familiar with. Adding stochastic shocks introduces randomness to our models, and this may seem like it complicates the road ahead. However, from a purely mechanical perspective, the difference is that I now have to maximize *expected* utility. To a large extent, the steps required to solve stochastic problems are the same as those required to solve deterministic problems.

The example below shows how a simple, two-outcome TFP shock (think high productivity vs. low productivity, or good weather vs. bad weather) embedded in a two-period model changes what I need to do – but not by much.

Example 6.1 Let's borrow an example from Heer and Maussner (2024): consider a two-period economy in which the representative household has instantaneous utility $u(C_t)$, where u is well behaved. Output in $t = 0$ is deterministic and given by $f(K_0)$; output in $t = 1$ is given by $A_1 f(K_1)$, where $A_1 = A^L$ with probability $\pi \in (0,1)$ and $A_1 = A^H > A^L$ with probability $1 - \pi$. The production function f is well behaved, K_0 is given, and $\delta = 1$. As the economy ends after $t = 1$, the household sets $C_1 = A_1 f(K_1)$. Hence, the household's expected utility is given by

$$\mathbb{E}_0\left[u(C_0) + \beta u(C_1)\right] = u\left[f(K_0) - K_1\right] + \beta\left[\pi u(A^L f(K_1)) + (1-\pi)u(A^H f(K_1))\right],$$

where $\mathbb{E}_0$ is the **expected value operator**. (More precisely, $\mathbb{E}_t$ represents the expected value *conditional* on period-t information; here, $\mathbb{E}_0$ is the operator that allows us to calculate expected utility conditional on the information available at $t = 0$.) Maximizing the right-hand side of the equation gives the first-order condition

$$-u'\left[f(K_0) - K_1\right] + \beta\left\{\pi u'\left[A^L f(K_1)\right]A^L f'(K_1) + (1-\pi)u'\left[A^H f(K_1)\right]A^H f'(K_1)\right\} = 0.$$

Rearrange a bit to get

$$u'(C_0) = \beta \mathbb{E}_0 u'(C_1) A_1 f'(K_1),$$

which is the stochastic analogue of the deterministic intertemporal condition.

As Example 6.1 shows, when TFP changes randomly over time, the economy's output is no longer deterministic: it fluctuates randomly for a given capital stock. Given what you know so far, by the end of this chapter you'll agree that adding randomness to the model doesn't complicate things at all.

The road ahead is as follows. First, Section 6.1 takes the ideas from Example 6.1 and puts them inside an SPP to generate what I call the stochastic benchmark SPP. Section 6.2 takes a detour to present minimal theory on stochastic processes – in particular, Markov processes – which offer the underlying theoretical structure for our random shocks. Finally, Section 6.3 revisits the stochastic benchmark SPP from Section 6.1; I show how to characterize it and obtain its steady-state values, which will be very handy in the chapters that follow.

6.1 The Stochastic Benchmark SPP with Full Depreciation

Example 6.1 is similar to something you may have encountered in intermediate microeconomics, but it's time to switch to a richer environment. Hence, let's return to the benchmark SPP (see Section 5.3.2), to which I (i) add stochastic TFP shocks and (ii) assume full depreciation (i.e., set $\delta = 1$). The SPP now reads

$$\begin{aligned} \max_{\{C_t, K_{t+1}\}_{t=0}^{\infty}} \quad & \mathbb{E}_0 \sum_{t=0}^{\infty} \beta^t u(C_t) \\ \text{subject to} \quad & A_t f(K_t) = C_t + K_{t+1}, \\ & C_t, K_{t+1} \geq 0, \end{aligned} \tag{6.1}$$

where K_0 is known by the planner. In SPP (6.1), the planner maximizes expected utility, as implied by the expectation operator $\mathbb{E}_0$. Moreover, output depends not only on capital but also on the realization of the stochastic variable A_t. (For now, just consider A_t as something random that affects the economy's output and cannot be controlled by the planner – like the weather.) Finally, assume the planner knows the value of A_t when it's time to choose C_t.

6.1.1 Stochastic Intertemporal Conditions

I can characterize the solution of the SPP by following the recipe for the deterministic case. Thus, consider the Lagrangian derived from the SPP (6.1):

$$\mathscr{L} = \mathbb{E}_0 \sum_{t=0}^{\infty} \beta^t \{u(C_t) + \lambda_t [A_t f(K_t) - C_t - K_{t+1}]\}. \tag{6.2}$$

Given the planner's informational constraints, I need to tackle the Lagrangian in a slightly different way. As a first step, I take first-order conditions with respect to C_0, K_1, and $\beta^0\lambda_0$:

$$\begin{aligned} C_0: &\quad \mathbb{E}_0\left[u'(C_0) - \lambda_0\right] = 0, \\ K_1: &\quad \mathbb{E}_0\left[-\lambda_0 + \beta\lambda_1 A_1 f'(K_1)\right] = 0, \\ \beta^0\lambda_0: &\quad \mathbb{E}_0\left[A_0 f(K_0) - C_0 - K_1\right] = 0. \end{aligned}$$

The variables C_0, K_1, λ_0, and A_0 are known at $t = 0$, so I can take them out of the expectations operator. I rewrite the equations as

$$\begin{aligned} u'(C_0) &= \lambda_0, \\ \lambda_0 &= \beta f'(K_1)\mathbb{E}_0\lambda_1 A_1, \\ A_0 f(K_0) &= C_0 + K_1, \end{aligned} \tag{6.3}$$

where I've used the fact that $\beta^0 = 1$. Note the feasibility constraint (6.3) is not stochastic; it holds with equality regardless of the realization of A_0.

Next, consider the problem that the planner faces when $t = 1$; as before, A_1 is known to the planner and he can take K_1 as given. The Lagrangian is

$$\mathscr{L} = \mathbb{E}_1 \sum_{t=1}^{\infty} \beta^{t-1}\left\{u(C_t) + \lambda_t\left[A_t f(K_t) - C_t - K_{t+1}\right]\right\}.$$

Using the same arguments as above, the first-order conditions with respect to C_1, K_1, and $\beta^0\lambda_1$ are

$$\begin{aligned} u'(C_1) &= \lambda_1, \\ \lambda_1 &= \beta f'(K_2)\mathbb{E}_1\lambda_2 A_2, \\ A_1 f(K_1) &= C_1 + K_2. \end{aligned}$$

As I repeat this process I see a pattern emerging: the sequences $\left\{C_t, K_{t+1}\right\}_{t=0}^{\infty}$ that solve (6.1) must satisfy

$$u'(C_t) = \lambda_t, \tag{6.4}$$

$$\lambda_t = \beta f'(K_{t+1})\mathbb{E}_t\lambda_{t+1}A_{t+1}, \tag{6.5}$$

$$A_t f(K_t) = C_t + K_{t+1}. \tag{6.6}$$

(Since K_{t+1} is known at period t, it is not placed inside the expectation operator.) While the procedure to derive equations (6.4)–(6.6) is different, I get the same results if I calculate the first-order conditions straight from the original Lagrangian function in equation (6.2). Since it is only a formality, I will always go straight into getting (6.4)–(6.6) without the one-period-at-a-time logic.

It follows that any interior solution must satisfy the intertemporal condition obtained by combining equations (6.4)–(6.6):

$$u'\left[A_t f(K_t) - K_{t+1}\right] = \beta f'(K_{t+1})\mathbb{E}_t u'\left[A_{t+1}f(K_{t+1}) - K_{t+2}\right]A_{t+1}. \tag{6.7}$$

Note equation (6.7) is a second-order difference equation, just like (5.18) in Chapter 5. I also need to consider the stochastic analogue of the transversality condition

$$\lim_{t\to\infty} \beta^t \mathbb{E}_t \lambda_t K_{t+1} = 0.$$

6.2 Modeling the Shocks: Markov Processes

Little is lost (and a lot is gained) by learning some basic concepts from the theory of stochastic processes. Two remarks: first, this section is not intended to provide every detail about Markov processes. Rather, it offers a "cookbook" approach to get you started; it is not a proper substitute for a formal course in stochastic processes. Second, this section draws from Heer and Maussner (2024).

6.2.1 Stochastic Processes

A **stochastic process** is a sequence of random variables, denoted $\{X_t\}_{t=0}^{\infty}$. The elements of the sequence (the X_ts) can take discrete or continuous values.

In addition, the elements of $\{X_t\}_{t=0}^{\infty}$ are **independent and identically distributed** (i.i.d.) if (i) the underlying probability distribution is the same for each X_t and (ii) the value of each X_t is independent of the value of X_s for all $s \neq t$. Under the i.i.d. assumption,

$$\mathrm{p}\left[X_1 = x_1, X_2 = x_2, \ldots, X_T = x_T\right] = \mathrm{p}\left[X_1 = x_1\right] \times \mathrm{p}\left[X_2 = x_2\right] \times \cdots \times \mathrm{p}\left[X_T = x_T\right].$$

Example 6.2 Suppose that we take a fair coin and flip it five times. Let $X_t = 1$ if the coin lands heads and $X_t = 0$ otherwise. In this case, the sequence $\{X_t\}_{t=1}^{5}$ is a stochastic process. Moreover, as the flips are drawn from the same coin, $\{X_t\}_{t=1}^{5}$ is also i.i.d. and, for a particular sequence, say, [heads, tails, tails, tails, heads], the probability of observing this exact sequence equals

$$\mathrm{p}\left[X_1 = 1, X_2 = 0, X_3 = 0, X_4 = 0, X_5 = 1\right] = \frac{1}{2} \times \frac{1}{2} \times \frac{1}{2} \times \frac{1}{2} \times \frac{1}{2} = \frac{1}{32}.$$

6.2.2 Markov Processes

Let $\{X_t\}_{t=0}^{\infty}$ denote a stochastic process. Suppose I want to know the probability that next period's random variable is $\bar{x}_{t+1}$, given that the history of random variables has been $\{\bar{x}_t, \bar{x}_{t-1}, \ldots, \bar{x}_0\}$ – a conditional probability. Formally, I want to calculate

$$\mathrm{p}\left[X_{t+1} = \bar{x}_{t+1} | X_t = \bar{x}_t, X_{t-1} = \bar{x}_{t-1}, \ldots, X_0 = \bar{x}_0\right].$$

A stochastic process $\{X_t\}_{t=0}^{\infty}$ is a **Markov process** whenever

$$\mathrm{p}\left[X_{t+1} = \bar{x}_{t+1} | X_t = \bar{x}_t, X_{t-1} = \bar{x}_{t-1}, \ldots, X_0 = \bar{x}_0\right] = \mathrm{p}\left[X_{t+1} = \bar{x}_{t+1} | X_t = \bar{x}_t\right]$$

or, in plain English, if tomorrow's realization of the random variable depends only on today's realization and not on its finite (or infinite) history.

What does a Markov process look like? Here's an example, which I'll use intensively in the material that follows.

Example 6.3 Let $\{X_t\}_{t=0}^{\infty}$ be a stochastic process defined by

$$X_t = (1-\rho)X + \rho X_{t-1} + \sigma\varepsilon_t, \tag{6.8}$$

where $\rho \in (0,1)$, $X \in \mathbb{R}$, $\sigma > 0$, and ε_t follows a standard Normal distribution. A process like (6.8) is known as a first-order **autoregressive process**, or AR(1) for short; it is clear that today's realization only depends on yesterday's value X_t (and a constant), which gives it the Markov property.
The steady state of the process requires me to set $X_t = X_{t-1} = X_{ss}$ and the shock ε_t to its unconditional mean (i.e., zero). Substituting these values in equation (6.8), I get

$$X_{ss} = (1-\rho)X + \rho X_{ss} + 0 \implies (1-\rho)X_{ss} = (1-\rho)X,$$

or $X_{ss} = X$. This fact implies that steady states are *nonstochastic* even if the underlying economy is. In addition, the expected value of X_{t+1} – conditional on all available information as of period t – is given by

$$\begin{aligned}\mathbb{E}_t\left[X_{t+1}\right] &= \mathbb{E}_t\left[(1-\rho)X + \rho X_t + \sigma\varepsilon_{t+1}\right] \\ &= \mathbb{E}_t\left[(1-\rho)X\right] + \mathbb{E}_t\left[\rho X_t\right] + \mathbb{E}_t\left[\sigma\varepsilon_{t+1}\right] \\ &= (1-\rho)X + \rho X_t. \end{aligned} \tag{6.9}$$

The result follows as (i) the first two terms on the right-hand side of (6.9) are known in period t and (ii) the expected value of ε_{t+1} as of time t equals its unconditional mean, which is zero.

Example 6.4 Let's obtain one draw from the AR process (6.8). Let $\rho = 0.85$, $X = 0$, and $\sigma = 1$. The sample time path for this process is shown in Figure 6.1. Note how the path of $\{X_t\}_{t=0}^{100}$ looks random but exhibits *persistence*: if $X_t > X_{ss}$ then the series tends to stay above X_{ss}, and vice versa. The degree of persistence obeys the value of ρ; as $\rho \to 0$, the stochastic process behaves more like an i.i.d. sequence.

Remark 6.1 Unless otherwise noted, all model innovations (i.e., the ε_t terms) will follow a standard Normal distribution. In this sense, parameter σ indicates the standard deviation of the underlying process.

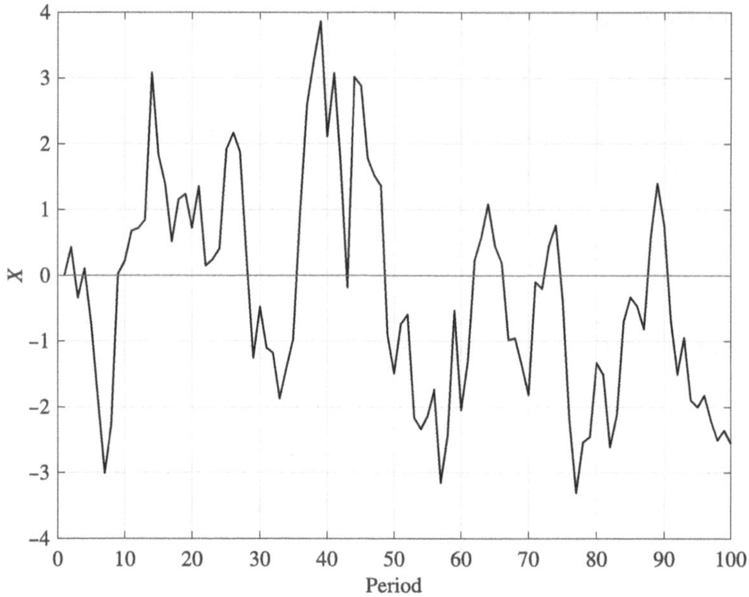

Figure 6.1 A sample AR(1) time path ($X = 0$, $\rho = 0.85$, $\sigma = 1$).

6.3 The Stochastic Benchmark SPP, Revisited

To wrap up everything I've covered so far, let's work out the stochastic benchmark SPP with full depreciation from beginning to end. In principle, every economic model in the book requires the same sequence of steps in order to find its solution. In this sense, having the blueprint of the steps to take is fairly convenient.

In addition, I put some structure into the TFP shock. Following the literature, I model the shock as a Markov process – more precisely, an AR(1) process. (While more complicated forms are possible, not much is lost by keeping things simple as I do here.)

Example 6.5 Consider the SPP given by

$$\begin{aligned} \max_{\{C_t, K_{t+1}\}_{t=0}^{\infty}} \quad & \mathbb{E}_0 \sum_{t=0}^{\infty} \beta^t \log C_t \\ \text{subject to} \quad & A_t K_t^{\alpha} = C_t + K_{t+1}, \\ & C_t, K_{t+1} \geq 0, \end{aligned} \tag{6.10}$$

where K_0 is known to the planner. In this problem, the TFP shock A_t evolves according to

$$\log A_t = \left(1 - \rho_A\right) \log A_{ss} + \rho_A \log A_{t-1} + \sigma_A \varepsilon_{At},$$

where $\rho_A \in \left(0, 1\right)$, A_0 is known, and $\sigma_A > 0$. The task at hand is to obtain the intertemporal and aggregate feasibility conditions for this problem.

To do so, set up the Lagrangian as

$$\mathscr{L} = \mathbb{E}_t \sum_{t=0}^{\infty} \beta^t \left[\log C_t + \lambda_t \left(A_t K_t^{\alpha} - C_t - K_{t+1} \right) \right].$$

(I'll take care of the technology process $\{A_t\}_{t=1}^{\infty}$ in a moment.) The first-order conditions with respect to C_t, K_{t+1}, and $\beta^t \lambda_t$ are

$$\begin{aligned} C_t^{-1} &= \lambda_t, \\ \lambda_t &= \alpha\beta K_{t+1}^{\alpha-1} \mathbb{E}_t \lambda_{t+1} A_{t+1}, \\ A_t K_t^{\alpha} &= C_t + K_{t+1}. \end{aligned}$$

Combining the first two equations and adding the law of motion for the technology process, the solution to the SPP (6.10) satisfies

$$C_t^{-1} = \alpha\beta K_{t+1}^{\alpha-1} \mathbb{E}_t C_{t+1}^{-1} A_{t+1}, \tag{6.11}$$

$$A_t K_t^{\alpha} = C_t + K_{t+1}, \tag{6.12}$$

given the evolution of the TFP shock

$$\log A_t = \left(1 - \rho_A\right) \log A_{ss} + \rho_A \log A_{t-1} + \sigma_A \varepsilon_{At}. \tag{6.13}$$

In the above, (6.11) is the intertemporal condition, (6.12) represents aggregate feasibility, and (6.13) is the stochastic process that governs the evolution of productivity.

Example 6.6 Let $A_{ss} = 1$. In the steady state, equation (6.11) becomes

$$C^{-1} = \alpha\beta K^{\alpha-1} C^{-1}.$$

Since steady states are nonstochastic, I don't have to worry about the expectation operator. Cancel the C^{-1} terms to get

$$1 = \alpha\beta K^{\alpha-1}, \tag{6.14}$$

which can be solved for K as a function of model parameters α and β; the solution is

$$K = (\alpha\beta)^{1/(1-\alpha)}.$$

Equation (6.12) becomes

$$C = K^{\alpha} - K \tag{6.15}$$

and equation (6.13) is no longer relevant in the steady state since

$$\log 1 = (1 - \rho_A) \log 1 + \rho_A \log 1 + 0$$

gives the equality $0 = 0$.

6.4 Up Next

What now? Let's take stock of what has happened so far. You now know:

- How to define an equilibrium, either in finite or infinite horizons.
- How to characterize the equilibrium; that is, how to find the first-order conditions of the model economy.
- If applicable, how to set up the equivalent SPP, either in finite or infinite horizons.
- What the steady state is and why we need infinite horizons to make this work.
- How infinite-horizon problems require a different solution method, that is, policy functions as opposed to sequences of numbers.
- How to introduce randomness into our models via stochastic shocks.

What's left out is how to combine these ideas in order to generate policy functions for *any* economic model. As it turns out, we are more than halfway there. We just need to make a small investment in linear algebra and a bit of scientific computing – and we'll get to do so in the next chapter.

6.5 Problems

6.5.1 Working with the Stochastic, Infinite-Horizon Benchmark SPP

Redo Example 6.5 but now assume that depreciation is less than unity; that is, the planner problem is now restricted by

$$A_t K_t^{\alpha} = C_t + K_{t+1} - (1 - \delta) K_t.$$

Briefly describe how the intertemporal and aggregate feasibility conditions change when we modify the problem in this way.

6.5.2 Investment-Specific Technological Progress

Redo Problem 6.5.1, but now assume the stochastic shocks affect the productivity of new capital goods (i.e., investment). More precisely, the planner is restricted by the following constraints:

$$K_t^{\alpha} = C_t + X_t,$$

together with the law of motion for capital:

$$K_{t+1} = (1 - \delta) K_t + \left(1 + \mu_t\right) X_t,$$

where μ_t is a shock to the marginal efficiency of investment. Derive the intertemporal and aggregate feasibility conditions for this economy. *Hint*: You may benefit from reading the papers by Greenwood et al. (1988), Greenwood, Hercowitz, and Krusell (1997), and Justiniano, Primiceri, and Tambalotti (2010).

6.5.3 Government Expenditure Shocks

Redo Problem 6.5.1, but now include a government sector that spends some stochastic fraction of output g_t every period. More precisely, the planner problem is now restricted by

$$K_t^\alpha = C_t + K_{t+1} - (1-\delta)K_t + g_t K_t^\alpha.$$

In this constraint, g_t satisfies

$$g_t = (1-\rho_g)g_{ss} + \rho_g g_{t-1} + \sigma_g \varepsilon_{gt},$$

where $\rho_g, g_{ss} \in (0,1)$, g_0 is known, and $\sigma_g > 0$. Derive the intertemporal and aggregate feasibility conditions for this economy.

7 Linear Systems

As of now, you should feel fairly comfortable setting up and solving finite-horizon competitive equilibrium (or social planner) problems. Of course, we hit a wall as soon as we want to explore the infinite-horizon case, as there is no way to handle systems of equations with an infinite number of equations and variables.

Sure, I just told you that the undetermined coefficients method works (and, moreover, that most infinite-horizon problems have a policy function associated with them), but its biggest drawback is that I need to get "lucky" with the guess – and that makes this solution method a long shot.

What I'll do instead is to look for answers elsewhere: not within the global solution methods offered by the field of dynamic programming, but within local solution methods that are valid within a neighborhood of the steady state.

Local solution methods approximate the equilibrium conditions around the economy's steady state; since all the model economies contained in this book are "well-behaved" (in the sense that their steady states are stable), I know that the economy will return to the steady state after receiving a shock, and thus I'm able to map the time dynamics from start to finish by relying on these approximate policy functions. (The fact that I use the undetermined coefficients method shows that the time invested in learning it was justified.) These tools are the ones we will use in the rest of the book.

The chapter proceeds as follows. Section 7.1 takes the benchmark SPP reviews from Chapter 6 and I use it to test Uhlig's rules, which are the tools that transform nonlinear equilibrium conditions into log-linear ones. Of course, log-linear equilibrium conditions are not the same as policy functions, but I share the way ahead (the method of undetermined coefficients) in Section 7.2. Finally, Section 7.3 adds stochastic shocks and shows how the method explained in the previous section still works in a more complicated model, at the cost of more work (and more algebra).

7.1 The Infinite-Horizon Benchmark SPP, Revisited

Consider, once again, the infinite-horizon benchmark SPP from Section 5.3.2, assuming $u(C_t) = \log C_t$ and $f(K_t) = K_t^{\alpha}$:

$$\max_{\{C_t, K_{t+1}\}_{t=0}^{\infty}} \quad \sum_{t=0}^{\infty} \beta^t \log C_t \tag{7.1}$$

$$\text{subject to} \quad K_t^\alpha = C_t + K_{t+1} - (1-\delta)K_t,$$
$$C_t \geq 0,$$

where the planner knows K_0. (Yes, the problem is deterministic, but this modeling choice is on purpose. I'll add randomness before the chapter is done.) If I perform the routine calculations – namely, (i) set up the Lagrangian function, (ii) take first-order conditions, and (iii) rearrange – I obtain an intertemporal condition

$$\begin{aligned} C_t^{-1} &= \beta C_{t+1}^{-1}\left(\alpha K_{t+1}^{\alpha-1} + 1 - \delta\right) \\ &= \alpha\beta C_{t+1}^{-1} K_{t+1}^{\alpha-1} + \beta(1-\delta)C_{t+1}^{-1} \end{aligned} \tag{7.2}$$

and an aggregate feasibility constraint

$$K_t^\alpha = C_t + K_{t+1} - (1-\delta)K_t. \tag{7.3}$$

Equations (7.2) and (7.3) are the equilibrium conditions associated with SPP (7.1). In the steady state, these equations become

$$1 = \alpha\beta K^{\alpha-1} + \beta(1-\delta), \tag{7.4}$$

$$K^\alpha = C + \delta K. \tag{7.5}$$

Example 7.1 Consider the steady-state conditions derived from SPP (7.1) and let the parameter values be as follows: $\alpha = 0.33$, $\beta = 0.99$, and $\delta = 0.02$. From (7.4), steady-state capital equals

$$K_{ss} = \left[\frac{\alpha\beta}{1-\beta(1-\delta)}\right]^{1/(1-\alpha)} = \left[\frac{(0.33)(0.99)}{1-(0.99)(1-0.02)}\right]^{1/(1-0.33)},$$

or $K_{ss} = 35.6565$. From (7.5), steady-state consumption equals

$$C_{ss} = K_{ss}^\alpha - \delta K_{ss} = (35.6565)^{0.33} - (0.02)(35.6565),$$

or $C_{ss} = 2.5393$.

Chapter 5 suggests that the undetermined coefficients method had promise, but repeating the steps for this SPP won't work because $\delta < 1$. Problem (7.1) is too nonlinear for me to get lucky with a guess.

While the theory of dynamic programming guarantees that a problem like (7.1) has a solution – that is, the policy functions exist – there is no obvious way to obtain them even though I already have the intertemporal and aggregate feasibility conditions (7.2) and (7.3). That being said, while I can't calculate the policy functions when these conditions are nonlinear, I *can* make things work provided these conditions are linear. In a nutshell, this is what local solution methods offer.

The first step is transforming the nonlinear equilibrium conditions (7.2) and (7.3) into linear expressions. There are a few ways to achieve this goal, and the most efficient way follows the work of Uhlig (1999).

7.1.1 Uhlig's Rules

Uhlig (1999) provides a straightforward set of rules, shown below. Given some variable Ω_t, I will use hats (e.g., $\widehat{\Omega}_t$) to denote percent deviations from steady state, so that

$$\widehat{\Omega}_t \equiv \frac{\Omega_t - \Omega_{ss}}{\Omega_{ss}}. \tag{7.6}$$

Equation (7.6) already provides the first result, namely,

Proposition 7.1 *Let Ω_t be any model variable set in levels. The following result holds exactly:*

$$\Omega_t = \Omega_{ss}\left(1 + \widehat{\Omega}_t\right). \tag{7.7}$$

Proof. Solve for Ω_t from the definition of $\widehat{\Omega}_t$, equation (7.6). □

Remark 7.2 Why do I need to specify "any model variable set in levels"? Because some variables are set in percent terms (e.g., tax rates) and in this case the notion of a percent deviation from steady state is not that useful (e.g., the percent change in a percentage). Rather, talking about the *level* deviation from steady state (i.e., $\Omega_t - \Omega_{ss}$) is a much better choice.

Sometimes the equilibrium conditions involve products of two (or more) variables, where one of the terms may be a nonlinear function of a variable. For example, in equation (7.2), the first term on the right-hand side reads $\alpha\beta C_{t+1}^{-1} K_{t+1}^{\alpha-1}$. To tackle these products, Proposition 7.1 becomes really useful, especially when I combine it with itself, as the next two results show.

Proposition 7.3 (Product Rule) *Let Ψ_t and Ω_t be two model variables. The product $\Psi_t\Omega_t$ is approximated as*

$$\Psi_t\Omega_t \approx \Psi_{ss}\Omega_{ss}\left(1 + \widehat{\Psi}_t + \widehat{\Omega}_t\right). \tag{7.8}$$

Proof. Use Proposition 7.1 to substitute for Ψ_t and Ω_t; the product becomes

$$\begin{aligned}\Psi_t\Omega_t &= \Psi_{ss}(1 + \widehat{\Psi}_t)\Omega_{ss}\left(1 + \widehat{\Omega}_t\right)\\ &= \Psi_{ss}\Omega_{ss}\left(1 + \widehat{\Psi}_t + \widehat{\Omega}_t + \widehat{\Psi}_t\widehat{\Omega}_t\right)\\ &\approx \Psi_{ss}\Omega_{ss}\left(1 + \widehat{\Psi}_t + \widehat{\Omega}_t\right),\end{aligned}$$

where the approximation in the third step follows after setting $\widehat{\Psi}_t\widehat{\Omega}_t = 0$ (the product should be very small, anyway). □

Proposition 7.4 (Exponentiation Rule) *Let Ω_t be a model variable and $a \in \mathbb{R}$. The exponentiation Ω_t^a is approximated as*

$$\Omega_t^a \approx \Omega_{ss}^a\left(1 + a\widehat{\Omega}_t\right). \tag{7.9}$$

Proof. Follows from repeated application of Proposition 7.3. □

These three rules cover most of what I need when log-linearizing equilibrium conditions, but occasionally I will draw on the following result:

Proposition 7.5 (Logarithmic Rule) *Let Ω_t be a model variable. The logarithm of Ω_t is approximated as*

$$\log \Omega_t \approx \log \Omega_{ss} + \widehat{\Omega}_t. \tag{7.10}$$

Proof. Start from $\log \Omega_t$ and use Proposition 7.1 to substitute for Ω_t in (7.10):

$$\begin{aligned}\log \Omega_t &= \log \left[\Omega_{ss}\left(1+\widehat{\Omega}_t\right)\right] \\ &= \log \Omega_{ss} + \log\left(1+\widehat{\Omega}_t\right) \\ &\approx \log \Omega_{ss} + \widehat{\Omega}_t,\end{aligned}$$

where the approximation in the third step follows the fact that $\log\left(1+u\right) \approx u$ when u is a small number. (See Appendix C for a refresher.) □

7.1.2 Putting the Rules to Work

The usefulness of Uhlig's rules is not obvious until they are put to work. Since I have a model at hand – the infinite-horizon benchmark SPP – now is a good time to use these rules.

As with most things in life, the rules may seem very complicated at first. Just know that with practice, they will seem as easy as the multiplication tables. (And every time you're struggling, remember that the alternatives are much harder.)

Example 7.2 Here I show how to calculate the log-linearized expression for the equilibrium conditions (7.2) and (7.3). Let's log-linearize equation (7.2), one term at a time.

First, let's work on the left-hand side of the expression. Using (7.9),

$$C_t^{-1} \approx C^{-1}\left(1-\widehat{C}_t\right).$$

Now let's go for the first term on the right-hand side of (7.2). This involves using a combination of (7.8) and (7.9):

$$\alpha\beta C_{t+1}^{-1}K_{t+1}^{\alpha-1} \approx \alpha\beta K^{\alpha-1}C^{-1}\left[1+(\alpha-1)\widehat{K}_{t+1}-\widehat{C}_{t+1}\right].$$

Finally, the second term on the right-hand side of the equation relies on (7.9) only:

$$\beta(1-\delta)C_{t+1}^{-1} \approx \beta(1-\delta)C^{-1}\left(1-\widehat{C}_{t+1}\right).$$

Altogether, I get

$$C^{-1}\left(1-\widehat{C}_t\right) = \alpha\beta K^{\alpha-1}C^{-1}\left[1+(\alpha-1)\widehat{K}_{t+1}-\widehat{C}_{t+1}\right] + \beta(1-\delta)C^{-1}\left(1-\widehat{C}_{t+1}\right).$$

Now it's time to simplify. Begin by multiplying all terms to get

$$C^{-1} - C^{-1}\widehat{C}_t = \alpha\beta K^{\alpha-1}C^{-1} + \alpha\beta K^{\alpha-1}C^{-1}(\alpha-1)\widehat{K}_{t+1}$$
$$- \alpha\beta K^{\alpha-1}C^{-1}\widehat{C}_{t+1} + \beta(1-\delta)C^{-1} - \beta(1-\delta)C^{-1}\widehat{C}_{t+1}.$$

This doesn't look like progress, but I'm getting there. Next, divide across by C^{-1}:

$$1 - \widehat{C}_t = \alpha\beta K^{\alpha-1} + \alpha\beta K^{\alpha-1}(\alpha-1)\widehat{K}_{t+1} - \alpha\beta K^{\alpha-1}\widehat{C}_{t+1} + \beta(1-\delta) - \beta(1-\delta)\widehat{C}_{t+1}.$$

Now look at the constant terms and compare them with (7.4) – they cancel out:

$$-\widehat{C}_t = \alpha\beta K^{\alpha-1}(\alpha-1)\widehat{K}_{t+1} - \alpha\beta K^{\alpha-1}\widehat{C}_{t+1} - \beta(1-\delta)\widehat{C}_{t+1}.$$

Gather common terms:

$$-\widehat{C}_t = \alpha\beta K^{\alpha-1}(\alpha-1)\widehat{K}_{t+1} - \left[\alpha\beta K^{\alpha-1} + \beta(1-\delta)\right]\widehat{C}_{t+1}.$$

Glance at the coefficient of the last term on the right-hand side of the equation. Looks familiar, right? It's equation (7.4) once again, and using that $\alpha\beta K^{\alpha-1} + \beta(1-\delta) = 1$, I get

$$-\widehat{C}_t = \alpha(\alpha-1)\beta K^{\alpha-1}\widehat{K}_{t+1} - \widehat{C}_{t+1}. \tag{7.11}$$

Similarly, I use (7.7)–(7.9) and the steady-state condition (7.5) to log-linearize the feasibility constraint. The equation becomes

$$\left[\alpha K^{\alpha} + (1-\delta)K\right]\widehat{K}_t = C\widehat{C}_t + K\widehat{K}_{t+1}. \tag{7.12}$$

Equations (7.11) and (7.12) are the expressions I'm looking for.

The log-linearized equations (as derived via Uhlig's rules) are given by equations (7.11) and (7.12). While the coefficients are nonlinear functions of parameters, both (7.11) and (7.12) are linear in $\widehat{C}_t$ and $\widehat{K}_t$. This is evident when I substitute for parameter values, as I do in Example 7.3.

Example 7.3 Given the parameter values and the steady-state values obtained in Example 7.1, equations (7.11) and (7.12) become

$$-\widehat{C}_t = -0.0200\widehat{K}_{t+1} - \widehat{C}_{t+1},$$
$$36.0167\widehat{K}_t = 2.5393\widehat{C}_t + 35.6565\widehat{K}_{t+1}.$$

It is clear that both expressions are linear in $\widehat{C}_t$, $\widehat{C}_{t+1}$, $\widehat{K}_t$, and $\widehat{K}_{t+1}$.

7.2 The Method of Undetermined Coefficients, Revisited

Here I take a second pass at the method of undetermined coefficients, using the linearized conditions (7.11) and (7.12). As I showed in Example 5.3, the method works as follows: I provide a guess for the policy function and then verify that the guess is correct.

7.2.1 Building a Second-Order Difference Equation

First, some housekeeping: define the auxiliary parameter $\gamma \equiv \alpha(\alpha - 1)\beta K_{ss}^{\alpha-1}$ to economize on notation. Then (7.11) becomes

$$-\widehat{C}_t = \gamma\widehat{K}_{t+1} - \widehat{C}_{t+1}. \tag{7.13}$$

Now take (7.12) and solve for $\widehat{C}_t$; I get

$$\widehat{C}_t = \left[\frac{\alpha K^{\alpha} + (1-\delta)K}{C}\right]\widehat{K}_t - \frac{K}{C}\widehat{K}_{t+1}.$$

Let $\omega \equiv \left[\alpha K^{\alpha} + (1-\delta)K\right]/C$; the equation now reads

$$\widehat{C}_t = \omega\widehat{K}_t - \frac{K}{C}\widehat{K}_{t+1}.$$

This equation puts consumption as a function of current and future capital; as such, it makes sense to plug it in (7.13):

$$-\left[\omega\widehat{K}_t - \frac{K}{C}\widehat{K}_{t+1}\right] = \gamma\widehat{K}_{t+1} - \left[\omega\widehat{K}_{t+1} - \frac{K}{C}\widehat{K}_{t+2}\right],$$

which is a second-order difference equation, just like equation (5.18). If I gather common terms and set equal to zero, the expression becomes

$$\frac{K}{C}\widehat{K}_{t+2} + \left[\gamma - \frac{K}{C} - \omega\right]\widehat{K}_{t+1} + \omega\widehat{K}_t = 0,$$

which is equivalent to

$$a_2\widehat{K}_{t+2} + a_1\widehat{K}_{t+1} + a_0\widehat{K}_t = 0 \tag{7.14}$$

where, obviously,

$$a_0 \equiv \omega,$$
$$a_1 \equiv \gamma - \frac{K}{C} - \omega,$$
$$a_2 \equiv \frac{K}{C}.$$

7.2.2 The Policy Function and the Quadratic Equation

Just as in Chapter 5, I guess that the policy function is such that the percent deviation of next-period capital from its steady state depends on the current value of the same variable; that is,

$$\widehat{K}_{t+1} = \varphi_{kk}\widehat{K}_t.$$

This expression implies

$$\begin{aligned}\widehat{K}_{t+2} &= \varphi_{kk}\widehat{K}_{t+1} \\ &= \varphi_{kk}\big(\varphi_{kk}\widehat{K}_t\big) \\ &= \varphi_{kk}^2\widehat{K}_t.\end{aligned}$$

Now plug these expressions into (7.14):

$$a_2\varphi_{kk}^2\widehat{K}_t + a_1\varphi_{kk}\widehat{K}_t + a_0\widehat{K}_t = 0 \tag{7.15}$$

and note I've transformed a second-order difference equation in $\widehat{K}_t$ into a quadratic equation of the form

$$a_2\varphi_{kk}^2 + a_1\varphi_{kk} + a_0 = 0, \tag{7.16}$$

which follows after dividing (7.15) across by $\widehat{K}_t$. This quadratic equation has two roots, and the last step in this process is choosing the root that solves the equation. Figuring out which root is the right one requires a bit of care, though.

Example 7.4 Given the parameters and steady-state values obtained in Example 7.1, the values for a_0, a_1, and a_2 are

$$\begin{aligned}a_0 &= 14.1838, \\ a_1 &= -28.2457, \\ a_2 &= 14.0419.\end{aligned}$$

The two roots that solve equation (7.16) are $\varphi_{kk,1} = 1.0439$ and $\varphi_{kk,2} = 0.9676$.

7.2.3 Picking the "Right" Root

Following on Example 7.4, the two roots that satisfy equation (7.16) are $\varphi_{kk,1} > 1$ and $\varphi_{kk,2} < 1$. Let's see if economic theory helps in determining which root is the right one.

To start, remember that model variables are cast as percent deviations from the steady state; following equation (7.7), the link between the capital stock in levels (K_t) and its percent deviation from steady state ($\widehat{K}_t$) is

$$K_t = K_{ss}\big(1 + \widehat{K}_t\big).$$

Suppose I pick the first root ($\varphi_{kk,1} > 1$) and let the model economy start from some arbitrary capital stock $K_0 < K_{ss}$. (Consequently, $\widehat{K}_0 < 0$.) Then, iterating over the policy function implies

$$\begin{aligned}\widehat{K}_1 &= \varphi_{kk,1}\widehat{K}_0, \\ \widehat{K}_2 &= \varphi_{kk,1}^2\widehat{K}_0,\end{aligned}$$

$$\vdots$$

$$\widehat{K}_t = \varphi_{kk,1}^t \widehat{K}_0.$$

So far, so good. However, the fact that $\varphi_{kk,1} > 1$ kicks in: given $\widehat{K}_0 < 0$, $\widehat{K}_t$ becomes more negative in each iteration. Eventually, the economy will reach a period $t = \tau$ for which $\widehat{K}_\tau < -1$, so that

$$K_\tau = K_{ss}\left(1 + \widehat{K}_\tau\right) < 0,$$

which doesn't make sense: the *level* of the capital stock is negative and, moreover, it becomes *more negative* every period – it explodes to negative infinity. Trying the same trick with $K_0 > K_{ss}$ doesn't help either, as the solution explodes to positive infinity.

Thus, let's try the other root, $\varphi_{kk,2} < 1$. Following the steps above, I arrive at a similar expression, namely,

$$\widehat{K}_t = \varphi_{kk,2}^t \widehat{K}_0,$$

but note $\varphi_{kk,2}^t \to 0$ as $t \to \infty$. Hence, $\widehat{K}_t \to 0$ too, and this fact implies

$$K_t = K_{ss}\left(1 + \widehat{K}_t\right) \to K_{ss}\left(1 + 0\right) = K_{ss}.$$

Thus, choosing $\varphi_{kk,2} < 1$ guarantees that the capital stock converges to its steady state – as theory implies – and so I've found the right root. The optimal policy function is

$$\widehat{K}_t = \varphi_{kk}\widehat{K}_t,$$

where $\varphi_k \equiv \varphi_{kk,2}$. Some comments:

- Usually, $\varphi_{kk,1} > 1$ is known as the *unstable root*, as it leads to an explosive solution for capital. Not surprisingly, $\varphi_{kk,2} < 1$ is known as the *stable root*, as it ensures convergence to the steady state. (The fact that one root is unstable and the other one is stable guarantees that the policy function is unique.)
- The policy function is linear in percent deviations from the steady state, which need not be the right measure for the task at hand. To transform these results into levels, note that

$$\widehat{K}_{t+1} = \varphi_{kk}\widehat{K}_t \tag{7.17}$$

  is equivalent to

$$\frac{K_{t+1} - K_{ss}}{K_{ss}} = \varphi_{kk}\left(\frac{K_t - K_{ss}}{K_{ss}}\right).$$

  If I solve for K_{t+1}, some algebra later I get

$$K_{t+1} = \left(1 - \varphi_{kk}\right)K_{ss} + \varphi_{kk}K_t,$$

  which is the policy function for the capital stock, but now set in levels.

Remark 7.6 Equation (7.17) can also be written as

$$K_{t+1} = K_{ss} + \varphi_{kk}\widetilde{K}_t,$$

where $\widetilde{K}_t \equiv K_t - K_{ss}$ represents the *level* deviation of capital from its steady state.

Example 7.5 Given the parameter values and the steady-state values obtained in Example 7.1, $\varphi_{kk} = 0.9676$. It's somewhat easy to code this procedure and use a computer program to see how the economy responds to certain shocks. In this case, the only exogenous variable is the capital stock, so let's think about, say, a natural disaster that destroys 1% of the installed capital stock in period 1. Using that $\widehat{K}_{t+1} = 0.9676\widehat{K}_t$ and setting $K_1 = 0.99K_{ss}$, Figure 7.1 shows the dynamic evolution of the economy – the **impulse-response function** – to the shock.

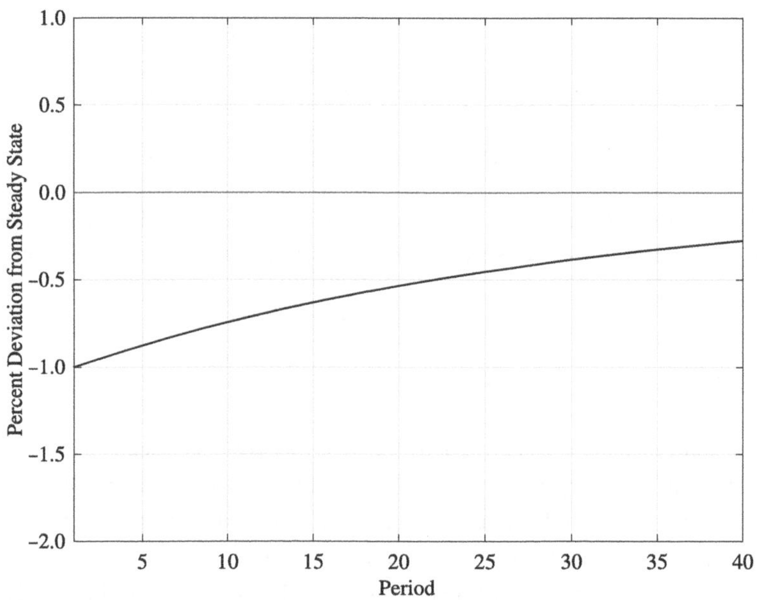

Figure 7.1 Impulse-response function of capital after a 1% decline in period 1.

7.3 Randomness, Revisited

Section 7.2 helps us understand how the method of undetermined coefficients works under linearized equilibrium conditions. But the example used there was lacking. Any realistic model economy requires the addition of stochastic shocks.

As it turns out, the main idea is still there, but the process that generates the policy functions is slightly different – and more cumbersome. For the sake of making things clear, let's move along and see how everything works out.

7.3.1 The Stochastic, Infinite-Horizon Benchmark SPP, Revisited

Consider the stochastic version of the infinite-horizon benchmark SPP (7.1):

$$\begin{aligned} \max_{\{C_t, K_{t+1}\}_{t=0}^{\infty}} \quad & \mathbb{E}_0 \sum_{t=0}^{\infty} \beta^t \log C_t \\ \text{subject to} \quad & A_t K_t^{\alpha} = C_t + K_{t+1} - (1-\delta) K_t, \\ & C_t \geq 0, \end{aligned} \tag{7.18}$$

where K_0 is known by the planner. In addition, the TFP shock A_t evolves according to

$$\log A_t = \left(1 - \rho_A\right) \log A_{ss} + \rho_A \log A_{t-1} + \sigma_A \varepsilon_{At},$$

where $\rho_A \in \left(0, 1\right)$, A_0 is known, and $\sigma_A > 0$. Following (7.18), I set up the Lagrangian as

$$\mathscr{L} = \mathbb{E}_t \sum_{t=0}^{\infty} \beta^t \left\{ \log C_t + \lambda_t \left[A_t K_t^{\alpha} - C_t - K_{t+1} + \left(1 - \delta\right) K_t \right] \right\}$$

and the first-order conditions with respect to C_t, K_{t+1}, and $\beta^t \lambda_t$ are

$$\begin{aligned} C_t^{-1} &= \lambda_t, \\ \lambda_t &= \beta\, \mathbb{E}_t \lambda_{t+1} \left(\alpha A_{t+1} K_{t+1}^{\alpha-1} + 1 - \delta \right), \\ A_t K_t^{\alpha} &= C_t + K_{t+1} - \left(1 - \delta\right) K_t. \end{aligned}$$

Substituting the multiplier λ_t, the system that characterizes equilibrium is given by

$$\begin{aligned} C_t^{-1} &= \beta\, \mathbb{E}_t C_{t+1}^{-1} \left(\alpha A_{t+1} K_{t+1}^{\alpha-1} + 1 - \delta \right), \\ A_t K_t^{\alpha} &= C_t + K_{t+1} - \left(1 - \delta\right) K_t. \end{aligned} \tag{7.19}$$

Staring at the system of equations, log-linearizing the right-hand side of (7.19) doesn't seem that appealing. Is there a strategy to simplify the process? Fortunately, the answer is yes: the divide-and-conquer method.

To start, note I'm allowed to do whatever I want with the system of equations *as long as it remains balanced*, in the sense that it has the same number of variables and equations. Following this advice, I introduce a new variable to the system, the (gross) net-of-depreciation rate of return on capital, denoted Q_{kt}:

$$Q_{kt} \equiv \alpha A_t K_t^{\alpha-1} + 1 - \delta.$$

This addition leads to a system in $\left\{C_t, K_t, Q_{kt}\right\}$, namely,

$$C_t^{-1} = \beta\, \mathbb{E}_t C_{t+1}^{-1} Q_{k,t+1}, \tag{7.20}$$

$$A_t K_t^{\alpha} = C_t + K_{t+1} - \left(1 - \delta\right) K_t, \tag{7.21}$$

$$Q_{kt} = \alpha A_t K_t^{\alpha-1} + 1 - \delta, \tag{7.22}$$

together with the law of motion for TFP,

$$\log A_t = \left(1 - \rho_A\right) \log A_{ss} + \rho_A \log A_{t-1} + \sigma_A \varepsilon_{At}. \tag{7.23}$$

Even though it doesn't look like it, solving this larger system is just as easy as solving the previous one.

7.3.2 The Steady State

Let $A_{ss} = 1$. Take (7.20)–(7.22) and impose steady-state conditions to get

$$1 = \beta Q_k, \tag{7.24}$$

$$K^\alpha = C + \delta K, \tag{7.25}$$

$$Q_k = \alpha K^{\alpha-1} + 1 - \delta. \tag{7.26}$$

From (7.24) I get

$$Q_k = \frac{1}{\beta}$$

and, from (7.26),

$$K = \left(\frac{\alpha}{Q_k - 1 + \delta}\right)^{1/(1-\alpha)}.$$

Finally, equation (7.25) yields

$$C = K^\alpha - \delta K.$$

7.3.3 Log-Linearizing the Equilibrium Conditions

I now transform the nonlinear system (7.20)–(7.23) into its equivalent linear representation. Let's start with the intertemporal condition (7.20); applying the rules gives

$$C^{-1}\left(1 - \widehat{C}_t\right) = \beta C^{-1} Q_k \mathbb{E}_t\left(1 - \widehat{C}_{t+1} + \widehat{Q}_{k,t+1}\right).$$

Divide across by C^{-1} and use that $\beta Q_k = 1$; some algebra later, I get

$$-\widehat{C}_t = -\mathbb{E}_t\widehat{C}_{t+1} + \mathbb{E}_t\widehat{Q}_{k,t+1}. \tag{7.27}$$

Equation (7.21) yields

$$K^\alpha\left(1 + \widehat{A}_t + \alpha\widehat{K}_t\right) = C\left(1 + \widehat{C}_t\right) + K\left(1 + \widehat{K}_{t+1}\right) - (1-\delta)K\left(1 + \widehat{K}_t\right).$$

Use the steady-state condition (7.25) to cancel the 1s in the expression; doing so and gathering terms, I get

$$K^\alpha\widehat{A}_t + \left(\alpha K^{\alpha-1} + 1 - \delta\right)K\widehat{K}_t = C\widehat{C}_t + K\widehat{K}_{t+1}.$$

Note the term in parenthesis in the second term of the left-hand side equals $Q_{k,ss}$ per equation (7.26); thus, the final version of the linearized expression is

$$K^\alpha\widehat{A}_t + Q_k K\widehat{K}_t = C\widehat{C}_t + K\widehat{K}_{t+1}. \tag{7.28}$$

Equation (7.22) results in

$$Q_k(1+\widehat{Q}_{kt}) = \alpha K^{\alpha-1}\left[1+\widehat{A}_t + (\alpha-1)\widehat{K}_t\right] + 1 - \delta.$$

Using (7.26) to cancel some terms, I arrive at

$$Q_k\widehat{Q}_{kt} = \alpha K^{\alpha-1}\widehat{A}_t + \alpha(\alpha-1)K^{\alpha-1}\widehat{K}_t. \tag{7.29}$$

Finally, equation (7.23) results in

$$\widehat{A}_t = \rho_A\widehat{A}_{t-1} + \sigma_A\varepsilon_{At}, \tag{7.30}$$

following Proposition 7.5.

7.3.4 The Policy Functions

Intuitively, the policy functions of the economy should depend on the state variables K_t and A_t. Thus, it seems natural to guess linear policy functions of the form

$$\widehat{K}_{t+1} = \varphi_{kk}\widehat{K}_t + \varphi_{ka}\widehat{A}_t, \tag{7.31}$$
$$\widehat{C}_t = \varphi_{ck}\widehat{K}_t + \varphi_{ca}\widehat{A}_t, \tag{7.32}$$
$$\widehat{Q}_{kt} = \varphi_{qk}\widehat{K}_t + \varphi_{qa}\widehat{A}_t. \tag{7.33}$$

The task at hand, then, is to find the six undetermined coefficients

$$\left\{\varphi_{kk}, \varphi_{ka}, \varphi_{ck}, \varphi_{ca}, \varphi_{qk}, \varphi_{qa}\right\}.$$

Fortunately, the strategy remains the same as in Section 7.2: plug the policy functions (7.31)–(7.33) into the linearized equilibrium conditions (7.27)–(7.29) and then solve. Of course, this process is more painful than before.

The Intertemporal Condition

Let's start with (7.27). Plugging as needed gives

$$-\underbrace{\left[\varphi_{ck}\widehat{K}_t + \varphi_{ca}\widehat{A}_t\right]}_{\widehat{C}_t} = -\mathbb{E}_t\underbrace{\left[\varphi_{ck}\widehat{K}_{t+1} + \varphi_{ca}\widehat{A}_{t+1}\right]}_{\widehat{C}_{t+1}} + \mathbb{E}_t\underbrace{\left[\varphi_{qk}\widehat{K}_{t+1} + \varphi_{qa}\widehat{A}_{t+1}\right]}_{\widehat{Q}_{k,t+1}}.$$

Gather terms on the right-hand side of the equation to get

$$-\varphi_{ck}\widehat{K}_t - \varphi_{ca}\widehat{A}_t = \left[-\varphi_{ck} + \varphi_{qk}\right]\mathbb{E}_t\widehat{K}_{t+1} + \left[-\varphi_{ca} + \varphi_{qa}\right]\mathbb{E}_t\widehat{A}_{t+1}.$$

Now use that (i) $\mathbb{E}_t\widehat{A}_{t+1} = \mathbb{E}_t\left[\rho_A\widehat{A}_t + \varepsilon_t\right] = \rho_A\widehat{A}_t$ and (ii) $\mathbb{E}_t\widehat{K}_{t+1} = \widehat{K}_{t+1} = \varphi_{kk}\widehat{K}_t + \varphi_{ka}\widehat{A}_t$:

$$-\varphi_{ck}\widehat{K}_t - \varphi_{ca}\widehat{A}_t = \left[-\varphi_{ck} + \varphi_{qk}\right]\left(\varphi_{kk}\widehat{K}_t + \varphi_{ka}\widehat{A}_t\right) + \left[-\varphi_{ca} + \varphi_{qa}\right]\rho_A\widehat{A}_t$$

and, gathering terms once again, I get

$$-\varphi_{ck}\widehat{K}_t - \varphi_{ca}\widehat{A}_t = \left(-\varphi_{ck} + \varphi_{qk}\right)\varphi_{kk}\widehat{K}_t + \left[\left(-\varphi_{ck} + \varphi_{qk}\right)\varphi_{ka} + \left(-\varphi_{ca} + \varphi_{qa}\right)\rho_A\right]\widehat{A}_t.$$

Pairing the coefficients for $\widehat{K}_t$ and $\widehat{A}_t$, I find that

$$-\varphi_{ck} = \left(-\varphi_{ck} + \varphi_{qk}\right)\varphi_{kk}$$

and

$$-\varphi_{ca} = \big(- \varphi_{ck} + \varphi_{qk} \big) \varphi_{ka} + \big(- \varphi_{ca} + \varphi_{qa} \big) \, \rho_A.$$

Finally, solve for φ_{ck} and φ_{ca}:

$$\begin{aligned} \varphi_{ck} &= \big(\varphi_{ck} - \varphi_{qk} \big) \varphi_{kk}, \\ \varphi_{ca} &= \big(\varphi_{ck} - \varphi_{qk} \big) \varphi_{ka} + \big(\varphi_{ca} - \varphi_{qa} \big) \, \rho_A. \end{aligned}$$

I'm not done yet, but I'm making progress.

The Aggregate Feasibility Condition

Moving on to (7.28), I have

$$K^{\alpha} \widehat{A}_t + Q_k K \widehat{K}_t = C \big[\underbrace{\varphi_{ck} \widehat{K}_t + \varphi_{ca} \widehat{A}_t}_{\widehat{C}_t} \big] + K \big[\underbrace{\varphi_{kk} \widehat{K}_t + \varphi_{ka} \widehat{A}_t}_{\widehat{K}_{t+1}} \big].$$

Rearrange the terms on the right-hand side to get

$$K^{\alpha} \widehat{A}_t + Q_k K \widehat{K}_t = \big[C \varphi_{ck} + K \varphi_{kk} \big] \widehat{K}_t + \big[C \varphi_{ca} + K \varphi_{ka} \big] \widehat{A}_t,$$

which means that the following equations must hold:

$$\begin{aligned} Q_k K &= C \varphi_{ck} + K \varphi_{kk}, \\ K^{\alpha} &= C \varphi_{ca} + K \varphi_{ka}. \end{aligned}$$

Just as above, solve for φ_{ck} and φ_{ca}:

$$\begin{aligned} \varphi_{ck} &= \frac{Q_k K}{C} - \frac{K}{C} \varphi_{kk}, \\ \varphi_{ca} &= \frac{K^{\alpha}}{C} - \frac{K}{C} \varphi_{ka}. \end{aligned}$$

The Rental Rate Equation

Finally, (7.29) becomes

$$Q_k \big[\underbrace{\varphi_{qk} \widehat{K}_t + \varphi_{qa} \widehat{A}_t}_{\widehat{Q}_{kt}} \big] = \alpha K^{\alpha - 1} \widehat{A}_t + \alpha K^{\alpha - 1} \widehat{K}_t.$$

Pairing coefficients yields

$$Q_k \varphi_{qk} = \alpha \big(\alpha - 1 \big) K^{\alpha - 1}$$

and

$$Q_k \varphi_{qa} = \alpha K^{\alpha - 1}.$$

Simplifying a bit, solve for φ_{qk} and φ_{qa}:

$$\begin{aligned} \varphi_{qk} &= \frac{\alpha \big(\alpha - 1 \big) K^{\alpha - 1}}{Q_k}, \\ \varphi_{qa} &= \frac{\alpha K^{\alpha - 1}}{Q_k}. \end{aligned}$$

7.3.5 The Quadratic Equation, Revisited

Let's bring back all equations that relate to $\widehat{K}_t$:

$$\varphi_{ck} = \left(\varphi_{ck} - \varphi_{qk}\right)\varphi_{kk}, \tag{7.34}$$

$$\varphi_{ck} = \frac{Q_k K}{C} - \frac{K}{C}\varphi_{kk}, \tag{7.35}$$

$$\varphi_{qk} = \frac{\alpha\left(\alpha - 1\right)K^{\alpha-1}}{Q_k}. \tag{7.36}$$

As I show below, the critical step is to solve for φ_{kk}. Plugging (7.35) and (7.36) in (7.34) I get

$$\frac{Q_k K}{C} - \frac{K}{C}\varphi_{kk} = \left[\frac{Q_k K}{C} - \frac{K}{C}\varphi_{kk} - \frac{\alpha\left(\alpha - 1\right)K^{\alpha-1}}{Q_k}\right]\varphi_{kk}.$$

Now let's expand:

$$\frac{Q_k K}{C} - \frac{K}{C}\varphi_{kk} = \frac{Q_k K}{C}\varphi_{kk} - \frac{K}{C}\varphi_{kk}^2 - \frac{\alpha\left(\alpha - 1\right)K^{\alpha-1}}{Q_k}\varphi_{kk}.$$

This equation, once again, is quadratic in φ_{kk}. Gathering common terms and setting equal to zero, I get

$$a_2\varphi_{kk}^2 + a_1\varphi_{kk} + a_0 = 0, \tag{7.37}$$

where

$$a_0 \equiv \frac{Q_k K}{C},$$

$$a_1 \equiv \frac{\alpha\left(\alpha - 1\right)K^{\alpha-1}}{Q_k} - \frac{Q_k K}{C} - \frac{K}{C},$$

$$a_2 \equiv \frac{K}{C}.$$

Just like in Section 7.2.3, the key is to choose the stable root that solves (7.37). Once I have this value, φ_{ck} is obtained from equation (7.35) and φ_{qk} follows (7.36).

7.3.6 A Linear Equation

Is the process for dealing with the equations that relate to $\widehat{A}_t$ just as bad as the last one? No. To see this, let's list all the equations that relate to $\widehat{A}_t$:

$$\varphi_{ca} = \left(\varphi_{ck} - \varphi_{qk}\right)\varphi_{ka} + \left(\varphi_{ca} - \varphi_{qa}\right)\rho_A, \tag{7.38}$$

$$\varphi_{ca} = \frac{K^{\alpha}}{C} - \frac{K}{C}\varphi_{ka}, \tag{7.39}$$

$$\varphi_{qa} = \frac{\alpha K^{\alpha-1}}{Q_k}. \tag{7.40}$$

Now plug (7.39) and (7.40) in (7.38):

$$\frac{K^{\alpha}}{C} - \frac{K}{C}\varphi_{ka} = \left(\varphi_{ck} - \varphi_{qk}\right)\varphi_{ka} + \left(\frac{K^{\alpha}}{C} - \frac{K}{C}\varphi_{ka} - \frac{\alpha K^{\alpha-1}}{Q_k}\right)\rho_A.$$

If you stare at the expression for a bit, you'll realize that this equation is a linear equation in φ_{ka} (note φ_{ck} and φ_{qk} are already known). Gathering terms and setting equal to zero yields

$$b_1\varphi_{ka} + b_0 = 0, \tag{7.41}$$

where

$$b_0 \equiv \frac{K^\alpha}{C} - \frac{K^\alpha \rho_A}{C} + \frac{\alpha K^{\alpha-1}\rho_A}{Q_k},$$
$$b_1 \equiv -\frac{K}{C} - \left(\varphi_{ck} - \varphi_{qk}\right) + \frac{K\rho_A}{C}.$$

Clearly, the solution to (7.41) is

$$\varphi_{ka} = -\frac{b_0}{b_1}.$$

From here, φ_{ca} follows (7.39) and φ_{qa} follows (7.40).

Example 7.6 Set the parameter values to $\alpha = 0.33$, $\beta = 0.99$, $\delta = 0.02$, and $\rho_A = 0.9$. Given these parameters, a_0, a_1, and a_2 take values

$$a_0 = 14.1838,$$
$$a_1 = -28.2457,$$
$$a_2 = 14.0419,$$

and so the stable root equals $\varphi_{kk} = 0.9676$. From here I calculate $\varphi_{ck} = 0.5966$ and $\varphi_{qk} = -0.0200$. In addition,

$$b_0 = 0.1549,$$
$$b_1 = -2.0207,$$

so that $\varphi_{ka} = 0.0767$, $\varphi_{ca} = 0.2044$, and $\varphi_{qa} = 0.0298$. These coefficients imply the policy functions

$$\widehat{K}_{t+1} = 0.9676\widehat{K}_t + 0.0767\widehat{A}_t,$$
$$\widehat{C}_t = 0.5966\widehat{K}_t + 0.2044\widehat{A}_t,$$
$$\widehat{Q}_{kt} = -0.0200\widehat{K}_t + 0.0298\widehat{A}_t.$$

Note how all variables depend positively on TFP and capital, except for the rental rate, for which $\partial\widehat{Q}_{kt}/\partial\widehat{K}_t < 0$. (This last result follows the fact that $Q_{kt} = \alpha K_t^{\alpha-1} + 1 - \delta$.)

Example 7.7 How does this stochastic economy respond to a TFP shock? Let's assume $\varepsilon_{At} = 1$ in period 1 and $\varepsilon_{At} = 0$ in all other periods. By doing this, I generate a one-standard-deviation shock to TFP in period 1, which dies off over time given $\rho_A < 1$. Figure 7.2 shows the impulse-response functions for TFP, capital, consumption, and the rental rate, given $\sigma_A = 0.007$.

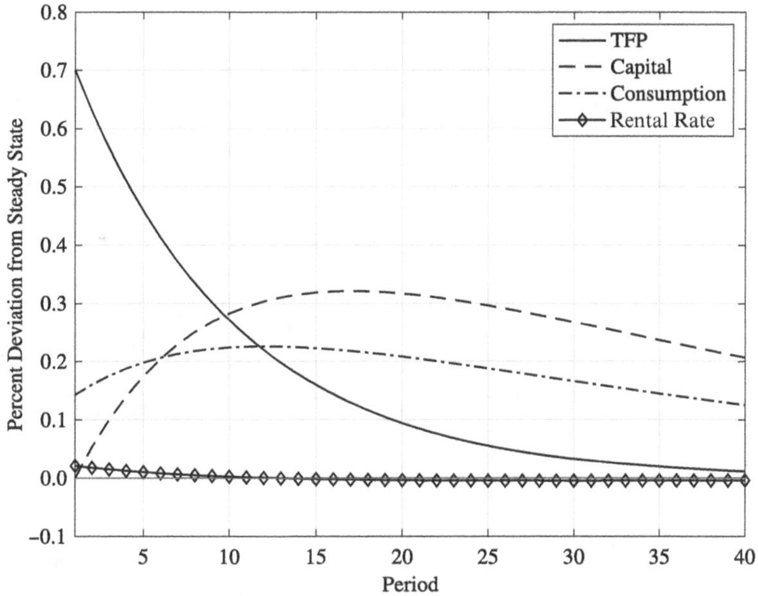

Figure 7.2 Impulse-response function of TFP, capital, consumption, and rental rate given a one-standard-deviation shock to ε_A in period 1 and $\sigma_A = 0.007$.

Example 7.8 It's easy to write code that simulates artificial data from the model: since ε_{At} follows a standard Normal distribution and $\sigma_A = 0.007$, Figure 7.3 shows one simulated path for TFP, while Figure 7.4 shows the implied paths for capital, consumption, and the rental rate after using the implied path for $\{A_t\}_{t=0}^{200}$.

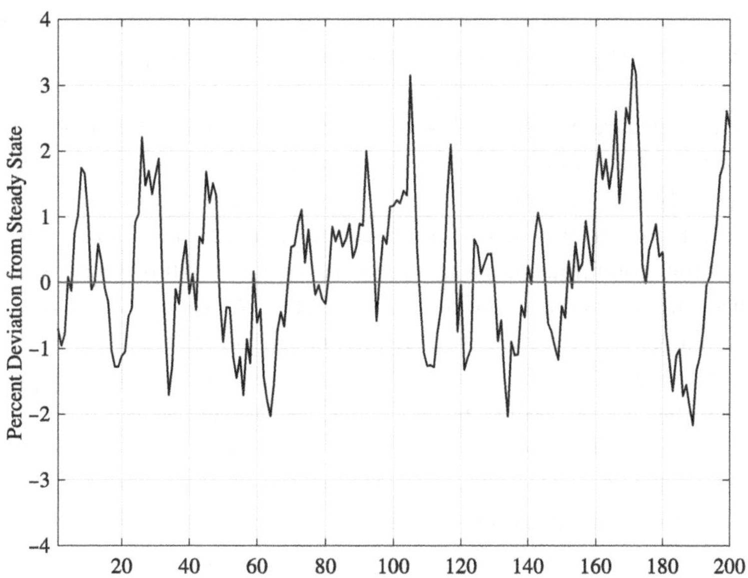

Figure 7.3 Simulated path of total factor productivity given $\sigma_A = 0.007$.

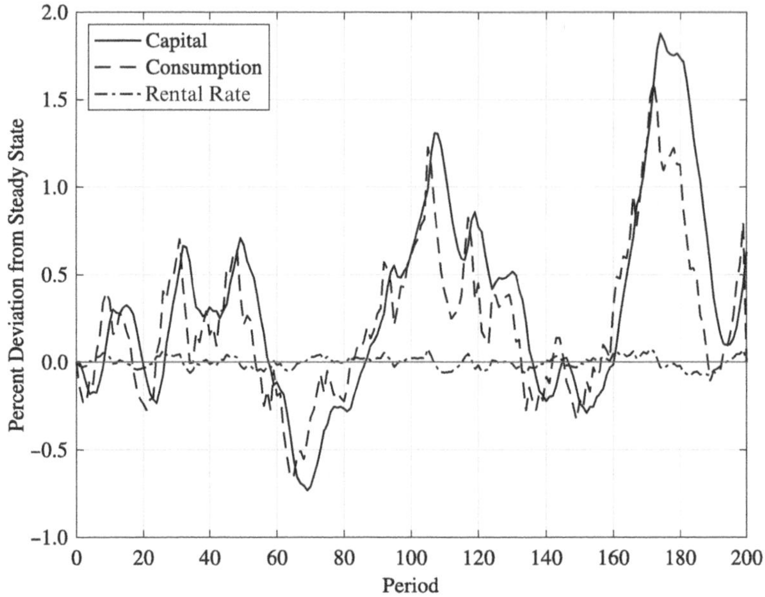

Figure 7.4 Simulated path of capital, consumption, and rental rate given the TFP sequence shown in Figure 7.3.

7.4 Up Next

By now you're probably thinking that the methodologies we've covered in this chapter are a cool way to unlock the potential of dynamic macro models, but you also know you don't want to redo all the algebra in Section 7.3 *every single time you work with a model.* And think about it: I've used a simple model with three variables (capital, consumption, and the rental rate). What if I were to use a model with 20 variables? It doesn't seem like following this path is the most efficient way to go.

Strictly speaking, there *is* a way forward, which relies on the tools shown in Appendix E. However, this path requires careful planning in order to map the log-linearized first-order conditions into a set of matrix equations. Thus, you might be thinking: do we always need to write all the steps from Section 7.3 (or derive the matrix equation system from Appendix E in order to solve a DSGE model)?

The answer, as it turns out, is "no." An analogy helps here: typically, we don't calculate the matrix product $\mathbf{b} = \left(\mathbf{X}^{\mathrm{T}}\mathbf{X}\right)^{-1}\mathbf{X}^{\mathrm{T}}\mathbf{y}$ every single time we need to get some regression coefficients. We use Stata, Eviews, or R. However, typing "`regress y X`" is meaningless if we don't know the theory that explains what's going on. Similarly, we don't solve dynamic macro models by calculating the system matrices every time we want to test a theory. We use Dynare. But as with econometrics, Dynare is meaningless if you don't know the theory behind what's going on. Fortunately, that's what we just did.

7.5 Bibliographic Notes

The discussion in this chapter follows the methodology proposed by Uhlig (1999); it's fairly powerful and can handle pretty much everything we throw its way. Of course, there are many other solution methods for linear systems; three of the most popular approaches – besides Uhlig (1999) – are Klein (2000), Christiano (2002), and Sims (2002). For a long time, the paper by Campbell (1994) was the gold standard on how to solve DSGE models, though his log-linearization routine still requires taking derivatives (it is not automated like Uhlig's). Campbell's take on the method of undetermined coefficients nicely complements the exposition in this chapter.

The book by McCandless (2008) offers a discussion on linear systems, just like the one in this chapter, and it goes deeper into explaining the contents of Appendix E. More advanced books that also discuss alternative solution methods are DeJong and Dave (2011) and Heer and Maussner (2024). Finally, the survey piece by Fernández-Villaverde et al. (2016) is a comprehensive (but fairly advanced) reference.

7.6 Problems

7.6.1 Solving a Stochastic CRRA Economy, Part I

Consider a dynamic economy with a representative household and a representative firm. The household chooses values of consumption C_t, leisure ℓ_t, and next-period capital K_{t+1} to solve

$$\begin{aligned} \max \quad & \mathbb{E}_0 \sum_{t=0}^{\infty} \beta^t \left[\frac{\left(C_t \ell_t^{\phi}\right)^{1-\eta} - 1}{1-\eta} \right] \\ \text{subject to} \quad & C_t + K_{t+1} - (1-\delta) K_t = r_{kt} K_t + w_t (1-\ell_t), \\ & C_t, K_{t+1} \geq 0, \end{aligned}$$

where K_0 is known by the planner. In the above, $\beta \in (0,1)$ is the household's discount factor, $\phi \geq 0$ is a leisure weight, $1/\eta > 1$ is the coefficient of relative risk aversion, and $\delta \in (0,1)$ is the depreciation rate.

Each period, the firm rents labor N_F and capital K_F from the household and uses these inputs to solve

$$\begin{aligned} \max \quad & Y_t - r_{kt} K_{Ft} - w_t N_{Ft} \\ \text{subject to} \quad & Y_t = A_t K_{Ft}^{\alpha} N_{Ft}^{1-\alpha}, \\ & K_{Ft}, N_{Ft} \geq 0, \end{aligned}$$

where $\alpha \in (0,1)$ is the income share of capital. TFP follows an AR(1) process of the form

$$\log A_t = (1-\rho_A) \log A_{ss} + \rho_A \log A_{t-1} + \sigma_A \varepsilon_{At},$$

where A_0 is given, $\rho_A \in (0,1)$ is an autocorrelation coefficient, and $\sigma_A > 0$.

1. For the economy described above, either write the definition of a CE or state the associated SPP, along with a brief justification of why it's possible to use the CE = PO equivalency.
2. Use your answer to part 1 to find the intratemporal, intertemporal, and aggregate feasibility conditions for this economy.
3. Use your answer to part 2 to find closed-form expressions for all of the economy's steady-state values. *Note*: Your solutions should be a function of model parameters only.

7.6.2 Solving a Stochastic CRRA Economy, Part II

Use Uhlig's rules and your answer to Problem 7.6.1 to derive the log-linearized equilibrium conditions for this economy.

7.6.3 Solving a Stochastic CRRA Economy, Part III

Let $\beta = 0.99$, $\phi = 1$, $\eta = 1.5$, $\delta = 0.02$, $\alpha = 0.36$, and $\rho_A = 0.9$. Use your answer to Problem 7.6.2 and the theory from Section 7.3 in order to derive policy functions for this economy. Offer a brief interpretation of your findings.

7.6.4 Solving a Stochastic CRRA Economy, Part IV

Generate the impulse-response functions for consumption, output, and hours worked after a one-time shock to TFP. Set $\sigma_A = 0.007$.

7.6.5 Solving a Stochastic CRRA Economy, Part V

Add investment as a new variable and plot its impulse-response function alongside the ones for consumption, output, investment, and hours you calculated in Problem 7.6.4. Are all these variables procyclical, as they are in the data? *Hint*: Investment obeys the law of motion for capital, $X_t = K_{t+1} - (1 - \delta) K_t$.

8 Dynare

At the end of the previous chapter, I asked whether we always needed to work through the long algebra of Section 7.3 or derive the matrix equation system from Appendix E. The answer, I argued, was "no." We don't solve dynamic macro models by calculating the system matrices every time we want to test a theory. We use Dynare. But again, Dynare is meaningless if you don't know the theory behind what's going on. This theory, fortunately, has been at the core of the previous chapters. Armed with this knowledge, it's okay to move toward specialized software that will make our lives easier.

Section 8.1 shares the history of Dynare and explains what you can do with it. The rest of the chapter, however, is meant to be worked out in front of the computer. Section 8.2 lays out the stochastic benchmark SPP and characterizes its equilibrium; in turn, these equations are the input that goes into Dynare. In Sections 8.3 and 8.4, I carefully explain both the inputs to and outputs from Dynare; Section 8.5 offers a detour to ask whether log-linearized equations are needed if Dynare doesn't need this step in the first place. Finally, Section 8.6 repeats the previous steps by showing how to capture a log-linear model (not the nonlinear version from Sections 8.3 and 8.4) into Dynare.

Before I begin, it's convenient to review the notation and guidelines that I'm using. Dynare commands and variables are identified in the text as they're shown in **`bold monospace`** font. Code that you actually have to type in the editor or the command window (and, when applicable, the output produced by the code) uses `plain monospace` font.

8.1 What is Dynare?

Dynare is an add-on program to Matlab (and, as of the time of writing, Julia) that solves and estimates DSGE models. It was developed not so long ago by a group of French researchers based at CEPREMAP (Centre Pour la Recherche Economique et ses Applications). It's fair to say that the importance (and user base) of Dynare has grown exponentially over time, most likely because (i) it's extremely powerful yet (ii) very easy to use.

So, what can Dynare do for us? Here's a short list:

- Solve almost any (representative-agent) DSGE model you may think of.
- Generate impulse-response functions.
- Calculate summary statistic tables.
- Estimate parameters via MLE and Bayesian estimation.

Of course, nothing is perfect, so Dynare can't (at least at the time of writing)

- Get you analytical log-linearized conditions.
- Solve models via value function iteration.
- Give you an idea for your research proposal.

As a well-established programming language, Dynare has a lot to offer – sometimes too much – but that's what the manual (Adjemian et al. 2024) is for. For now I'll focus on the solution and stochastic simulation of DSGE models, leaving (Bayesian) estimation for Chapter 16.

8.2 A Nonlinear Example

The goal of this chapter is to test Dynare with an actual DSGE model, so I will return to the model economy from Section 7.3.1, reproduced below for your convenience. For the time being, I look at the nonlinear model itself (which is *not* the log-linearized version – that will be addressed in Section 8.5).

8.2.1 The Stochastic, Infinite-Horizon Benchmark SPP, One More Time

Consider an economy with inelastic labor supply and stochastic technology shocks, where I assume logarithmic utility and a Cobb–Douglas production function. This economy is mapped to the SPP

$$\begin{aligned}
\max_{\{C_t,K_{t+1}\}_{t=0}^{\infty}} \quad & \mathbb{E}_0 \sum_{t=0}^{\infty} \beta^t \log C_t \\
\text{subject to} \quad & A_t K_t^{\alpha} = C_t + K_{t+1} - (1-\delta)K_t, \\
& C_t \geq 0,
\end{aligned}$$

where K_0 is known by the planner. The technology shock follows

$$\log A_t = \big(1-\rho_A\big)\log A_{ss} + \rho_A \log A_{t-1} + \sigma_A \varepsilon_{At},$$

where A_t is a stochastic shock affecting period-t output (with steady state $A = 1$), A_0 is given, $\rho_A \in \big(0,1\big)$ is a persistence parameter, and $\sigma_A > 0$.

8.2.2 Equilibrium Conditions

As shown in Chapter 7, the equilibrium conditions for this economy are characterized by an intertemporal and and aggregate feasibility condition, given by

$$C_t^{-1} = \beta\,\mathbb{E}_t C_{t+1}^{-1}\left(\alpha A_{t+1} K_{t+1}^{\alpha-1} + 1 - \delta\right),$$
$$A_t K_t^{\alpha} = C_t + K_{t+1} - \left(1 - \delta\right) K_t.$$

I now add more variables to the system of equations. First, output Y_t, which is

$$Y_t = A_t K_t^{\alpha}.$$

Second, the real gross net-of-depreciation rate of return on capital

$$Q_{kt} \equiv \alpha A_t K_t^{\alpha-1} + 1 - \delta = \alpha Y_t K_t^{-1} + 1 - \delta,$$

where the last equality follows the definition of output.

To complete the extensions, I incorporate investment as a model variable, which comes directly from the law of motion for capital:

$$X_t = K_{t+1} + \left(1 - \delta\right) K_t.$$

All together, the model's equilibrium conditions are given by

$$Y_t = A_t K_t^{\alpha}, \tag{8.1}$$
$$Q_{kt} = \alpha Y_t K_t^{-1} + 1 - \delta, \tag{8.2}$$
$$C_t^{-1} = \beta \mathbb{E}_t C_{t+1}^{-1} Q_{k,t+1}, \tag{8.3}$$
$$Y_t = C_t + X_t, \tag{8.4}$$
$$X_t = K_{t+1} + \left(1 - \delta\right) K_t. \tag{8.5}$$

I also include the technology process

$$\log A_t = \left(1 - \rho_A\right) \log A_{ss} + \rho_A \log A_{t-1} + \sigma_A \varepsilon_{At}. \tag{8.6}$$

8.2.3 Steady State

In the steady state, the equilibrium conditions become

$$Y = K^{\alpha}, \tag{8.7}$$
$$Q_k = \alpha Y K^{-1} + 1 - \delta, \tag{8.8}$$
$$1 = \beta Q_k, \tag{8.9}$$
$$Y = C + X, \tag{8.10}$$
$$X = \delta K, \tag{8.11}$$

where I've already used that $A_{ss} = 1$. For reasons that will be apparent in a moment, it's convenient to derive closed-form expressions for the steady-state variables. To do this, start from equation (8.9), which gives me the steady-state value for the (gross) net-of-depreciation rate of return:

$$Q_{k,ss} = \frac{1}{\beta}.$$

The way ahead may not be clear, but I always find it convenient to put all model variables in terms of one variable (say, K_{ss}) and go from there. Following this suggestion, equation (8.8) yields

$$Y_{ss} = \left(\frac{Q_{k,ss} - 1 + \delta}{\alpha} \right) K_{ss} = \omega_Y K_{ss}, \tag{8.12}$$

where $\omega_Y \equiv \left(Q_{k,ss} - 1 + \delta\right)/\alpha$. While I don't currently have a value for Y_{ss}, I will do so once I have an expression for K_{ss}. Now let's look at equation (8.7): plugging the expression above in the left-hand side, I get

$$\omega_Y K_{ss} = K_{ss}^{\alpha},$$

which I rearrange to

$$K_{ss} = \frac{1}{\omega_Y^{1/(1-\alpha)}}.$$

This last expression gives me both K_{ss} and Y_{ss}. Then, trivially, I get X_{ss} from (8.11),

$$X_{ss} = \delta K_{ss},$$

and (8.10) implies

$$C_{ss} = Y_{ss} - X_{ss}.$$

I now have steady-state values for the six model variables.

8.3 Dynare Scripts

By construction, all Dynare files need to be identified with a `mod` extension, for example `indivisible.mod` or `ckm2007.mod`. (If it helps, think of a Stata `do` file.)

The main unit of a `mod` file is a **block**. Happily, all `mod` files have the same structure (blocks), namely,

1. Preamble.
2. Model.
3. Steady state.
4. Shocks.
5. Simulation and/or estimation.

I now dive into each block, one step at a time. For your convenience, the full `mod` file I'll be working with is shared in Appendix F.1.

8.3.1 Preamble Block

Being the first block in the code, the preamble block allows me to define the variables I use in the model. The only detail is that Dynare asks me to distinguish between endogenous and exogenous variables. Once this is done, I provide a list of model parameters, assign them values, and move along.

This being said, Dynare handles exogenous variables differently relative to the logic I've set up in earlier chapters. For example, here's the law of motion for TFP, equation (8.6):

$$\log A_t = \left(1 - \rho_A\right) \log A_{ss} + \rho_A \log A_{t-1} + \sigma_A \varepsilon_{At}.$$

Our current understanding is that A_t is an exogenous state variable. However, Dynare takes A_t to be an *endogenous* variable and makes ε_{At} the exogenous one.

Taking this detail into account, here's how to write the preamble block in Dynare:

```
/*
nonlinear.mod
Implementation of the stochastic, infinite horizon benchmark SPP.
*/

close all

// PREAMBLE: VARIABLE AND PARAMETER DEFINITIONS

// Endogenous variables (6)
var Y A K Qk C X ;

// Exogenous variables (1)
varexo epsilon_A ;

// Parameters (6)
parameters beta delta alpha rho_A sigma_A A_ss ;

    beta = 0.99 ;
    delta = 0.08 ;
    alpha = 0.33 ;
    rho_A = 0.85 ;
    sigma_A = 0.007 ;
    A_ss = 1 ;
```

(Code 8.1)

Some notes:

- All Dynare instructions end with a semicolon (;); failure to do so will make the compiler crash, as it won't know where an instruction ends and another begins.

- The double slash `//` introduces a comment in Dynare; nothing to the right will be read by the compiler. Typically, this instruction is meant for single-line comments; longer remarks can be block-commented by the start and end block-quote commands `/*` and `*/`, respectively (I use these at the very top of the code to describe what the **mod** file is doing).
- The variable declaration parts are obvious in the code: endogenous variables follow **var** while exogenous variables follow **varexo**. I do not need to put all model variables in one line; for readability, I may use as many **var** and **varexo** commands as needed. Finally, parameters are declared with the instruction **parameters** and their values follow one at a time.

8.3.2 Model Block

The beauty of Dynare comes from one simple idea: wysiwyg ("what you see is what you get"). There is no need to do anything beyond calculating the first-order conditions, and I get to input them to Dynare just as they look in the calculations I do by hand. An example helps a lot here.

Example 8.1 Consider the intertemporal condition, equation (8.3), which is

$$C_t^{-1} = \beta\,\mathbb{E}_t C_{t+1}^{-1} Q_{k,t+1}.$$

The expression that goes into the model block is

```
1/C = beta*Qk(+1)/C(+1) ;
```

There are minor differences between the first-order condition calculated by hand and the one that goes into Dynare. First, I change C_t^{-1} to its equivalent $1/C_t$. (Strictly speaking, this is not really needed, but computationally speaking, a division is "less expensive" than an exponentiation – and it takes fewer keystrokes to type.) Second, variables dated in $t+1$ are declared by adding a "`(+1)`" after the variable name; thus, $Q_{k,t+1}$ becomes `Qk(+1)`. Not surprisingly, variables dated in $t-1$ are declared by adding a "`(-1)`" instead.

Armed with this knowledge, the code inside the model block is given by

```
// MODEL BLOCK

model ;
    Y = A*K(-1)^alpha ;
    Qk = alpha*Y/K(-1) + 1 - delta ;
    1/C = beta*Qk(+1)/C(+1) ;
    Y = C + X ;
    X = K - (1-delta)*K(-1) ;
```

```
    log(A) = (1-rho_A)*log(A_ss) + rho_A*log(A(-1))
         + sigma_A*epsilon_A ;
end ;
```

(Code 8.2)

which is consistent with equations (8.1)–(8.6).

Remark 8.1 Maybe you're wondering why I set the production function as

$$Y_t = A_t K_{t-1}^{\alpha}$$

and not as

$$Y_t = A_t K_t^{\alpha}.$$

The reason is that Dynare's timing convention requires measuring all variables when they are decided: in this case, today's capital was chosen yesterday, and so the right notation is `K(-1)` and not `K`. That said, this is a minor issue that is easily fixed with an extra command in the preamble block. (See the manual for details.)

8.3.3 Steady-State Block

In this block, I provide an initial guess for the model's steady-state values and Dynare takes care of the rest via a Newton-based procedure (see Online Appendix 2). For small models, this approach is often the most efficient, but as its complexity increases, typing the model's closed-form solutions speeds up the process considerably – and avoids crashes due to bad initial guesses.

Using a Steady State Guess

If I want to guess the steady-state values, I just add this bit to the code:

```
// STEADY STATE BLOCK

initval ;
    A = 1 ;
    K = 7 ;
    Qk = 0.1 ;
    C = 1.5 ;
    Y = 2 ;
    X = 0.5 ;
end ;

steady ;
check ;
```

(Code 8.3)

Of course, just as with any Newton-style solver, getting the "right" guess is critical: there is no guarantee that Dynare will find the steady state if the initial values are too far away from the solution.

Moving along, the **steady** command tells Dynare to compute the steady state based on the guesses (or closed-form solutions) you have provided. Then, the **check** command verifies that given the parameter values you have provided, the model has a stable solution (this idea rhymes with "quadratic equation" – more on this topic in Section 8.4.3).

Using Closed-Form Solutions

Most of the time I will have calculated closed-form solutions for all steady-state values, like in Section 8.2.3. In this case, I write instead

```
// STEADY STATE BLOCK

steady_state_model ;
    A = A_ss ;
    Qk = 1/beta ;
    omega_y = (Qk - 1 + delta)/alpha ;
    K = 1/omega_y^(1/(1 - alpha)) ;
    Y = A*K^alpha ;
    X = delta*K ;
    C = Y - X ;
end ;

steady ;
check ;
```

(Code 8.4)

Note I define (and later use) the auxiliary parameter **omega_y** (i.e., ω_Y in equation (8.12)); as long as Dynare knows the relationship between parameter and steady-state values, everything works as expected.

8.3.4 Shocks Block

This block allows me to provide the statistical properties (e.g., the variances or standard deviations) of the model's exogenous innovations. Without this information, I cannot simulate or generate the model's impulse-response functions.

I've said this before, but it's worth mentioning again: model innovations are not the same as model shocks. Think that for the TFP process, equation (8.6):

$$\log A_t = \left(1 - \rho_A\right) \log A_{ss} + \rho_A \log A_{t-1} + \sigma_A \varepsilon_{At},$$

Dynare cares about ε_{At} only, and I need to tell the program how this innovation is distributed. Put differently, Dynare needs to know either the standard deviation of ε_{At} (i.e., σ_A) or its variance (σ_A^2).

What does the shocks block look like? Here's the code for our example, where I tell Dynare that the variance of ε_{At} is simply 1, given my ongoing assumption that all innovations follow a standard Normal distribution:

```
// SHOCKS BLOCK

shocks ;
    var epsilon_A = 1 ;
end ;
```

(Code 8.5)

8.3.5 Simulation Block

The simulation block is self-explanatory. For now, my goal is to generate the model's impulse-response functions and statistical properties, so I only need to include two options (and a variable list) into the simulation command. (Sure, there are a lot of options, but not all of them are needed right now. Though I fear I'm repeating myself, see the manual for details.) I let Dynare know that

- I want 40 periods in the impulse-response function plots.
- The solution method is a first-order (linear) approximation.
- I want the impulse-response graph to have the following ordering: TFP, capital, rental rate, output, consumption, and investment. (If I don't add this list, Dynare will plot all model variables in the order they're declared in the preamble block.)

Here's what I need to put in the code:

```
// SIMULATION BLOCK

stoch_simul(irf=40, order=1) A K Qk Y C X ;
```

(Code 8.6)

8.4 Dynare Output

Armed with computer code, I need to run it. First, it's useful to verify that Dynare is already installed on the computer. I verify this by going to the command prompt and typing `dynare` in Matlab, or `using Dynare` in Julia. If everything is installed as it should be, Matlab returns this text:

```
>> dynare

This is Dynare version 6.0.

USAGE: dynare FILENAME[.mod,.dyn] [OPTIONS]
```

```
The dynare command executes instruction included in FILENAME.mod.
See the reference manual for the available options.
```

(Code 8.7)

Failure to see this message means that Dynare is not installed on your computer; if this is the case, go to the Dynare download page and follow the instructions for your operating system. (Julia doesn't return any output, so if you don't get any prompt, you're good to go.)

Once installed, Dynare does the heavy lifting. Assuming that you followed the convention in Section 8.3.1 and named your file `nonlinear.mod`, all that's left to do is to go to the command prompt and type

```
>> dynare nonlinear
```

if using Matlab, or

```
julia> context =@dynare "nonlinear.mod"
```

if using Julia. After pressing the return key, output will start showing up on your screen. Given the way I've set up the code, the following components will appear:

1. Preprocessor output.
2. Steady-state results.
3. Eigenvalues and model summary.
4. Matrix of covariance of exogenous shocks.
5. Policy and transition functions.
6. Theoretical moments.
7. Matrix of correlations.
8. Coefficients of autocorrelation.
9. Impulse-response function graphs.

Let's take it slowly and dissect each of these output components. When applicable, I'll throw in a couple of comments on how to solve (debug) the most typical issues with Dynare code.

8.4.1 Preprocessor Output

If you typed up your model correctly and there are no major issues, you should expect to see this (big) chunk of text:

```
>> dynare nonlinear
Starting Dynare (version 6.0).
Calling Dynare with arguments: none
Starting preprocessing of the model file ...
Found 6 equation(s).
```

```
Evaluating expressions...
Computing static model derivatives (order 1).
Normalizing the static model...
Finding the optimal block decomposition of the static model...
2 block(s) found:
  1 recursive block(s) and 1 simultaneous block(s).
  the largest simultaneous block has 5 equation(s)
                                 and 5 feedback variable(s).
Computing dynamic model derivatives (order 1).
Normalizing the dynamic model...
Finding the optimal block decomposition of the dynamic model...
2 block(s) found:
  1 recursive block(s) and 1 simultaneous block(s).
  the largest simultaneous block has 5 equation(s)
                                 and 5 feedback variable(s).
Preprocessing completed.
Preprocessing time: 0h00m00s.
```

(Code 8.8)

Debugging: A Missing Variable

If I mess something up when typing or setting up the model, Dynare will let me know right away. For example, suppose I forget to add TFP to the endogenous variable declaration in the preamble, so that I only have

```
// Endogenous variables (6)
var Y K Qk C X ;
```

Obviously, as two of the model block equations invoke A_t, Dynare will let me know that something doesn't add up:

```
>> dynare nonlinear
Starting Dynare (version 6.0).
Calling Dynare with arguments: none
Starting preprocessing of the model file ...
ERROR: nonlinear.mod: line 29, col 9: Unknown symbol: A
ERROR: nonlinear.mod: line 34, col 9: Unknown symbol: A
ERROR: nonlinear.mod: line 34, cols 46-50: Unknown symbol: A
Preprocessing time: 0h00m00s.
Error using dynare (line 297)
Dynare: preprocessing failed
```

(Code 8.9)

Note how the software tells you the exact position (line and column) where the error is, and what the problem is (i.e., "`Unknown symbol: A`").

Debugging: A Missing Semicolon

A fairly common error is forgetting to end a Dynare command with a semicolon (`;`): the software won't know why two instructions are merged and will let you know. For example, suppose I forget to close the endogenous variable declaration line with a semicolon and I just move on to the exogenous variable declaration part:

```
// Endogenous variables (6)
var Y A K Qk C X

// Exogenous variables (1)
varexo epsilon_A ;
```

Here, Dynare tells me something is not right:

```
>> dynare nonlinear
Starting Dynare (version 6.0).
Calling Dynare with arguments: none
Starting preprocessing of the model file ...
ERROR: nonlinear.mod: line 14, cols 1-6: syntax error,
       unexpected VAREXO
Preprocessing time: 0h00m00s.
Error using dynare (line 297)
Dynare: preprocessing failed
```

(Code 8.10)

Cleary, the problem is that Dynare is still reading endogenous variables, but thinks that I've decided to name one of them "**`varexo`**," which is a restricted (system) name.

The bottom line? Dynare is pretty good at spotting errors in your code, and also letting you know where (and what) the problem is.

8.4.2 Steady-State Results

Remember the "**`steady`**" command in the steady-state block? Here's where I get to see whether my guess or closed-form solutions worked out – or not.

Let's show the software output when there is good news. Starting from the closed-form solution (see the **`steady_state_model`** part in Section 8.3.3), I should see this chunk of text on the screen:

```
STEADY-STATE RESULTS:

Y    1.89533
A    1
K    6.94175
Qk   1.0101
```

```
C    1.33999
X    0.55534
```

(Code 8.11)

which are the values of the stationary equilibrium.

Debugging: A Bad Initial Guess

As I mentioned above, providing an initial guess and letting Dynare do the heavy lifting is often reasonable for small models, but even then, things may go wrong when the guess is not good. Now, just because I'm trying to make a point here, suppose my initial (and definitely wrong) guess is

```
initval ;
    A = 0 ;
    K = 7 ;
    Qk = 1 ;
    C = 1 ;
    Y = 2 ;
    X = 1 ;
end ;
```

(Code 8.12)

If I run the code, I get an error message right after the preprocessor output:

```
Residuals of the static equations:
Equation number 1: Y  :        2.000000
Equation number 2: Qk :       -0.014286
Equation number 3: 3  :        0.010000
Equation number 4: 4  :        0.000000
Equation number 5: X  :        0.440000
Equation number 6: 6  :             NaN

Error using print_info (line 33)
The steady state has NaNs or Inf.
Error in steady (line 143)
    print_info(info,options_.noprint, options_);
Error in nonlinear.driver (line 286)
steady;
Error in dynare (line 310)
    evalin('base',[fname '.driver']);
```

(Code 8.13)

By now you probably know that something is wrong, but since you're starting from a guess, most likely you don't know that setting $A_{ss} = 0$ is to blame. The moral of the story is that it's often better to solve analytically for the steady-state values.

Debugging: A Typo in the Closed-Form Solutions

Next, suppose I derive the closed-form solutions correctly on paper, but type up the wrong sign when copying to the Dynare code. More precisely, suppose, instead of writing $C_{ss} = Y_{ss} - X_{ss}$, I mix up the signs and type

```
C = Y + X ;
```

What happens? Let's see the output. The preprocessor part will run correctly, but the steady-state results won't add up:

```
Residuals of the static equations:
Equation number 1: Y  :        0.000000
Equation number 2: Qk :        0.000000
Equation number 3: 3  :        0.000000
Equation number 4: 4  :       -1.110680
Equation number 5: X  :        0.000000
Equation number 6: 6  :        0.000000

Error using print_info (line 33)
The steadystate file did not compute the steady state
Error in steady (line 143)
    print_info(info,options_.noprint, options_);
Error in nonlinear.driver (line 270)
steady;
Error in dynare (line 310)
    evalin('base',[fname '.driver']);
```

(Code 8.14)

What's going on here? It looks a bit cryptic, but Dynare is letting me know that given my steady-state guesses, the fourth equation is not arriving at $0 = 0$. Now, which one is my fourth equation? That depends on how I captured the model. Let's copy and paste from the model block:

```
Y = A*K(-1)^alpha ;
Qk = alpha*Y/K(-1) + 1 - delta ;
1/C = beta*Qk(+1)/C(+1) ;
Y = C + X ;
X = K - (1-delta)*K(-1) ;
log(A) = (1-rho_A)*log(A_ss) + rho_A*log(A(-1))
     + sigma_A*epsilon_A ;
```

(Code 8.15)

The fourth equation corresponds to the aggregate feasibility constraint, and Dynare is telling you that

$$Y_{ss} - C_{ss} - X_{ss} = -1.1107,$$

instead of zero. Since this equation is the only one giving you trouble, and Y_{ss} and X_{ss} seem to work okay elsewhere, you may conclude that the problem lies in C_{ss} and go back to double-check what's going on. (Or not. Debugging is an art, not a science.)

8.4.3 Eigenvalues and Model Summary

The eigenvalues output tells you whether your model satisfies the "right conditions" for a stable solution to exist. Most of the time, this part will move along and you will see something like this on your computer screen:

```
EIGENVALUES:
         Modulus                Real           Imaginary
            0.85                0.85                   0
          0.9029              0.9029                   0
           1.119               1.119                   0
        1.15e+18           -1.15e+18                   0

There are 2 eigenvalue(s) larger than 1 in modulus for 2
     forward-looking
variable(s)
The rank condition is verified.
```

(Code 8.16)

Since I don't want to open up a can of worms (but if you do, see Blanchard & Kahn 1980), it's enough to know that I need to have the same number of eigenvalues outside the unit circle (i.e., with modulus greater than 1) as I have forward-looking variables – in our case, there are two: consumption and the real interest rate. If this condition is satisfied, then the model is stable and a non-explosive solution exists. We then say that "the Blanchard–Kahn conditions are met." (If this idea still doesn't ring a bell, it's time to review Section 7.2.3.)

As for the model summary output, this part simply gives me a "bird's-eye" view of the model:

```
MODEL SUMMARY

  Number of variables:          6
  Number of stochastic shocks:  1
  Number of state variables:    2
  Number of jumpers:            2
  Number of static variables:   2
```

(Code 8.17)

8.4.4 Matrix of Covariance of Exogenous Shocks

In this case, as the model only has one exogenous shock (ε_{At}), there's not a lot to see. For larger models, this section helps to confirm that the links between the exogenous shocks are exactly as I want them.

In the meantime, this output is what I get from Dynare:

```
MATRIX OF COVARIANCE OF EXOGENOUS SHOCKS
Variables     epsilon_A
epsilon_A      1.000000
```

(Code 8.18)

8.4.5 Policy and Transition Functions

A key part of Dynare's output consists of the model's policy and transition functions (for the endogenous and exogenous variables, respectively). These policy functions are slightly different to what I've shared before, so a bit of care is needed when interpreting the output. Here's what I get out of the software:

```
POLICY AND TRANSITION FUNCTIONS
                    A           K          Qk           Y           C           X
Constant     1.000000    6.941752    1.010101    1.895330    1.339990    0.555340
A(-1)        0.850000    1.220422    0.076586    1.611030    0.390608    1.220422
K(-1)        0           0.902867   -0.008696    0.090101    0.107234   -0.017133
epsilon_A    0.007000    0.010051    0.000631    0.013267    0.003217    0.010051
```

(Code 8.19)

Remark 8.2 What do the values in the table mean? First, Dynare's policy functions calculate the evolution of the variable as a function of the *level deviations* from the steady state (instead of percent deviations throughout). Hence, the policy function for, say, capital takes the form

$$K_t = 6.941752 + 0.902867\widetilde{K}_{t-1} + 1.220422\widetilde{A}_{t-1} + 0.010051\varepsilon_{At},$$

where tilde variables (e.g., $\widetilde{K}_t$) are level deviations from the steady state, that is

$$\widetilde{K}_t \equiv K_t - K_{ss}.$$

(See Remark 7.6.) Just to be safe, here's the policy function for consumption:

$$C_t = 1.339990 + 0.107234\widetilde{K}_{t-1} + 0.390608\widetilde{A}_{t-1} + 0.003217\varepsilon_{At},$$

and the one for TFP:

$$A_t = 1 + 0.85\widetilde{A}_{t-1} + 0.007\varepsilon_{At}.$$

8.4.6 Theoretical Moments

As coded above, this chunk of output provides the theoretical moments for the model variables. I get

```
THEORETICAL MOMENTS
VARIABLE          MEAN  STD. DEV.    VARIANCE
A               1.0000     0.0133      0.0002
K               6.9418     0.1223      0.0150
Qk              1.0101     0.0011      0.0000
Y               1.8953     0.0327      0.0011
C               1.3400     0.0173      0.0003
X               0.5553     0.0180      0.0003
```

(Code 8.20)

If I want to compute empirical moments, I use simulated data instead. To do this, let's modify the `stoch_simul` command so that it tells Dynare to generate 150,000 artificial data points, drop the first 50,000, and then calculate empirical moments for the remaining 100,000. I write instead

```
stoch_simul(irf=40, order=1, periods = 150000, drop = 50000) A K Qk Y C X ;
```

and get

```
MOMENTS OF SIMULATED VARIABLES
VARIABLE        MEAN     STD. DEV.       VARIANCE       SKEWNESS       KURTOSIS
A           0.999993      0.013236       0.000175       0.006205       0.043462
K           6.941665      0.121236       0.014698       0.000287       0.092484
Qk          1.010101      0.001054       0.000001       0.006386      -0.026254
Y           1.895310      0.032542       0.001059       0.003272       0.058429
C           1.339978      0.017192       0.000296       0.000620       0.085467
X           0.555332      0.017910       0.000321       0.007152       0.038792
```

(Code 8.21)

As expected, the first and second moments are almost identical. That said, I now get information about the third and fourth moments, which I didn't have when only computing theoretical moments.

8.4.7 Matrix of Correlations

The next output component tells us the correlation structure between the model's endogenous variables. This output offers a convenient quick check that allows us to see whether variables are procyclical, countercyclical, or acyclical.

```
MATRIX OF CORRELATIONS
Variables            A         K        Qk         Y         C         X
A               1.0000    0.6706    0.5600    0.9610    0.7833    0.9954
K               0.6706    1.0000   -0.2391    0.8496    0.9864    0.5964
```

```
Qk            0.5600  -0.2391   1.0000   0.3090  -0.0763   0.6368
Y             0.9610   0.8496   0.3090   1.0000   0.9247   0.9301
C             0.7833   0.9864  -0.0763   0.9247   1.0000   0.7201
X             0.9954   0.5964   0.6368   0.9301   0.7201   1.0000
```

(Code 8.22)

From the table, the correlation between output and consumption is 0.92, which shows consumption is a procyclical variable, just as in the data. A similar story happens for investment (correlation = 0.93).

Finally, as in Section 8.4.6, changing the `stoch_simul` command to compute empirical moments will yield a matrix of correlation for simulated variables instead (not shown).

8.4.8 Coefficients of Autocorrelation

The output also gives us estimates of the coefficients of autocorrelation for all model variables; these values offer yet another one of the standard set of statistical measures used to compare model fit. The output received is

```
COEFFICIENTS OF AUTOCORRELATION
Order          1       2       3       4       5
A         0.8500  0.7225  0.6141  0.5220  0.4437
K         0.9918  0.9710  0.9409  0.9041  0.8627
Qk        0.7812  0.6019  0.4556  0.3366  0.2404
Y         0.9142  0.8351  0.7622  0.6952  0.6336
C         0.9807  0.9516  0.9154  0.8743  0.8300
X         0.8289  0.6855  0.5654  0.4651  0.3813
```

(Code 8.23)

All variables are very persistent. And just like in Section 8.4.6, changing the `stoch_simul` command to compute empirical moments will yield a matrix of autocorrelation of simulated variables (not shown).

8.4.9 Impulse-Response Function Graphs

The final output component is the set of impulse-response functions for the model variables – there is one set for each exogenous shock. (Here, ε_{At} is the only shock.) I show these graphs in Figure 8.1.

Qualitatively, the model variables follow the same path as in Figure 7.1. Just remember that the y-axis measures *level* deviations from the steady state (Remark 8.2) and not *percent* deviations from the steady state as in Chapter 7.

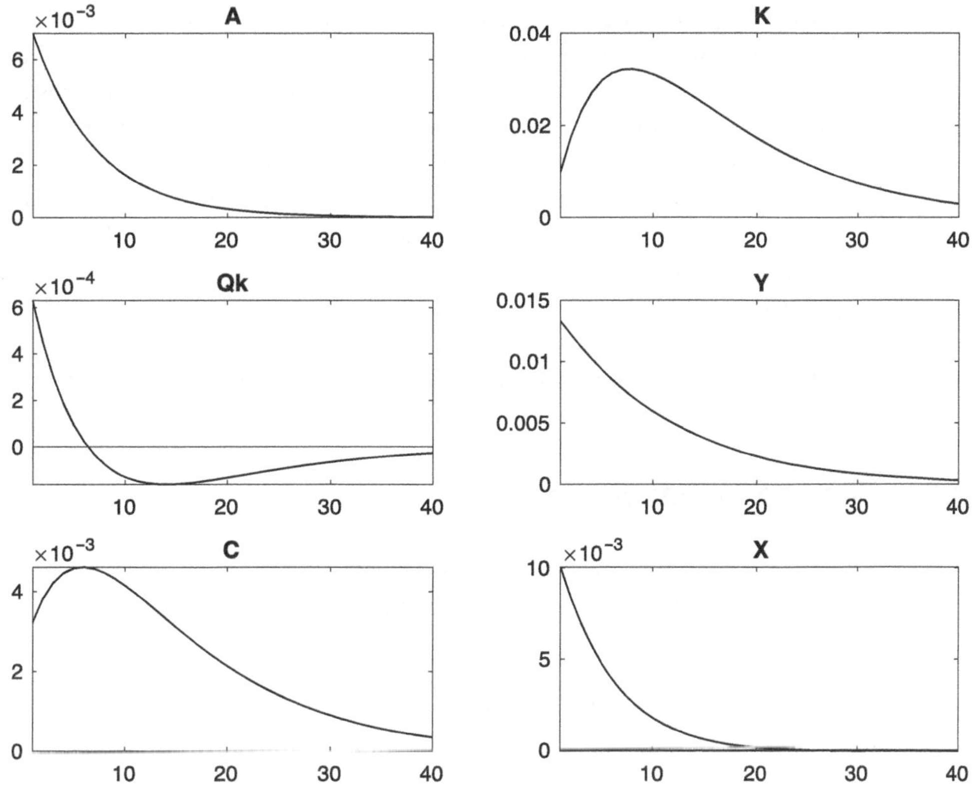

Figure 8.1 Impulse-response functions given a one-standard-deviation shock to ε_{At} in period 1 and $\sigma_A = 0.007$. Nonlinear model.

8.5 Intermezzo V: Do We Need Log-Linearized Equations?

From the ideas presented so far in this chapter, it may seem that learning how to log-linearize is a thing of the past. However, this is not necessarily the case, as it depends on what I want to do:

1. In most cases, I do not need to log-linearize the equilibrium conditions. That said, it's convenient to provide closed-form solutions for the steady-state values. When simulating models, the main issue is failing to provide a good initial guess for the Newton procedure.
2. However, sometimes I *need* to log-linearize before putting the equilibrium conditions in Dynare. For example, here's the pricing equation for the plain-vanilla New Keynesian model I'll present in Chapter 14:

$$P_t^*(i) = \frac{\omega}{\omega - 1} \frac{\mathbb{E}_t \sum_{s=0}^{\infty} \theta^s M_{t,t+s} mc_{t+s} P_{t+s}^{\omega} Y_{t+s}}{\mathbb{E}_t \sum_{s=0}^{\infty} \theta^s M_{t,t+s} P_{t+s}^{\omega-1} Y_{t+s}},$$

where $P_t^*(i)$ is the price that firm i sets when it gets the chance to optimize, $\omega > 1$ is the elasticity of substitution between good varieties, $\theta \in (0, 1)$ is the probability that the firm cannot change its price every period, $M_{t,t+s}$ is the household's stochastic discount factor, and mc_t is the firm's marginal cost in nominal terms. (Don't worry if these terms don't make sense to at the moment, they will be introduced at the right time.) For now, what matters is that this equation takes the ratio of two infinite sums, and consequently I cannot cast this particular equation into Dynare. (Well, not exactly; there are tricks for this too, and I'll share them when I'm dealing with the New Keynesian model. But you get the idea.)

3. Looking at *linearized* expressions sometimes yields more insights relative to looking at their nonlinear equivalents. You may be surprised about what you find (or not).

8.6 The Log-Linear Model File

I now put the log-linearized model into Dynare, recycling most of the hard work I've done so far. The model's log-linearized equilibrium conditions are

$$\widehat{Y}_t = \widehat{A}_t + \alpha \widehat{K}_t, \tag{8.13}$$

$$Q_k \widehat{Q}_{kt} = \alpha K^{\alpha-1} \widehat{A}_t + \alpha(\alpha - 1) K^{\alpha-1} \widehat{K}_t, \tag{8.14}$$

$$\widehat{C}_t = \mathbb{E}_t \widehat{C}_{t+1} - \mathbb{E}_t \widehat{Q}_{k,t+1}, \tag{8.15}$$

$$Y_{ss} \widehat{Y}_t = C_{ss} \widehat{C}_t + X_{ss} \widehat{X}_t, \tag{8.16}$$

$$\delta \widehat{X}_t = \widehat{K}_{t+1} - (1 - \delta) \widehat{K}_t, \tag{8.17}$$

together with the log-linearized equation for the stochastic process, which is

$$\widehat{A}_t = \rho_A \widehat{A}_{t-1} + \sigma_A \varepsilon_{At}. \tag{8.18}$$

The `mod` file that solves (8.13)–(8.18) is presented in Appendix F.2.

8.6.1 Preamble Block

Other than changing the file's name (I'll use `loglinear.mod`), everything looks just like before.

8.6.2 Model Block

Besides the obvious fact that I need to input the equilibrium conditions in log-linear form, I immediately bump into a somewhat unique situation: there are steady-state values in most of the expressions – see, for example, equation (8.16). Since the steady states are determined in a separate block (and, moreover, the steady state of all variables in a log-linearized model equals zero), it's not obvious what to do.

The solution, however, is fairly simple. First, I tell Dynare that I'm using a linearized model (so that it doesn't try to linearize again) and then introduce **model local variables** (i.e., valid only within the model block) with the pound ("`#`") sign. This logic is better explained with some actual code:

```
// MODEL BLOCK

model(linear) ;
    # Qk_SS = 1/beta ;
    # ome_y = (Qk_SS - 1 + delta)/alpha ;
    # K_SS = 1/ome_y^(1/(1 - alpha)) ;
    # Y_SS = A_ss*K_SS^alpha ;
    # X_SS = delta*K_SS ;
    # C_SS = Y_SS - X_SS ;

    Y = A + alpha*K(-1) ;
    Qk_SS*Qk = alpha*K_SS^(alpha - 1)*A
                + alpha*(alpha - 1)*K_SS^(alpha - 1)*K(-1) ;
    C = C(+1) - Qk(+1) ;
    Y_SS*Y = C_SS*C + X_SS*X ;
    delta*X = K - (1 - delta)*K(-1) ;
    A = rho_A*A(-1) + sigma_A*epsilon_A ;
end ;
```

(Code 8.24)

What's going on here? First, I modify the `model` command by adding the "`linear`" option. Second, I declare the steady-state values as local variables; note I use names that don't overlap with Dynare's own steady-state variables.

8.6.3 Steady-State Block

Not a lot to do here, other than adjust the values, since the steady state of a log-linearized model is zero. (Alternatively, the percent deviation from steady state at the steady state is, well, zero.)

```
// STEADY STATE BLOCK

steady_state_model ;
    Y = 0 ;
    A = 0 ;
    K = 0 ;
    Qk = 0 ;
    C = 0 ;
    X = 0 ;
end ;

steady ;
check ;
```

(Code 8.25)

8.6.4 Shocks Block and Simulation Block

No changes here, so I move along.

8.6.5 Dynare Output

Since there are no changes to the pieces of software output – only to their values – I just copy and paste the relevant parts from Dynare.

```
>> dynare loglinear

STEADY-STATE RESULTS:

Y     0
A     0
K     0
Qk    0
C     0
X     0

EIGENVALUES:
         Modulus              Real          Imaginary
            0.85              0.85                  0
          0.9029            0.9029                  0
           1.119             1.119                  0
             Inf               Inf                  0

There are 2 eigenvalue(s) larger than 1 in modulus for 2
     forward-looking
variable(s)
The rank condition is verified.

MODEL SUMMARY

  Number of variables:          6
  Number of stochastic shocks:  1
  Number of state variables:    2
  Number of jumpers:            2
  Number of static variables:   2

MATRIX OF COVARIANCE OF EXOGENOUS SHOCKS
Variables    epsilon_A
epsilon_A     1.000000
```

```
POLICY AND TRANSITION FUNCTIONS
                    A          K         Qk          Y          C          X
 A(-1)       0.850000   0.175809   0.075820   0.850000   0.291501   2.197612
 K(-1)       0          0.902867  -0.059764   0.330000   0.555519  -0.214158
 epsilon_A   0.007000   0.001448   0.000624   0.007000   0.002401   0.018098

THEORETICAL MOMENTS
VARIABLE          MEAN  STD. DEV.   VARIANCE
A               0.0000     0.0133     0.0002
K               0.0000     0.0176     0.0003
Qk              0.0000     0.0010     0.0000
Y               0.0000     0.0173     0.0003
C               0.0000     0.0129     0.0002
X               0.0000     0.0324     0.0010

MATRIX OF CORRELATIONS
Variables           A         K        Qk         Y         C         X
A              1.0000    0.6706    0.5600    0.9610    0.7833    0.9954
K              0.6706    1.0000   -0.2391    0.8496    0.9864    0.5964
Qk             0.5600   -0.2391    1.0000    0.3090   -0.0763    0.6368
Y              0.9610    0.8496    0.3090    1.0000    0.9247    0.9301
C              0.7833    0.9864   -0.0763    0.9247    1.0000    0.7201
X              0.9954    0.5964    0.6368    0.9301    0.7201    1.0000

COEFFICIENTS OF AUTOCORRELATION
Order          1        2        3        4        5
A         0.8500   0.7225   0.6141   0.5220   0.4437
K         0.9918   0.9710   0.9409   0.9041   0.8627
Qk        0.7812   0.6019   0.4556   0.3366   0.2404
Y         0.9142   0.8351   0.7622   0.6952   0.6336
C         0.9807   0.9516   0.9154   0.8743   0.8300
X         0.8289   0.6855   0.5654   0.4651   0.3813
```

(Code 8.26)

By inspection, the values are very similar to their nonlinear counterparts in Section 8.4, though minor differences show up given that the linear and log-linear approximations are not identical. The last piece of output concerns the impulse-response function graphs, which are shown in Figure 8.2. The paths are identical, but the magnitudes are different, which is a consequence of expressing everything as a percent deviation from the steady state. (Remember that Figure 8.1 plots level deviations, not percent deviations.)

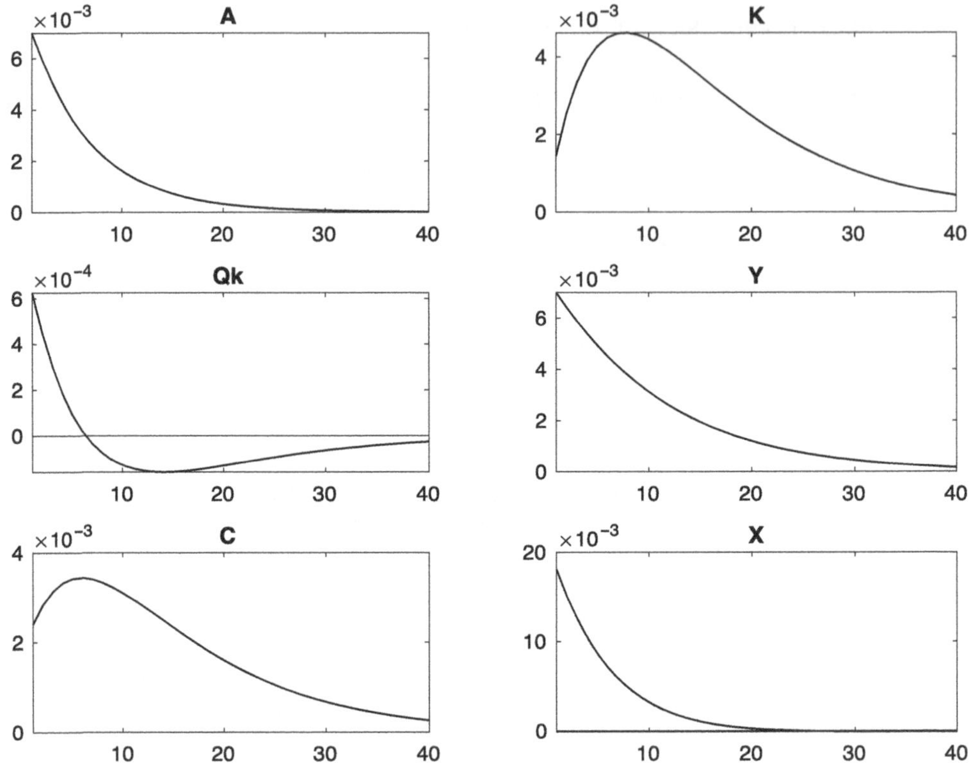

Figure 8.2 Impulse-response functions given a one-standard-deviation shock to ε_{At} in period 1 and $\sigma_A = 0.007$. Log-linear model.

8.7 Up Next

You now know how Dynare works and the many things it can do for us. The next step, of course, is to put this knowledge to good use. While the field of DSGE macro is vast – it's no exaggeration to say that covering all the bases would increase the length of this book by a sizable margin – there are a few models that are used over and over in the literature. Even though some of the source papers were published in the 1980s, the ideas are still borrowed by state-of-the-art work. If we pay attention to a select few contributions, we will be able to understand how everything fits together.

Before embarking on this trip, there is one detail that must be addressed. If you think about it, everything that we have done so far depends crucially on parameter values. Indeed, steady states – and, in turn, policy functions – will change whenever, say, δ changes from 0.05 to 0.08. So, how should we pick these parameter values?

This discussion should make it obvious that the issue of **parametrization** is important for our models. At this time, it's fair to say that the literature tells us to choose parameter values in two steps: first, we **calibrate** some parameters, and then we estimate the rest. While "calibration" is considered a bad word in some circles, it remains a useful tool in applied ones. The next chapter offers a crash course on calibration, which will complement the material on (Bayesian) estimation at the end of the book.

8.8 Bibliographic Notes

The code templates shared in this chapter barely scratch the surface of what Dynare can do. We'll get a few extra ideas over the next chapters – including details on Bayesian econometrics – but for now these templates are good enough to cover the majority of what representative-agent DSGE models have to offer.

As mentioned above, the Dynare manual (Adjemian et al. 2024) offers a wealth of information that is better digested over the long run; the Dynare forums (found on Dynare's webpage) are a great place to look for answers – most likely someone already asked the same question or faced the same problem you're currently struggling with. Finally, a very good (and also very lengthy) companion is the piece by Fernández-Villaverde et al. (2016), which goes into detail on many topics not covered in this basic introduction to Dynare (e.g., higher-order approximations).

8.9 Problems

8.9.1 The Role of Structural Parameters

Use the nonlinear model code from Appendix F.1 to perform the following experiments. Changing one parameter at a time, discuss the effects over the model's theoretical moments when you change the baseline parameters (i.e., $\beta = 0.99$, $\delta = 0.08$, $\alpha = 0.33$, $\rho_A = 0.85$, $\sigma_A = 0.007$) as follows:

1. $\beta \in \{0.25, 0.75, 0.9\}$.
2. $\delta \in \{0, 0.02, 0.2\}$.
3. $\alpha \in \{0.25, 0.5, 0.75\}$.
4. $\rho_A \in \{0.25, 0.75, 0.9\}$.
5. $\sigma_A \in \{0, 0.002, 0.02\}$.

8.9.2 Investment-Specific Technological Progress, Revisited

Consider a variant of the model in this chapter, where stochastic shocks affect the productivity of new capital goods (i.e., investment). More precisely, the planner is restricted by the following constraints:

$$
\begin{aligned}
K_t^{\alpha} &= C_t + X_t, \\
K_{t+1} &= (1-\delta)K_t + (1+\mu_t)X_t,
\end{aligned}
$$

where μ_t is a shock to the marginal efficiency of investment. Modify the nonlinear model code from Appendix F.1 to incorporate this new formulation. Discuss how your results differ relative to the baseline model. *Hint*: You may benefit from reviewing Problem 6.5.2.

8.9.3 Government Expenditure Shocks, Revisited

Redo Problem 8.9.2 but now include a government sector that spends some stochastic fraction of output g_t every period. More precisely, the planner problem is now restricted by

$$K_t^\alpha = C_t + K_{t+1} - (1-\delta)K_t + g_t K_t^\alpha.$$

In this constraint, g_t satisfies

$$g_t = (1-\rho_g)g_{ss} + \rho_g g_{t-1} + \sigma_g \varepsilon_{gt},$$

where $\rho_g, g_{ss} \in (0,1)$ and $\sigma_g > 0$. *Hint*: You may benefit from reviewing Problem 6.5.3.

8.9.4 Comparing Nonlinear and Log-Linear Models

Redo both Problems 8.9.2 and 8.9.3 but now use the log-linear model code from Appendix F.2. Are your results qualitatively similar to those from the nonlinear model? How about quantitatively similar?

9 Parametrization I: Calibration

We now know a lot about setting up and solving dynamic macroeconomic models. However, it's easy to overlook that nearly every result we obtain – statistical properties of the data, impulse response functions, and so on – depends crucially on the values that model parameters take.

Getting the "right" values is not a function of how well the model fits the data given parameters (that's closer to a Bayesian approach, which comes later in the book); rather, it's about getting the values that make the model's predictions match real-world observations, in a way that I'll clarify below.

The **calibration** procedure is one of several tools we can use to tackle parametrization. This method was introduced in the paper by Kydland and Prescott (1982); while the Bayesian approach is now dominant, calibration is still used in the literature and can provide a useful first pass when determining whether further work on a model is worth our time.

The ideas behind calibration require a bit of theory – not that there's much to it – which I present in Section 9.1. In Section 9.2 I fully calibrate the DSGE model we used in Chapter 8. Section 9.3 contains an empirical application that is related to the calibration process but is otherwise hard to fit elsewhere. Finally, I should add that the material in these notes gets inspiration from Canova (2007) and DeJong and Dave (2011).

9.1 Some Theory

In a nutshell, the calibration exercise "picks" parameter values $\theta \in \Theta$ in such a way that the model under consideration is able to replicate certain real-world features, which I get to pick.

More formally, let $\left\{Y_t\right\}_{t=1}^{T}$ denote a sample of observed data and $\left\{Y_t^m\right\}_{t=1}^{T}$ denote a sample of artificial data created by the model. We want

$$\Upsilon\left(\left\{Y_t\right\}_{t=1}^{T}\right) = \Upsilon\left(\left\{Y_t^m\right\}_{t=1}^{T}\right) \tag{9.1}$$

to hold, where Υ denotes a set of real-world features used to identify the parameter vector Θ. The function Υ can include long-run averages, ratios, volatilities, and so on.

Remark 9.1 Calibrated parameters are very different from estimated parameters, in the sense that we cannot calculate standard errors or some other measure to assess their statistical significance. As opposed to maximum likelihood or Bayesian estimation, a calibration exercise assumes that parameters follow a degenerate distribution with a certain mean (the calibrated value) and zero variance. Of course, there is no revision based on the model's likelihood function that can provide improved parameter values given the entire dataset.

9.2 Test Run: The Stochastic, Infinite-Horizon Benchmark SPP

Here I use the same benchmark SPP as in Chapter 8 (with one small change, which I explain below) to illustrate how calibration works. Before anything, I need to make the following remark.

Remark 9.2 Calibration is an *art*, not a science. There are many ways in which I can use the ideas behind calibration to parametrize a model.

For convenience, I repeat the setup of the benchmark SPP. The economy under study has inelastic labor supply and stochastic technology shocks, and I assume logarithmic utility and a Cobb–Douglas production function. I incorporate investment as a model variable and add the law of motion for capital to keep the system balanced. The associated SPP is given by

$$\begin{aligned} \max_{\{C_t, X_t\}_{t=0}^{\infty}} \quad & \mathbb{E}_0 \sum_{t=0}^{\infty} \beta^t \log C_t \\ \text{subject to} \quad & \bar{s} A_t K_t^{\alpha} = C_t + X_t, \\ & K_{t+1} = (1 - \delta) K_t + X_t, \\ & C_t \geq 0, \end{aligned}$$

where, as usual, the planner knows K_0 and the technology shock follows

$$\log A_t = (1 - \rho_A) \log A_{ss} + \rho_A \log A_{t-1} + \sigma_A \varepsilon_{At},$$

where A_t is a stochastic shock affecting period-t output (with steady state $A = 1$), A_0 is given, $\rho_A \in (0, 1)$ is a persistence parameter, and $\sigma_A > 0$.

The only difference relative to the SPP from Chapter 8 is the addition of a *scaling parameter* ($\bar{s} > 0$) multiplying the firm's output; this parameter will ensure that the steady-state value of output equals the value that I choose.

I calculated the economy's equilibrium conditions in Chapter 8. These are mostly the same, except for the addition of the $\bar{s}$ term, and are now given by

$$Y_t = \bar{s} A_t K_t^{\alpha}, \tag{9.2}$$

$$Q_{kt} = \alpha \bar{s} Y_t K_t^{-1} + 1 - \delta, \tag{9.3}$$

$$C_t^{-1} = \beta \, \mathbb{E}_t C_{t+1}^{-1} Q_{k,t+1}, \tag{9.4}$$

$$Y_t = C_t + X_t, \tag{9.5}$$

$$X_t = K_{t+1} + (1 - \delta) K_t, \tag{9.6}$$

as well as the technology process

$$\log A_t = \left(1 - \rho_A\right) \log A_{ss} + \rho_A \log A_{t-1} + \sigma_A \varepsilon_{At}. \tag{9.7}$$

Note how equations (9.2) and (9.3) now include parameter $\bar{s}$. In addition, the model's steady-state conditions, derived from equations (9.2)–(9.6), are

$$Y = \bar{s} K^{\alpha}, \tag{9.8}$$

$$Q_k = \alpha \bar{s} Y K^{-1} + 1 - \delta, \tag{9.9}$$

$$1 = \beta Q_k, \tag{9.10}$$

$$Y = C + X, \tag{9.11}$$

$$X = \delta K, \tag{9.12}$$

where I've already used that $A_{ss} = 1$; note that equation (9.7) collapses to 0=0. (At this time it's clear that the role of $\bar{s}$ is to adjust the value of steady-state output Y: if the model doesn't include $\bar{s}$ then, necessarily, Y_{ss} equals whatever value K_{ss}^{α} takes.)

And here's the plot twist: in Chapter 8, I solved for the closed-form solutions of the steady-state equations. Once this was done, I picked parameter values, plugged them into the steady-state solutions, and moved along. When performing a calibration exercise, the process is reversed: the steady-state equations (9.8)–(9.12) are used to pin down *target* parameter values or ratios that I want the model to replicate. (If you were wondering when the "big ratios" from Chapter 1 would come in handy, this is the time.)

Formally, the calibration process works as follows. First, I choose a set of target moments that I want the model to replicate. (For example, I will require that the steady-state ratio of investment to output agrees with the Great Moderation "big ratio" value.) Then I divide the parameter vector Θ into two sets: a set of exogenously given parameters whose values I pick based on external sources and a set of parameters that need to be solved within the model, conditional on the exogenously given parameters and the target moments I have chosen for the model.

Since this explanation is getting too verbose, let's just get to work. Without loss of generality, I'll do an annual-frequency calibration. For reference purposes, the parameter vector Θ is given by

$$\Theta = \left\{\alpha, \delta, \beta, \bar{s}, \rho_A, \sigma_A\right\}.$$

9.2.1 Targeted Moments

I have complete freedom of choosing the data moments I want the model to replicate (i.e., the function Υ from Section 9.1), which gives context to Remark 9.2.

I start with the low-hanging fruit: in this calibration, I want the steady-state output to take a value of 1 (i.e., $Y_{ss} = 1$). This choice will make it easy to work with the "big ratios" from Chapter 1.

Remark 9.3 When working through a calibration exercise, *it is of utmost importance to match model objects with their real-world counterparts*. What does this mean? If you think about it, the benchmark SPP describes a closed economy without a government sector. This detail means that model-based output equals the sum of model consumption and model investment. However, in the real world, GDP is defined as the sum of consumption, investment, government expenditure, and net exports. Therefore, if I blindly use national income and product accounts (NIPA) data to calculate my targets, I would be biasing the results because real-world (i.e., targeted) GDP is not consistent with model GDP.

Is this the end of the road? No. It just means that I need to be very careful with how I pick my targets so that $\Upsilon\left(\left\{Y_t\right\}_{t=1}^{T}\right) = \Upsilon\left(\left\{Y_t^m\right\}_{t=1}^{T}\right)$ per (9.1).

The Revised Big Ratios

I use annual NIPA data in nominal terms (more precisely, NIPA Table 1.1.5, downloaded from the Bureau of Economic Analysis). I define (nominal) "model-adjusted output" as the sum of *observed* nominal consumption (line 2 in Table 1.1.5) and nominal investment (line 7); in this sense, model-adjusted output is necessarily smaller than real-world nominal output – and the big ratios will be different too. If I calculate the average ratios of observed consumption and investment to model-adjusted output (which approximate the steady state), I get that

$$\frac{C_{ss}}{Y_{ss}} = C_{ss} = 0.7904 \text{ and } \frac{X_{ss}}{Y_{ss}} = X_{ss} = 0.2096.$$

Note also that by normalizing the value of steady-state output to unity, the ratios C_{ss}/Y_{ss} and X_{ss}/Y_{ss} are equivalent to C_{ss} and X_{ss}, respectively.

For the model's capital-to-output ratio, I use the Fixed Assets Table 1.1 (also downloaded from the Bureau of Economic Analysis) and obtain the value of nominal fixed assets (line 2) from there. I divide this value over model-adjusted output and take the average of the ratios. I get

$$\frac{K_{ss}}{Y_{ss}} = K_{ss} = 3.4827.$$

Overall, my targeted moments are

$$\begin{aligned} Y_{ss} &= 1.0000, \\ C_{ss} &= 0.7904, \\ X_{ss} &= 0.2096, \\ K_{ss} &= 3.4827. \end{aligned}$$

9.2.2 Parameters Determined Exogenously

I put $\left\{\alpha, \rho_A, \sigma_A\right\}$ in this set. I now explain how each of these parameters is selected.

Capital Share (α)

In a Cobb–Douglas production function, parameter α represents the share of capital income relative to GDP. While technically straightforward, getting a good approximation for α is kind of difficult, since trying to measure either the capital or labor shares straight out of NIPA data presents some inaccuracies that can bias the result. (For example, when thinking about the labor share of income, proprietors' income is often underreported.) Hence, the literature usually follows Gollin (2002), who concludes that choosing a value for α within the interval $[0.2, 0.35]$ is an empirically sound strategy. For the calculations below, I take $\alpha = 0.33$.

TFP Process Parameters (ρ_A and σ_A)

To obtain values for ρ_A and σ_A, start from equation (9.2) and solve for A_t:

$$A_t = \frac{Y_t}{\bar{s}K_t^\alpha}.$$

The expression above shows what's also known in the literature as the **Solow residual**. This variable allows me to derive a time series for TFP since I already have values for the capital stock and model-adjusted output, as well as a value for α. I don't, however, know what $\bar{s}$ equals – but this issue will be addressed below.

For now, let's assume I know the value of $\bar{s}$. Then, ρ_A and σ_A can be calculated as follows.

Step 1 Run the ordinary least squares (OLS) regression

$$\log A_t = a_0 + a_1 t + u_{At},$$

where $t = 0, 1, 2, \ldots$ is a time trend.

Step 2 Use the estimated coefficients to obtain the detrended TFP values. (In this sense, u_{At} is equivalent to $\widehat{A}_t$ in our terminology.)

Step 3 Run the AR(1) regression

$$u_{At} = b_0 + b_1 u_{A,t-1} + v_{At}. \tag{9.13}$$

Here, b_1 is my estimate for ρ_A and the variance of the regression residuals v_{At} can stand in for σ_A^2.

9.2.3 Parameters to be Solved within the Model

The remaining model parameters, namely $\{\delta, \beta, \bar{s}\}$, are put in this set. I now explain what "to be solved within the model" means.

Depreciation Rate (δ)

Take the steady-state version of the law of motion for capital, equation (9.12), reproduced below for convenience:

$$X_{ss} = \delta K_{ss}.$$

From this expression I can solve for δ quite easily:

$$\delta = \frac{X_{ss}}{K_{ss}}.$$

And here's where the phrase "to be solved within the model" becomes meaningful: I take a model equilibrium condition *and* some targeted moments to pin down the value of the depreciation rate. Plugging values from Section 9.2.1, I get

$$\delta = \frac{X_{ss}}{K_{ss}} = \frac{0.2096}{3.4827} = 0.0602,$$

which is the calibrated value of the depreciation rate.

Scaling Coefficient ($\bar{s}$)

Equation (9.8) tells me that the following relation must hold in the steady state:

$$Y = \bar{s}K^{\alpha}.$$

My targeted moments include $Y_{ss} = 1$ and $K_{ss} = 3.4827$; hence, getting the value for $\bar{s}$ is immediate, since

$$\bar{s} = \frac{Y}{K^{\alpha}} = \frac{1}{3.4827^{0.33}}$$

or $\bar{s} = 0.6625$. Note this value allows me to run the regressions that uncover parameters ρ_A and σ_A.

Discount Factor (β)

The process to obtain parameter β is straightforward but a bit convoluted. Since I'm still "solving within the model," I need to use one of the steady-state conditions. The first expression I need is equation (9.9), namely,

$$Q_k = \alpha\bar{s}\frac{Y}{K} + 1 - \delta.$$

I already have values for the K_{ss}/Y_{ss} ratio (see my targeted moments) and δ, so calculating $Q_{k,ss}$ is straightforward:

$$Q_k = \alpha\bar{s}\frac{Y}{K} + 1 - \delta = \left(0.33\right)\left(0.6625\right)\frac{1}{3.4827} + 1 - 0.0602 = 1.0026.$$

Armed with a value for the rental rate, equation (9.10) allows me to solve for β:

$$1 = \beta Q_k \implies \beta = \frac{1}{Q_k} = \frac{1}{1.0026}$$

or $\beta = 0.9974$.

9.2.4 Closing the Loop: TFP Process Parameters

Just for completeness: running the regression in Section 9.2.2, namely equation (9.13), yields estimates $\rho_A = 0.9020$ and $\sigma_A = 0.0193$.

9.2.5 Back to Dynare

I now have a fully calibrated set of parameters that I can use in Dynare. How does a model using these parameters compare to the real world? Table 9.1 gives us the details (in short: pretty good). While the model's volatilities are smaller than those in the data, the model does a good job of replicating the facts that consumption is less volatile than output ($\sigma_{CY} = 0.43$ in the model vs. 0.51 in the data) and that investment is more volatile than GDP ($\sigma_{XY} = 3.20$ in the model vs. 3.28 in the data). The volatility of capital, however, is much smaller in the model than in the data.

Table 9.1 Business cycle statistics (data vs. model). I present three statistics for each variable j: the correlation of the variable with respect to output (denoted $\rho_{j,Y}$), the standard deviation of the variable (σ_j), and the relative standard deviation of the variable with respect to output ($\sigma_{j,Y} \equiv \sigma_j/\sigma_Y$). "Data" columns are calculated over HP-detrended values for the sample 1985Q1 to 2019Q4 ($\lambda = 7.25$); "model" columns are obtained from Dynare's simulation of the benchmark SPP. I use the calibration strategy described in this section.

	Data			Model		
Variable	$\rho_{j,Y}$	σ_j	$\sigma_{j,Y}$	$\rho_{j,Y}$	σ_j	$\sigma_{j,Y}$
Output	1.0000	0.0159	1.0000	1.0000	0.0124	1.0000
Consumption	0.9190	0.0081	0.5107	0.9875	0.0053	0.4274
Investment	0.9682	0.0520	3.2767	0.9969	0.0397	3.2016
Capital	0.8395	0.0116	0.7298	0.5961	0.0025	0.2016

Regarding correlations, the model is consistent with the data: all model variables are procyclical, yet consumption and investment appear to be more procyclical than in the data – and capital much less. (For reference, the calibration and Dynare codes are found alongside the online materials for the book.)

Remark 9.4 Since my goal is to compare the business cycle statistics coming out of the calibrated model with those from the real world, I need to be careful or Remark 9.3 will come back and bite me. The business cycle statistics found in Table 9.1 have been logged and detrended with a Hodrick–Prescott filter with parameter $\lambda = 7.25$, following Ravn and Uhlig (2002); this different parameter follows the fact that I'm using annual data. This means that I must give the same treatment to the model variables, which come out of a *nonlinear* model. Fortunately, this is easy to do: I just need to add two options to the `stoch_simul` command in Dynare. It should read

```
stoch_simul(irf=40, order=1, loglinear, hp_filter = 7.25) Y A K Qk C X ;
```

The first two options (`irf=40, order=1`) are the same ones I used in Chapter 8. The third option (`loglinear`) tells Dynare to log all variables and then perform the approximation; this choice performs a log-linear approximation without the need to do manual log-linearization of equilibrium conditions. The last option (`hp_filter = 7.25`) generates HP-filtered statistics on the model's log-linearized variables, thus making model and data directly comparable.

9.3 Building a Time Series for the Capital Stock

Getting a time series for the capital stock is sometimes a problematic ordeal. While the Bureau of Economic Analysis offers the Fixed Assets tables, the data may not be in the frequency (why not quarterly data?) that we need. Moreover, if the task at hand requires analyzing a country other than the United States, at best we can get a very limited capital stock series, while at worst we won't get a thing.

Fortunately, there is a procedure that can be used to build a series for the capital stock and the depreciation rate that relies on investment and depreciation data – both of which are often available in national accounts. This method is called the **perpetual inventory method**. The method is based on the law of motion for capital that you already know, namely,

$$K_{t+1} = \left(1 - \delta\right) K_t + X_t. \tag{9.14}$$

The inputs are time series for GDP, investment, and depreciation expenditures (for time periods $t = 1, \dots, N$). I combine the $N - 1$ equations (9.14) with an initial guess for δ and the initial capital stock K_1 (relative to $t = 1$ in the investment series). To complete the system, I add two equations. The first one is the depreciation-to-output ratio over the data sample:

$$\frac{1}{N} \sum_{t=1}^{N} \frac{\delta K_t}{Y_t} \equiv dky. \tag{9.15}$$

Since getting K_1 can be problematic, we often use a rule of thumb to get things running: impose that the capital-to-output ratio in the initial period matches the average capital-to-output ratio over some subset of the sample. This is

$$\frac{K_1}{Y_1} = \frac{1}{n} \sum_{t=N_1}^{n} \frac{K_t}{Y_t}, \tag{9.16}$$

where $N_1 \geq 1$ and $n \leq N$, with at least one strict inequality. Note equations (9.14)–(9.16) are a system of $N + 1$ equations in $N + 1$ variables. The online materials for the book provide Matlab code that uses US data to show how we can apply the perpetual inventory method to build a capital stock series starting from NIPA data.

9.4 Up Next

We are now armed with the benchmark SPP – problem (7.1) – and we know a way to solve and parametrize it on a computer. So far, so good.

The problem we face is that this benchmark SPP is not up to par for thinking about business cycle fluctuations or the effects of economic policy. For example, the benchmark SPP only includes one stochastic shock (TFP) and has no policy components (though we briefly looked at the effects of government expenditure and taxation in Chapters 1 and 2); it does not give us any details about government debt or deficits, or monetary policy altogether.

While this may seem disappointing, the material covered so far gives us the foundation to build richer models that can address these shortcomings. In general, the modeling changes can be divided into two broad categories, namely,

1. Real frictions.
2. Nominal rigidities.

What are the differences? Models that incorporate real rigidities are fairly similar to the benchmark SPP, but we add distortions that modify how the frictionless SPP works. For example, we may incorporate labor supply, give the household a preference for keeping its standard of living, or impose adjustment costs that make investment more expensive for the firm. Note, however, that none of these frictions involve nominal features.

When we add monetary features, we need to distinguish between real and nominal quantities. Models that incorporate these frictions are said to exhibit nominal rigidities, and they are the object of Part IV. It's safe to say that most of the DSGE literature nowadays looks at models with nominal rigidities – though this doesn't mean that real frictions are no longer used. On the contrary, the newest set of papers combine real and nominal frictions under the New Keynesian label.

9.5 Bibliographic Notes

As mentioned earlier in the chapter, the paper by Kydland and Prescott (1982) was the first one to present a calibration exercise. The literature quickly caught on and most papers published in the 1980s followed Kydland and Prescott's steps. Kydland and Prescott (1991) provide a thoughtful discussion of the connections between general equilibrium and econometrics – and also calibration. On the other hand, Hansen and Heckman (1996) offer a critique of using calibration as a parametrization tool.

The 1990s introduced new parametrization techniques: limited-information methods (like the generalized method of moments, GMM) or full-information tools (maximum likelihood estimation, MLE). Later, the 2000s brought the required computational power to implement Bayesian estimation methods.

Even with these advances, researchers still rely on calibration for assigning values to some parameters, while estimating the rest. For an example of parametrization using GMM, see Christiano and Eichenbaum (1992); for MLE, the paper by McGrattan (1994) is a good starting point. A good piece that relies on Bayesian estimation is Schmitt-Grohé and Uribe (2012).

In some cases, data availability prevents us from using the perpetual inventory method. Blades (2015) presents a "short-cut method" that considerably reduces the data requirements for estimating a capital stock.

Finally, the books by Canova (2007) and DeJong and Dave (2011) are good complements to the ideas developed above.

9.6 Problems

9.6.1 An Alternative Calibration Strategy

Modify the calibration strategy presented in the chapter as follows. Instead of setting the value of σ_A to be the standard deviation of the residuals in equation (9.13), play with its value until the standard deviation of model GDP equals that of real-world GDP. Derive all other parameters in the same way. Calculate the last three columns of Table 9.1; what, if anything, changes? *Hint*: By construction, the standard deviation of model GDP should equal 0.0159; check your work if this is not the case.

9.6.2 The Capital Stock in Other Countries

Use the results from Problem 1.7.2 and the perpetual inventory method from Section 9.3 to generate a capital stock series for another country. If data are available, compare the series you generated with a series obtained from another source. Comment on the differences that you find.

Part III

Real Frictions

10 The Canonical Real Business Cycle Model

We now know how to work with a DSGE model, although our benchmark SPP model (developed in Chapter 7) is far from realistic. This chapter – and the ones that follow – aim to improve this shortcoming.

As a first step, let's take into account the fact that people work, and that sometimes they lose their jobs. Our benchmark SPP is silent about this feature of the real world, since households always choose to work full-time (i.e., their labor supply equals the time endowment h). Moreover, this logic implies that households can never be unemployed, which obviously clashes with reality.

To overcome this shortcoming, our first task is to incorporate labor supply into the model. While we have looked at this concept in earlier chapters (Chapters 2 and 3 come to mind), we didn't elaborate on how to deal with labor supply inside a full-fledged DSGE model. This is what we do in this chapter.

Before moving on, a history intermezzo comes in handy. Real business cycle (RBC) theory started with the celebrated paper "Time to build and aggregate fluctuations" by Kydland and Prescott (1982). The paper offers what is essentially a Solow growth model (more precisely, a neoclassical growth model) augmented with stochastic productivity shocks; moreover, it gets rid of policy altogether, as there is no government or monetary authority. The question they ask is: to what extent can productivity shocks help the model to qualitatively and quantitatively replicate observed business cycle fluctuations (i.e., the co-movements we discussed in Chapter 1)?

To their surprise (and, I believe, many other economists as well), the answer was "to a great degree." Why was this a surprise? To answer this question, we have to return to the conventional economic wisdom of the late 1970s and early 1980s: government intervention is important, if not essential. But Kydland and Prescott introduce a model that replicates the *quantitative* behavior of the US economy without the need for government expenditure or money supply. (Clearly, this had the inconvenient implication that fiscal and monetary policy was irrelevant. And this was as close to heresy as one could get at the time – but that's another story. For now, it suffices to say that Kydland and Prescott's contribution changed the way in which macroeconomists model the economy. As we will see in the chapters ahead, it is easy to add fiscal and monetary policy to an RBC framework and, as it turns out, fiscal and monetary policy *are* relevant after all.)

Back to our goals: in Section 10.1 I go ahead and introduce labor supply into our benchmark SPP in a natural way, adding leisure to the utility function and looking at the consequences of letting the household decide on the intratemporal margin (i.e., current-period leisure vs. current-period consumption). In this sense, the household responds to changes in TFP; as this variable affects the marginal product of labor, it generates changes in the market wage and induces income and substitution effects over the household's choice of consumption and labor. This modeling choice leads to what I call the **canonical RBC model** (or RBC model for short).

The RBC model is a useful starting point, but the underlying modeling choice still assumes the household is always employed; after all, the Inada conditions prevent the household from setting optimal leisure equal to h! I take a first step toward solving this issue in Section 10.2, when I introduce the **indivisible labor supply** model of Hansen (1985). This model incorporates the fact that most people either work full-time (say, 8 hours per day) or not at all (they are unemployed).

To do this, I modify the canonical RBC model as follows: instead of thinking about a representative household, we now incorporate a large number of them, so that a fraction of them work while the remaining one is unemployed. Once this setup is in place, the logic of **labor lotteries** of Rogerson (1988) kicks in and helps us overcome the problem of nonconvex choice sets. While somewhat old, this methodology is often used by papers on the research frontier.

The bottom line for this chapter (and also, the book) is simple: if we want to work with economic models that capture as much of reality as possible, we cannot rely on models that ignore labor supply. We must add a choice between leisure and work, and that's just what this chapter does.

10.1 The Canonical RBC Model

In what follows, the household now derives utility from leisure and, consequently, must choose some optimal level of leisure demand (which implicitly defines an optimal level of labor supply). Incidentally, a model like this one is said to have **divisible labor supply**, to distinguish between the inelastic labor supply scenario (the household does not enjoy leisure, so labor is inelastically supplied as long as the wage rate is non-negative, just like in Chapter 7) and the indivisible labor supply case that I present in Section 10.2. Also, the material that follows is based on Hansen (1985), the book by McCandless (2008), and, quite obviously, Kydland and Prescott (1982).

10.1.1 Model Economy

The canonical RBC model consists of a representative household and a representative firm. I discuss each kind of agent below.

Household

The household owns the capital stock and has a time endowment (normalized to one unit time) each period. It chooses infinite sequences of consumption C_t, leisure ℓ_t, and investment X_t to maximize

$$\mathbb{E}_0 \sum_{t=0}^{\infty} \beta^t u(C_t, \ell_t),$$

where $\beta \in (0, 1)$ is a time discount factor. The household's utility function takes the form

$$u(C_t, \ell_t) = \log C_t + \phi \log \ell_t, \tag{10.1}$$

where $\phi > 0$ is a parameter that determines the relative importance of leisure in the utility function. The law of motion for capital follows

$$K_{t+1} = (1 - \delta) K_t + X_t,$$

where $\delta \in (0, 1)$ is the depreciation rate of physical capital.

Representative Firm

A representative firm produces the final good using the CRS technology

$$F(K_{Ft}, N_{Ft}) = K_{Ft}^{\alpha} N_{Ft}^{1-\alpha}.$$

In particular, output can be consumed or invested following

$$A_t F(K_{Ft}, N_{Ft}) = Y_t = C_t + X_t,$$

where A_t denotes TFP and follows the Markov process

$$\log A_t = (1 - \rho_A) \log A_{ss} + \rho_A \log A_{t-1} + \sigma_A \varepsilon_{At},$$

where A_t is a stochastic shock affecting period-t output (with steady state $A = 1$), A_0 is given, $\rho_A \in (0, 1)$ is a persistence parameter, and $\sigma_A > 0$. To avoid unnecessary complications, I assume A_t is observed before making period-t decisions.

The Social Planner Problem

Given the assumptions so far, the welfare theorems (Theorems 4.2 and 4.3) guarantee that the solution to the associated SPP also solves the decentralized economy's equilibrium. The SPP is given by

$$\begin{aligned} \max \quad & \mathbb{E}_0 \sum_{t=0}^{\infty} \beta^t \left[\log C_t + \phi \log (1 - N_t) \right] \\ \text{subject to} \quad & A_t K_t^{\alpha} N_t^{1-\alpha} = C_t + X_t, \\ & K_{t+1} = (1 - \delta) K_t + X_t, \\ & C_t \geq 0, \\ & K_0 \text{ given} \end{aligned} \tag{10.2}$$

and I also need to include the TFP process

$$\log A_t = (1 - \rho_A) \log A_{ss} + \rho_A \log A_{t-1} + \sigma_A \varepsilon_{At}.$$

10.1.2 Equilibrium Conditions

Since the plan is to use Dynare to solve the model, I might as well derive the equilibrium conditions from the SPP (10.2). Setting the Lagrangian is easy: letting λ_t denote the multiplier on the aggregate feasibility constraint and ζ_t be the multiplier on the law of motion for capital (LMK), I get

$$\begin{aligned}
C_t &: \quad C_t^{-1} - \lambda_t = 0, \\
N_t &: \quad -\phi(1 - N_t)^{-1} + \lambda_t\left[(1 - \alpha)A_t K_t^{\alpha} N_t^{-\alpha}\right] = 0, \\
X_t &: \quad -\lambda_t + \zeta_t = 0, \\
K_{t+1} &: \quad -\zeta_t + \beta\,\mathbb{E}_t\left\{\lambda_{t+1}\left[\alpha A_{t+1} K_{t+1}^{\alpha-1} N_{t+1}^{1-\alpha}\right] + (1 - \delta)\zeta_{t+1}\right\} = 0, \\
\beta^t\lambda_t &: \quad A_t K_t^{\alpha} N_t^{1-\alpha} - C_t - X_t = 0, \\
\beta^t\zeta_t &: \quad K_{t+1} - (1 - \delta)K_t - X_t = 0.
\end{aligned}$$

I include the definition of output (i.e., $Y_t = A_t K_t^{\alpha} N_t^{1-\alpha}$) as an extra equation and, just for fun, I add the real wage rate, which must equal the marginal product of labor in equilibrium. This is

$$w_t = (1 - \alpha)A_t K_t^{\alpha} N_t^{-\alpha} = (1 - \alpha)Y_t N_t^{-1}, \tag{10.3}$$

where the second equality uses the definition of output to put wages as a function of output and labor only. (Note, incidentally, that the real wage is proportional to labor productivity, which is defined as Y_t/N_t.) Having output as a model variable, I rewrite the model's intratemporal condition as

$$\phi C_t N_t = (1 - \alpha)Y_t(1 - N_t).$$

Similarly, the intertemporal condition is now given by

$$C_t^{-1} = \alpha\beta\,\mathbb{E}_t Y_{t+1} K_{t+1}^{-1} C_{t+1}^{-1} + \beta(1 - \delta)\mathbb{E}_t C_{t+1}^{-1}.$$

Substituting for the multipliers, the set of equilibrium conditions – now including the expression for the wage rate in equation (10.3) – is then

$$Y_t = A_t K_t^{\alpha} N_t^{1-\alpha}, \tag{10.4}$$

$$w_t = (1 - \alpha)Y_t N_t^{-1}, \tag{10.5}$$

$$\phi C_t N_t = (1 - \alpha)Y_t(1 - N_t), \tag{10.6}$$

$$C_t^{-1} = \alpha\beta\,\mathbb{E}_t Y_{t+1} K_{t+1}^{-1} C_{t+1}^{-1} + \beta(1 - \delta)\mathbb{E}_t C_{t+1}^{-1}, \tag{10.7}$$

$$Y_t = C_t + X_t, \tag{10.8}$$

$$K_{t+1} = (1 - \delta)K_t + X_t. \tag{10.9}$$

Of course, I also include the TFP equation

$$\log A_t = (1 - \rho_A)\log A_{ss} + \rho_A \log A_{t-1} + \sigma_A \varepsilon_{At}. \tag{10.10}$$

10.1.3 Steady-State Conditions

Since I now include labor in the list of model variables, it's useful to show how to derive the closed-form solutions for the model's steady-state values. In the steady state, equations (10.4)–(10.9) are

$$Y = K^{\alpha} N^{1-\alpha}, \tag{10.11}$$

$$w = (1-\alpha) Y N^{-1}, \tag{10.12}$$

$$\phi C N = (1-\alpha) Y (1-N), \tag{10.13}$$

$$1 = \alpha \beta Y K^{-1} + \beta (1-\delta), \tag{10.14}$$

$$Y = C + X, \tag{10.15}$$

$$X = \delta K, \tag{10.16}$$

where I've already used that $A_{ss} = 1$; note equation (10.10) collapses to 0=0. Note that (10.11)–(10.16) are a system of six equations in $\{Y, K, N, C, X, w\}$.

To derive a closed-form solution for the system, start from equation (10.14): solving for Y_{ss} as a function of K_{ss}, I get

$$Y_{ss} = \left[\frac{1-\beta(1-\delta)}{\alpha\beta}\right] K_{ss} = \omega_Y K_{ss},$$

where $\omega_Y \equiv [1-\beta(1-\delta)]/(\alpha\beta)$. Equation (10.16) already sets X_{ss} as a function of K_{ss}, so it's natural to plug this equation alongside the expression for output in (10.15) in order to get C_{ss} as a function of K_{ss}:

$$C_{ss} = \omega_Y K_{ss} - \delta K_{ss} = (\omega_Y - \delta) K_{ss} = \omega_C K_{ss},$$

where $\omega_C \equiv \omega_Y - \delta$. Since I already have expressions for Y_{ss} and C_{ss}, I now plug both expressions into (10.13):

$$\phi \omega_C K_{ss} N_{ss} = (1-\alpha) \omega_Y K_{ss} (1 - N_{ss}).$$

Divide across by K_{ss} to get one equation in N_{ss}; after some algebra, I get

$$N_{ss} = \frac{(1-\alpha)\omega_Y}{\phi\omega_C + (1-\alpha)\omega_Y}$$

and, with this value at hand, I solve for K_{ss} from (10.11):

$$\omega_Y K_{ss} = K_{ss}^{\alpha} N_{ss}^{1-\alpha},$$

where, to reiterate, N_{ss} is known from the previous step. A bit of algebra later, I get

$$K_{ss} = \frac{N_{ss}}{\omega_Y^{1/(1-\alpha)}},$$

which is the last step in the chain. The steady-state wage can be derived from (10.12).

10.1.4 Dynare Output

If I follow the steps outlined in Chapter 8, I get a ton of output that describes how the divisible labor model behaves. (The associated `mod` file can be found alongside the online materials for the book.) The parametrization I used follows Hansen (1985): the discount factor β is set to 0.99, the leisure utility weight ϕ equals 2, the depreciation rate is set to $\delta = 0.025$, and the capital share of income α equals 0.36. For the TFP process, the autocorrelation parameter ρ_A is set to 0.95 and the volatility of the innovation σ_A takes value 0.00712.

Business Cycle Properties

I combine the moments and correlations to generate (part of) what's know as a "Kydland–Prescott" table (or business cycle properties table), as shown in Table 10.1. Columns (a) and (c) show standard deviations and columns (b) and (d) show the correlation of the variable with respect to output; both sets of statistics are generated for real-world data and that coming from the model.

Table 10.1 Business cycle statistics (data vs. model). For each variable, columns (a), (c), and (e) show standard deviations and columns (b), (d), and (f) show the correlation of the variable with respect to output. "Data" columns are taken from Hansen (1985); "model" columns are obtained from Dynare's simulation of the canonical RBC model; I use Hansen's parametrization to derive the values in columns (c) and (d), while I set the leisure weight to zero in columns (e) and (f).

	Data		Model, $\phi = 2$		Model, $\phi = 0$	
Variable	(a)	(b)	(c)	(d)	(e)	(f)
Output	1.76	1.00	1.46	1.00	0.98	1.00
Consumption	1.29	0.85	0.47	0.87	0.35	0.90
Investment	8.60	0.92	4.56	0.99	2.96	0.99
Capital	0.63	0.04	0.44	0.32	0.30	0.32
Hours worked	1.66	0.76	0.75	0.98	0.00	—
Productivity	1.18	0.42	0.74	0.98	0.98	1.00

While not perfect, the model fits (some of) the business cycle facts. To start, all model variables are predicted to be procyclical (their correlation with output is positive), just like in the data (except for capital, which is virtually acyclical). That said, the predicted correlation of output and hours is too high in the model (0.98 vs. 0.76), and so is the case for output and productivity (0.98 vs. 0.42).

Turning to the volatility of the variables, the model predicts smoother cycles relative to the data. For example, model output is less volatile than in the data (1.46 vs. 1.76), and model investment is almost half as volatile in the model relative to the data. (To be fair, the model does hit the qualitative feature of investment being more volatile than output, but it fails from a quantitative perspective.)

Impulse-Response Function Graphs

Before moving on, let's acknowledge that Dynare's graphs are lacking. Matlab's capabilities are much better, so I use them instead. Figure 10.1 shows the impulse-response function graph for all the model's endogenous variables given a one-standard-deviation shock to TFP. Note how the graph is very consistent with the information shown in Table 10.1. (The Matlab script used to generate Figure 10.1 can also be found alongside the online materials for the book.)

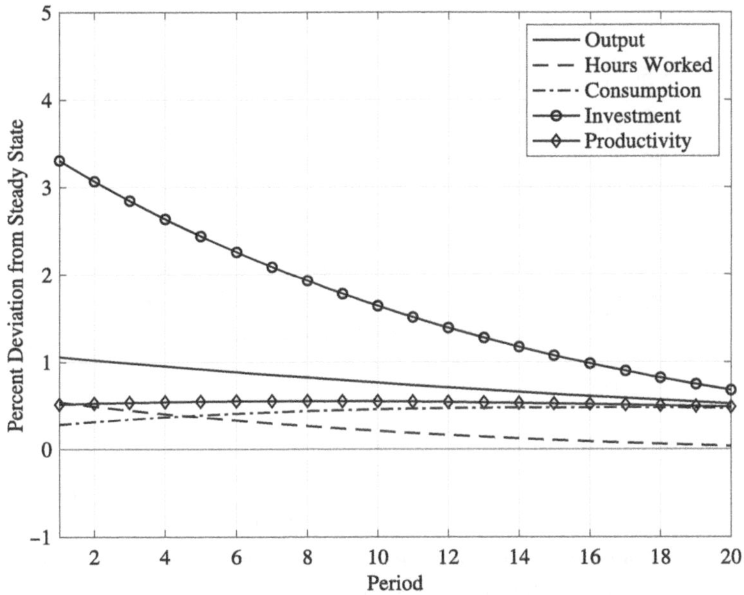

Figure 10.1 Canonical RBC model: impulse-response functions given a one-standard-deviation shock to ε_{At}. Model parametrization with $\phi = 2$.

As TFP increases by one standard deviation, all model variables jump up on impact, though some more than others. Investment goes up by about 3.5% (relative to steady state), while output does so about 1%. Hours worked jump up by 0.5%, then slowly decline back to steady state. Both consumption and productivity follow inverted-U patterns; by period 20, these variables are still above their steady state.

Example 10.1 Now that I have a working model that includes labor supply, I can put it to use by running some experiments. One such experiment is to compare the statistical properties (and IRFs) of an equivalent model in which the household doesn't care about leisure. To do this, I re-parametrize the model by setting $\phi = 0$, which effectively eliminates the importance of leisure in the utility function.

Columns (e) and (f) in Table 10.1 show how the model's behavior changes. To start, the volatility of all variables falls considerably, which is a consequence of hours worked being constant and equal to the time endowment $h = 1$. Regarding correlations, that of consumption increases to 0.9 (from 0.87) and the other ones remain identical at the second decimal.

Figure 10.2 shows the effect of this parameter change in the associated impulse-response functions. Compared with Figure 10.1, all model variables now rise by less on impact; as expected, the paths for productivity and output overlap, since labor productivity (Y/N) equals output when $N = 1$.

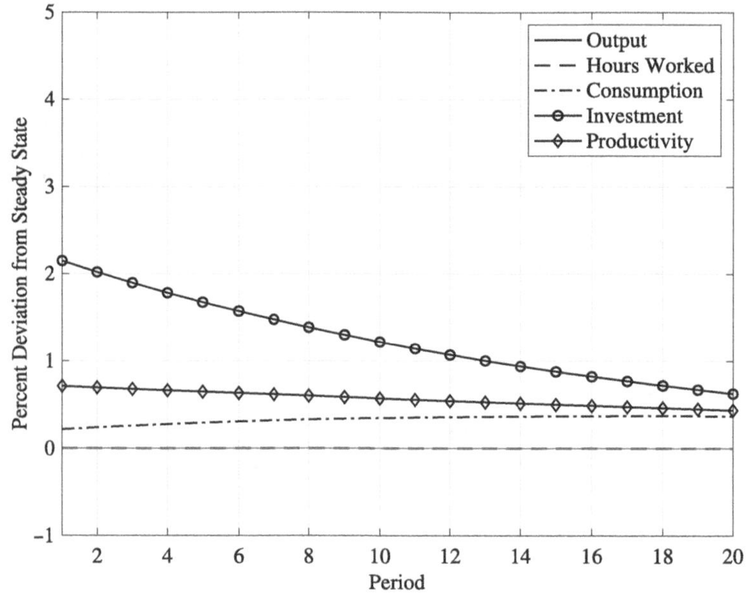

Figure 10.2 Canonical RBC model: impulse-response functions given a one-standard-deviation shock to ε_{At}. Model parametrization with $\phi = 0$.

In this setup, output increases by less relative to the case when $\phi = 2$. But if hours are not changing, then the only way output can adjust to a positive TFP shock is via capital accumulation, which takes time. It is also true that steady-state output and consumption are much higher in the $\phi = 0$ economy: $Y_{ss} = 3.70$ and $C_{ss} = 2.75$, compared to $Y_{ss} = 1.11$ and $C_{ss} = 0.83$ in the $\phi = 2$ one.

10.2 An Improvement: Indivisible Labor Supply

While the canonical RBC model is a workhorse, it's useful to check whether our findings are robust to a different specification. I now share one such robustness check (which is also very easy to implement): the indivisible labor model.

For some background, the economic models I have introduced assume that (i) the household puts all its time endowment as labor (via inelastic labor supply, as in Chapter 7) or (ii) the household is always employed but chooses how much of its time to work – that is, the optimization is done over the *intensive margin* (i.e., the variation in hours worked for a particular household, as in the canonical RBC model). In both of these cases, there is no room for unemployment and, consequently, it is not possible to account for some (or most) of the properties from the labor market.

The model described in Example 10.1 provides an example of inelastic labor supply. In this case, the household works as long as the wage received is strictly positive – which always holds given the assumptions imposed over the production technology. In the RBC case, the model is able to replicate the business cycle features only because we require a strong dependence on leisure substitution across time in response to wage or interest rate changes (in turn, generated by the changes in technology). However, studies using micro-level data fail to detect the right amount of intertemporal substitution to account for the large aggregate fluctuations in hours.

To tackle these issues, Hansen (1985) takes the canonical RBC model and introduces a significant nonconvexity – indivisible labor – into it. In this model, agents either work some positive number of hours or none at all, just as in the real world. In a way, Hansen's model asks the following question: which dimension is more important when accounting for the dynamics of aggregate hours? Agents moving in or out of the labor force (the *extensive margin*), or agents adjusting the number of hours to work in a day?

In order to get Hansen's model to work, I need to modify the economic environment. Instead of a representative household, I assume the economy is inhabited by a unit measure of identical households, indexed by $i \in [0, 1]$. The reason for this modeling choice is simple: if a representative household opts to stay out of the labor market, the representative firm produces zero output, which makes the household consume zero goods, and the entire equilibrium breaks down. I need to have a very large number of households (actually, infinitely many) that are *ex ante* identical but *ex post* heterogeneous. This heterogeneity arises in equilibrium as some households will be working and others will not, given a labor lottery that decides which households work and which ones don't.

Labor lotteries are a theoretical device originally proposed by Rogerson (1988). There are two positive features we get out of adding this friction to the model. First, we allow for unemployment. Second, the elasticity of substitution between leisure in different time periods now allows for large aggregate fluctuations in hours (relative to productivity) without a large value for the elasticity. Put differently, the "representative agent" (not the individuals in the economy) has an elasticity of substitution equal to infinity. This idea will be clarified below.

10.2.1 Model Economy

The economy consists of a unit measure of (ex ante) identical households and a representative firm. Both the firm and each individual household look just as the representative ones discussed in Section 10.1.

As mentioned above, the main assumption of the indivisible labor model is that households can work either full-time or no time, and full-time work implies an amount $h \geq N_0 > 0$ of hours worked. While this assumption makes sense, the "work full-time or don't work" assumption creates a problem, since the production set of the economy is no longer convex. To understand what this concept means, think that all of the production possibilities sets we've use are convex because the representative household could vary hours as desired.

Why Nonconvexities Matter

Maybe the discussion above regarding convex sets was unclear. Here's a short detour that aims to explain why nonconvexities in production possibilities sets matter. First things first: a set is **convex** if for any two points within the set it is possible to draw a straight line between them – and the line lies completely within the set.

Example 10.2 A line in $\mathbb{R}$ is a convex set. A solid circle in $\mathbb{R}^2$ is also a convex set, and so is a solid sphere in $\mathbb{R}^3$. However, a solid torus (fancy math lingo for "donut") in $\mathbb{R}^3$ is not a convex set.

Example 10.3 Let's borrow an example from Williamson (2017): suppose the representative household cannot vary hours of work as it chooses. In particular, it must choose between working $N_0 > 0$ hours and not working at all (so that leisure is equal to total hours h). Suppose further the household pays a (lump-sum) tax T if it works and receives a benefit b when not working, interpreted as an unemployment insurance payment. In this case, the budget constraint consists of two points in $\left(C, \ell\right)$ space, namely, $\left(N_0, wN_0 - T\right)$ and $\left(h, b\right)$, as shown in Figure 10.3. Clearly, the budget set is not convex.

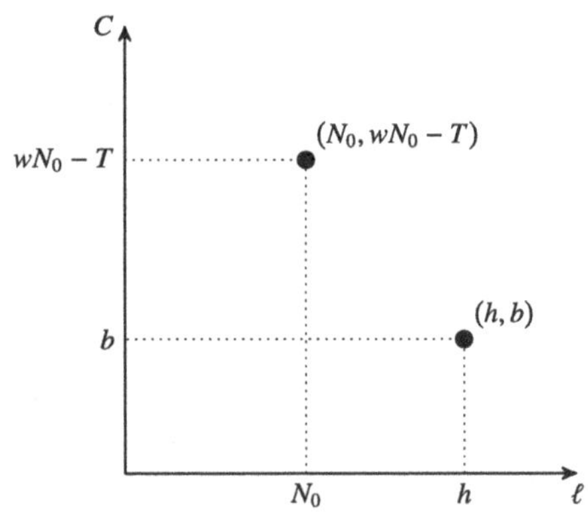

Figure 10.3 A nonconvex budget set: the household can only choose between two points – full work or no work.

Labor Lotteries and Households

To make the model work, I need to find a way to "convexify" the budget set. The solution proposed by Hansen involves labor lotteries. Now, the easiest way to understand how these lotteries work is to imagine a contract traded between the firm and a household, say, household i. In this contract, the household agrees to work N_0 hours with probability

$p(i)$; given this probability, a lottery then determines whether the household works or not. In turn, the firm agrees to pay the household regardless of the outcome of the lottery: work or no work, the household gets paid for the *expected* amount of time worked, which equals $p(i)N_0$. Hence, the contract works as a kind of unemployment insurance for all households.

Remark 10.1 In Chapter 4, I argued that the second welfare theorem (Theorem 4.3) requires a lot more technical finesse than the first welfare theorem (Theorem 4.2). Here's why: the key step in finding a set of market prices that can support the Pareto-optimal allocation that the planner desires requires the use of the *hyperplane separation theorem* (HST). For the theorem to run, we need to have two disjoint nonempty convex sets. Otherwise, the HST doesn't run, and so the second welfare theorem doesn't run, and we can't use the SPP to work things out.

Back to labor lotteries: under these assumptions, the relevant budget constraint for household i is

$$C_t(i) + X_t(i) = w_t p_t(i) N_0 + r_{kt} K_t(i). \tag{10.17}$$

Since all households are ex ante identical, they will all choose the same probability of work, so that $p_t(i) = p_t$ for all i. However, there will be *ex post* heterogeneity, in the sense that some households will work N_0 hours and some others won't work at all. From equation (10.1), household i's expected utility in period t is

$$p_t \underbrace{\left[\log C_t(i) + \phi \log(1 - N_0)\right]}_{\text{utility if working}} + (1 - p_t) \underbrace{\left[\log C_t(i) + \phi \log 1\right]}_{\text{utility if not working}},$$

which I can rearrange as

$$p_t \log C_t(i) + \phi p_t \log(1 - N_0) + (1 - p_t) \log C_t(i).$$

(Note I've used that $\log 1 = 0$.) Gathering common terms and simplifying, I get an expression that serves as an updated utility function $v : \mathbb{R}_+ \times [0,1] \to \mathbb{R}_+$ representing these preferences, given by

$$v[C_t(i), p_t] = \log C_t(i) + [\phi \log(1 - N_0)] p_t. \tag{10.18}$$

The Social Planner Problem

Since all households are ex ante identical, I can rely on an SPP that looks at the welfare of a "representative agent" with utility function (10.18) and budget constraint (10.17). (As a consequence, I no longer need the "i" index for each household.) In this setting, per-capita hours are given by $N_t = p_t N_0$. Incorporating the aggregation constraints of the economy, the associated SPP requires the planner to choose sequences $\{C_t, X_t, p_t\}_{t=0}^{\infty}$ to solve

$$\max \quad \mathbb{E}_0 \sum_{t=0}^{\infty} \beta^t v(C_t, p_t) \tag{10.19}$$

$$\text{subject to} \quad A_t K_t^{\alpha} N_t^{1-\alpha} = C_t + X_t,$$

$$
\begin{aligned}
K_{t+1} &= (1-\delta)K_t + X_t, \\
N_t &= p_t N_0, \\
C_t &\geq 0, \\
K_0 &\text{ given}
\end{aligned}
$$

and where TFP evolves following

$$\log A_t = (1-\rho_A)\log A_{ss} + \rho_A \log A_{t-1} + \sigma_A \varepsilon_{At}.$$

Hansen claims the "representative agent" will have an infinite elasticity of substitution between leisure in different periods. To see this, combine the time constraint $N_t = 1 - \ell_t$ with the labor supply equation $N_t = p_t N_0$ and solve for p_t:

$$1 - \ell_t = p_t N_0 \implies p_t = \frac{1-\ell_t}{N_0}.$$

Using this expression in (10.18) yields a utility function that depends on leisure, since

$$
\begin{aligned}
v(C_t, \ell_t) &= \log C_t + \phi \log(1-N_0)\left(\frac{1-\ell_t}{N_0}\right) \\
&= \log C_t + \frac{\phi \log(1-N_0)}{N_0} - \left[\frac{\phi \log(1-N_0)}{N_0}\right]\ell_t \\
&= \log C_t + \varphi \ell_t, \qquad (10.20)
\end{aligned}
$$

where the last equality uses the fact that any positive monotone transformation of a utility function keeps the same preference ordering. Since the leisure term in equation (10.20) is linear, there is an infinite elasticity of substitution between leisure in different periods, and so the claim follows.

Remark 10.2 Parameter φ is not really a parameter, in the sense that (10.20) shows φ is a function of the model's "primitive" parameters, namely,

$$\varphi \equiv -\frac{\phi \log(1-N_0)}{N_0}.$$

10.2.2 Equilibrium Conditions

Hansen relied on a linear-quadratic approximation to the value function (i.e., dynamic programming) in order to solve the model. Let's look at how the methods covered so far can help in solving the model.

First I characterize the SPP contained in (10.19), after substituting for (10.20) and $\ell_t = 1 - N_t$. The first-order conditions are

$$
\begin{aligned}
Y_t &= A_t K_t^{\alpha} N_t^{1-\alpha}, \qquad (10.21) \\
\varphi C_t N_t &= (1-\alpha) Y_t, \qquad (10.22) \\
C_t^{-1} &= \alpha\beta\, \mathbb{E}_t Y_{t+1} K_{t+1}^{-1} C_{t+1}^{-1} + \beta(1-\delta)\mathbb{E}_t C_{t+1}^{-1}, \qquad (10.23) \\
Y_t &= C_t + X_t, \qquad (10.24)
\end{aligned}
$$

$$K_{t+1} = (1-\delta)K_t + X_t. \tag{10.25}$$

I also need to add the stochastic process

$$\log A_t = (1-\rho_A)\log A_{ss} + \rho_A \log A_{t-1} + \sigma_A \varepsilon_{At}. \tag{10.26}$$

By inspection, the only difference between the equilibrium conditions of the divisible labor model (see Section 10.1.2) and the ones above is equation (10.22); for completeness, equation (10.6) reads

$$\phi C_t N_t = (1-\alpha)Y_t(1-N_t).$$

Put differently, the divisible and indivisible labor models are identical except for the intratemporal equation.

10.2.3 Steady-State Conditions

Imposing the steady state in equations (10.21)–(10.25) above yields

$$Y = K^{\alpha}N^{1-\alpha}, \tag{10.27}$$

$$\varphi CN = (1-\alpha)Y, \tag{10.28}$$

$$1 = \alpha\beta YK^{-1} + \beta(1-\delta), \tag{10.29}$$

$$Y = C + X, \tag{10.30}$$

$$X = \delta K. \tag{10.31}$$

As usual, (10.26) is not included in the list of steady-state equations. I follow the same process as in Section 10.1.3 to calculate the steady-state values. From (10.29) I get Y_{ss} as a function of K_{ss}:

$$Y_{ss} = \left[\frac{1-\beta(1-\delta)}{\alpha\beta}\right]K_{ss} \equiv \omega_y K_{ss}.$$

Equation (10.31) directly determines steady-state investment, since $X_{ss} = \delta K_{ss}$. Use this expression in (10.30) to get C_{ss} as a function of K_{ss}:

$$C_{ss} = \omega_y K_{ss} - \delta K_{ss} = (\omega_y - \delta)K_{ss} \equiv \omega_c K_{ss}.$$

Now use this expression in (10.28) to solve for N_{ss} directly:

$$\varphi\omega_C N_{ss} = (1-\alpha)\omega_y \implies N_{ss} = \frac{(1-\alpha)\omega_y}{\varphi\omega_c}. \tag{10.32}$$

Since equation (10.32) gives me a closed-form solution for steady-state labor, I can use all of the above in (10.27) to solve for K_{ss}:

$$\omega_y K_{ss} = K_{ss}^{\alpha}N_{ss}^{1-\alpha} \implies K_{ss} = \frac{N_{ss}}{\omega_y^{1/1-\alpha}}.$$

With the value of K_{ss} at hand, it's easy to back out the other steady-state values.

10.2.4 Dynare Output

Since there is only one equation that changes between the divisible and indivisible labor models, getting Dynare to run is a trivial matter. (The associated `mod` file is contained in the online materials for the book.)

Business Cycle Properties

Tables 10.1 and 10.2 are qualitatively similar, though there are quantitative differences. To start, all variables – except for productivity – are more volatile under indivisible labor. At the same time, consumption and productivity are now less correlated with output, while investment and hours worked remain the same.

Impulse-Response Functions

As with the information found in Table 10.2, the impulse-response function graph (shown in Figure 10.4) is qualitatively similar – but not quantitatively so. Clearly, investment reaches a higher peak on impact under an indivisible labor model; output and hours worked are higher as well, yet the difference is not that dramatic. Also, productivity seems to be more hump-shaped (and persistent) relative to the divisible labor framework.

Table 10.2 Business cycle facts (data vs. model). For each variable, columns (a) and (c) show standard deviations and columns (b) and (d) show the correlation of the variable with respect to output. "Data" columns are taken from Hansen (1985); "model" columns are obtained from Dynare's simulation of the indivisible labor supply model. I use Hansen's parametrization to derive the values in columns (c) and (d).

	Data		Model	
Variable	(a)	(b)	(c)	(d)
Output	1.76	1.00	1.90	1.00
Consumption	1.29	0.85	0.57	0.84
Investment	8.60	0.92	6.10	0.99
Capital	0.63	0.04	0.58	0.31
Hours worked	1.66	0.76	1.46	0.98
Productivity	1.18	0.42	0.57	0.84

Summing Up

It is clear that changing the model's labor specification (from divisible to indivisible) creates some subtle but important changes in its behavior. Moreover, doing so only involves a modification in one key model condition – the intratemporal condition! As we will see in the chapters that follow, making adjustments to the canonical RBC model is key to generating models that are able to replicate business cycle fluctuations.

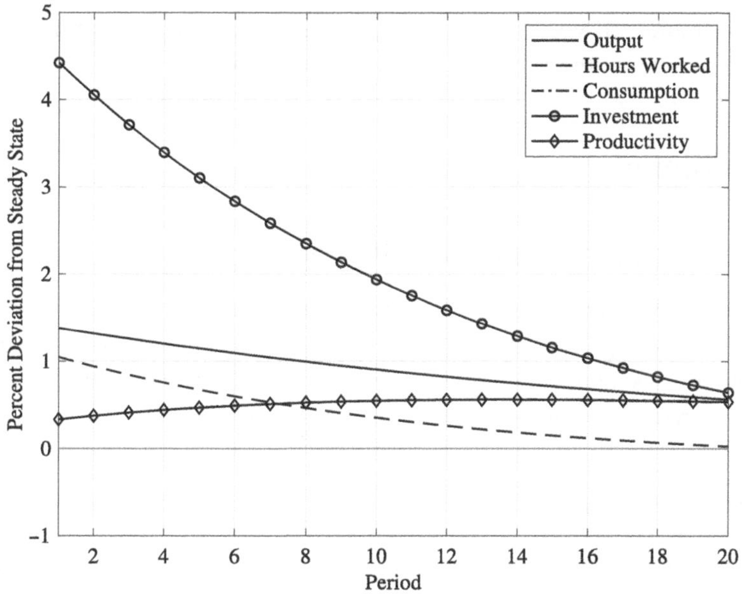

Figure 10.4 Indivisible labor supply model: impulse-response functions given a one-standard-deviation shock to ε_{At}.

10.3 Up Next

We're moving along nicely in terms of expanding our model economies toward the real world. Armed with knowledge about the labor market, the next step is to talk about different frictions that can improve the performance of the canonical RBC model. Hang in there.

10.4 Bibliographic Notes

King and Rebelo (1999) show how a model that relies on the indivisible labor formulation is key to replicating business cycle features. Reading the earlier works of King, Plosser, and Rebelo (1988, 2002) can provide useful background on the divisible labor model.

As mentioned throughout the chapter, Hansen (1985) and Rogerson (1988) are the key references to understand the material we've just covered. Interestingly, if you look at Hansen's Table 1 (where he lays out the Kydland–Prescott statistics), you may see that the model statistics are slightly different from the ones contained in Table 10.1. Hansen relied on a linear-quadratic approximation to the problem's value function, which can account for these small discrepancies in the values.

Although our initial motivation was to account for movements in and out of the labor market (both on the intensive and extensive margins), none of the models presented in the chapter really allow us to achieve this goal. The divisible labor market model only looks at the intensive market, and the indivisible labor model does so at the extensive margin. Is there a way to analyze both? The answer is yes, but doing so would take us too far afield. If you are curious, the starting point to learn **search models** from a DSGE perspective are the papers by Merz (1995) and Andolfatto (1996).

10.5 Problems

10.5.1 Calibrating the Canonical RBC Model

Use the ideas from Chapter 9 to calibrate the canonical RBC model from this chapter. *Hint*: To help you find a value for ϕ, use the fact that households work about 30% of available time as a targeted moment (i.e., set $N_{ss} = 0.3$). How different are your parameters compared to the parametrization I use in this chapter?

10.5.2 Leisure Shocks

Consider a variation of the canonical RBC model. In this environment, the household receives stochastic shocks to the marginal utility of leisure, which generate changes in the household's optimal labor supply. More precisely, the social planner consumer chooses values of consumption C_t, labor supply N_t, and investment X_t to solve

$$\begin{aligned}
\max \quad & \mathbb{E}_0 \sum_{t=0}^{\infty} \beta^t \left[\log C_t + \phi_t \log\left(1 - N_t\right) \right] \\
\text{subject to} \quad & A_t K_t^{\alpha} N_t^{1-\alpha} = C_t + X_t, \\
& K_{t+1} = \left(1 - \delta\right) K_t + X_t, \\
& C_t \geq 0, \\
& K_0 \text{ given.}
\end{aligned}$$

The problem is identical to the one described in Section 10.1.1 except for the addition of a **leisure shock** ϕ_t, which evolves following

$$\phi_t = (1 - \rho_\phi)\phi_{ss} + \rho_\phi \phi_{t-1} + \sigma_\phi \varepsilon_{\phi t}.$$

Assume that ϕ_0 is given, $\rho_\phi > 0$ is an autocorrelation coefficient, and $\sigma_\phi > 0$.

1. Use the SPP described above to find the intratemporal, intertemporal, and aggregate feasibility conditions for this economy.
2. Use your answer to part 1 to find closed-form expressions for all of the economy's steady-state values.
3. Let $\beta = 0.99$, $\delta = 0.025$, $\alpha = 0.36$, $\rho_A = 0.95$, $\sigma_A = 0.007$, $A_{ss} = 1$, $\rho_\phi = 0.75$, $\sigma_\phi = 0.015$, and $\phi_{ss} = 2$. Use Dynare to derive the model's impulse-response functions after a shock to ε_ϕ.
4. Compare the impulse-response functions coming from a shock to leisure with those coming from a TFP shock. What are the key differences?

10.5.3 Parameter Sensitivity in the Canonical RBC Model

Consider another variation of the canonical RBC model. We have a dynamic economy with a representative consumer and a representative firm. The representative consumer chooses values of consumption C_t, leisure ℓ_t, and next-period capital K_{t+1} to solve

$$\begin{aligned} \max \quad & \mathbb{E}_0 \sum_{t=0}^{\infty} \beta^t \left[\frac{\left(C_t \ell_t^{\phi}\right)^{1-\eta} - 1}{1-\eta} \right] \\ \text{subject to} \quad & C_t + K_{t+1} - (1-\delta)K_t = r_{kt}K_t + w_t(1-\ell_t), \\ & C_t \geq 0, \\ & K_0 \text{ given.} \end{aligned}$$

In the above, $\beta \in (0,1)$ is the consumer's discount factor, $\phi \geq 0$ is a leisure weight, $\eta > 1$ is the coefficient of relative risk aversion, and $\delta \in (0,1)$ is the depreciation rate.

Each period, the representative firm rents labor N_F and capital K_F from the consumer and uses these inputs to produce the final good. The firm chooses the level of inputs to solve

$$\begin{aligned} \max \quad & Y_t - r_{kt}K_{Ft} - w_t N_{Ft} \\ \text{subject to} \quad & Y_t = A_t K_{Ft}^{\alpha} N_{Ft}^{1-\alpha}, \\ & K_{Ft}, N_{Ft} \geq 0, \end{aligned}$$

where $\alpha \in (0,1)$ is the income share of capital. TFP follows an AR(1) process of the form

$$\log A_t = (1-\rho_A)\log A_{ss} + \rho_A \log A_{t-1} + \sigma_A \varepsilon_{At},$$

where A_0 is given, $\rho_A > 0$ is an autocorrelation coefficient, and $\sigma_A > 0$.

1. Write the definition of a competitive equilibrium *or* state the associated SPP, along with a brief justification of why you can go ahead and use the CE = PO equivalency.
2. Use your answer to part 1 to find the intratemporal, intertemporal, and aggregate feasibility conditions for this economy.
3. Use your answer to part 2 to find closed-form expressions for all of the economy's steady-state values.
4. Let $\beta = 0.99$, $\phi = 1$, $\eta = 1.5$, $\delta = 0.02$, $\alpha = 0.33$, $\rho_A = 0.9$, and $\sigma_A = 0.007$. Use Dynare to derive the model's impulse-response functions and Kydland–Prescott statistics. Offer a brief interpretation of your findings.
5. Use your code from part 4 to generate impulse-response functions that show how the model responds when the leisure weight ϕ takes values in the set $\{0.5, 1.5, 3, 6\}$. Compare with the baseline case ($\phi = 1$) and discuss your results.
6. Use your code from part 4 to generate impulse-response functions that show how the model responds when the coefficient of relative risk aversion η takes values in the set $\{0.5, 1.5, 2, 3\}$. Compare with the baseline case ($\eta = 1.5$) and discuss your results.

11 Habit Persistence and Preference Shocks

Up to now, our models have worked under the assumption that the household derives utility from consumption and leisure enjoyed in the *current* period. Put simply, the instantaneous utility function u takes the form

$$u\left(C_t, \ell_t\right)$$

with $u_C, u_\ell > 0$. However, this methodological choice has not always been the case. In their paper, Kydland and Prescott (1982) assume that it's not only the current leisure choice that matters – the (infinite) history of leisure choices also affects current-period utility. As it turns out, this modeling choice didn't have too much of an effect on the RBC agenda, so it was quickly dropped out of subsequent papers after researchers recognized that looking at the household's decisions over current leisure was enough to get the job done.

Some years later, Mehra and Prescott (1985) documented a "puzzle" in the intersection of macroeconomic theory and financial economics – the **equity premium puzzle**. (In economics, a discrepancy between theory and data is called a puzzle.) The equity premium puzzle arises because a standard dynamic model (like the ones we've been using so far) cannot account for the large difference between the return on risky (e.g., equity) and safe (e.g., government bonds) assets *unless* we are willing to accept unrealistic parameter estimates that have no counterpart in empirical studies.

While the equity premium puzzle is still an open debate, the literature has offered plenty of solutions – some of which have been adopted by macroeconomists *even though said models have no financial components*. One such solution is the addition (or, more precisely, reintroduction) of past choices in current utility, bundled under the label of **habit persistence** models (in consumption).

At the most basic level, habit persistence imposes a link between yesterday's and today's consumption choices; to see this, suppose that the instantaneous utility function now takes the form

$$u(C_t, C_{t-1}, \ell_t).$$

In this case, the marginal utility of consumption no longer depends on what is consumed today; rather, yesterday's consumption has an influence on today's utility – and today's consumption. Kocherlakota (1996) puts it this way:

> Thus, the marginal utility of period t consumption is an increasing function of period $(t-1)$ consumption. Note that there are two pieces to this formula for marginal utility. The first term captures

the fact that if I buy a BMW rather than a Yugo today, then I am certainly better off today; however, the second piece models the notion that having the BMW "spoils" me and reduces my utility from all future car purchases.

Even though habit persistence is a *real* (not nominal) friction, it has found a place in many New Keynesian models, building what McGrattan (2004) calls the "triple-sticky" model (sticky prices, sticky wages, and sticky consumption – i.e., habit persistence). In this sense, knowing how this friction modifies the basic model is an important step ahead.

I should add that there are two kinds of habit persistence: internal and external. The former links the household's own consumption to its utility, while the latter compares the average consumption in the economy to the household's own consumption. As internal habits are more frequently used in the literature, I only look at this case and discuss external habits in the Bibliographic Notes section.

This chapter is on the short side, but as many DSGE models choose to include habit persistence, knowing how it works (and why it gets included in the first place) is important. In what follows, Section 11.1 presents the implementation of internal habits in a canonical RBC model, and Section 11.2 shows how to take the model into Dynare.

11.1 A Model with Internal Habit Persistence

Consider an RBC economy consisting of a representative household and a representative firm. As usual, both the consumer and the firm are price takers. The household chooses infinite sequences of consumption C_t, investment X_t, and hours worked N_t to maximize the objective function

$$\mathbb{E}_0 \sum_{t=0}^{\infty} \beta^t u\left(C_t, C_{t-1}, N_t\right),$$

where $\beta \in (0,1)$ is the household's discount factor and where the instantaneous utility function u takes the form

$$u\left(C_t, C_{t-1}, N_t\right) = \log\left(C_t - \varkappa C_{t-1}\right) + \phi \log\left(1 - N_t\right).$$

In the above, parameter $\varkappa \geq 0$ governs the household's habit persistence while parameter $\phi > 0$ represents the relative importance of consumption and leisure. The household's endowment consists of an initial capital stock K_0 and a time endowment of $h = 1$ units of time every period, which it can devote either to work or to leisure. Labor is paid at a rate w_t per hour. Finally, I assume the household is in charge of the investment decision; capital accumulation follows

$$K_{t+1} = \left(1 - \delta\right) K_t + X_t,$$

where $\delta \in \left(0, 1\right)$ is the depreciation rate of physical capital. Each period, the household rents capital K_t to the representative firm and obtains a rental rate of r_{kt} per unit.

The representative firm uses a CRS technology F to produce output, following

$$Y_t = A_t F\left(K_{Ft}, N_{Ft}\right) = A_t K_{Ft}^{\alpha} N_{Ft}^{1-\alpha}.$$

In the above, A_t is a stochastic productivity shock, K_{Ft} denotes the firm's capital input, and N_{Ft} denotes its labor input. The process for A_t follows

$$\log A_t = (1 - \rho_A) \log A_{ss} + \rho_A \log A_{t-1} + \sigma_A \varepsilon_{At},$$

where $\rho_A \in (0, 1)$, A_0 is given, A_{ss} is the steady-state level of the productivity shock, and $\sigma_A > 0$.

I move along the following lines. First, I set up the SPP that solves this economy and then use it to characterize the model's solution. Once this is done, I find the model's steady state and cast the model in Dynare.

11.1.1 The Social Planner Problem

As there are no distortions in this economy, I can directly state and solve an SPP and I do this next. The SPP for this economy is

$$\begin{aligned}
\max \quad & \mathbb{E}_0 \sum_{t=0}^{\infty} \beta^t \left[\log \left(C_t - \varkappa C_{t-1}\right) + \phi \log \left(1 - N_t\right) \right] \\
\text{subject to} \quad & C_t + X_t = A_t K_t^{\alpha} N_t^{1-\alpha}, \\
& K_{t+1} = (1 - \delta) K_t + X_t, \\
& C_t \geq 0, \\
& K_0 \text{ given},
\end{aligned}$$

together with the TFP process

$$\log A_t = (1 - \rho_A) \log A_{ss} + \rho_A \log A_{t-1} + \sigma_A \varepsilon_{At}.$$

Relative to the RBC model covered in Chapter 10, the only difference lies in the objective function, which now includes a lagged consumption term to incorporate habit persistence.

11.1.2 Characterizing the Solution

A potential point of confusion is the role of the habit term C_{t-1} in the Lagrangian function. Here's where knowing which variables are states and which are controls can help. In the canonical RBC model, I take the derivative with respect to K_{t+1} (the control variable) and not with respect to K_t (the state variable); this follows as the household needs to pick tomorrow's capital today – today's capital is predetermined and was chosen yesterday. Using a similar logic, the household chooses C_t even though the habit (state) variable is C_{t-1}. The associated Lagrangian is then

$$\begin{aligned}
\mathscr{L} = \mathbb{E}_0 \sum_{t=0}^{\infty} \beta^t \Big\{ & \log \left(C_t - \varkappa C_{t-1}\right) + \phi \log \left(1 - N_t\right) \\
& + \lambda_t \left(A_t K_t^{\alpha} N_t^{1-\alpha} - C_t - X_t\right) + \zeta_t \left[(1 - \delta) K_t + X_t - K_{t+1} \right] \Big\}.
\end{aligned}$$

The first-order conditions are

$$
\begin{aligned}
C_t: &\quad \frac{1}{C_t - \varkappa C_{t-1}} - \lambda_t + \beta \mathbb{E}_t \left(\frac{-\varkappa}{C_{t+1} - \varkappa C_t} \right) = 0, \\
N_t: &\quad -\phi (1 - N_t)^{-1} + \lambda_t \left[(1-\alpha) A_t K_t^{\alpha} N_t^{-\alpha} \right] = 0, \\
X_t: &\quad -\lambda_t + \zeta_t = 0, \\
K_{t+1}: &\quad -\zeta_t + \beta \mathbb{E}_t \lambda_{t+1} \left(\alpha A_{t+1} K_{t+1}^{\alpha-1} N_{t+1}^{1-\alpha} \right) + \beta \mathbb{E}_t \zeta_{t+1} (1-\delta) = 0, \\
\lambda_t: &\quad A_t K_t^{\alpha} N_t^{1-\alpha} - C_t - X_t = 0, \\
\zeta_t: &\quad (1-\delta) K_t + X_t - K_{t+1} = 0.
\end{aligned}
$$

Just as in earlier chapters, I add output as a model variable ($Y_t = A_t K_t^{\alpha} N_t^{1-\alpha}$). After substituting $\zeta_t = \lambda_t$, the equations become

$$Y_t = A_t K_t^{\alpha} N_t^{1-\alpha}, \tag{11.1}$$

$$\frac{1}{C_t - \varkappa C_{t-1}} = \lambda_t + \beta \varkappa \mathbb{E}_t \left(\frac{1}{C_{t+1} - \varkappa C_t} \right), \tag{11.2}$$

$$\phi N_t = (1-\alpha) \lambda_t Y_t (1 - N_t), \tag{11.3}$$

$$\lambda_t = \beta \mathbb{E}_t \lambda_{t+1} \left(\alpha Y_{t+1} K_{t+1}^{-1} + 1 - \delta \right), \tag{11.4}$$

$$Y_t = C_t + X_t, \tag{11.5}$$

$$K_{t+1} = (1-\delta) K_t + X_t. \tag{11.6}$$

Finally, I add the law of motion for technology:

$$\log A_t = (1 - \rho_A) \log A_{ss} + \rho_A \log A_{t-1} + \sigma_A \varepsilon_{At}. \tag{11.7}$$

11.1.3 The Steady State

Let variables without subscripts denote steady-state values. Given $A_{ss} = 1$, the steady-state equations associated with (11.1)–(11.6) are

$$Y = K^{\alpha} N^{1-\alpha}, \tag{11.8}$$

$$\frac{1}{(1-\varkappa) C} = \lambda + \frac{\beta \varkappa}{(1-\varkappa) C}, \tag{11.9}$$

$$\phi N = (1-\alpha) \lambda Y (1 - N), \tag{11.10}$$

$$1 = \beta \left(\alpha Y K^{-1} + 1 - \delta \right), \tag{11.11}$$

$$Y = C + X, \tag{11.12}$$

$$X = \delta K. \tag{11.13}$$

As usual, note that equation (11.7) collapses to 0=0. To solve (11.8)–(11.13), first take (11.11) and solve for Y_{ss}:

$$Y = \left[\frac{1 - \beta(1-\delta)}{\alpha \beta} \right] K \equiv \omega_Y K. \tag{11.14}$$

Now take (11.13) and (11.14) and substitute in (11.12). Solving for C_{ss} yields

$$C = \left(\omega_Y - \delta\right) K \equiv \omega_C K. \tag{11.15}$$

I can solve (11.9) for λ_{ss}. If I do so, I obtain

$$\lambda = \frac{1 - \beta \varkappa}{(1 - \varkappa) C}. \tag{11.16}$$

If I substitute (11.14)–(11.16) in (11.10), a bit of algebra later I get

$$N = \frac{(1 - \alpha)(1 - \beta \varkappa)\omega_Y}{\phi(1 - \varkappa)\omega_C + (1 - \alpha)(1 - \beta \varkappa)\omega_Y}. \tag{11.17}$$

The last step is to plug the expression for Y and the value of N, equations (11.14) and (11.17), respectively, into the production function, equation (11.8). Solving for K gives

$$K = \frac{N}{\omega_Y^{1/(1-\alpha)}}. \tag{11.18}$$

With the value of K at hand, from equation (11.18), it is straightforward to obtain the steady-state values for $\{X, Y, C, \lambda\}$.

11.1.4 Intermezzo VI: Log-Linearizing the Consumption FOC

While I will go ahead and put the entire model into Dynare, it is useful to know how to log-linearize the first-order condition for consumption, equation (11.2). The difficulty lies with the two terms with fractions. Looking back at Chapter 7, Uhlig's rules are not helpful in this situation.

The solution, once again, is to use a divide-and-conquer strategy. Instead of trying to tackle equation (11.2) directly, I divide this expression into two parts. First, I introduce a new variable ς_t:

$$\varsigma_t = C_t - \varkappa C_{t-1} \tag{11.19}$$

and then rewrite (11.2) using this new variable:

$$\frac{1}{\varsigma_t} = \lambda_t + \beta \varkappa \mathbb{E}_t \left(\frac{1}{\varsigma_{t+1}} \right).$$

I rewrite this expression more compactly as

$$\varsigma_t^{-1} = \lambda_t + \beta \varkappa \mathbb{E}_t \varsigma_{t+1}^{-1}. \tag{11.20}$$

By inspection, equations (11.19) and (11.20) are now easily log-linearized using Uhlig's rules. I get

$$\varsigma_{ss} \widehat{\varsigma}_t = C_{ss} \widehat{C}_t - \varkappa C_{ss} \widehat{C}_{t-1},$$
$$-\varsigma_{ss}^{-1} \widehat{\varsigma}_t = \lambda_{ss} \widehat{\lambda}_t - \beta \varkappa \varsigma_{ss}^{-1} \mathbb{E}_t \widehat{\varsigma}_{t+1},$$

which is the log-linear equivalent of equation (11.2).

11.2 Dynare Code

Here I share the code that implements the model with habit persistence in Dynare. The only change (a quality-of-life improvement) is the addition of an auxiliary variable, `denom`, which equals the denominator in equation (11.2). While not strictly necessary, it makes typing the first-order conditions a bit easier.

```
/*
habit.mod
Canonical RBC model with habit persistence.
*/

close all

// PREAMBLE: VARIABLE AND PARAMETER DEFINITIONS

// Endogenous variables (8)
var Y A K N denom C lambda X ;

// Exogenous variables (1)
varexo epsilon_A ;

// Parameters (10)
parameters alpha phi beta delta varkappa ;
parameters rho_A A_ss sigma_A ;

    alpha = 0.33 ;
    phi = 2 ;
    beta = 0.99 ;
    delta = 0.025 ;
    varkappa = 0.85 ;
    rho_A = 0.9 ;
    A_ss = 1 ;
    sigma_A = 0.01 ;

// MODEL BLOCK

model ;
    Y = A*K(-1)^alpha*N^(1 - alpha) ;
    denom = C - varkappa*C(-1) ;
    1/denom = lambda + beta*varkappa/denom(+1) ;
    phi*N = (1 - alpha)*lambda*Y*(1 - N) ;
    lambda = beta*lambda(+1)*(alpha*Y(+1)/K + 1 - delta) ;
    Y = C + X ;
```

```
    K = (1 - delta)*K(-1) + X ;
    log(A) = (1 - rho_A)*log(A_ss) + rho_A*log(A(-1))
             + sigma_A*epsilon_A ;
end ;

// STEADY STATE BLOCK

steady_state_model ;
    A = A_ss ;
    omega_y = (1 - beta*(1 - delta))/(alpha*beta) ;
    omega_c = omega_y - delta ;
    N = (1 - alpha)*(1 - beta*varkappa)*omega_y /
            (phi*(1 - varkappa)*omega_c
            + (1 - alpha)*(1 - beta*varkappa)*omega_y) ;
    K = N/omega_y^(1/(1 - alpha)) ;
    Y = omega_y*K ;
    X = delta*K ;
    C = omega_c*K ;
    denom = (1 - varkappa)*C ;
    lambda = (1 - beta*varkappa)/((1 - varkappa)*C) ;
end ;

steady ;
check ;

// SHOCKS BLOCK

shocks ;
    var epsilon_A = 1 ;
end ;

// SIMULATION BLOCK

stoch_simul(irf=40, order=1) ;
```

(Code 11.1)

11.3 Up Next

We have two key frictions down, and there are two more to go. The ability to add labor supply is important, and reducing the variability of consumption by adding habit persistence also helps replicate real-world behavior. However, we are still missing two key frictions, namely, those that affect investment and capital and those surrounding fiscal policy. Fortunately, the next two chapters take care of filling in these gaps.

11.4 Bibliographic Notes

The exposition in this chapter follows the papers by Boldrin, Christiano, and Fisher (2001) and Schmitt-Grohé and Uribe (2012). Some examples of "triple-sticky" models include Galí and Rabanal (2004), Christiano, Eichenbaum, and Evans (2005), and Smets and Wouters (2007). (Of course, we have to wait until Part IV to see how sticky prices and wages work.)

As mentioned in the introduction to this chapter, the equity premium puzzle has motivated many tools that are now frequently used in macroeconomic models, including habit persistence. Unlike *internal* habits – the version I cover in this chapter – *external* habits induce the household to "catch up" with the average level of consumption in the economy (hence the moniker, "catching up with the Joneses"). See Abel (1990) for an initial contribution and Ravn, Schmitt-Grohé, and Uribe (2006) for a more modern exposition of what external habits can achieve. For a comprehensive review of the equity premium puzzle, see the survey by Kocherlakota (1996).

11.5 Problems

11.5.1 The Effects of Habit Persistence

Use Code 11.1 – which includes habit persistence – to compare its results with those of an equivalent model without this friction by setting $\varkappa = 0$. How does consumption behave with and without habit persistence? *Hint*: Look at the impulse-response function. Are there any other variables that qualitatively (or quantitatively) change as you vary the value of $\varkappa$? If yes, provide some intuition that explains their behavior.

11.5.2 Preference Shocks

Consider a variation on Problem 10.5.2. In this new environment, the household receives stochastic shocks to the discount factor β *and* to the marginal utility of leisure. More precisely, the social planner consumer chooses values of consumption C_t, labor supply N_t, and investment X_t to solve

$$\begin{aligned} \max \quad & \mathbb{E}_0 \sum_{t=0}^{\infty} \beta^t z_t \left[\log C_t + \phi_t \log \left(1 - N_t\right)\right] \\ \text{subject to} \quad & A_t K_t^{\alpha} N_t^{1-\alpha} = C_t + X_t, \\ & K_{t+1} = \left(1-\delta\right) K_t + X_t, \\ & C_t \geq 0, \\ & K_0 \text{ given.} \end{aligned}$$

The problem is identical to Problem 10.5.2 except for the addition of the **discount factor shock** z_t, which evolves following

$$\log z_t = (1-\rho_z)\log z_{ss} + \rho_z \log z_{t-1} + \sigma_z \varepsilon_{zt},$$

where z_{ss} and z_0 are given, $\rho_z > 0$ is an autocorrelation coefficient, and $\sigma_z > 0$.

1. Use the SPP described above to find the intratemporal, intertemporal, and aggregate feasibility conditions for this economy.
2. Use your answer to part 1 to find closed-form expressions for all of the economy's steady-state values.
3. Let $\beta = 0.99$, $\delta = 0.025$, $\alpha = 0.36$, $\rho_A = 0.95$, $\sigma_A = 0.007$, $A_{ss} = 1$, $\rho_\phi = 0.75$, $\sigma_\phi = 0.015$, $\phi_{ss} = 2$, $\rho_z = 0.8$, $\sigma_z = 0.025$, and $z_{ss} = 1$. Use Dynare to derive the model's impulse-response functions after a shock to ε_z.
4. Compare the impulse-response functions coming from a preference shock to those coming from (i) a TFP shock and (ii) a leisure shock. What are the key differences?

12 Investment Adjustment Costs and Variable Capacity Utilization

This chapter introduces two frictions that at first seem unrelated, yet share the common feature of being connected to capital accumulation and investment. In Section 12.1 I introduce the notion of **variable capacity utilization**. In the canonical RBC model, the full stock of capital is used for production in every period and the only way to reduce the amount of capital that goes into the production process is via disinvestment. (And even then, letting the capital stock depreciate takes time.) This strategy, of course, can be very impractical; what if the capital that's tossed away is highly specialized? Instead, firms may opt to reduce the **utilization rate** of their capital stock. When demand is low, it's much better to shut down the factory equipment for a few hours every day instead of getting rid of it at fire-sale prices; conversely, when demand is high, the firm can use its capital at maximum capacity (which, as we will see, will have an impact over the depreciation rate). In this sense, I must distinguish between the capital stock itself and the flow of *capital services*, defined as the product of the utilization rate and the capital stock. As expected, the utilization rate is highly procyclical and serves to better match the data, as shown by King and Rebelo (1999).

At this point I also introduce shocks to the **marginal efficiency of investment** (MEI). To get some context, in the canonical RBC model one unit of investment yields one unit of capital – and the capital stock is of a homogeneous quality. In the real world this logic doesn't quite hold: when a firm decides to upgrade its old computer hardware, the *real* price of the new capital goods is much lower than what it replaces and, at the same time, the firm now gets "more capital for the same price." (This is the idea behind, say, Moore's law for semiconductors.) Incorporating an MEI shock complements the role of TFP shocks (and, according to some authors, shocks to investment are far more important in replicating the quantitative features of the data).

Next, in Section 12.2 I look at **investment adjustment costs**. The main idea is that there are limits to how fast the capital stock can increase without incurring additional expenses. For example, while it is feasible to build (say) a new industrial warehouse in a quarter, doing so will be much costlier than building it over the course of a year. Model-wise, deviations of investment *relative to its steady-state level* are costly, and this generates tradeoffs at the firm level – since adding more capital generates future revenue but incurs additional costs today. Put differently, investment is no longer frictionless, as was the case in the canonical RBC model. A consequence of this friction is that the response of investment is less volatile in response to TFP shocks.

12.1 Variable Capacity Utilization

Besides the ideas shared in the introduction, there are two reasons why it's convenient to add variable capacity utilization to an RBC model. First, a model with a single shock (TFP) only has one driver of fluctuations. As King and Rebelo (1999) show, an RBC model requires very persistent TPF shocks in order to qualitatively replicate the features observed in the data. However, the fact that there is only one shock – technology – means that recessions are periods when firms "forget how to do things," which is a very unpalatable conclusion.

The second reason still relates to TFP shocks, but in a different context. Suppose that a researcher measures TFP via the Solow residual. As I showed in Chapter 9, this variable equals the difference between measured capital and labor inputs and measured GDP. Assuming that the production technology takes a Cobb–Douglas form, the researcher would "back out" the value of A via

$$A = \frac{Y}{K^{\alpha}N^{1-\alpha}}.$$

So far, so good. But what happens if the inputs of production remain idle during the period? Maybe capital is not fully utilized or the labor force is invited to work less during a downturn. In this case, capital and labor *services* would go down. However, if the researcher is unable to measure said level of services, he would incorrectly infer that TFP has gone down. Put differently, given

$$Y = A\left(\upsilon K\right)^{\alpha}\left(eN\right)^{1-\alpha},$$

an unobserved fall in υ (utilization) or e (effort) – keeping A constant – would be interpreted as a drop in TFP.

Models with variable capacity utilization seek to address this potential pitfall. In what follows, I take the model from Greenwood et al. (1988) as a starting point and explain how to modify the canonical RBC model into one that not only includes variable capacity utilization but also shocks to the marginal efficiency of investment.

12.1.1 The Social Planner Problem

Consider a canonical RBC model that consists of a representative firm and a representative household. The firm uses capital services and labor in order to produce the final good, following

$$Y_t = A_t\bar{K}_t^{\alpha}N_t^{1-\alpha},$$

where $\bar{K}_t = \upsilon_t K_t$ represents capital services, $\upsilon > 0$ denotes the utilization rate of capital (selected by the household), and K_t is the stock of physical capital. As usual, A_t denotes TFP and is given by

$$\log A_t = \left(1-\rho_A\right)\log A_{ss} + \rho_A \log A_{t-1} + \sigma_A\varepsilon_{At}, \qquad (12.1)$$

where $\rho_A \in \left(0,1\right)$, A_0 is known, A_{ss} denotes the steady-state level of TFP, and $\sigma_A > 0$.

The household chooses decision rules for consumption, labor, investment, and the utilization rate to solve

$$\begin{aligned}
\max \quad & \mathbb{E}_0 \sum_{t=0}^{\infty} \beta^t \left\{ \frac{1}{1-\eta} \left[\left(C_t - \frac{1}{1+\chi} N_t^{1+\chi} \right)^{1-\eta} - 1 \right] \right\} \\
\text{subject to} \quad & C_t + X_t = r_{kt} \upsilon_t K_t + w_t N_t, \\
& K_{t+1} = \left[1 - \delta(\upsilon_t)\right] K_t + (1 + \mu_t) X_t, \\
& \delta(\upsilon_t) = \frac{1}{\varpi} \upsilon_t^{\varpi}.
\end{aligned}$$

In this problem, $1/\eta > 0$ is the intertemporal elasticity of substitution, $1/\chi > 0$ is the Frisch elasticity of labor supply, $\delta(\upsilon)$ is the depreciation function – which depends on the utilization rate – and $\varpi > 1$ represents the elasticity of depreciation with respect to utilization. The term μ_t represents the shock to the marginal efficiency of investment; I assume μ_t follows the AR(1) process

$$\mu_t = \rho_\mu \mu_{t-1} + \sigma_\mu \varepsilon_{\mu t}, \tag{12.2}$$

where $\rho_\mu \in (0, 1)$, μ_0 is known, and $\sigma_\mu > 0$.

Since the assumptions that guarantee the equivalence between the first and second welfare theorems hold, I set the associated SPP and work over it instead of defining a competitive equilibrium. After substituting the law of motion for capital into the budget constraint and substituting for $\bar{K}_t$ on the firm's side, the Lagrangian function that corresponds to this SPP is given by

$$\begin{aligned}
\mathscr{L} = \mathbb{E}_0 \sum_{t=0}^{\infty} \beta^t \Bigg\{ & \frac{1}{1-\eta} \left[\left(C_t - \frac{1}{1+\chi} N_t^{1+\chi} \right)^{1-\eta} - 1 \right] \\
& + \lambda_t \left[A_t (\upsilon_t K_t)^{\alpha} N_t^{1-\alpha} - C_t - \frac{K_{t+1}}{1+\mu_t} + \left(1 - \frac{1}{\varpi} \upsilon_t^{\varpi}\right) \frac{K_t}{1+\mu_t} \right] \Bigg\}.
\end{aligned} \tag{12.3}$$

12.1.2 Characterization of Equilibrium

The first-order conditions associated with problem (12.3) are

$$\begin{aligned}
C_t: \quad & \left(C_t - \frac{1}{1+\chi} N_t^{1+\chi} \right)^{-\eta} - \lambda_t = 0, \\
N_t: \quad & - \left(C_t - \frac{1}{1+\chi} N_t^{1+\chi} \right)^{-\eta} N_t^{\chi} + \alpha \lambda_t A_t (\upsilon_t K_t)^{\alpha} N_t^{-\alpha} = 0, \\
\upsilon_t: \quad & \alpha A_t \upsilon_t^{\alpha-1} K_t^{\alpha} N_t^{1-\alpha} - \frac{K_t \upsilon_t^{\varpi-1}}{1+\mu_t} = 0, \\
K_{t+1}: \quad & - \frac{\lambda_t}{1+\mu_t} + \beta \mathbb{E}_t \lambda_{t+1} \left[\alpha A_{t+1} \upsilon_{t+1}^{\alpha} K_{t+1}^{\alpha-1} N_{t+1}^{1-\alpha} + \left(1 - \frac{1}{\varpi} \upsilon_{t+1}^{\varpi}\right) \frac{1}{1+\mu_{t+1}} \right] = 0,
\end{aligned}$$

$$\lambda_t: \quad A_t(\upsilon_t K_t)^{\alpha} N_t^{1-\alpha} - C_t - \frac{K_{t+1}}{1+\mu_t} + \left(1 - \frac{1}{\varpi}\upsilon_t^{\varpi}\right)\frac{K_t}{1+\mu_t} = 0.$$

I now add the production function as a new equation, namely,

$$Y_t = A_t(\upsilon_t K_t)^{\alpha} N_t^{1-\alpha} \tag{12.4}$$

and rewrite the first-order conditions as

$$\left(C_t - \frac{1}{1+\chi}N_t^{1+\chi}\right)^{-\eta} = \lambda_t, \tag{12.5}$$

$$\left(C_t - \frac{1}{1+\chi}N_t^{1+\chi}\right)^{-\eta} N_t^{\chi} = \alpha\frac{\lambda_t Y_t}{N_t},$$

$$\alpha\frac{Y_t}{\upsilon_t} = \frac{K_t \upsilon_t^{\varpi-1}}{1+\mu_t},$$

$$\frac{\lambda_t}{1+\mu_t} = \beta\,\mathbb{E}_t\lambda_{t+1}\left[\alpha\frac{Y_{t+1}}{K_{t+1}} + \left(1 - \frac{1}{\varpi}\upsilon_{t+1}^{\varpi}\right)\frac{1}{1+\mu_{t+1}}\right],$$

$$Y_t = C_t + \frac{K_{t+1}}{1+\mu_t} - \left(1 - \frac{1}{\varpi}\upsilon_t^{\varpi}\right)\frac{K_t}{1+\mu_t}.$$

For the final step, I substitute (12.5) in the remaining equations. After some algebra, the system of equations describing equilibrium in this economy is

$$\alpha Y_t = N_t^{1+\chi}, \tag{12.6}$$

$$\alpha Y_t = \frac{K_t \upsilon_t^{\varpi}}{1+\mu_t}, \tag{12.7}$$

$$\frac{1}{1+\mu_t}\left(C_t - \frac{1}{1+\chi}N_t^{1+\chi}\right)^{-\eta} = \beta\,\mathbb{E}_t\left(C_{t+1} - \frac{1}{1+\chi}N_{t+1}^{1+\chi}\right)^{-\eta} \times,$$

$$\left[\alpha\frac{Y_{t+1}}{K_{t+1}} + \left(1 - \frac{1}{\varpi}\upsilon_{t+1}^{\varpi}\right)\frac{1}{1+\mu_{t+1}}\right], \tag{12.8}$$

$$Y_t = C_t + \frac{K_{t+1}}{1+\mu_t} - \left(1 - \frac{1}{\varpi}\upsilon_t^{\varpi}\right)\frac{K_t}{1+\mu_t}. \tag{12.9}$$

How to interpret these expressions? Equation (12.6) is the intratemporal tradeoff between current-period consumption and current-period leisure. Similarly, equation (12.7) describes the intratemporal tradeoff that exists from increasing the utilization rate (thus yielding more output) vis-à-vis its cost in terms of capital depreciation. Finally, equation (12.8) is the standard intertemporal condition and equation (12.9) is the aggregate feasibility constraint. These four equations – together with the TFP and investment shock processes, equations (12.1) and (12.2) – describe the model's equilibrium.

12.1.3 The Steady State

In the steady state, equations (12.4) and (12.6)–(12.9) become

$$
\begin{aligned}
Y &= \left(\upsilon K\right)^{\alpha} N^{1-\alpha}, \\
\alpha Y &= N^{1+\chi}, \\
\alpha Y &= \frac{K\upsilon^{\varpi}}{1+\mu}, \\
\frac{1}{1+\mu} &= \beta\left[\alpha\frac{Y}{K} + \left(1 - \frac{1}{\varpi}\upsilon^{\varpi}\right)\frac{1}{1+\mu}\right], \\
Y &= C + \left(\frac{1}{\varpi}\upsilon^{\varpi}\right)\frac{K}{1+\mu}.
\end{aligned}
$$

Now for some simplifications: I set $\mu_{ss} = 0$ (the steady state is deterministic) and I also observe that $\upsilon^{\varpi}/\varpi \equiv \delta > 0$, where δ is the depreciation rate in the steady state. The system becomes

$$Y = \left(\upsilon K\right)^{\alpha} N^{1-\alpha}, \tag{12.10}$$

$$\alpha Y = N^{1+\chi}, \tag{12.11}$$

$$\alpha Y = K\upsilon^{\varpi}, \tag{12.12}$$

$$1 = \alpha\beta\frac{Y}{K} + \beta\left(1-\delta\right), \tag{12.13}$$

$$Y = C + \delta K, \tag{12.14}$$

$$\delta = \frac{1}{\varpi}\upsilon^{\varpi}, \tag{12.15}$$

which gives me a system of six equations in $\left\{Y, K, N, \upsilon, C, \varpi\right\}$. To solve for the steady-state values, start from (12.13) and rearrange to get

$$\frac{Y}{K} = \frac{1-\beta\left(1-\delta\right)}{\alpha\beta}. \tag{12.16}$$

I can rewrite (12.16) as

$$Y \equiv \omega_Y K. \tag{12.17}$$

Combine (12.12) with (12.16) to solve for υ_{ss}^{ϖ}:

$$\frac{\upsilon^{\varpi}}{\alpha} = \frac{Y}{K} \Longrightarrow \upsilon^{\varpi} = \frac{1-\beta\left(1-\delta\right)}{\beta}. \tag{12.18}$$

From (12.15), solve for ϖ:

$$\varpi = \frac{\upsilon^{\varpi}}{\delta},$$

where δ is a known value and υ^{ϖ} follows (12.18). Take (12.15) once again, but now solve for υ:

$$\delta = \frac{1}{\varpi}\upsilon^{\varpi} \Longrightarrow \upsilon = \left(\delta\varpi\right)^{1/\varpi}.$$

This takes care of υ_{ss}. Next, take (12.14) and rearrange as

$$\omega_Y K - \delta K = C \implies C = \left(\omega_Y - \delta\right) K \equiv \omega_C K, \tag{12.19}$$

so that equation (12.19) gives me C_{ss} as a function of K_{ss}. Do the same with (12.11):

$$\alpha \omega_Y K = N^{1+\chi} \implies N = \left(\alpha \omega_Y K\right)^{1/(1+\chi)} \equiv \omega_N K^{1/(1+\chi)}, \tag{12.20}$$

where $\omega_N \equiv \left(\alpha \omega_Y\right)^{1/(1+\chi)}$. Finally, plug the steady-state expressions (12.17) and (12.20) into (12.10):

$$\omega_Y K = \left(\upsilon K\right)^{\alpha} \left[\omega_N K^{1/(1+\chi)}\right]^{1-\alpha}.$$

Solving for K_{ss} gives

$$K = \left(\frac{\upsilon^{\alpha} \omega_N^{1-\alpha}}{\omega_Y}\right)^{(1+\chi)/[(1-\alpha)\chi]}.$$

All other steady-state values follow from here.

12.2 Investment Adjustment Costs

Investment adjustment costs, as their name suggests, make it costly for the firm to change its scope of investment relative to its steady-state value. There are a few ways to accomplish this, but the literature often uses the formulation put forward by Christiano et al. (2005), which modifies the law of motion for capital so it takes the form

$$K_{t+1} = \left(1 - \delta\right) K_t + \left[1 - \Phi\left(\frac{X_t}{X_{t-1}}\right)\right] X_t,$$

where function Φ satisfies $\Phi(1) = \Phi'(1) = 0$ and $\Phi''(1) \equiv \xi > 0$. Note that when function Φ is omitted, I have the regular law of motion for capital, $K_{t+1} = \left(1 - \delta\right) K_t + X_t$.

To set ideas, I now present a simplified version of the model in Christiano et al. (2005), which emphasizes both investment adjustment costs and variable capacity utilization. As a bonus, this version presents an alternative functional form for the variable depreciation term (relative to the one found in Section 12.1). As usual, the model economy has two agents: a representative household and a representative firm. Since there are no distortions, I set up the SPP and move along.

Remark 12.1 In their paper, Christiano et al. (2005) do not provide a functional form for function Φ. The quadratic form I present below follows Schmitt-Grohé and Uribe (2012).

12.2.1 The Social Planner Problem

The social planner chooses decision rules for consumption C_t, hours worked N_t, capital utilization υ_t, and investment X_t to solve

$$\max \quad \mathbb{E}_0 \sum_{t=0}^{\infty} \beta^t \left[\log C_t + \phi \log\left(1 - N_t\right)\right]$$

$$\text{subject to} \quad Y_t = A_t(v_t K_t)^\alpha N_t^{1-\alpha}, \tag{12.21}$$

$$Y_t = C_t + X_t, \tag{12.22}$$

$$K_{t+1} = (1 - \delta(v_t))K_t + \left[1 - \Phi\left(\frac{X_t}{X_{t-1}}\right)\right] X_t,$$

$$\delta(v_t) = \delta_0 + \delta_1(v_t - 1) + \frac{\delta_2(v_t - 1)^2}{2}, \tag{12.23}$$

$$\Phi\left(\frac{X_t}{X_{t-1}}\right) = \frac{\xi}{2}\left(\frac{X_t}{X_{t-1}} - 1\right)^2, \tag{12.24}$$

where $\delta_0, \delta_1, \delta_2, \xi > 0$. While the variable depreciation equation (12.23) is different relative to the one proposed by Greenwood et al. (1988), it still represents an increasing and convex function and satisfies $\delta(1) = \delta_0 > 0$.

Finally, I also incorporate the TFP process

$$\log A_t = (1 - \rho_A)\log A_{ss} + \rho_A \log A_{t-1} + \sigma_A \varepsilon_{At}. \tag{12.25}$$

12.2.2 Characterization of Equilibrium

The associated Lagrangian is

$$\mathscr{L} = \mathbb{E}_0 \sum_{t=0}^{\infty} \beta^t \Bigg\{ \log C_t + \phi \log(1 - N_t) + \lambda_t \left[A_t(v_t K_t)^\alpha N_t^{1-\alpha} - C_t - X_t\right]$$
$$+ \lambda_t \zeta_t \left[(1 - \delta(v_t))K_t + \left[1 - \frac{\xi}{2}\left(\frac{X_t}{X_{t-1}} - 1\right)^2\right] X_t - K_{t+1}\right]\Bigg\},$$

where I have combined equations (12.21) and (12.22) to simplify the problem. Without loss of generality, I use $\lambda_t \zeta_t$ as the Lagrange multiplier for the law of motion for capital. The set of first-order conditions, which already incorporate (12.23) and (12.24) where appropriate, are

$$C_t: \quad C_t^{-1} - \lambda_t = 0,$$

$$N_t: \quad -\phi(1 - N_t)^{-1} + (1 - \alpha)\lambda_t A_t (v_t K_t)^\alpha N_t^{-\alpha} = 0,$$

$$v_t: \quad \alpha \lambda_t A_t v_t^{\alpha-1} K_t^\alpha N_t^{1-\alpha} - \lambda_t \zeta_t (\delta_1 + \delta_2(v_t - 1)) = 0,$$

$$X_t: \quad -\lambda_t + \lambda_t \zeta_t \left\{1 - \frac{\xi}{2}\left(\frac{X_t}{X_{t-1}} - 1\right)^2 + X_t\left[-\xi\left(\frac{X_t}{X_{t-1}} - 1\right)\left(\frac{1}{X_{t-1}}\right)\right]\right\},$$
$$+ \beta\, \mathbb{E}_t \lambda_{t+1} \zeta_{t+1} \left\{X_{t+1}\left[-\xi\left(\frac{X_{t+1}}{X_t} - 1\right)\left(-\frac{X_{t+1}}{X_t^2}\right)\right]\right\} = 0,$$

$$K_{t+1}: \quad -\lambda_t \zeta_t + \beta\, \mathbb{E}_t \lambda_{t+1}\left[\alpha A_{t+1} v_{t+1}^\alpha K_{t+1}^{\alpha-1} N_{t+1}^{1-\alpha} + \zeta_{t+1}(1 - \delta(v_{t+1}))\right] = 0,$$

along with the first-order conditions with respect to the multipliers λ_t and $\lambda_t \zeta_t$. I substitute $\lambda_t = C_t^{-1}$ and the definition of Y_t where needed. After rearranging, I get the updated system

$$Y_t = A_t(v_t K_t)^\alpha N_t^{1-\alpha}, \tag{12.26}$$

$$\phi C_t N_t = (1-\alpha)Y_t(1-N_t), \tag{12.27}$$

$$\zeta_t = \beta \mathbb{E}_t \frac{C_t}{C_{t+1}} \left[\frac{\alpha Y_{t+1}}{K_{t+1}} + \zeta_{t+1}(1-\delta(\upsilon_{t+1})) \right], \tag{12.28}$$

$$1 = \zeta_t \left[1 - \frac{\xi}{2} \left(\frac{X_t}{X_{t-1}} - 1 \right)^2 - \xi \left(\frac{X_t}{X_{t-1}} - 1 \right) \left(\frac{X_t}{X_{t-1}} \right) \right]$$
$$+ \xi \beta \mathbb{E}_t \frac{C_t}{C_{t+1}} \zeta_{t+1} \left(\frac{X_{t+1}}{X_t} - 1 \right) \left(\frac{X_{t+1}}{X_t} \right)^2, \tag{12.29}$$

$$\alpha Y_t = \zeta_t \upsilon_t (\delta_1 + \delta_2(\upsilon_t - 1)), \tag{12.30}$$

$$Y_t = C_t + X_t, \tag{12.31}$$

$$K_{t+1} = (1-\delta(\upsilon_t))K_t + \left[1 - \frac{\xi}{2} \left(\frac{X_t}{X_{t-1}} - 1 \right)^2 \right] X_t, \tag{12.32}$$

together with the stochastic process (12.25).

12.2.3 The Steady State

I set $A_{ss} = u_{ss} = 1$; most of the complicated terms cancel out and equations (12.26)–(12.32) become

$$Y = K^{\alpha} N^{1-\alpha}, \tag{12.33}$$

$$\phi CN = (1-\alpha)Y(1-N), \tag{12.34}$$

$$\zeta = \beta \left[\frac{\alpha Y}{K} + \zeta(1-\delta_0) \right], \tag{12.35}$$

$$1 = \zeta, \tag{12.36}$$

$$\alpha Y = \zeta \delta_1, \tag{12.37}$$

$$Y = C + X, \tag{12.38}$$

$$K = (1-\delta_0)K + X. \tag{12.39}$$

I now solve the system (12.33)–(12.39). From (12.36) I immediately get that $\zeta_{ss} = 1$ and I substitute where appropriate. Next, from (12.35), I solve for Y_{ss} as a function of K_{ss}. Some algebra later, I get

$$Y = \left[\frac{1-\beta(1-\delta_0)}{\alpha\beta} \right] K \equiv \omega_Y K.$$

I can trivially rearrange (12.39) to get X_{ss} as a function of K_{ss}:

$$X = \delta_0 K \equiv \omega_X K$$

and then use the previous two results in (12.38) and solve for C_{ss} as a function of K_{ss}:

$$C = \omega_Y K - \omega_X K \equiv \omega_C K.$$

Next, I use the expressions for C_{ss} and Y_{ss} in (12.34) to solve for N_{ss}:

$$N = \frac{(1-\alpha)\omega_Y}{\phi\omega_C + (1-\alpha)\omega_Y}.$$

Finally, I substitute the value for N_{ss} and the expression for Y_{ss} in (1.13) to solve for K_{ss}:

$$K = \frac{N}{\omega_Y^{1/(1-\alpha)}}.$$

Working backwards, I use this value to obtain C, Y, and X. Note also that the value of δ_1 is endogenous, as it is pinned down in the steady state. This value equals

$$\delta_1 = \alpha Y = \alpha\omega_Y K.$$

12.3 Up Next

As of now I've covered most of the frictions that don't rely on nominal factors; modern macroeconomic models often include one (or all) of labor supply (divisible or indivisible), habit persistence, variable capacity utilization, and investment adjustment costs. Moreover, models in the New Keynesian tradition – begin RBC models with price stickiness – rely on these features as well.

That being said, we are still missing one major friction: fiscal policy. As to *why* we need to talk about it, the real world is full of examples of taxes on different activities or goods, and governments use tax revenue resources to fund their activities. Moreover, distortionary taxes often change the relevant tradeoffs that are present within a model. Knowing how policy decisions interact with equilibrium outcomes is an important step before wrapping up this part of the book.

12.4 Bibliographic Notes

Variable capacity utilization falls into the broader category of **factor hoarding models**. Burnside and Eichenbaum (1996) offer one of the earliest contributions and they also include variable effort (i.e., labor hoarding). However, the literature has paid most attention to capital hoarding (capacity utilization), perhaps because of its ability to help the canonical RBC model fit the data; see King and Rebelo (1999, sections 5–8) for additional details.

As mentioned in the text, variable capacity utilization often carries a variable depreciation term – the more intensively capital is used, the higher the depreciation rate. While Greenwood et al. (1988) introduce the functional form presented in Section 12.1, most recent papers use the specification found in Christiano et al. (2005).

Shocks to the marginal utility of investment have been added to RBC models since they appeared in the paper by Greenwood et al. (1988). In that contribution, the shocks are stationary and work just as regular TFP shocks. However, when we allow these shocks to have a *trend*, they can capture other dynamic features of the economy under the name of **investment-specific technological change**. Many authors claim that these shocks are more important than TFP shocks in accounting for business cycle fluctuations; related papers include Greenwood et al. (1997), Justiniano et al. (2010, 2011), and Furlanetto, Natvik, and Seneca (2013).

Regarding investment adjustment costs, I mentioned that the specification with the Φ-function (Christiano et al. 2005) is the most used in the literature. An alternative formulation that relies on the investment-to-capital ratio follows Lucas and Prescott (1971); while it succeeds in its goal of making changes to investment costly, it doesn't allow the model to replicate the (empirical) "hump-shaped" response of investment to monetary policy shocks like the one proposed by Christiano et al. (2005).

Finally, a side note. This book relies on Dynare to derive the policy functions that generate the equilibrium paths, and these operations only require the model's first-order conditions as they come out of the Lagrangian function or the firm's profit maximization problem. However, sometimes we need to log-linearize these expressions, which becomes an algebra nightmare given the complexity in the first-order conditions. Equations (12.29) and (12.32) are good examples of this complexity. Solis-Garcia (2021) presents a method to ease the log-linearization process, which relies on the basic fact that the product of second-order terms is zero when dealing with a linear expansion.

12.5 Problems

12.5.1 Greenwood et al. (1988) Meet Dynare

Take the model from Section 12.1 and implement it in Dynare. Use parameter values $\alpha = 0.29$, $\beta = 0.96$, $\delta = 0.1$, $\chi = 0.6$, $\eta = 1.001$, $\rho_A = \rho_\mu = 0.9$, and $\sigma_A = \sigma_\mu = 0.01$. How does investment respond to a shock to TFP? To a shock to the marginal efficiency of investment? *Hint*: Remember that in this model, ϖ is a function of other parameters. You will need to define model local variables (see Section 8.6.2) in order to get ϖ inside your model block.

12.5.2 A Model with and without Investment Adjustment Costs

Take the model from Section 12.2 and implement it in Dynare. Use parameter values $\alpha = 0.36$, $\beta = 0.99$, $\delta_0 = 0.025$, $\delta_2 = 0.02$, $\xi = 2.5$, $\rho_A = 0.9$, and $\sigma_A = 0.01$. How does investment respond to a shock to TFP? How does your answer change if you set $\xi = 0$ and redo the analysis? Based on your previous answers, how do adjustment costs change the model's equilibrium?

12.5.3 Lucas and Prescott (1971) Meet Dynare

As mentioned in the Bibliographic Notes, Lucas and Prescott (1971) offer an adjustment investment cost structure that depends on the ratio of investment to capital, so that

$$K_{t+1} = (1 - \delta) K_t + \Phi \left(\frac{I_t}{K_t} \right) K_t.$$

Kehoe (2003) suggests a function Φ of the form

$$\Phi(x) = \frac{\delta^{1-a} x^a + (a-1)\delta}{a}.$$

Take this model and implement it in Dynare. Assume that the household has a standard divisible labor utility function; the firm side is as usual except for this investment adjustment structure. Use parameter values $\alpha = 0.36$, $\beta = 0.99$, $\delta = 0.025$, $\rho_A = 0.9$, and $\sigma_A = 0.01$. In this formulation, parameter $a \in (0,1)$ is key; the case $a = 1$ corresponds to zero adjustment costs. Following Fernández de Cóordoba and Kehoe (2000), Kehoe picks $a = 0.9$, and you should too. Compared to your solution to Problem 12.5.2, how does investment respond to a shock to TFP?

13 Fiscal Policy

Up to now, the material we've covered has (strategically) ignored all matters related to fiscal policy. This is not because of oversight, of course; rather, it is because adding fiscal policy is an easy task once we know how DSGE models work, yet can add a lot of unnecessary details that obscure the basics without adding to our understanding of DSGE tools.

The reason why we want to look at how the government runs things hardly requires justification. All governments around the world spend resources in order to achieve a variety of goals (e.g., national defense, infrastructure, or bureaucrat paychecks), and they necessarily have to extract these resources (tax revenue) from households and firms. Moreover, the ways in which the fiscal instruments interact with the economy (not only with private sector decisions but also with other policy instruments) can generate some surprises if we don't treat this issue with the care it deserves.

Fortunately, we now have all the tools to offer an introduction to fiscal policy. We do so in three steps. First, in Section 13.1 I look at the effects of adding a flow of (stochastic) government expenditure into the model. The intuition is straightforward: assuming expenditure is paid with lump-sum taxes, output should increase given the associated (negative) income effect. The household has to pay more taxes and, given consumption and leisure being normal goods, it purchases less of both goods. Less leisure means more labor, which increases output. Consumption falls too, in order to accommodate the increase in expenditure.

In Section 13.2, I add another layer to our fiscal policy framework – a set of distortionary income taxes levied over the household's consumption and also over its capital and labor income. This regime is more interesting, as it brings substitution effects into the mix. Once the underlying logic is settled, I discuss several interesting policy structures that rely on richer tax systems and automatic stabilizers. The third (and final) pass at fiscal policy adds government debt into the mix; I share this model in Section 13.3.

I should caution that while fiscal policy contributes to business cycle fluctuations, it is not the main cause behind them. For example, a tax on labor income reduces the after-tax wage and can make the household work less (Prescott 2004 makes this point) and allows us to understand the *levels* of some variables. However, policy of this nature (taxes and expenditure) cannot account for the quarter-to-quarter movements in economic variables. King and Rebelo (1999, pp. 973–4) mention that

Shocks to fiscal and monetary policy have been long standing suspects in the search for business cycles. It is thus natural to ask what are the effects of these shocks in the standard RBC model.

Shocks to government spending cannot, by themselves, produce realistic patterns of comovement among macroeconomic variables. This result stems from the fact that an increase in government expenditures (financed with lump-sum taxes) gives rise to a negative wealth effect that induces consumption to fall at the same time that labor and output rise. Thus, if government spending were the only shock in the model, consumption would be countercyclical.

Changes in labor and capital income taxes have effects that are similar to productivity shocks. However, these taxes change infrequently making them poor candidates for sources of business cycle fluctuations.

13.1 A First Pass: Stochastic Government Expenditure

Consider an RBC model with three kinds of agents: a representative household, a representative firm, and a government. I'll discuss each of these and then present the associated model equilibrium. While I could rely on an SPP (there are no distortionary taxes yet), I will return to the notion of a competitive equilibrium in order to provide a refresher on this concept.

13.1.1 Household

The representative household chooses sequences of consumption C_t, investment X_t, and labor supply N_t to solve the UMP

$$\begin{aligned} \max \quad & \mathbb{E}_0 \sum_{t=0}^{\infty} \beta^t \left[\log C_t + \phi \log \left(1 - N_t\right) \right] & (13.1) \\ \text{subject to} \quad & C_t + X_t = r_{kt} K_t + w_t N_t - Z_t, \\ & Z_t = T_t, \\ & K_{t+1} = \left(1 - \delta\right) K_t + X_t, \\ & C_t \geq 0, \\ & K_0 \text{ given.} \end{aligned}$$

As usual, $\beta \in \left(0, 1\right)$ is a discount factor and $\phi \geq 0$ controls the relative weight of consumption and leisure. The term Z_t denotes the tax obligations of the household, which, for the time being, only include a lump-sum tax payment T_t. I assume the household behaves competitively and takes the processes for prices $\left\{r_{kt}, w_t\right\}$ and fiscal policy $\left\{T_t\right\}$ as given.

13.1.2 Firm

Each period, the representative firm rents capital and labor inputs K_{Ft} and N_{Ft} from the household to solve the PMP

$$\max \quad \Pi_t \equiv Y_t - r_{kt} K_{Ft} - w_t N_{Ft} \tag{13.2}$$

$$\text{subject to} \qquad Y_t = A_t K_{Ft}^{\alpha} N_{Ft}^{1-\alpha},$$
$$K_{Ft}, N_{Ft} \geq 0.$$

In the above, $\alpha \in (0, 1)$ denotes the capital share and A_t represents TFP. I assume the process for TFP satisfies

$$\log A_t = (1 - \rho_A) \log A_{ss} + \rho_A \log A_{t-1} + \sigma_A \varepsilon_{At}, \tag{13.3}$$

where A_0 is known, $A_{ss} = 1$, $\rho_A \in (0, 1)$ is a persistence parameter, and $\sigma_A > 0$. I assume the firm behaves competitively and takes the processes for prices $\{r_{kt}, w_t\}$ as given.

13.1.3 Government

The government is required to spend a stochastic amount of goods G_t. For simplicity, I require the government to balance its budget every period. (I will incorporate debt in Section 13.3.) The government budget constraint is thus given by

$$G_t = T_t. \tag{13.4}$$

To keep things simple, I assume total government expenditure G_t is a fraction of output, following

$$G_t = g_t Y_t, \tag{13.5}$$

where $g_t \in (0, 1)$ is a stochastic process that characterizes the government's fiscal policy. In turn, $\{g_t\}$ follows

$$g_t = (1 - \rho_g) g_{ss} + \rho_g g_{t-1} + \sigma_g \varepsilon_{gt}. \tag{13.6}$$

In equation (13.6), g_{ss} denotes the steady-state value of the government expenditure to output ratio, $\rho_g \in (0, 1)$ is a persistence parameter, and $\sigma_g > 0$. I now proceed to characterize the solution using the definition of a competitive equilibrium.

13.1.4 Equilibrium

The model's equilibrium can be defined as follows:

Definition 13.1 A competitive equilibrium consists of prices $\mathcal{P} \equiv \{r_{kt}^*, w_t^*\}$, allocations for the household $\mathcal{A}_H \equiv \{C_t^*, X_t^*, N_t^*\}$ and the firm $\mathcal{A}_F \equiv \{K_{Ft}^*, N_{Ft}^*\}$, and government policy $\{T_t^*\}$ such that, given the set of exogenous variables $\{A_t, g_t\}$,

1. The elements in $\mathcal{A}_H$ solve the household's UMP (13.1):

$$\max \qquad \mathbb{E}_0 \sum_{t=0}^{\infty} \beta^t \left[\log C_t + \phi \log (1 - N_t) \right]$$
$$\text{subject to} \qquad C_t + X_t = r_{kt} K_t + w_t N_t - Z_t,$$
$$Z_t = T_t,$$
$$K_{t+1} = (1 - \delta) K_t + X_t,$$

$$C_t \geq 0,$$
$$K_0 \text{ given.}$$

2. The elements in $\mathcal{A}_F$ solve the firm's period-by-period PMP (13.2):

$$\begin{aligned} \max \quad & \Pi_t \equiv Y_t - r_{kt}K_{Ft} - w_t N_{Ft} \\ \text{subject to} \quad & Y_t = A_t K_{Ft}^{\alpha} N_{Ft}^{1-\alpha}, \\ & K_{Ft}, N_{Ft} \geq 0. \end{aligned}$$

3. The government's policy instruments balance its period-by-period budget constraint (13.4):

$$G_t = T_t.$$

4. All markets clear:

$$K_t^* = K_{Ft}^*,$$
$$N_t^* = N_{Ft}^*.$$

As usual, I rely on Walras's Law to omit the goods market clearing condition.

13.1.5 Characterizing the Equilibrium

I start from the firm's problem; it's easy to verify that the first-order conditions with respect to capital and labor inputs are, respectively,

$$r_{kt}K_{Ft} = \alpha A_t K_{Ft}^{\alpha} N_{Ft}^{1-\alpha},$$
$$w_t N_{Ft} = (1-\alpha) A_t K_{Ft}^{\alpha} N_{Ft}^{1-\alpha}.$$

(To keep notation light, I'll refrain from using asterisks to denote equilibrium values.) I impose market clearing (i.e., set $K_t = K_{Ft}$ and $N_t = N_{Ft}$) and use that Y_t denotes aggregate output; the firm's equilibrium conditions then become

$$Y_t = A_t K_t^{\alpha} N_t^{1-\alpha}, \tag{13.7}$$
$$r_{kt}K_t = \alpha Y_t, \tag{13.8}$$
$$w_t N_t = (1-\alpha) Y_t. \tag{13.9}$$

Moving on to the household, I set up a Lagrangian function – note I've substituted for tax payments Z_t in the budget constraint:

$$\begin{aligned} \mathscr{L} = \mathbb{E}_0 \sum_{t=0}^{\infty} \beta^t \{ & \log C_t + \phi \log (1 - N_t) \\ & + \lambda_t \left[r_{kt}K_t + w_t N_t - T_t - C_t - X_t \right] + \zeta_t \left[(1-\delta) K_t + X_t - K_{t+1} \right] \}, \end{aligned}$$

where λ_t and ζ_t are Lagrange multipliers. The household's first-order conditions with respect to consumption, investment, labor supply, and next-period capital are, respectively,

$$\lambda_t = C_t^{-1}, \tag{13.10}$$

$$\lambda_t = \zeta_t, \tag{13.11}$$

$$\frac{\phi}{1 - N_t} = \lambda_t w_t, \tag{13.12}$$

$$\zeta_t = \beta \, \mathbb{E}_t \left[\lambda_{t+1} r_{k,t+1} + (1 - \delta) \zeta_{t+1} \right]. \tag{13.13}$$

I also need to add the budget constraint

$$C_t + X_t = r_{kt} K_t + w_t N_t - T_t \tag{13.14}$$

and the law of motion for capital:

$$K_{t+1} = (1 - \delta) K_t + X_t. \tag{13.15}$$

Finally, I combine the government's budget constraint with the household budget constraint, equations (13.4) and (13.14), to get

$$r_{kt} K_t + w_t N_t = C_t + X_t + G_t.$$

If I use (13.5), (13.8), and (13.9) in the equation above, I obtain the aggregate feasibility constraint, given by

$$(1 - g_t) Y_t = C_t + X_t. \tag{13.16}$$

Thus, the equilibrium in this economy is described by equations (13.5), (13.7)–(13.13), (13.15), and (13.16); I also need to add the laws of motion (13.3) and (13.6).

Remark 13.2 I keep both λ_t and ζ_t as part of the model's endogenous variables; while it is possible to substitute them out, Dynare doesn't care about the number of endogenous variables I have around. As the model is complicated enough that I can easily make an algebra mistake, I rather avoid the embarrassment and ask Dynare to do the heavy lifting for me.

13.1.6 Steady State

In the steady state, equations (13.5), (13.7)–(13.13), (13.15), and (13.16) become

$$\begin{aligned}
G &= gY, \\
Y &= K^{\alpha} N^{1-\alpha}, \\
r_k K &= \alpha Y, \\
wN &= (1 - \alpha) Y, \\
\lambda &= C^{-1}, \\
\lambda &= \zeta, \\
\phi &= \lambda w (1 - N), \\
1 &= \beta (r_k + 1 - \delta), \\
\delta K &= X, \\
(1 - g) Y &= C + X,
\end{aligned}$$

where I've already imposed the steady-state TFP value $A_{ss} = 1$. I end up with a system of 10 equations in $\{G, Y, K, N, r_k, w, \lambda, C, \zeta, X\}$.

13.2 Consumption and Income Taxes

The model I just shared served well to (re-)introduce government expenditure and to refresh the notion of a competitive equilibrium, but it is too basic for the purposes at hand. Thus, I extend it slightly by requiring the household to pay capital and labor income taxes alongside sales (i.e., consumption) taxes. Even though the model is fairly similar to that in Section 13.1, I err on the side of caution and list the household, firm, and government problems once again.

13.2.1 Household

The representative household chooses decision rules for consumption, investment, and labor supply to solve

$$\begin{aligned}
\max \quad & \mathbb{E}_0 \sum_{t=0}^{\infty} \beta^t \left[\log C_t + \phi \log \left(1 - N_t\right) \right] \qquad (13.17)\\
\text{subject to} \quad & C_t + X_t = r_{kt} K_t + w_t N_t - Z_t, \\
& Z_t = \tau_{ct} C_t + \tau_{kt} r_{kt} K_t + \tau_{nt} w_t N_t + T_t, \\
& K_{t+1} = \left(1 - \delta\right) K_t + X_t, \\
& C_t \geq 0, \\
& K_0 \text{ given.}
\end{aligned}$$

The main difference lies in the distortionary taxes that affect the household's choice of consumption, capital, and labor. I assume $\tau_{jt} \in [0, 1)$ for $j = c, k, n$. I keep the lump-sum tax T_t as a measure for balancing the government's budget in case the tax revenue exceeds expenditure (or vice versa). Finally, I assume the household behaves competitively and takes the processes for prices $\{r_{kt}, w_t\}$ and fiscal policy $\{\tau_{ct}, \tau_{kt}, \tau_{nt}, T_t\}$ as given.

13.2.2 Firm

The representative firm operates in the same form as described in Section 13.1.2, so I move along.

13.2.3 Government

The government is required to spend a stochastic amount G_t. I still assume a balanced budget every period, but the budget itself is different; it now reads

$$G_t = \tau_{ct} C_t + \tau_{kt} r_{kt} K_t + \tau_{nt} w_t N_t + T_t. \qquad (13.18)$$

Remark 13.3 I should reiterate that the processes $\{\tau_{ct}, \tau_{kt}, \tau_{nt}\}$ are taken as exogenous. If I don't make this assumption, then I need to specify *how* the government chooses these values and what goal it uses to do so – which is a much harder problem to solve. (**Ramsey problems**, which fall under the field of optimal taxation, deal with these issues.)

As in Section 13.1.3, I assume total government expenditure is a fraction of output

$$G_t = g_t Y_t,$$

where $g_t \in (0, 1)$ follows

$$g_t = (1 - \rho_g) g_{ss} + \rho_g g_{t-1} + \sigma_g \varepsilon_{gt}. \tag{13.19}$$

Note equation (13.19) is identical to (13.6) in the previous section. Finally, I need to state the laws of motion for the tax rates. To keep things simple, I assume these take the form

$$\tau_{jt} = (1 - \rho_j)\tau_{j,ss} + \rho_j \tau_{j,t-1} + \sigma_j \varepsilon_{jt},$$

where $\rho_j \in (0, 1)$ and $\sigma_j > 0$, for $j = k, n, c$, take on the usual meanings. I assume all steady-state tax rates $\tau_{j,ss}$ are known.

13.2.4 Equilibrium

The definition of a tax-distorted competitive equilibrium (TDCE) is as follows:

Definition 13.4 A TDCE consists of prices $\mathcal{P} \equiv \{r_{kt}^*, w_t^*\}$, allocations for the household $\mathcal{A}_H \equiv \{C_t^*, X_t^*, N_t^*\}$ and the firm $\mathcal{A}_F \equiv \{K_{Ft}^*, N_{Ft}^*\}$, and government policy $\{T_t^*\}$ such that, given the set of exogenous variables $\{A_t, g_t, \tau_{ct}, \tau_{kt}, \tau_{nt}\}$,

1. The elements in $\mathcal{A}_H$ solve the household's UMP (13.17):

$$\begin{aligned} \max \quad & \mathbb{E}_0 \sum_{t=0}^{\infty} \beta^t \left[\log C_t + \phi \log (1 - N_t) \right] \\ \text{subject to} \quad & C_t + X_t = r_{kt} K_t + w_t N_t - Z_t, \\ & Z_t = \tau_{ct} C_t + \tau_{kt} r_{kt} K_t + \tau_{nt} w_t N_t + T_t, \\ & K_{t+1} = (1 - \delta) K_t + X_t, \\ & C_t \geq 0, \\ & K_0 \text{ given.} \end{aligned}$$

2. The elements in $\mathcal{A}_F$ solve the firm's period-by-period PMP (13.2):

$$\begin{aligned} \max \quad & \Pi_t \equiv Y_t - r_{kt} K_{Ft} - w_t N_{Ft} \\ \text{subject to} \quad & Y_t = A_t K_{Ft}^{\alpha} N_{Ft}^{1-\alpha}, \\ & K_{Ft}, N_{Ft} \geq 0. \end{aligned}$$

3. The government's policy instruments balance its period-by-period budget constraint (13.18):

$$G_t = \tau_{ct} C_t + \tau_{kt} r_{kt} K_t + \tau_{nt} w_t N_t + T_t.$$

4. All markets clear:

$$K_t^* = K_{Ft}^*,$$
$$N_t^* = N_{Ft}^*.$$

13.2.5 Characterizing the Equilibrium

The firm's first-order conditions with respect to capital and labor inputs are, respectively,

$$Y_t = A_t K_t^{\alpha} N_t^{1-\alpha}, \quad (13.20)$$
$$r_{kt} K_t = \alpha Y_t, \quad (13.21)$$
$$w_t N_t = (1-\alpha) Y_t, \quad (13.22)$$

where I've added the definition of output to simplify the equilibrium expressions.

Similarly, I tackle the household's UMP with a Lagrangian function; this looks like

$$\mathscr{L} = \mathbb{E}_0 \sum_{t=0}^{\infty} \beta^t \{ \log C_t + \phi \log(1 - N_t) + \lambda_t [(1 - \tau_{kt}) r_{kt} K_t + (1 - \tau_{nt}) w_t N_t - T_t - (1 + \tau_{ct}) C_t - X_t] + \zeta_t [(1 - \delta) K_t + X_t - K_{t+1}] \},$$

where λ_t and ζ_t are Lagrange multipliers. The household's first-order conditions are

$$C_t: \quad C_t^{-1} - \lambda_t (1 + \tau_{ct}) = 0, \quad (13.23)$$
$$N_t: \quad -\phi (1 - N_t)^{-1} + \lambda_t (1 - \tau_{nt}) w_t = 0, \quad (13.24)$$
$$X_t: \quad -\lambda_t + \zeta_t = 0, \quad (13.25)$$
$$K_{t+1}: \quad -\zeta_t + \beta \mathbb{E}_t \lambda_{t+1} (1 + \tau_{k,t+1}) r_{k,t+1} + \beta \mathbb{E}_t \zeta_{t+1} (1 - \delta) = 0, \quad (13.26)$$
$$\lambda_t: \quad (1 - \tau_{kt}) r_{kt} K_t + (1 - \tau_{nt}) w_t N_t - T_t - (1 + \tau_{ct}) C_t - X_t = 0, \quad (13.27)$$
$$\zeta_t: \quad (1 - \delta) K_t + X_t - K_{t+1} = 0. \quad (13.28)$$

Next, I combine the government's budget constraint, equation (13.18), with the household budget constraint (13.27) and the marginal products of labor/capital equations (13.21) and (13.22). I get

$$(1 - g_t) Y_t = C_t + X_t. \quad (13.29)$$

The equilibrium in this economy is characterized by equations (13.20)–(13.26), (13.28), and (13.29), together with the laws of motion for the model's exogenous processes $\{A_t, g_t, \tau_{kt}, \tau_{nt}, \tau_{ct}\}$.

13.2.6 Steady State

I now derive the closed-form steady-state solutions for the model variables. In the steady state, the equilibrium conditions are

$$Y = K^{\alpha} N^{1-\alpha}, \quad (13.30)$$
$$r_k K = \alpha Y, \quad (13.31)$$

$$wN = (1 - \alpha)Y, \tag{13.32}$$
$$C^{-1} = \lambda(1 + \tau_c), \tag{13.33}$$
$$\phi = \lambda(1 - \tau_n)w(1 - N), \tag{13.34}$$
$$\lambda = \zeta, \tag{13.35}$$
$$\zeta = \beta\lambda(1 + \tau_k)r_k + \beta\zeta(1 - \delta), \tag{13.36}$$
$$K = (1 - \delta)K + X, \tag{13.37}$$
$$(1 - g)Y = C + X, \tag{13.38}$$
$$G = gY. \tag{13.39}$$

The solution is slightly more complicated relative to the model in Section 13.1. First, (13.35) tells me that I can substitute $\zeta = \lambda$ where needed. Using this fact, equation (13.36) gives

$$r_k = \frac{1 - \beta(1 - \delta)}{\beta(1 - \tau_k)}.$$

Substituting in (13.31), I get

$$Y = \frac{r_k}{\alpha}K \equiv \omega_Y K. \tag{13.40}$$

Since equation (13.37) tells me $X = \delta K$, I use this result and (13.40) in (13.38) to deduce

$$C = \left[(1 - g)\omega_Y - \delta\right]K \equiv \omega_C K.$$

If I use this result in (13.33), I get

$$\lambda = \frac{1}{(1 + \tau_c)\omega_C K}$$

and I can plug this into (13.34) to derive an expression for the wage rate as a function of K and N. After a bit of algebra, this expression is

$$w = \frac{\phi(1 + \tau_c)\omega_C K}{(1 - \tau_n)(1 - N)}.$$

I'm almost done: I combine this last result with (13.40) in (13.32) to get a closed-form solution for labor:

$$N = \frac{(1 - \alpha)\omega_Y(1 - \tau_n)}{\phi(1 + \tau_c)\omega_C + (1 - \alpha)\omega_Y(1 - \tau_n)}$$

and finally, use this value in (13.30) to get the closed-form solution for capital:

$$K = \frac{N}{\omega_Y^{1/(1-\alpha)}}.$$

All steady-state values follow from here. Appendix G presents Dynare code that replicates the model I just derived.

13.3 A Model with Government Debt

While instructive, the previous two models assume that the government uses lump-sum taxes to clear the budget in every period. In the real world, this is not the case: governments rely on debt to balance the budget.

This section also uses the canonical RBC model as a starting point. Relative to the previous models in this chapter, the difference is that the government now issues debt, purchased by the household, that promises to pay a real interest rate (denoted r) in the following period. In this sense, there are two main changes to the model:

1. On the household side, government debt (bonds) now compete with capital accumulation as a device for saving. As will be shown shortly, this implies that the return on both assets should be the same (in expectation).
2. On the government side, distortionary taxes still generate the tax revenue that's used to fund expenditure and debt repayment. However, care must be taken so that the total government debt doesn't explode over time; the easiest way to accomplish this goal is to make tax rates, government expenditure, and transfers a function of the total debt in the economy.

The setup of the economy is slightly repetitive, but it helps to identify the differences between a model with debt and one without. To keep things easy, I assume the household pays a single tax over total income (capital and labor), as opposed to a different tax rate for each income source. I should add that the modeling below follows Leeper and Yang (2008) and Leeper, Plante, and Traum (2010).

13.3.1 Household

The representative household chooses decision rules for consumption C_t, investment X_t, labor supply N_t, and savings S_t to solve

$$\begin{aligned} \max \quad & \mathbb{E}_0 \sum_{t=0}^{\infty} \beta^t \left[\log C_t + \phi \log \left(1 - N_t\right) \right] \qquad (13.41) \\ \text{subject to} \quad & C_t + X_t + S_t = r_{kt} K_t + w_t N_t + \left(1 + r_{t-1}\right) S_{t-1} - Z_t, \\ & Z_t = \tau_t \left(r_{kt} K_t + w_t N_t \right) - T_t, \\ & K_{t+1} = \left(1 - \delta\right) K_t + X_t, \\ & C_t, S_t \geq 0, \\ & K_0, S_0 \text{ given.} \end{aligned}$$

As usual, $\beta \in \left(0, 1\right)$ is a discount factor and $\phi \geq 0$ controls the relative weight of consumption and leisure. The term $\left(1 + r_{t-1}\right) S_{t-1}$ denotes interest and principal payments, where r_{t-1} is the risk-free rate offered by government bonds (and is also nonstochastic as it is determined in period $t - 1$). The household pays a tax rate τ_t over total income (capital and labor), and receives lump-sum transfers T_t. As usual, I assume the household behaves competitively and takes the processes for prices $\{r_{kt}, r_t, w_t\}$ and fiscal policy $\{\tau_t, T_t\}$ as given.

13.3.2 Firm

Not surprisingly, the representative firm operates in the same form as described in Section 13.1.2, so once again, I move along.

13.3.3 Government

The government issues new debt B_t and levies taxes over total income in order to finance an exogenous sequence of consumption G_t, debt repayments $r_{t-1}B_{t-1}$, and lump-sum transfers T_t. The government budget constraint, given by

$$\begin{aligned} G_t + r_{t-1}B_{t-1} &= B_t + Z_t \\ &= B_t + \tau_t\left(r_{kt}K_t + w_tN_t\right) - T_t, \end{aligned} \tag{13.42}$$

must hold in every period. In this policy arrangement, with (13.42), government debt is in charge of balancing the budget.

What is new to this arrangement is the need for policy rules that set the fiscal instruments (i.e., government expenditure, transfers, and the tax rate) as a function of the level of debt *relative to its steady-state value*. This arrangement ensures that debt does not accumulate too fast and that an equilibrium exists. If these sentences are too verbose, perhaps I should just write out what I mean. The tax rate, transfers, and expenditure are now endogenous processes and follow

$$\log\left(\frac{\tau_t}{\tau_{ss}}\right) = a_\tau \log\left(\frac{s_{t-1}^B}{s_{ss}^B}\right), \tag{13.43}$$

$$\log\left(\frac{s_t^T}{s_{ss}^T}\right) = a_T \log\left(\frac{s_{t-1}^B}{s_{ss}^B}\right), \tag{13.44}$$

$$\log\left(\frac{s_t^G}{s_{ss}^G}\right) = a_G \log\left(\frac{s_{t-1}^B}{s_{ss}^B}\right), \tag{13.45}$$

where $s_t^B \equiv B_t/Y_t$, $s_t^T \equiv T_t/Y_t$, $s_t^G \equiv G_t/Y_t$, $a_\tau \geq 0$, and $a_T, a_G \leq 0$. The key characteristic of (13.43)–(13.45) is that these policy variables are a function of the current debt-to-GDP ratio relative to its steady-state counterpart. In this sense, if the debt ratio rises relative to its steady state, taxes rise *and* transfers and government expenditure fall until the system is back to the "right" ratio of debt to GDP.

Remark 13.5 In principle, there is nothing that prevents me from adding other terms to the policy rules in (13.43)–(13.45); for example, I could devise a countercyclical (Keynesian) policy of the form

$$\log\left(\frac{\tau_t}{\tau_{ss}}\right) = a_\tau \log\left(\frac{s_{t-1}^B}{s_{ss}^B}\right) + b_\tau \log\left(\frac{Y_{t-1}}{Y_{ss}}\right),$$

$$\log\left(\frac{s_t^T}{s_{ss}^T}\right) = a_T \log\left(\frac{s_{t-1}^B}{s_{ss}^B}\right) + b_T \log\left(\frac{Y_{t-1}}{Y_{ss}}\right),$$

$$\log\left(\frac{s_t^G}{s_{ss}^G}\right) = a_G \log\left(\frac{s_{t-1}^B}{s_{ss}^B}\right) + b_G \log\left(\frac{Y_{t-1}}{Y_{ss}}\right),$$

where $a_\mathcal{T}, b_\mathcal{T} \geq 0$ and $a_T, b_T, a_G, b_G \leq 0$. The terms in these policy rules that depend on output are often called **automatic stabilizers**.

13.3.4 Equilibrium and Steady State

Relative to the definition of equilibrium in Section 13.2, the main difference lies in the addition of the policy rules (13.43)–(13.45); most of what's contained in Definition 13.4 goes through without changes. The same can be said about the derivation of closed-form steady-state values for all the model variables. (See Problem 13.6.4 for details.)

That being said, this framework allows me to introduce a very important object, the **stochastic discount factor**, which will be used frequently when working with New Keynesian models. I look at this concept next.

13.3.5 The Stochastic Discount Factor

Take the household's UMP (13.41) and consider the associated Lagrangian function. This is

$$\begin{aligned}\mathscr{L} = \mathbb{E}_0 \sum_{t=0}^{\infty} \beta^t \{ & \log C_t + \phi \log(1 - N_t) \\ & + \lambda_t [(1 - \tau_t)(r_{kt} K_t + w_t N_t) + (1 + r_{t-1}) S_{t-1} - C_t - X_t - S_t] \\ & + \zeta_t [(1 - \delta) K_t + X_t - K_{t+1}] \}.\end{aligned}$$

In particular, the first-order conditions with respect to consumption and savings are

$$\begin{aligned} C_t : \quad & C_t^{-1} - \lambda_t = 0, \\ S_t : \quad & -\lambda_t + \beta \mathbb{E}_t \lambda_{t+1} (1 + r_t) = 0. \end{aligned}$$

Intuitively, the first-order condition with respect to savings shows the tradeoff between the cost of purchasing one extra bond – a utility loss of λ_t, the marginal utility of consumption – and the (future) benefit of doing so, namely, a return of $1 + r_t$, adjusted for future marginal utility (λ_{t+1}) and discounted for present value using the discount rate β.

If I combine both expressions, I get

$$\frac{1}{C_t} = \beta(1 + r_t)\mathbb{E}_t \frac{1}{C_{t+1}}, \tag{13.46}$$

where the $1 + r_t$ term in (13.46) is outside the expectation operator since it is known at time t. Finally, I rearrange once more to

$$1 = \mathbb{E}_t \left[\beta \frac{C_t}{C_{t+1}} (1 + r_t)\right]$$

or, in its final form,

$$1 = \mathbb{E}_t [M_{t,t+1} (1 + r_t)], \tag{13.47}$$

where $M_{t,t+1} \equiv \beta C_t/C_{t+1}$. The term $M_{t,t+1}$ in (13.47) is the household's stochastic discount factor. The name follows as, in this example, the household's current valuation of $1 + r_t$ units of consumption tomorrow equals one unit of consumption today. Put differently, the household *discounts* tomorrow's payoffs by a factor equal to $M_{t,t+1}$.

More precisely, the stochastic discount factor depends on the value of β and the household's marginal utilities:

$$M_{t,t+1} = \beta \frac{\lambda_{t+1}}{\lambda_t},$$

where λ_t is the Lagrange multiplier attached to the household's budget constraint in any given UMP.

I close this section by proving the following result.

Proposition 13.6 *Define the stochastic discount factor between periods t and $t+s$ as $M_{t,t+s} \equiv \beta^s \lambda_{t+s}/\lambda_t$, where λ_t is the Lagrange multiplier attached to the household's budget constraint. Then the following statements hold true:*

1. $M_{t,t+s} = M_{t,t+1} \times M_{t+1,t+2} \times \cdots \times M_{t+s-2,t+s-1} \times M_{t+s-1,t+s}$.
2. $M_{t,t} = 1$.

Proof. To show item 1 holds, I use the definition to expand the equation:

$$\beta^s \frac{\lambda_{t+s}}{\lambda_t} = \underbrace{\left(\beta \frac{\lambda_{t+1}}{\lambda_t}\right) \times \left(\beta \frac{\lambda_{t+2}}{\lambda_{t+1}}\right) \times \cdots \times \left(\beta \frac{\lambda_{t+s-1}}{\lambda_{t+s-2}}\right) \times \left(\beta \frac{\lambda_{t+s}}{\lambda_{t+s-1}}\right)}_{s \text{ terms}}.$$

Many terms cancel out and the result follows. To prove item 2, I use the definition again, but now specialized to $s = 0$:

$$m_{t,t+0} = \beta^0 \frac{\lambda_{t+0}}{\lambda_t} = \frac{\lambda_t}{\lambda_t} = 1,$$

as needed. □

13.4 Up Next

We have now covered a suite of real frictions that allow us to work with most of the literature that relies on RBC models – and New Keynesian models too. These frictions appear again and again and, while their *particular* formulations may differ slightly, the idea remains the same.

What's left is to understand the second large class of frictions: nominal ones. Throughout Parts II and III, we have implicitly assumed that there is no money – all exchange is set in terms of goods (put differently, we have a barter economy). The real world is not like that. People trade pieces of paper in exchange for goods.

Moreover, econometricians have consistently shown that changes in the *quantity* of money (or alternatively, the nominal interest rate set by the central bank) – a nominal shock – have effects on real quantities, like output, consumption, and so on. Even though these effects are short-lived (the quantity theory of money seems to hold in the long run), RBC models with money are unable to get the kind of behavior that econometricians uncover in the real world.

The main reason why we don't see this action is because prices remain flexible throughout. Market clearing is immediate and, as a consequence, any change in the money supply is instantaneously translated into a change in prices – and market clearing does the rest.

New Keynesian economists argue that prices – and wages – are sticky in the short run. Under this logic, monetary policy (a nominal shock) is effective in changing the model's equilibrium. The precise way in which this mechanism works is too complicated to explain in one paragraph, so it will have to wait until the next chapter.

13.5 Bibliographic Notes

For a long time, models with fiscal policy – and distortionary taxes in particular – were not considered in the literature. The reason was not because of a lack of interest; rather, the computational techniques available at the time relied on the equivalence between the first and second welfare theorems. As this equivalence breaks down under distortionary taxes, the conclusion follows.

Baxter and King (1993), Braun (1994), and McGrattan (1994) are among the earliest contributions that combine RBC models and a rich fiscal structure. Fast-forward some years, and the work of Eric Leeper and coauthors stands among the most important when thinking about fiscal policy and government expenditure multipliers; some of his most relevant works are Leeper (2010), Leeper et al. (2010), Leeper, Walker, and Yang (2013), and Leeper, Traum, and Walker (2017). Some other relevant papers include McGrattan and Prescott (2005), McGrattan and Ohanian (2010), McGrattan (2012, 2023).

Finally, Chari and Kehoe (1999) remains a good reference for understanding how Ramsey problems work, and how they differ from the methodology presented in this chapter.

13.6 Problems

13.6.1 Public Goods

(Inspired by Braun 1994.) Suppose the representative household derives utility from the level of government expenditure (say, state parks). In particular, suppose the instantaneous utility function u takes the form

$$u(C, N, G) = \log C + \phi \log \left(1 - N\right) + aG,$$

where $a \in \mathbb{R}$.

1. Modify the model from Section 13.1 to incorporate this change. You don't need to redo the problem from scratch, but carefully explain the changes you would make to the equilibrium conditions above.
2. Can you think of any reason why a could be negative? *Hint*: Think beyond state parks.

13.6.2 Public Infrastructure

(Inspired by Baxter and King 1993.) Suppose the representative firm's technology benefits from government expenditure (think highways, for example). In particular, suppose the production function F takes the form

$$F(K, N, G) = K^{\alpha} N^{1-\alpha} G^{\vartheta},$$

where $\vartheta > 0$. While $\alpha + (1 - \alpha) + \vartheta > 1$, the firm still exhibits *private* constant returns to scale. How would you modify the equilibrium conditions to incorporate this change? You don't need to redo the problem from scratch, but carefully explain the changes you would make to the equilibrium conditions above.

13.6.3 A Model with Consumption and Income Taxes, Revisited

Use the Dynare code of Appendix G to comment on the equilibrium effects of taxation. Be sure to compare how the model responds when taxes are set to their steady-state values vis-à-vis when they are set to zero. Comment on what you find. *Note*: This exercise is open-ended on purpose. See how many things you can find!

13.6.4 A Model with Government Debt, Revisited

1. Define a competitive equilibrium for the model economy in Section 13.3.
2. Using your answer to part 1, characterize the competitive equilibrium.
3. Find closed-form solutions to the model's steady-state variables.
4. Implement the model in Dynare. Use parameter values $\alpha = 0.33$, $\phi = 2$, $\beta = 1/1.05$, $\delta = 0.1$, $A_{ss} = 1$, $\tau_{ss} = 0.3$, $s_{ss}^{B} = 0.376$, $s_{ss}^{G} = 0.2$, $s_{ss}^{T} = 0.0812$, $a_{\tau} = 0.15$, $a_T = -0.341$, $a_G = -0.119$, $\rho_A = 0.9$, and $\sigma_A = 0.01$.

Note that in this environment there is only one stochastic shock (TFP).

13.6.5 Automatic Stabilizers

Redo Problem 13.6.4 but now add the automatic stabilizer terms discussed in Remark 13.5. When taking the problem to Dynare, keep the same parameter values and let $b_{\tau} = 0.025$, $b_T = -0.025$, and $b_G = -0.025$. How do the model's impulse-response functions differ from those generated by Problem 13.6.4?

13.6.6 Tax Rules

Consider the three-tax model from Section 13.2 and modify it as follows: suppose the tax rates $\{\tau_{kt}, \tau_{nt}\}$ are now given by

$$\tau_{kt} = (1 - \rho_k)\tau_k + \rho_k \tau_{k,t-1} + \varepsilon_{kt} + \psi_k \varepsilon_{nt},$$
$$\tau_{nt} = (1 - \rho_n)\tau_n + \rho_n \tau_{n,t-1} + \varepsilon_{nt} + \psi_n \varepsilon_{kt},$$

where $\psi_k, \psi_n > 0$. This formulation corresponds to the case in which both tax rates move together. Include these new rules in the Dynare code of Appendix G; set $\psi_k = \psi_n = 0.85$. How do the model's impulse-response functions differ from those generated by Problem 13.6.4?

Part IV

Nominal Frictions

14 The Canonical New Keynesian Model

Learning **New Keynesian** (NK) models seems like a daunting task. (It is, sorry.) That said, this fact comes not from a difficulty of the concept itself but rather because (i) there are a lot of things going around at the same time (compared to the relatively easier models we've seen earlier in the book) and (ii) the algebra to work out a lot of results is messy to say the least.

To ease the process, I break down the full-blown model into bite-size pieces so that it's easier to concentrate on the details. First, in Section 14.1 I show how a dynamic market equilibrium under **monopolistic competition** works; this is relevant as monopolistic competition is the market structure of choice when dealing with NK models.

In a second step, in Section 14.2 I add a representative household and a government/central bank in order to build the **canonical NK model**, define an equilibrium, and characterize its solution. In the next chapter, I log-linearize the equilibrium conditions (which is far from trivial), and show how to compress everything into the three-equation system that is the workhorse of NK economics: an IS curve, a Phillips curve, and a Taylor rule.

I should add that this chapter (and the next one) borrows from Galí (2015) and McCandless (2008), though the derivations are mostly the same no matter where you look in the literature.

14.1 A Model of Monopolistic Competition

I start by laying out a monopolistically competitive market; to keep my focus on the modeling pieces that matter, I (i) assume prices are flexible, just as in the previous chapters in the book, and (ii) leave out the household and government. (I get rid of these simplifications in Section 14.2.)

Thus, consider an environment with a continuum of monopolistically competitive firms, indexed by $i \in [0, 1]$, each producing a differentiated intermediate good. The output of all firms is combined ("bundled") by a final goods firm; in turn, the final good that is produced is the one consumed by the representative household (which, again, is omitted from this section on purpose).

As a reference, a good example of a monopolistically competitive market is the market for restaurants. In any given city, there are many restaurants and each of them sells a differentiated product; moreover, each restaurant has a certain degree of market power since they are the sole producers of their own dishes.

14.1.1 The Final Goods Firm

The first agent in the market is a price-taking (competitive) final goods firm. The firm's inputs are the goods produced by the intermediate goods firms, denoted $Y_t(i)$. In turn, these inputs are combined to produce the final good Y_t, sold at the aggregate price level P_t (to be determined below).

The final goods firm chooses the mix of intermediate goods $\{Y_t(i)\}_{i\in[0,1]}$ in order to maximize its nominal profits, given by

$$P_tY_t - \int_0^1 P_t(i)Y_t(i)\,\mathrm{d}i. \tag{14.1}$$

In this expression, the term $\int P_t(i)Y_t(i)\,\mathrm{d}i$ denotes total costs; the equation just states that the final goods firm's profits equal total revenue (P_tY_t) minus total costs. In turn, the bundling technology Y_t takes the form

$$Y_t = \left[\int_0^1 Y_t(i)^{\frac{\omega-1}{\omega}}\,\mathrm{d}i\right]^{\frac{\omega}{\omega-1}}, \tag{14.2}$$

where $\omega > 1$ denotes the elasticity of substitution between intermediate goods.

14.1.2 The Intermediate Goods Firms

Each period, intermediate goods firm i chooses a labor demand $N_t(i)$ and a price $P_t(i)$ in order to maximize its nominal profits, given by

$$P_t(i)Y_t(i) - W_tN_t(i), \tag{14.3}$$

where W_t denotes the nominal wage rate, taken as given by all firms. Firm i's output follows the production technology

$$Y_t(i) = A_tN_t(i), \tag{14.4}$$

where A_t is a TFP shock (shared by all intermediate goods firms). The TFP shock follows

$$\log A_t = (1-\rho_A)A_{ss} + \rho_A \log A_{t-1} + \sigma_A\varepsilon_{At},$$

where A_{ss} is the steady state of TFP (satisfying $A_{ss} = 1$), A_0 is given, $\rho_A \in (0,1)$ is a persistence parameter, and $\sigma_A > 0$.

Remark 14.1 The canonical NK model typically abstracts from capital accumulation to ease the algebra, and I'll stick to tradition. (Adding capital back into the model is not that bad once the mechanics of the model are clearly understood.)

14.1.3 Characterization of Equilibrium

I keep things simple and characterize the equilibrium without invoking a definition. I start with the final goods firm and then move to the intermediate goods firms; Section 14.1.4 shows how aggregation works in this model.

Final Goods Firm

If I substitute the bundling technology (14.2) into equation (14.1), I get that the final goods firm's PMP is given by

$$\max_{\{Y_t(i)\}_{i\in[0,1]}} \quad P_t\left[\int_0^1 Y_t(i)^{\frac{\omega-1}{\omega}}\,\mathrm{d}i\right]^{\frac{\omega}{\omega-1}} - \int_0^1 P_t(i)Y_t(i)\,\mathrm{d}i.$$

Before embarking on a long algebra ride, remember that the final goods firm aims to find the optimal demand for each intermediate good – that is, the value $Y_t(i)$.

The first-order condition with respect to $Y_t(i)$ is

$$\left(\frac{\omega}{\omega-1}\right)P_t\left[\int_0^1 Y_t(i)^{\frac{\omega-1}{\omega}}\,\mathrm{d}i\right]^{\frac{\omega}{\omega-1}-1}\left(\frac{\omega-1}{\omega}\right)Y_t(i)^{\frac{\omega-1}{\omega}-1} - P_t(i) = 0$$

or, canceling the constant terms and working the algebra in the exponents:

$$P_t\left[\int_0^1 Y_t(i)^{\frac{\omega-1}{\omega}}\,\mathrm{d}i\right]^{\frac{1}{\omega-1}} Y_t(i)^{-\frac{1}{\omega}} - P_t(i) = 0.$$

Now solve for $Y_t(i)$:

$$Y_t(i)^{-\frac{1}{\omega}} = \frac{P_t(i)}{P_t}\left[\int_0^1 Y_t(i)^{\frac{\omega-1}{\omega}}\,\mathrm{d}i\right]^{-\frac{1}{\omega-1}}$$

and rearrange the exponents to get

$$\begin{aligned} Y_t(i) &= \left(\frac{P_t(i)}{P_t}\right)^{-\omega}\left[\int_0^1 Y_t(i)^{\frac{\omega-1}{\omega}}\,\mathrm{d}i\right]^{\frac{\omega}{\omega-1}} \\ &= \left(\frac{P_t(i)}{P_t}\right)^{-\omega} Y_t, \end{aligned} \tag{14.5}$$

where the second equality uses the definition of the bundling technology, equation (14.2). Equation (14.5) describes the final goods firm's optimal demand for intermediate good i. By inspection, the final goods firm buys more of the intermediate good as output (Y_t, here denoting aggregate demand) increases. Moreover, its demand for the intermediate good also depends on the relative price ratio $P_t(i)/P_t$; as this value enters with a negative exponent, increases in $P_t(i)$ will reduce the demand for the good.

To solve for the aggregate price level of the economy, plug equation (14.5) into (14.2) to get

$$Y_t = \left[\int_0^1 \left(\frac{P_t(i)}{P_t} \right)^{1-\omega} Y_t^{\frac{\omega-1}{\omega}} \, \mathrm{d}i \right]^{\frac{\omega}{\omega-1}}$$

$$= \left[P_t^{\omega-1} Y_t^{\frac{\omega-1}{\omega}} \int_0^1 P_t(i)^{1-\omega} \, \mathrm{d}i \right]^{\frac{\omega}{\omega-1}}$$

$$= P_t^{\omega} Y_t \left[\int_0^1 P_t(i)^{1-\omega} \, \mathrm{d}i \right]^{\frac{\omega}{\omega-1}} .$$

Canceling the Y_t terms and solving for P_t yields

$$P_t^{-\omega} = \left[\int_0^1 P_t(i)^{1-\omega} \, \mathrm{d}i \right]^{\frac{\omega}{\omega-1}} .$$

Rearrange one last time to get

$$P_t = \left[\int_0^1 P_t(i)^{1-\omega} \, \mathrm{d}i \right]^{\frac{1}{1-\omega}} , \tag{14.6}$$

which is the aggregate price level. Equation (14.6) offers a fairly intuitive result: the aggregate price level in the economy is a geometric average of all intermediate good prices, where the weight is given by the elasticity of substitution ω.

Intermediate Goods Firms

Optimization takes place over two steps: each firm has to choose (i) how much labor to hire in order to minimize costs and (ii) the price to set for its product in order to maximize profits. Since neither pricing nor labor choice have an intertemporal component, these decisions are made independently of one another.

Labor Demand To find the firm's labor demand, I exploit the dual problem of *cost minimization*: each period, the firm picks a value for the labor input $N_t(i)$ to minimize its labor costs subject to the demand for its good and its production technology. More formally, the firm solves

$$\min_{N(i)} \quad W_t N_t(i)$$

$$\text{subject to} \quad Y_t(i) = \left(\frac{P_t(i)}{P_t} \right)^{-\omega} Y_t,$$

$$Y_t(i) = A_t N_t(i),$$

where W_t is the nominal wage rate, which is the same for all intermediate goods firms. The associated Lagrangian is given by

$$\mathcal{L} = -W_t N_t(i) + \Lambda_t(i)\left[A_t N_t(i) - \left(\frac{P_t(i)}{P_t}\right)^{-\omega} Y_t\right],$$

with first-order condition

$$-W_t + \Lambda_t(i)A_t = 0.$$

The multiplier $\Lambda_t(i)$ represents firm i's (nominal) **marginal cost**: this follows as the Lagrange multiplier measures how much the objective function – which equals labor costs – increases when the production constraint is relaxed. (See Appendix H for details.)

Note the nominal wage rate and TFP values are the same for all firms; hence, marginal cost should be identical among all firms too. I can then rewrite the equation as

$$W_t = \Lambda_t A_t. \tag{14.7}$$

Equation (14.7) is an implicit labor demand equation.

Price Setting Each period, the firm chooses a price $P_t(i)$ to maximize its nominal profits, defined as total revenue minus labor costs, subject to the demand for its good and its optimal labor demand, given by equation (14.7). More formally, the firm solves

$$\max_{P_t(i)} \quad P_t(i)Y_t(i) - W_t N_t(i) \tag{14.8}$$

$$\text{subject to} \quad Y_t(i) = \left(\frac{P_t(i)}{P_t}\right)^{-\omega} Y_t,$$

$$W_t = \Lambda_t A_t.$$

To solve this problem, I first substitute the relevant expressions into (14.8):

$$\max_{P_t(i)} \quad P_t(i)\left(\frac{P_t(i)}{P_t}\right)^{-\omega} Y_t - \Lambda_t A_t N_t(i),$$

and then use (14.4), (14.5), and (14.7) in the rightmost term. I get

$$\max_{P_t(i)} \quad P_t(i)\left(\frac{P_t(i)}{P_t}\right)^{-\omega} Y_t - \Lambda_t\left(\frac{P_t(i)}{P_t}\right)^{-\omega} Y_t,$$

where the first-order condition is

$$(1-\omega)P_t(i)^{-\omega}P_t^{\omega}Y_t - (-\omega)\Lambda_t P_t(i)^{-\omega-1}P_t^{\omega}Y_t = 0.$$

Canceling terms and multiplying throughout by $P_t(i)^{1+\omega}$ gives

$$(1-\omega)P_t(i) + \omega\Lambda_t = 0$$

or, rearranging,

$$P_t(i) = \frac{\omega}{\omega-1}\Lambda_t. \tag{14.9}$$

Equation (14.9) shows the optimal price charged by the intermediate goods firm. Since $\omega > 1$, it follows that $\omega/(\omega - 1) > 1$, and thus price is higher than marginal cost (i.e., we have a **markup**, consistent with what you know about monopolistic competition). Moreover, since ω is a parameter and Λ_t is the same for all firms, it follows that all intermediate goods firms charge the same price. Note finally that if $\omega \to \infty$ (so that all intermediate goods are perfectly substitutable), then $P_t(i) \to \Lambda_t$, just as in a perfectly competitive environment.

14.1.4 Aggregation

The last task remaining is to aggregate all quantities in the market. From the discussion above, all firms charge the same price for their goods and face the same wages and TFP. Hence, it makes sense to assume a symmetric equilibrium – all intermediate goods firms behave the same.

I start from the aggregate production function, equation (14.2):

$$Y_t = \left[\int_0^1 Y_t(i)^{\frac{\omega-1}{\omega}}\,\mathrm{d}i\right]^{\frac{\omega}{\omega-1}}.$$

Since $Y_t(i)$ is the same for all firms, I treat this term as a constant. Hence,

$$Y_t = \left[Y_t(i)^{\frac{\omega-1}{\omega}}\int_0^1 \mathrm{d}i\right]^{\frac{\omega}{\omega-1}} = Y_t(i). \tag{14.10}$$

At the same time, the intermediate goods firm production function is

$$Y_t(i) = A_t N_t(i).$$

Integrating over i yields

$$\int_0^1 Y_t(i)\,\mathrm{d}i = \int_0^1 A_t N_t(i)\,\mathrm{d}i \implies Y_t(i) = A_t \int_0^1 N_t(i)\,\mathrm{d}i \implies Y_t = A_t N_t,$$

where the last step in the process uses equation (14.10) and the labor market clearing condition

$$N_t = \int_0^1 N_t(i)\,\mathrm{d}i.$$

To determine the equilibrium price level, I start from equation (14.6). Since all firms charge the same price, it follows that

$$P_t = \left[P_t(i)^{1-\omega}\int_0^1 \mathrm{d}i\right]^{\frac{1}{1-\omega}}$$

and this fact implies that the aggregate price level is given by

$$P_t = P_t(i), \tag{14.11}$$

where each intermediate firm's price is

$$P_t(i) = \frac{\omega}{\omega - 1}\Lambda_t. \tag{14.12}$$

Labor demand is characterized by

$$W_t = \Lambda_t A_t. \tag{14.13}$$

Dividing (14.13) throughout by P_t and using (14.9) yields an expression for the real wage W_t/P_t, namely,

$$\frac{W_t}{P_t} = \frac{\omega - 1}{\omega}A_t. \tag{14.14}$$

Given $(\omega - 1)/\omega < 1$, it follows that real wages are less than the marginal product of labor (i.e., A_t).

14.1.5 Up Next

This process concludes the first pass at a monopolistically competitive market. The canonical NK model, however, adds sticky prices to this environment. Why does this change make a big difference? Because the intermediate goods firm must now take into account the fact that its own price need not adjust *even though all other prices in the economy keep changing*. Put differently, conditional on being able to adjust its price, a firm's pricing decision depends not only on current conditions but also on those that it will face in the future.

14.2 The Canonical New Keynesian Model

I use the work from the previous section to build the canonical NK model. As a reminder, the model consists of a representative household, a final goods firm, a continuum of intermediate goods firms – indexed by $i \in [0, 1]$ – and a government/central bank. Following tradition, the model operates in a *cashless* environment (see Woodford 2003); money serves only as a unit of account and monetary policy works through the (gross) nominal interest rate on government bonds R_t, set by the central bank according to a Taylor rule.

14.2.1 Household

The representative household chooses sequences of consumption C_t, hours worked N_t, and savings S_t to solve

$$\begin{aligned} \max \quad & \mathbb{E}_0 \sum_{t=0}^{\infty} \beta^t \left(\frac{C_t^{1-\eta}}{1-\eta} - \phi \frac{N_t^{1+\chi}}{1+\chi} \right) \\ \text{subject to} \quad & P_t C_t + S_t = W_t N_t + R_{t-1} S_{t-1} + D_t - P_t T_t. \end{aligned}$$

I assume the period-t price of bonds is 1 and their associated *gross* nominal rate of return is R_t, whose value is known at the time the bonds are purchased. The term D_t denotes nominal profits, in turn equal to the sum of profits coming from the final goods and intermediate goods firms. Finally, the term $P_t T_t$ denotes nominal lump-sum taxes.

14.2.2 Final Goods Firm

The final goods firm looks just as in Section 14.1.1, so I move along.

14.2.3 Intermediate Goods Firms

The intermediate goods firm problem in the canonical NK model looks similar, but is not identical, to that in Section 14.1.2.

The difference lies in the pricing rule governing intermediate firms' decisions, which I now discuss. Under a **Calvo rule** (Calvo 1983), a measure $1-\theta$ of firms are randomly selected each period; these firms – and only these firms – are allowed to adjust their price in the period, which I denote by $P_t^*(i)$. ("Reset their price" is also used in the literature.) The remaining firms set their prices according to a (predetermined) rule of thumb; to keep things simple, I assume these firms keep the same prices as in the previous period, so that the price they offer satisfies

$$P_t(i) = P_{t-1}(i).$$

Thus, while a firm's period-t profits are still given by (14.3), namely,

$$P_t(i)Y_t(i) - W_t N_t(i),$$

the value of $P_t(i)$ need not change every period. More precisely, a Calvo pricing structure implies that each firm keeps the price from last period with probability θ. In particular, once set at period t, the firm's price will be the same in period $t+1$ with probability θ, in period $t+2$ with probability θ^2, and so on. Hence, an intermediate goods firm needs to take this feature into account when choosing its optimal price.

Other than the Calvo rule, the production technology (14.4) and TFP process are the same as in Section 14.1.2.

14.2.4 Government/Central Bank

The government in this model borrows using one-period bonds and uses lump-sum taxes and new bond issuances to pay its debts. The budget constraint is given by

$$R_{t-1}B_{t-1} = B_t + P_t T_t.$$

The central bank sets the gross nominal interest rate R_t by following a **Taylor rule** of the form

$$R_t = R_{ss}\left(\frac{\Pi_t}{\Pi_{ss}}\right)^{\nu_\pi}\left(\frac{Y_t}{Y_{ss}}\right)^{\nu_y}, \tag{14.15}$$

where Π_t denotes the *gross* inflation rate and parameters $\nu_\pi, \nu_y > 0$ characterize the responsiveness of the nominal interest rate to deviations of inflation and output with respect to their steady-state values.

14.2.5 Equilibrium

An equilibrium is sort of easy to figure out by now.

Definition 14.2 A competitive equilibrium consists of prices $\mathcal{P} \equiv \{R_t, W_t, P_t\}$, allocations for the household $\mathcal{A}_H \equiv \{C_t, N_t, S_t\}$, the final goods firm $\mathcal{A}_F \equiv \{Y_t(i)\}$, each intermediate goods firm $\mathcal{A}_I(i) = \{P_t(i), N_t(i)\}$, and government policy $\{T_t\}$ such that, given an exogenous process for A_t,

1. For the representative household, the elements in $\mathcal{A}_H$ solve its UMP:

$$\begin{aligned} \max \quad & \mathbb{E}_0 \sum_{t=0}^{\infty} \beta^t \left(\frac{C_t^{1-\eta}}{1-\eta} - \phi \frac{N_t^{1+\chi}}{1+\chi} \right) \\ \text{subject to} \quad & P_t C_t + S_t = W_t N_t + R_{t-1} S_{t-1} + D_t - P_t T_t. \end{aligned}$$

2. For the final goods firm, the elements in $\mathcal{A}_F$ solve its PMP:

$$\begin{aligned} \max \quad & P_t Y_t - \int_0^1 P_t(i) Y_t(i) \, di \\ \text{subject to} \quad & Y_t = \left[\int_0^1 Y_t(i)^{\frac{\omega-1}{\omega}} \, di \right]^{\frac{\omega}{\omega-1}}. \end{aligned}$$

3. For each intermediate goods firm, the elements in $\mathcal{A}_I(i)$ solve its PMP:

$$\begin{aligned} \max \quad & P_t(i) Y_t(i) - W_t N_t(i) \\ \text{subject to} \quad & Y_t(i) = A_t N_t(i). \end{aligned}$$

4. The government's policy satisfies its budget constraint:

$$R_{t-1} B_{t-1} = B_t + P_t T_t$$

and sets the nominal interest rate via the Taylor rule

$$R_t = R_{ss} \left(\frac{\Pi_t}{\Pi_{ss}} \right)^{\nu_\pi} \left(\frac{Y_t}{Y_{ss}} \right)^{\nu_y}.$$

5. All markets clear:

$$\begin{aligned} S_t &= B_t, \\ N_t &= \int_0^1 N_t(i) \, di. \end{aligned}$$

(Note I exclude the goods market clearing condition because of Walras's Law.)

14.2.6 Characterization of Equilibrium

Household

The household's first-order conditions (see Problem 14.5.2) are given by

$$\begin{aligned} \frac{W_t}{P_t} &= \phi C_t^{\eta} N_t^{\chi}, \\ 1 &= \beta R_t \mathbb{E}_t \left[\left(\frac{C_{t+1}}{C_t} \right)^{-\eta} \frac{P_t}{P_{t+1}} \right], \\ P_t C_t + S_t &= W_t N_t + R_{t-1} S_{t-1} + D_t - P_t T_t, \end{aligned} \tag{14.16}$$

where the first equation can be loosely interpreted as a labor supply condition, the second one as a savings supply function.

Final Goods Firm

The relevant equations are the bundling technology, the demand function for intermediate goods, and the aggregate price-level equation, reproduced below for convenience:

$$Y_t = \left[\int_0^1 Y_t(i)^{\frac{\omega-1}{\omega}} \mathrm{d}i \right]^{\frac{\omega}{\omega-1}}, \tag{14.17}$$

$$Y_t(i) = \left(\frac{P_t(i)}{P_t} \right)^{-\omega} Y_t, \tag{14.18}$$

$$P_t = \left[\int_0^1 P_t(i)^{1-\omega} \mathrm{d}i \right]^{\frac{1}{1-\omega}}. \tag{14.19}$$

Equations (14.7)–(14.19) are identical to (14.2), (14.5), and (14.6).

Intermediate Goods Firms

Okay, it's time for good news and bad news.

Labor Demand On the good news end, as the intermediate goods firms' production technology and cost minimization problem have not changed, the relevant first-order condition that characterizes labor demand is still

$$W_t = \Lambda_t A_t. \tag{14.20}$$

Equation (14.20) is the same as (14.7).

Price Setting, Part I On to the bad news: the price-setting problem is hard. Why? Because of the Calvo pricing structure.

To set ideas, consider an intermediate goods firm that is able to reset its price in the current period. I assume the firm chooses the price that maximizes the (expected) present value of its profit flows, discounted with the household's stochastic discount factor $M_{t,t+s}$. More precisely,

Proposition 14.3 *The intermediate goods firm's price-setting problem takes the form*

$$\max_{P_t(i)} \quad \mathbb{E}_t \sum_{s=0}^{\infty} \theta^s M_{t,t+s} \left[\frac{P_t(i)}{P_{t+s}} \left(\frac{P_t(i)}{P_{t+s}} \right)^{-\omega} Y_{t+s} - mc_{t+s} \left(\frac{P_t(i)}{P_{t+s}} \right)^{-\omega} Y_{t+s} \right]. \tag{14.21}$$

Staring at something like equation (14.21) for the first time can be intimidating, so instead of a formal proof I offer a walk-through that explains how equation (14.21) comes to be.

Some preliminaries: recall that the intermediate goods firm no longer maximizes profits per period; the fact that its price need not be optimal (because of price stickiness) prevents it from doing so. Instead, the firm is better off by maximizing the *present discounted value* of its stream of future profits; as to which is the right discount rate, the household's stochastic discount factor $M_{t,t+s}$, adjusted for the probability of keeping the same price (i.e., θ), seems like an appropriate choice.

As a first step, let's define the firm's nominal profits in period $t+s$, $s \geq 0$; these are given by

$$P_{t+s}(i) Y_{t+s}(i) - W_{t+s} N_{t+s}(i).$$

Now, the Calvo rule implies that $P_{t+s}(i) = P_t(i)$ for as long as the firm cannot reset its price. Hence, if the firm has the option to reset its price in the current period, it will choose the value $P_t(i)$ that maximizes the expected present value of its profit flows, which equals

$$\mathbb{E}_t \{ \theta^0 M_{t,t+0} [P_t(i) Y_t(i) - W_t N_t(i)] + \theta^1 M_{t,t+1} [P_t(i) Y_{t+1}(i) - W_{t+1} N_{t+1}(i)] \\ + \theta^2 M_{t,t+2} [P_t(i) Y_{t+2}(i) - W_{t+2} N_{t+2}(i)] + \cdots \}.$$

Note (i) the firm's own price $P_t(i)$ remains constant over time and (ii) the expression above represents the present discounted value of *nominal* profits. To put this expression in real terms, I divide the total revenue and total cost terms by the aggregate price level in that period. Hence, the present value of the expression now reads

$$\mathbb{E}_t \left\{ \theta^0 M_{t,t+0} \left[\frac{P_t(i)}{P_t} Y_t(i) - \frac{W_t}{P_t} N_t(i) \right] + \theta^1 M_{t,t+1} \left[\frac{P_t(i)}{P_{t+1}} Y_{t+1}(i) - \frac{W_{t+1}}{P_{t+1}} N_{t+1}(i) \right] \right. \\ \left. + \theta^2 M_{t,t+2} \left[\frac{P_t(i)}{P_{t+2}} Y_{t+2}(i) - \frac{W_{t+2}}{P_{t+2}} N_{t+2}(i) \right] + \cdots \right\}.$$

Next, I use that $W_t = \Lambda_t A_t$ for all t (remember that the firm's wage-setting problem has not changed) and the definition of the intermediate goods firm's output $Y_t(i) = A_t N_t(i)$ to get

$$\mathbb{E}_t\Bigg\{\theta^0 M_{t,t+0}\left[\frac{P_t(i)}{P_t}Y_t(i)-\frac{\Lambda_t}{P_t}Y_t(i)\right]+\theta^1 M_{t,t+1}\left[\frac{P_t(i)}{P_{t+1}}Y_{t+1}(i)-\frac{\Lambda_{t+1}}{P_{t+1}}Y_{t+1}(i)\right]$$
$$+\theta^2 M_{t,t+2}\left[\frac{P_t(i)}{P_{t+2}}Y_{t+2}(i)-\frac{\Lambda_{t+2}}{P_{t+2}}Y_{t+2}(i)\right]+\cdots\Bigg\}.$$

The last step requires me to substitute the demand for each intermediate good, equation (14.18). I get

$$\mathbb{E}_t\Bigg\{\theta^0 M_{t,t+0}\left[\frac{P_t(i)}{P_t}\left(\frac{P_t(i)}{P_t}\right)^{-\omega}Y_t-\frac{\Lambda_t}{P_t}\left(\frac{P_t(i)}{P_t}\right)^{-\omega}Y_t\right]$$
$$+\theta^1 M_{t,t+1}\left[\frac{P_t(i)}{P_{t+1}}\left(\frac{P_t(i)}{P_{t+1}}\right)^{-\omega}Y_{t+1}-\frac{\Lambda_{t+1}}{P_{t+1}}\left(\frac{P_t(i)}{P_{t+1}}\right)^{-\omega}Y_{t+1}\right]$$
$$+\theta^2 M_{t,t+2}\left[\frac{P_t(i)}{P_{t+2}}\left(\frac{P_t(i)}{P_{t+2}}\right)^{-\omega}Y_{t+2}-\frac{\Lambda_{t+2}}{P_{t+2}}\left(\frac{P_t(i)}{P_{t+2}}\right)^{-\omega}Y_{t+2}\right]+\cdots\Bigg\}.$$

Putting the expression above into a sum operator and letting $mc_{t+s}=\Lambda_{t+s}/P_{t+s}$ denote *real* marginal costs, I obtain equation (14.21), as claimed.

Price Setting, Part II Before taking derivatives, I rearrange the terms in the intermediate goods firm's objective function by getting rid of the fractions. A bit of algebra shows that equation (14.21),

$$\max_{P_t(i)}\quad \mathbb{E}_t\sum_{s=0}^{\infty}\theta^s M_{t,t+s}\left[\frac{P_t(i)}{P_{t+s}}\left(\frac{P_t(i)}{P_{t+s}}\right)^{-\omega}Y_{t+s}-mc_{t+s}\left(\frac{P_t(i)}{P_{t+s}}\right)^{-\omega}Y_{t+s}\right],$$

is equivalent to

$$\max_{P_t(i)}\quad \mathbb{E}_t\sum_{s=0}^{\infty}\theta^s M_{t,t+s}\left[P_t(i)^{1-\omega}P_{t+s}^{\omega-1}Y_{t+s}-mc_{t+s}P_t(i)^{-\omega}P_{t+s}^{\omega}Y_{t+s}\right]. \tag{14.22}$$

At this point I take the derivative of (14.22) with respect to the firm's price, $P_t(i)$; the first-order condition equals

$$\mathbb{E}_t\sum_{s=0}^{\infty}\theta^s M_{t,t+s}\left[(1-\omega)P_t(i)^{-\omega}P_{t+s}^{\omega-1}Y_{t+s}-(-\omega)mc_{t+s}P_t(i)^{-\omega-1}P_{t+s}^{\omega}Y_{t+s}\right]=0.$$

There are several terms that don't depend on s; taking them out of the sum operator, I get

$$(1-\omega)P_t(i)^{-\omega}\mathbb{E}_t\sum_{s=0}^{\infty}\theta^s M_{t,t+s}P_{t+s}^{\omega-1}Y_{t+s}=-\omega P_t(i)^{-\omega-1}\mathbb{E}_t\sum_{s=0}^{\infty}\theta^s M_{t,t+s}mc_{t+s}P_{t+s}^{\omega}Y_{t+s}.$$

Finally, solve for $P_t(i)=P_t^*(i)$ to obtain the expression for the optimal reset price

$$P_t^*(i)=\frac{\omega}{\omega-1}\frac{\mathbb{E}_t\sum_{s=0}^{\infty}\theta^s M_{t,t+s}mc_{t+s}P_{t+s}^{\omega}Y_{t+s}}{\mathbb{E}_t\sum_{s=0}^{\infty}\theta^s M_{t,t+s}P_{t+s}^{\omega-1}Y_{t+s}}. \tag{14.23}$$

Here, $P_t^*(i)$ is the price that firm i sets when it gets the chance to adjust its price. The nature of the Calvo pricing structure implies that all firms that can reset their price will pick the same value; after all, they share the same probability of resetting their price and face the same future prices, wages, and TFP. Hence, I set $P_t^*(i) = P_t^*$ as the optimal reset price.

Government/Central Bank

The only thing that's needed is for the government's budget constraint

$$R_{t-1}B_{t-1} = B_t + P_tT_t$$

to hold, and for the central bank to set interest rates following the Taylor rule (14.15).

14.2.7 Aggregation, Market Clearing, and Stationarity

I'm not done yet, as I need to take care of several issues before moving on. Obviously, both aggregation and market clearing must happen. But looking closely at the model's equilibrium conditions, there are still prices within; as these trend over time, I also must get rid of this trend and make all equations stationary.

At this point, it's convenient to list the model's equilibrium conditions, which can be divided into five groups. First, the conditions coming from household optimization:

$$\frac{W_t}{P_t} = \phi C_t^{\eta} N_t^{\chi}, \tag{14.24}$$

$$1 = R_t \mathbb{E}_t \left(M_{t,t+1} \frac{P_t}{P_{t+1}} \right), \tag{14.25}$$

$$P_tC_t + S_t = W_tN_t + R_{t-1}S_{t-1} + D_t - P_tT_t, \tag{14.26}$$

$$M_{t-1,t} = \beta \left(\frac{C_t}{C_{t-1}} \right)^{-\eta}, \tag{14.27}$$

where equation (14.24) can be taken as a labor supply condition. Equation (14.25) is a savings supply function equivalent to (14.16), but now including the household's stochastic discount factor, equation (14.27), as a model variable. Equation (14.26) is the household's budget constraint. The second group includes the conditions coming from the final goods firm:

$$Y_t = \left[\int_0^1 Y_t(i)^{\frac{\omega-1}{\omega}} \, di \right]^{\frac{\omega}{\omega-1}}, \tag{14.28}$$

$$Y_t(i) = \left(\frac{P_t(i)}{P_t} \right)^{-\omega} Y_t, \tag{14.29}$$

$$P_t = \left[\int_0^1 P_t(i)^{1-\omega} \, di \right]^{\frac{1}{1-\omega}}. \tag{14.30}$$

In the above, (14.28) represents the bundling technology, (14.29) is the demand for intermediate goods, and (14.30) is the aggregate price level equation. In the third group, I add those from the intermediate goods firms:

$$Y_t(i) = A_t N_t(i), \tag{14.31}$$

$$W_t = P_t mc_t A_t, \tag{14.32}$$

$$P_t^* = \frac{\omega}{\omega - 1} \frac{\mathbb{E}_t \sum_{s=0}^{\infty} \theta^s M_{t,t+s} mc_{t+s} P_{t+s}^{\omega} Y_{t+s}}{\mathbb{E}_t \sum_{s=0}^{\infty} \theta^s M_{t,t+s} P_{t+s}^{\omega-1} Y_{t+s}}, \tag{14.33}$$

where (14.31) is the intermediate goods production function, (14.32) is a labor demand equation, and (14.33) is the optimal reset price; note (14.32) follows as $\Lambda_t / P_t = mc_t$. Fourth, add the government and central bank constraints

$$R_{t-1} B_{t-1} = B_t + P_t T_t, \tag{14.34}$$

$$R_t = R_{ss} \left(\frac{\Pi_t}{\Pi_{ss}} \right)^{\nu_\pi} \left(\frac{Y_t}{Y_{ss}} \right)^{\nu_y}, \tag{14.35}$$

where (14.34) is the government budget constraint and (14.35) is the Taylor rule. Finally, add the market clearing conditions

$$S_t = B_t, \tag{14.36}$$

$$N_t = \int_0^1 N_t(i)\, \mathrm{d}i, \tag{14.37}$$

where, to reiterate, I use Walras's Law to skip the market clearing condition on the goods market. (But see below.)

I now proceed to reduce the dimension of the system.

Goods Market Clearing

Moving on, I impose the bond market clearing condition (14.36) on the government budget constraint (14.34); then, combining with the household's budget (14.26), I get

$$P_t C_t + B_t = W_t N_t + R_{t-1} B_{t-1} + D_t - \left(R_{t-1} B_{t-1} - B_t \right),$$

which simplifies to

$$P_t C_t = W_t N_t + D_t. \tag{14.38}$$

I still need to work out the firm profits term D_t. As mentioned earlier, these profits come from the final goods firm and the intermediate goods firms. More precisely,

$$D_t = \underbrace{P_t Y_t - \int_0^1 P_t(i) Y_t(i)\, \mathrm{d}i}_{\text{Final goods firm}} + \underbrace{\int_0^1 \left[P_t(i) Y_t(i) - W_t N_t(i) \right] \mathrm{d}i}_{\text{Intermediate goods firms}}.$$

I rework this expression as

$$
\begin{aligned}
D_t &= P_tY_t - \int_0^1 P_t(i)Y_t(i)\,\mathrm{d}i + \int_0^1 P_t(i)Y_t(i)\,\mathrm{d}i - \int_0^1 W_tN_t(i)\,\mathrm{d}i \\
&= P_tY_t - W_t\int_0^1 N_t(i)\,\mathrm{d}i \\
&= P_tY_t - W_tN_t,
\end{aligned}
$$

where the last equality follows the labor market clearing condition, equation (14.37). Using this expression in the simplified budget constraint, equation (14.38), gives

$$P_tC_t = W_tN_t + \left(P_tY_t - W_tN_t\right) = P_tY_t,$$

or

$$C_t = Y_t. \tag{14.39}$$

Equation (14.39) is the goods market clearing condition.

Price-Level Equation

I now revise the aggregate price-level equation (14.30) by incorporating some of the results derived above. As a refresher, the Calvo rule implies that every period, a fraction $1-\theta$ of firms gets to change their prices to P_t^*, while the rest must charge the same price as in the previous period. Hence, the aggregate price level is a combination of both firms' prices, namely,

$$P_t^{1-\omega} = \int_0^{1-\theta} \left(P_t^*\right)^{1-\omega}\mathrm{d}i + \int_{1-\theta}^1 P_{t-1}^{1-\omega}(i)\,\mathrm{d}i.$$

Since P_t^* is a constant (the optimal price is identical for all firms that can reset in period t), the integral poses no problem. It seems, however, that the last term on the right-hand side of the equation will be an issue, as it still depends on the particular firm i's price from last period. Fortunately, the Calvo pricing structure takes care of this matter. Since the set of firms that keep their prices is randomly selected each period, the average price from the last period is equivalent to the share θ of all firms that kept their old price. More precisely,

$$\int_{1-\theta}^1 P_{t-1}^{1-\omega}(i)\,\mathrm{d}i = \theta\int_0^1 P_{t-1}(i)^{1-\omega}\,\mathrm{d}i = \theta P_{t-1}^{1-\omega},$$

where the last equality follows from the fact that the integral of the firm's prices in $t-1$ is just P_{t-1}. Hence, I can rewrite the aggregate price level as

$$P_t^{1-\omega} = \left(1-\theta\right)\left(P_t^*\right)^{1-\omega} + \theta P_{t-1}^{1-\omega}. \tag{14.40}$$

Equation (14.40) shows that the aggregate price level is a weighted average of reset and sticky prices.

Price Dispersion

Surprisingly, the Calvo pricing structure introduces a distortion over the aggregate production function, known as **price dispersion**. To see why this is the case, start from the intermediate goods firm's production function, equation (14.31), and note that

$$Y_t(i) = A_t N_t(i) \iff N_t(i) = \frac{Y_t(i)}{A_t}.$$

If I integrate over i, I get

$$\int_0^1 N_t(i)\,\mathrm{d}i = \int_0^1 \frac{Y_t(i)}{A_t}\,\mathrm{d}i.$$

From here, note the left side of the equation equals N_t per the labor market clearing condition (14.37). In addition, I can use the demand for intermediate goods coming out of the final goods firm, equation (14.29), to substitute for $Y_t(i)$; this process results in

$$N_t = \int_0^1 \left(\frac{P_t(i)}{P_t}\right)^{-\omega} \frac{Y_t}{A_t}\,\mathrm{d}i.$$

Neither output Y_t nor TFP A_t depends on i, so they can be taken out of the integrals. The expression becomes

$$N_t = \frac{Y_t}{A_t}\int_0^1 \left(\frac{P_t(i)}{P_t}\right)^{-\omega} \mathrm{d}i.$$

Rearranging, I find that the aggregate production function takes the form

$$Y_t = \left(\frac{A_t}{\Delta_t}\right) N_t, \tag{14.41}$$

where Δ_t in (14.41) is a measure of price dispersion, given by

$$\Delta_t = \int_0^1 \left(\frac{P_t(i)}{P_t}\right)^{-\omega} \mathrm{d}i. \tag{14.42}$$

As can be inferred from (14.42), the price dispersion measure Δ_t has a lower bound of 1, which occurs when prices are flexible; indeed, when prices are not sticky, equation (14.11) shows $P_t(i) = P_t$ and so $\Delta_t = 1$. When prices are sticky, however, $\Delta_t > 1$ and so $A_t/\Delta_t < A_t$, just as if a TFP shock had occurred. As is obvious from the expressions above, this distortion vanishes when log-linearizing the model around a zero-inflation steady state. (But not after linearization!) As most of the literature opts to log-linearize, I choose to leave this notion alone, but note that any approximation that is *not* a log-linear one should consider this term.

The Optimal Reset Price

In Section 8.5 I asked whether log-linearization was needed at all; one of the arguments *in favor* of learning this tool was the price reset equation (14.33). Indeed, this expression is the ratio of two infinite sums and, as a consequence, is impossible to put into Dynare – as currently written.

That said, there *is* a way to implement the price reset equation without the need to log-linearize – it just takes some extra steps. While most (if not all) the New Keynesian literature uses log-linearized expressions, I share this alternative derivation that allows me to put the system into Dynare without requiring a log-linearization step.

The key is transforming this ratio of infinite sums into a ratio of *recursive* expressions that are equivalent to the infinite sums. To see how this is achieved, start from equation (14.33), which I can rewrite as

$$P_t^* = \frac{\omega}{\omega - 1} \frac{NUM_t}{DEN_t},$$

where (very creatively) I use NUM_t and DEN_t to denote the numerator and denominator of the fraction. The task ahead is to show that both NUM_t and DEN_t have a recursive structure.

I start from NUM_t; if I play with the terms inside the summation operator, I get that

$$\begin{aligned} NUM_t &= \mathbb{E}_t \sum_{s=0}^{\infty} \theta^s M_{t,t+s} mc_{t+s} P_{t+s}^{\omega} Y_{t+s} \\ &= \theta^0 M_{t,t+0} mc_t P_t^{\omega} Y_t + \mathbb{E}_t \sum_{s=1}^{\infty} \theta^s M_{t,t+s} mc_{t+s} P_{t+s}^{\omega} Y_{t+s} \\ &= mc_t P_t^{\omega} Y_t + \mathbb{E}_t \sum_{s=1}^{\infty} \theta^s M_{t,t+s} mc_{t+s} P_{t+s}^{\omega} Y_{t+s}, \end{aligned}$$

where the second equality just extracts the first term (for $s = 0$) from the sum operator and the third equality uses that $\theta^0 = 1$ and $M_{t,t} = 1$ per Proposition 13.6. Note, however, that I can work the last term on the right-hand side to read

$$\begin{aligned} \mathbb{E}_t \sum_{s=1}^{\infty} \theta^s M_{t,t+s} mc_{t+s} P_{t+s}^{\omega} Y_{t+s} &= \mathbb{E}_t \sum_{s=1}^{\infty} \theta^s M_{t,t+1} M_{t+1,t+s} mc_{t+s} P_{t+s}^{\omega} Y_{t+s} \\ &= \theta\, \mathbb{E}_t \sum_{s=1}^{\infty} \theta^{s-1} M_{t,t+1} M_{t+1,t+s} mc_{t+s} P_{t+s}^{\omega} Y_{t+s} \\ &= \theta\, \mathbb{E}_t \sum_{s=0}^{\infty} \theta^s M_{t,t+1} M_{t+1,t+1+s} mc_{t+1+s} P_{t+1+s}^{\omega} Y_{t+1+s}. \end{aligned} \tag{14.43}$$

What happened? The first equality uses the properties of the stochastic discount factor (again, Proposition 13.6) to write $M_{t,t+s} = M_{t,t+1} M_{t+1,t+s}$. The second equality factors out θ from the sum operator, and the third equality relabels all the summation indices so that s starts at 0, not 1. For the next-to-last step, I rely on the following result, the **Law of Iterated Expectations** (LIE), which I state without proof (this version of the LIE is borrowed from Sargent and Ljungqvist 2018):

Proposition 14.4 *For any random variable z and two information sets J, I with $J \subset I$, $\mathbb{E}\left[\mathbb{E}(z|I)|J\right] = \mathbb{E}(z|J)$.*

If this result is a bit over the top, here's an analogy: *tomorrow's* forecast of the weather for the following day is just *today's* forecast of the weather two days ahead. In a more macroeconomic setting, the LIE says that $\mathbb{E}_t\left[\mathbb{E}_{t+1}\left(x_{t+2}\right)\right] = \mathbb{E}_t x_{t+2}$.

Why do I care about this result? Because Proposition 14.4 allows me to rewrite equation (14.43) as

$$\theta\,\mathbb{E}_t\mathbb{E}_{t+1}\sum_{s=0}^{\infty}\theta^s M_{t,t+1}M_{t+1,t+1+s}mc_{t+1+s}P_{t+1+s}^{\omega}Y_{t+1+s}$$

and, given that $M_{t,t+1}$ is known in period $t+1$, I can rewrite this expression as

$$\theta\,\mathbb{E}_t M_{t,t+1}\mathbb{E}_{t+1}\sum_{s=0}^{\infty}\theta^s M_{t+1,t+1+s}mc_{t+1+s}P_{t+1+s}^{\omega}Y_{t+1+s}.$$

Putting everything together, I note that

$$NUM_t = mc_t P_t^{\omega} Y_t + \theta\,\mathbb{E}_t M_{t,t+1}\underbrace{\mathbb{E}_{t+1}\sum_{s=0}^{\infty}\theta^s M_{t+1,t+1+s}mc_{t+1+s}P_{t+1+s}^{\omega}Y_{t+1+s}}_{=NUM_{t+1}},$$

and so I can express NUM_t recursively as

$$NUM_t = mc_t P_t^{\omega} Y_t + \theta\,\mathbb{E}_t M_{t,t+1} NUM_{t+1}.$$

Following a similar logic (see Problem 14.5.4), I can also show that

$$DEN_t = P_t^{\omega-1} Y_t + \theta\,\mathbb{E}_t M_{t,t+1} DEN_{t+1}.$$

Hence, the price reset equation (14.33) can be replaced by the following three equations:

$$P_t^* = \frac{\omega}{\omega-1}\frac{NUM_t}{DEN_t}, \tag{14.44}$$

$$NUM_t = mc_t P_t^{\omega} Y_t + \theta\,\mathbb{E}_t M_{t,t+1} NUM_{t+1}, \tag{14.45}$$

$$DEN_t = P_t^{\omega-1} Y_t + \theta\,\mathbb{E}_t M_{t,t+1} DEN_{t+1}. \tag{14.46}$$

Note how (14.45) and (14.46) allow for a recursive setup of the optimal reset price (14.44).

Imposing Stationarity

At this time, it's convenient to list the equilibrium conditions of the model after all the substitutions above have been made:

$$\frac{W_t}{P_t} = \phi C_t^{\eta} N_t^{\chi}, \tag{14.47}$$

$$1 = R_t \mathbb{E}_t \left(M_{t,t+1} \frac{P_t}{P_{t+1}} \right), \tag{14.48}$$

$$M_{t-1,t} = \beta \left(\frac{C_t}{C_{t-1}} \right)^{-\eta}, \tag{14.49}$$

$$W_t = P_t mc_t A_t, \tag{14.50}$$

$$R_{t-1} B_{t-1} = B_t + P_t T_t, \tag{14.51}$$

$$R_t = R_{ss} \left(\frac{\Pi_t}{\Pi_{ss}} \right)^{\nu_\pi} \left(\frac{Y_t}{Y_{ss}} \right)^{\nu_y}, \tag{14.52}$$

$$C_t = Y_t, \tag{14.53}$$

$$P_t^{1-\omega} = (1-\theta) \left(P_t^* \right)^{1-\omega} + \theta P_{t-1}^{1-\omega}, \tag{14.54}$$

$$Y_t = \left(\frac{A_t}{\Delta_t} \right) N_t, \tag{14.55}$$

$$\Delta_t = \int_0^1 \left(\frac{P_t(i)}{P_t} \right)^{-\omega} \mathrm{d}i, \tag{14.56}$$

$$P_t^* = \frac{\omega}{\omega - 1} \frac{NUM_t}{DEN_t}, \tag{14.57}$$

$$NUM_t = mc_t P_t^{\omega} Y_t + \theta \, \mathbb{E}_t M_{t,t+1} NUM_{t+1}, \tag{14.58}$$

$$DEN_t = P_t^{\omega-1} Y_t + \theta \, \mathbb{E}_t M_{t,t+1} DEN_{t+1}. \tag{14.59}$$

As I mentioned above, I still need to address the fact that some of the equilibrium conditions have trending prices. To fix this issue, I rely on the notion of (gross) inflation. Since

$$\Pi_t = \frac{P_t}{P_{t-1}}, \tag{14.60}$$

I can transform price ratios into gross inflation terms; the expressions that must be adjusted are (14.47), (14.48), (14.50), (14.54), and (14.56)–(14.59); (14.51) outlines how taxes must offset wealth effects from interest changes, but isn't explicitly needed to solve the model. Equations (14.49), (14.52)–(14.53), and (14.55) need no further modification.

I can reach out for some low-hanging fruit in (14.47) and (14.50); if I define the real wage as W_t/P_t, then simple algebra results in

$$w_t = \phi C_t^{\eta} N_t^{\chi},$$
$$w_t = mc_t A_t.$$

Next, if I combine equations (14.60) and (14.48), I get

$$1 = R_t \mathbb{E}_t \left(M_{t,t+1} \Pi_{t+1}^{-1} \right).$$

The remaining equations, namely, (14.54) and (14.56)–(14.59), are slightly harder to put in stationary terms and so I go one step at a time. For (14.54), note that if I divide across by $P_t^{1-\omega}$, I get

$$\frac{P_t^{1-\omega}}{P_t^{1-\omega}} = (1-\theta)\frac{\left(P_t^*\right)^{1-\omega}}{P_t^{1-\omega}} + \theta\frac{P_{t-1}^{1-\omega}}{P_t^{1-\omega}}.$$

Let $\Pi_t^* \equiv P_t^*/P_t$ denote the relative reset price, then I can rewrite the expression above as

$$1 = (1-\theta)\left(\Pi_t^*\right)^{1-\omega} + \theta\,\Pi_t^{\omega-1}.$$

Next, let's look at the price dispersion equation. The same logic used to derive the price equation (14.54) results in

$$\begin{aligned}
\Delta_t &= \int_0^1 \left(\frac{P_t(i)}{P_t}\right)^{-\omega} \mathrm{d}i \\
&= \int_0^{1-\phi} \left(\frac{P_t^*}{P_t}\right)^{-\omega} \mathrm{d}i + \int_{1-\phi}^1 \left(\frac{P_{t-1}(i)}{P_t}\right)^{-\omega} \mathrm{d}i \\
&= (1-\phi)\left(\Pi_t^*\right)^{-\omega} + \int_{1-\phi}^1 \left(\frac{P_{t-1}(i)}{P_t}\right)^{-\omega} \left(\frac{P_{t-1}}{P_{t-1}}\right)^{-\omega} \mathrm{d}i,
\end{aligned}$$

where the last equality follows the definition of the relative reset price. If I zoom into the last term in the expression, I get

$$\begin{aligned}
\int_{1-\phi}^1 \left(\frac{P_{t-1}(i)}{P_t}\right)^{-\omega} \left(\frac{P_{t-1}}{P_{t-1}}\right)^{-\omega} \mathrm{d}i &= \int_{1-\phi}^1 \left(\frac{P_{t-1}(i)}{P_{t-1}}\right)^{-\omega} \left(\frac{P_{t-1}}{P_t}\right)^{-\omega} \mathrm{d}i \\
&= \Pi_t^{\omega} \int_{1-\phi}^1 \left(\frac{P_{t-1}(i)}{P_{t-1}}\right)^{-\omega} \mathrm{d}i \\
&= \phi\Pi_t^{\omega} \underbrace{\int_0^1 \left(\frac{P_{t-1}(i)}{P_{t-1}}\right)^{-\omega} \mathrm{d}i}_{=\Delta_{t-1}},
\end{aligned}$$

and so the stationary price-level equation looks like

$$\Delta_t = (1-\theta)\left(\Pi_t^*\right)^{-\omega} + \phi\Pi_t^{\omega}\Delta_{t-1},$$

which is not only stationary but also recursive.

I now move on to equation (14.58), which is given by

$$NUM_t = mc_t P_t^{\omega} Y_t + \theta\,\mathbb{E}_t M_{t,t+1} NUM_{t+1}.$$

Define a new (stationary) variable, num_t, as

$$num_t = \frac{NUM_t}{P_t^{\omega}}.$$

Clearly, $NUM_t = P_t^{\omega}\, num_t$. Substituting in the original expression, I get

$$P_t^{\omega}\, num_t = mc_t P_t^{\omega} Y_t + \theta\,\mathbb{E}_t M_{t,t+1} P_{t+1}^{\omega}\, num_{t+1}.$$

Now divide across by P_t^{ω}:

$$num_t = mc_t Y_t + \theta\,\mathbb{E}_t M_{t,t+1}\left(\frac{P_{t+1}^{\omega}}{P_t^{\omega}}\right) num_{t+1}.$$

Using the definition of gross inflation, the stationary form of the equation is

$$num_t = mc_t Y_t + \theta\, \mathbb{E}_t M_{t,t+1} \Pi_{t+1}^{\omega} num_{t+1}.$$

Setting $den_t = DEN_t / P_t^{\omega-1}$, the steps above lead me to

$$den_t = Y_t + \theta\, \mathbb{E}_t M_{t,t+1} \Pi_{t+1}^{\omega-1} den_{t+1},$$

and this takes care of equation (14.59).

What's left is to put equation (14.57) in stationary terms. To do so, note I can rewrite the expression as

$$P_t^* = \frac{\omega}{\omega-1} \frac{NUM_t}{DEN_t} \frac{P_t^{\omega-1}}{P_t^{\omega-1}}$$

and, using some clever algebra, I get

$$P_t^* = \frac{\omega}{\omega-1} \frac{num_t}{den_t} P_t.$$

If I divide across by P_t, then

$$\frac{P_t^*}{P_t} = \frac{\omega}{\omega-1} \frac{num_t}{den_t} \implies \Pi_t^* = \frac{\omega}{\omega-1} \frac{num_t}{den_t},$$

which concludes the process.

14.2.8 Taking Stock

Summing up, the stationary system is

$$\begin{aligned}
w_t &= \phi C_t^{\eta} N_t^{\chi}, \\
1 &= R_t \mathbb{E}_t \left(M_{t,t+1} \Pi_{t+1}^{-1} \right), \\
M_{t-1,t} &= \beta \left(\frac{C_t}{C_{t-1}} \right)^{-\eta}, \\
C_t &= Y_t, \\
1 &= (1-\theta) \left(\Pi_t^* \right)^{1-\omega} + \theta\, \Pi_t^{\omega-1}, \\
Y_t &= \left(\frac{A_t}{\Delta_t} \right) N_t, \\
\Delta_t &= (1-\theta) \left(\Pi_t^* \right)^{-\omega} + \phi \Pi_t^{\omega} \Delta_{t-1}, \\
w_t &= mc_t A_t, \\
\Pi_t^* &= \frac{\omega}{\omega-1} \frac{num_t}{den_t}, \\
num_t &= mc_t Y_t + \theta\, \mathbb{E}_t M_{t,t+1} \Pi_{t+1}^{\omega} num_{t+1}, \\
den_t &= Y_t + \theta\, \mathbb{E}_t M_{t,t+1} \Pi_{t+1}^{\omega-1} den_{t+1}, \\
R_t &= R_{ss} \left(\frac{\Pi_t}{\Pi_{ss}} \right)^{\nu_\pi} \left(\frac{Y_t}{Y_{ss}} \right)^{\nu_y},
\end{aligned}$$

which is a system of 12 equations in $\{w_t, C_t, N_t, R_t, M_{t_1,t}, \Pi_t, Y_t, \Pi_t^*, \Delta_t, mc_t, num_t, den_t\}$. (Note I do not count A_t toward the total as it is an exogenous variable.)

14.3 Up Next

It has been quite a bit of material, but we've covered the canonical New Keynesian model. Are we done? No. Typically, the literature uses the log-linearized version of the model, which results in the "three-equation system" of the IS curve, the Phillips curve, and the Taylor rule. The steps required to get to this setup are nontrivial, though, and are the main goal of the next chapter.

14.4 Bibliographic Notes

The canonical NK model has been built over time, slowly, perhaps starting with the contribution of Yun (1996). More extensive discussions of the model can be found in the survey papers by Clarida, Galí, and Gertler (1999) and Galí (2018), as well as the textbook-length treatises by Woodford (2003), Galí (2015), and Walsh (2017).

As should be clear by now, the key distinction between RBC and NK models relies on the price stickiness. While the Calvo pricing structure is the most used formulation, it is not the only one. The approaches of Taylor (1980) and Rotemberg (1982) also generate price stickiness: the former assumes firms set prices in a staggered fashion (e.g., a first group of firms set prices in January, the next group in February, and so on) while the latter assumes firms can adjust prices as long as they pay a cost when doing so (the cost being proportional to the change in the price). Castelnuovo, and Rossi (2011) mention that both the Calvo and Rotemberg structures yield fairly similar dynamics when linearizing around a zero-inflation steady state.

Walsh (2017, Chapter 8) has a concise but thorough discussion about price dispersion and the mechanism that explains why Δ_t acts like a TFP shock. For a normative view on monetary policy under price distortions, see Yun (2005).

14.5 Problems

14.5.1 Working with a Large Number of Intermediate Goods Firms

Suppose that instead of having a continuum of intermediate goods firms, we have a large (but finite) number N of them.

1. How would equation (14.2) look in this case? Does this new production function remind you of anything you've seen before?
2. How would equation (14.6) look in this case? How can you interpret the price-level equation?

14.5.2 The Household's Utility Maximization Problem

Verify that the household's first-order conditions are given by

$$\frac{W_t}{P_t} = \phi C_t^{\eta} N_t^{\chi},$$

$$1 = R_t \mathbb{E}_t \left[\left(\frac{C_{t+1}}{C_t} \right)^{-\eta} \frac{P_t}{P_{t+1}} \right],$$

$$P_t C_t + S_t = W_t N_t + R_{t-1} S_{t-1} + D_t - P_t T_t.$$

14.5.3 Various Easy Proofs

1. Verify that in a zero-inflation steady state, the discount factor β and the risk-free interest rate R satisfy $1 = \beta R$.
2. Show that when $\theta = 0$ (what does this mean?), equation (14.23) collapses to the pricing condition (14.12), namely, $P_t^* = [\omega/(\omega - 1)]\Lambda_t$. Why does this make sense?
3. Show that in the steady state, equation (14.23) becomes $P^* = [\omega/(\omega - 1)]\,\Lambda$, even if $\theta > 0$. Why does this make sense?

14.5.4 On the Optimal Reset Price

Verify that

$$DEN_t = \mathbb{E}_t \sum_{s=0}^{\infty} \theta^s M_{t,t+s} P_{t+s}^{\omega-1} Y_{t+s}$$

can be set recursively as shown in equation (14.46), namely,

$$DEN_t = P_t^{\omega-1} Y_t + \theta\, \mathbb{E}_t M_{t,t+1} DEN_{t+1}.$$

14.5.5 The Steady States of the Nonlinear NK Model

Let $A_{ss} = 1$. Starting from the stationary equilibrium conditions listed in Section 14.2.8, verify that the closed-form steady-state values are as follows: $R = 1/\beta$, $M = \beta$, $mc = (\omega - 1)/\omega$, $w = mc$, $\Pi^* = \Pi = \Delta = 1$, and $N = C = Y = \left[(\omega - 1)/(\omega\phi)\right]^{1/(\eta+\chi)}$.

15 The Log-Linearized New Keynesian Model

In the next sections, I provide details on how to log-linearize the equilibrium conditions of the canonical NK model (which is far from trivial) and show how to compress everything into the three-equation system that is the workhorse of NK economics: an IS curve, a Phillips curve, and a Taylor rule.

Not surprisingly, this process is not trivial, and I take it one step at a time. Roughly speaking, Section 15.1 takes a first pass at deriving both the IS curve and the Phillips curve, while Section 15.2 works the rest of the equilibrium conditions.

However, there is still work to be done. The results that I obtain by the end of Section 15.2 yield an IS curve that depends on output and a Phillips curve that is a function of the marginal cost. While both of these expressions are technically correct, the literature often opts to put these relationships in terms of the output gap, which is (roughly) the difference between observed and potential output. This transformation is also far from trivial, and I discuss it in Section 15.4. Once all these steps are done, I arrive at the log-linearized NK model that remains a workhorse of the DSGE literature.

Most of the New Keynesian literature chooses to log-linearize around a *zero-inflation steady state*. I will follow tradition in what comes next (but see the Bibliographic Notes).

Remark 15.1 An implication of this choice of steady state is that the value of inflation equals its level deviation from the steady state – that is,

$$\pi_t = \widetilde{\pi}_t + \pi_{ss} = \widetilde{\pi}_t,$$

where a tilde above a variable denotes a level deviation relative to steady state (see Section 15.1.2). In addition, given that $\pi_t = P_t/P_{t-1} - 1$, the approximation of inflation around the zero-inflation steady state is

$$\widetilde{\pi}_t - \pi_{ss} = \frac{P_{ss}}{P_{ss}}\left(1 + \widehat{P}_t - \widehat{P}_{t-1}\right) - 1 \implies \widetilde{\pi}_t = \widehat{P}_t - \widehat{P}_{t-1}.$$

(As $\pi_{ss} = 0$, it is not possible to calculate the percent deviation from steady state.) Since $\pi_t = \widetilde{\pi}_t$, I will use $\pi_t = \widehat{P}_t - \widehat{P}_{t-1}$ throughout the chapter.

15.1 Log-Linearization, Part I

To start, here are the NK model's equilibrium conditions:

$$\frac{W_t}{P_t} = \phi C_t^{\eta} N_t^{\chi}, \tag{15.1}$$

$$1 = (1 + i_t)\mathbb{E}_t \left(M_{t,t+1} \frac{P_t}{P_{t+1}} \right), \tag{15.2}$$

$$M_{t-1,t} = \beta \left(\frac{C_t}{C_{t-1}} \right)^{-\eta}, \tag{15.3}$$

$$Y_t = \left[\int_0^1 Y_t(i)^{\frac{\omega-1}{\omega}} \, \mathrm{d}i \right]^{\frac{\omega}{\omega-1}}, \tag{15.4}$$

$$P_t^{1-\omega} = (1-\theta)\left(P_t^*\right)^{1-\omega} + \theta P_{t-1}^{1-\omega}, \tag{15.5}$$

$$Y_t(i) = A_t N_t(i), \tag{15.6}$$

$$W_t = \Lambda_t A_t, \tag{15.7}$$

$$P_t^* = \frac{\omega}{\omega - 1} \frac{\mathbb{E}_t \sum_{s=0}^{\infty} \theta^s M_{t,t+s} mc_{t+s} P_{t+s}^{\omega} Y_{t+s}}{\mathbb{E}_t \sum_{s=0}^{\infty} \theta^s M_{t,t+s} P_{t+s}^{\omega-1} Y_{t+s}}, \tag{15.8}$$

$$C_t = Y_t, \tag{15.9}$$

$$N_t = \int_0^1 N_t(i) \, \mathrm{d}i. \tag{15.10}$$

Note these expressions don't coincide with the ones found in Section 14.2.8; this is on purpose, as it allows me to show that there are several ways to deal with trending prices. Note also that I no longer need (i) the bond market clearing condition, equation (14.36), nor (ii) the household's and government's budget constraints, equations (14.26) and (14.34), as they have been combined to obtain the goods market clearing condition (15.9). In addition, equation (15.2) uses the nominal interest rate i_t instead of the gross rate R_t.

The road ahead requires me to log-linearize these expressions, and this is what I do next. (For a refresher, see Section 7.1.1.)

15.1.1 The NK Phillips Curve, Marginal-Cost Version

I start with the easy stuff, tackling the price-level equation (15.5). As a preliminary step, let's impose steady-state conditions. I get

$$P^{1-\omega} = (1-\theta)\left(P^*\right)^{1-\omega} + \theta P^{1-\omega}$$

which, after a bit of algebra, proves the following result:

Lemma 15.2 *In the steady state, $P = P^*$.*

(As I assume steady-state inflation equals zero, this result makes sense.) Now, log-linearizing the expression yields

$$P^{1-\omega}\left[1+(1-\omega)\widehat{P}_t\right]=(1-\theta)\left(P^*\right)^{1-\omega}\left[1+(1-\omega)\widehat{P}_t^*\right]+\theta P^{1-\omega}\left[1+(1-\omega)\widehat{P}_{t-1}\right].$$

If I use the result from Lemma 15.2 and cancel terms, I end up with

$$\widehat{P}_t=(1-\theta)\widehat{P}_t^*+\theta\widehat{P}_{t-1}. \tag{15.11}$$

Now, before log-linearizing the pricing rule (15.8), I lay out two results that I will need in a moment. First, here's a nice result from mathematics that you may already know (so I present it without proof):

Lemma 15.3 *Let $a\in\mathbb{R}$ and $|x|<1$. Then $\sum_{k=0}^{\infty}ax^k=a/(1-x)$.*

Next, I establish the steady-state value of the real marginal cost mc:

Lemma 15.4 *In the steady state, $mc_{ss}=(\omega-1)/\omega$.*

Proof. The steady-state version of equation (15.8) is

$$P^*=\frac{\omega}{\omega-1}\frac{\sum_{s=0}^{\infty}\theta^s\beta^s mcP^{\omega}Y}{\sum_{s=0}^{\infty}\theta^s\beta^s P^{\omega-1}Y},$$

where I've used that in the steady state, the stochastic discount factor is simply

$$M_{ss}=\beta^s\left(\frac{C_{ss}}{C_{ss}}\right)^{-\eta}=\beta^s.$$

Some of the terms in the reset price equation do not depend on s, so I can take them out of the sum operators. After rearranging terms, I get

$$(\omega-1)P^*P^{\omega-1}Y\sum_{s=0}^{\infty}(\theta\beta)^s=\omega\, mcP^{\omega}Y\sum_{s=0}^{\infty}(\theta\beta)^s.$$

Note that $\theta\beta\in(0,1)$. If I set $a=1$ then the conditions for Lemma 15.3 to work are satisfied, and therefore

$$\sum_{s=0}^{\infty}(\theta\beta)^s=\frac{1}{1-\theta\beta}.$$

Using this result in the reset price equation yields

$$\frac{(\omega-1)P^*P^{\omega-1}Y}{1-\theta\beta}=\frac{\omega\, mcP^{\omega}Y}{1-\theta\beta}.$$

Finally, I use the result from Lemma 15.2; the equation is now

$$\frac{(\omega-1)P^{\omega}Y}{1-\theta\beta}=\frac{\omega\, mcP^{\omega}Y}{1-\theta\beta}.$$

Canceling terms, I obtain $mc_{ss}=(\omega-1)/\omega$, as needed. □

Now I can go ahead and log-linearize equation (15.8). First, I rewrite it as

$$\mathbb{E}_t \sum_{s=0}^{\infty} \theta^s M_{t,t+s} P_t^* P_{t+s}^{\omega-1} Y_{t+s} = \frac{\omega}{\omega-1} \mathbb{E}_t \sum_{s=0}^{\infty} \theta^s M_{t,t+s} mc_{t+s} P_{t+s}^{\omega} Y_{t+s}$$

and log-linearizing, I get

$$\begin{aligned} &\mathbb{E}_t \sum_{s=0}^{\infty} \theta^s \beta^s P^* P^{\omega-1} Y \big[1 + \widehat{M}_{t,t+s} + \widehat{P}_t^* + (\omega-1)\widehat{P}_{t+s} + \widehat{Y}_{t+s}\big] \\ &= \Big(\frac{\omega}{\omega-1}\Big) \mathbb{E}_t \sum_{s=0}^{\infty} \theta^s \beta^s mc P^{\omega} Y \big[1 + \widehat{M}_{t,t+s} + \widehat{mc}_{t+s} + \omega \widehat{P}_{t+s} + \widehat{Y}_{t+s}\big]. \end{aligned}$$

Looking at the left-hand side of the expression, I can take the "1" and the $\widehat{P}_t^*$ terms out of the sum operator since they do not depend on s. I get

$$\frac{P^{\omega}Y}{1-\theta\beta} + \frac{P^{\omega}Y}{1-\theta\beta}\widehat{P}_t^* + P^{\omega} Y \mathbb{E}_t \sum_{s=0}^{\infty} (\theta\beta)^s \big[\widehat{M}_{t,t+s} + (\omega-1)\widehat{P}_{t+s} + \widehat{Y}_{t+s}\big],$$

where once again I've used the results from Lemmas 15.2 and 15.3. Regarding the right-hand side, I take the "1" term out of the sum operator and rewrite it as

$$\Big(\frac{\omega}{\omega-1}\Big)\frac{mcP^{\omega}Y}{1-\theta\beta} + \Big(\frac{\omega}{\omega-1}\Big) mcP^{\omega} Y \mathbb{E}_t \sum_{s=0}^{\infty} (\theta\beta)^s \big[\widehat{M}_{t,t+s} + \widehat{mc}_{t+s} + \omega\widehat{P}_{t+s} + \widehat{Y}_{t+s}\big].$$

I use the result from Lemma 15.4: substituting $mc_{ss} = (\omega - 1)/\omega$ where needed, the expression becomes

$$\begin{aligned} &\Big(\frac{\omega}{\omega-1}\Big)\Big(\frac{\omega-1}{\omega}\Big)\frac{P^{\omega}Y}{1-\theta\beta} \\ &+ \Big(\frac{\omega}{\omega-1}\Big)\Big(\frac{\omega-1}{\omega}\Big) P^{\omega} Y \mathbb{E}_t \sum_{s=0}^{\infty} (\theta\beta)^s \big[\widehat{M}_{t,t+s} + \widehat{mc}_{t+s} + \omega\widehat{P}_{t+s} + \widehat{Y}_{t+s}\big] \end{aligned}$$

or, after canceling terms,

$$\frac{P^{\omega}Y}{1-\theta\beta} + P^{\omega} Y \mathbb{E}_t \sum_{s=0}^{\infty} (\theta\beta)^s \big[\widehat{M}_{t,t+s} + \widehat{mc}_{t+s} + \omega\widehat{P}_{t+s} + \widehat{Y}_{t+s}\big].$$

Now I put both sides together:

$$\begin{aligned} &\frac{P^{\omega}Y}{1-\theta\beta} + \frac{P^{\omega}Y}{1-\theta\beta}\widehat{P}_t^* + P^{\omega} Y \mathbb{E}_t \sum_{s=0}^{\infty} (\theta\beta)^s \big[\widehat{M}_{t,t+s} + (\omega-1)\widehat{P}_{t+s} + \widehat{Y}_{t+s}\big] \\ &= \frac{P^{\omega}Y}{1-\theta\beta} + P^{\omega} Y \mathbb{E}_t \sum_{s=0}^{\infty} (\theta\beta)^s \big[\widehat{M}_{t,t+s} + \widehat{mc}_{t+s} + \omega\widehat{P}_{t+s} + \widehat{Y}_{t+s}\big]. \end{aligned}$$

Clearly, the constant terms cancel out, and so do the $\widehat{M}_{t,t+s}$, $\omega\widehat{P}_{t+s}$, and $\widehat{Y}_{t+s}$ terms inside the summations. Cleaning up,

$$\frac{P^{\omega}Y}{1-\theta\beta}\widehat{P}_t^{*} - P^{\omega}Y\mathbb{E}_t\sum_{s=0}^{\infty}(\theta\beta)^s\widehat{P}_{t+s} = P^{\omega}Y\mathbb{E}_t\sum_{s=0}^{\infty}(\theta\beta)^s\,\widehat{mc}_{t+s},$$

or

$$\frac{P^{\omega}Y}{1-\theta\beta}\widehat{P}_t^{*} = P^{\omega}Y\mathbb{E}_t\sum_{s=0}^{\infty}(\theta\beta)^s\left(\widehat{P}_{t+s} + \widehat{mc}_{t+s}\right).$$

Multiplying across by $(1-\theta\beta)P^{\omega}Y$ gives

$$\widehat{P}_t^{*} = (1-\theta\beta)\mathbb{E}_t\sum_{s=0}^{\infty}(\theta\beta)^s\left(\widehat{P}_{t+s} + \widehat{mc}_{t+s}\right), \tag{15.12}$$

which is the log-linearized reset price equation.

The Marginal-Cost Phillips Curve?

Armed with the log-linearized pricing rule, equation (15.12), I can substitute it into the aggregate price-level equation (15.11). This yields

$$\widehat{P}_t = (1-\theta)(1-\theta\beta)\mathbb{E}_t\sum_{s=0}^{\infty}(\theta\beta)^s\left(\widehat{P}_{t+s} + \widehat{mc}_{t+s}\right) + \theta\widehat{P}_{t-1}. \tag{15.13}$$

Equation (15.13) is technically correct, yet close inspection shows that its current inception is not useful: I still have an infinite amount of forward-looking terms on the right-hand side, which makes it impossible to put into Dynare. I still need to find a way to reduce the dimensionality of the expression, and this is what I do next.

Lag Operators and Quasi-Differencing

To fix this issue, I rely on **lag operators**. These tools are fairly easy to use and can help us quite a bit with the task at hand. Denote the lag operator by $\mathbb{L}$; to understand what this operator does, I offer some examples. Given some real-valued variables x_t and y_{t+1} and some number $a \in \mathbb{R}$,

$$\mathbb{L}x_t = x_{t-1},$$
$$(1 + a\mathbb{L})y_{t+1} = y_{t+1} + ay_t.$$

From time to time (such as right now), it's convenient to use the *inverse* lag operator $\mathbb{L}^{-1}$, which yields a variable's lead instead of lag:

$$\mathbb{L}^{-1}x_t = x_{t+1},$$
$$(1 + a\mathbb{L}^{-1})y_{t+1} = y_{t+1} + ay_{t+2}.$$

For further applications and theory, see Sargent (1987, chap. IX).

Armed with the notion of (inverse) lag operators, I now introduce a method known as **quasi-differencing**. Put simply, the method works by multiplying the Phillips curve equation (15.13) by a lag polynomial in order to eliminate most of the terms inside the infinite sums.

To get the method working, I multiply both sides of (15.13) by the lag polynomial $\left(1-\theta\beta\mathbb{L}^{-1}\right)$. I start with the left-hand side; multiplication by $\left(1-\theta\beta\mathbb{L}^{-1}\right)$ yields

$$\left(1-\theta\beta\mathbb{L}^{-1}\right)\widehat{P}_t=\widehat{P}_t-\theta\beta\,\mathbb{E}_t\widehat{P}_{t+1}. \tag{15.14}$$

Now do the same for the second term on the right-hand side:

$$\left(1-\theta\beta\mathbb{L}^{-1}\right)\theta\widehat{P}_{t-1}=\theta\widehat{P}_{t-1}-\theta^2\beta\widehat{P}_t \tag{15.15}$$

and the first term on that side too:

$$\begin{aligned}&\left(1-\theta\beta\mathbb{L}^{-1}\right)\left[\left(1-\theta\right)\left(1-\theta\beta\right)\mathbb{E}_t\sum_{s=0}^{\infty}\left(\theta\beta\right)^s\left(\widehat{P}_{t+s}+\widehat{mc}_{t+s}\right)\right]\\&=\left(1-\theta\right)\left(1-\theta\beta\right)\mathbb{E}_t\sum_{s=0}^{\infty}\left(\theta\beta\right)^s\left(\widehat{P}_{t+s}+\widehat{mc}_{t+s}\right)\\&\quad-\theta\beta\left(1-\theta\right)\left(1-\theta\beta\right)\mathbb{E}_t\sum_{s=0}^{\infty}\left(\theta\beta\right)^s\left(\widehat{P}_{t+1+s}+\widehat{mc}_{t+1+s}\right).\end{aligned} \tag{15.16}$$

This sure doesn't seem like an improvement, but it is. To see why, open up the sum in the first term on the right-hand side of (15.16):

$$\begin{aligned}&\left(1-\theta\right)\left(1-\theta\beta\right)\mathbb{E}_t\sum_{s=0}^{\infty}\left(\theta\beta\right)^s\left(\widehat{P}_{t+s}+\widehat{mc}_{t+s}\right)\\&=\left(1-\theta\right)\left(1-\theta\beta\right)\mathbb{E}_t\left[\widehat{P}_t+\widehat{mc}_t+\left(\theta\beta\right)\left(\widehat{P}_{t+1}+\widehat{mc}_{t+1}\right)+\cdots\right].\end{aligned}$$

Before doing the same to the second term on the right-hand side of (15.16), plug the $\left(\theta\beta\right)$ term inside the summation to get

$$\begin{aligned}&-\theta\beta\left(1-\theta\right)\left(1-\theta\beta\right)\mathbb{E}_t\sum_{s=0}^{\infty}\left(\theta\beta\right)^s\left(\widehat{P}_{t+1+s}+\widehat{mc}_{t+1+s}\right)\\&=-\left(1-\theta\right)\left(1-\theta\beta\right)\mathbb{E}_t\sum_{s=0}^{\infty}\left(\theta\beta\right)^{s+1}\left(\widehat{P}_{t+1+s}+\widehat{mc}_{t+1+s}\right).\end{aligned}$$

Opening the sum yields

$$\begin{aligned}&-\left(1-\theta\right)\left(1-\theta\beta\right)\mathbb{E}_t\sum_{s=0}^{\infty}\left(\theta\beta\right)^{s+1}\left(\widehat{P}_{t+1+s}+\widehat{mc}_{t+1+s}\right)\\&=-\left(1-\theta\right)\left(1-\theta\beta\right)\mathbb{E}_t\left[\left(\theta\beta\right)\left(\widehat{P}_{t+1}+\widehat{mc}_{t+1}\right)+\left(\theta\beta\right)^2\left(\widehat{P}_{t+2}+\widehat{mc}_{t+2}\right)+\cdots\right].\end{aligned}$$

Putting both parts together, note almost all of the terms cancel out:

$$\begin{aligned}&\left(1-\theta\right)\left(1-\theta\beta\right)\mathbb{E}_t\left[\widehat{P}_t+\widehat{mc}_t+\left(\theta\beta\right)\left(\widehat{P}_{t+1}+\widehat{mc}_{t+1}\right)+\cdots\right]\\&\quad-\left(1-\theta\right)\left(1-\theta\beta\right)\mathbb{E}_t\left[\left(\theta\beta\right)\left(\widehat{P}_{t+1}+\widehat{mc}_{t+1}\right)+\left(\theta\beta\right)^2\left(\widehat{P}_{t+2}+\widehat{mc}_{t+2}\right)+\cdots\right].\end{aligned} \tag{15.17}$$

Combine (15.14), (15.15), and (15.17) to get

$$\widehat{P}_t-\theta\beta\,\mathbb{E}_t\widehat{P}_{t+1}=\left(1-\theta\right)\left(1-\theta\beta\right)\left(\widehat{P}_t+\widehat{mc}_t\right)+\theta\widehat{P}_{t-1}-\theta^2\beta\widehat{P}_t. \tag{15.18}$$

Algebra shows that $(1-\theta)(1-\theta\beta) = 1-\theta\beta-\theta+\theta^2\beta$. I use this fact to break up the $\widehat{P}_t$ term in the first component of the right-hand side in (15.18):

$$\widehat{P}_t - \theta\beta\,\mathbb{E}_t\widehat{P}_{t+1} = \left(\widehat{P}_t - \theta\beta\widehat{P}_t - \theta\widehat{P}_t + \theta^2\beta\widehat{P}_t\right) + (1-\theta)(1-\theta\beta)\widehat{mc}_t + \theta\widehat{P}_{t-1} - \theta^2\beta\widehat{P}_t.$$

Some terms cancel out: group by common factors and rewrite as

$$\theta\left(\widehat{P}_t - \widehat{P}_{t-1}\right) = (1-\theta)(1-\theta\beta)\widehat{mc}_t + \theta\beta\,\mathbb{E}_t\left(\widehat{P}_{t+1} - \widehat{P}_t\right). \tag{15.19}$$

The Marginal-Cost Phillips Curve

From Remark 15.1, I know that $\pi_t = \widehat{P}_t - \widehat{P}_{t-1}$. If I divide equation (15.19) by θ and substitute for π_t, I arrive at the **New Keynesian Phillips curve** (marginal-cost version), which is

$$\pi_t = \frac{(1-\theta)(1-\theta\beta)}{\theta}\widehat{mc}_t + \beta\,\mathbb{E}_t\pi_{t+1}. \tag{15.20}$$

Equation (15.20) says current inflation is a function of two factors: current-period real marginal costs and expected inflation.

The fact that higher real marginal costs raise inflation is obvious – current prices go up when firms' costs increase. What is not obvious is the reason behind higher expected inflation increasing prices today; this fact follows the Calvo pricing rule. If inflation is expected to increase in the following period, a firm that can reset its price today will take this information into account: since it may not be able to adjust prices tomorrow, it decides (optimally) to adjust prices today. Hence, inflation is forward-looking in the NK model.

15.1.2 The NK IS Curve, Aggregate-Output Version

I now move to the second key component of the canonical NK model, the IS curve. To derive it, note first that I can substitute the goods market clearing condition (15.9) into the stochastic discount factor (15.3); this last expression now reads

$$M_{t-1,t} = \beta\left(\frac{Y_t}{Y_{t-1}}\right)^{-\eta}.$$

Now substitute the revised stochastic discount factor into the household's Euler equation (15.2):

$$1 = \beta(1+i_t)\mathbb{E}_t\left[\left(\frac{Y_{t+1}}{Y_t}\right)^{-\eta}\frac{P_t}{P_{t+1}}\right]. \tag{15.21}$$

Before moving forward, I need to introduce a set of results that are fairly interesting on their own – and very useful in what follows.

Extra Notes on Uhlig's Rules

In this section I offer an extra set of rules for cases where we want to work with the *level deviations* (as opposed to percent deviations) from the steady state. This operation is often required when working with variables that are already in percent terms (like interest rates or tax rates) or variables that can take a value of zero in the steady state (in our case, inflation).

Level vs. Percent Deviations In what follows, let Ω_t and Ψ_t be variables for which we want to calculate percent deviations and V_t and U_t be variables for which we want to calculate level deviations.

Note that the level deviation from the steady state for variable V_t is defined as $\widetilde{V}_t \equiv V_t - V_{ss}$, which leads to the equivalent of Uhlig's Rule 1 (Proposition 7.1):

Proposition 15.5 *Let V_t be a real-valued variable. The following results hold exactly:*

$$V_t = \widetilde{V}_t + V_{ss} \tag{15.22a}$$

$$= V_{ss}\left(1 + \frac{1}{V_{ss}}\widetilde{V}_t\right). \tag{15.22b}$$

Proof. Follows directly after solving for V_t from the definition of $\widetilde{V}_t$. □

Depending on the application, I may want to use (15.22a) or (15.22b); clearly, if $V_{ss} = 0$ then using (15.22b) is not a good idea. In general, (15.22a) is useful when the term to be log-linearized is not multiplied by any other variable; (15.22b) works best under a product rule (Rule 2, Proposition 7.3), as shown by the result below:

Proposition 15.6 *Let V_t, U_t, and Ω_t be three variables. Then*

1. *The product of the percent variables V_t and U_t can be approximated as*

$$V_tU_t \approx V_{ss}U_{ss}\left(1 + \frac{1}{V_{ss}}\widetilde{V}_t + \frac{1}{U_{ss}}\widetilde{U}_t\right).$$

2. *The product of the level variable Ω_t and the percent variable V_t can be approximated as*

$$\Omega_tV_t \approx \Omega_{ss}V_{ss}\left(1 + \widehat{\Omega}_t + \frac{1}{V_{ss}}\widetilde{V}_t\right).$$

The equivalents of the exponentiation (Rule 3) and logarithmic rules (Rule 4) are fairly similar; as their proofs are trivial, I omit them:

Proposition 15.7 *Let V_t be a variable and $b \in \mathbb{R}$. The exponentiation V_t^b can be approximated as*

$$V_t^b \approx V_{ss}^b\left(1 + \frac{b}{V_{ss}}\widetilde{V}_t\right).$$

Proposition 15.8 *Let V_t be a variable. The logarithm of V_t can be approximated as*

$$\log V_t \approx \log V_{ss} + \frac{1}{V_{ss}}\widetilde{V}_t.$$

Finally, in some circumstances, I need to log-linearize more complicated expressions of the form

$$(1+\Omega_t)(1-V_t)\Psi_t. \tag{15.23}$$

While I can always cross-multiply and apply the rules above, this procedure loses its appeal since it is no longer fast and concise. The following result shows how to get a hybrid of Rule 2 when level and percent variables coexist in the same expression.

Proposition 15.9 *Let Ω_t and Ψ_t be level variables and V_t be a percent variable. An expression like* (15.23) *can be approximated by*

$$(1+\Omega_t)(1-V_t)\Psi_t \approx (1+\Omega_{ss})(1-V_{ss})\Psi_{ss}\left(1+\frac{\Omega_{ss}}{1+\Omega_{ss}}\widehat{\Omega}_t - \frac{1}{1-V_{ss}}\widetilde{V}_t + \widehat{\Psi}_t\right). \tag{15.24}$$

The Aggregate-Output IS Curve

Here's equation (15.21):

$$1 = \beta(1+i_t)\mathbb{E}_t\left[\left(\frac{Y_{t+1}}{Y_t}\right)^{-\eta}\frac{P_t}{P_{t+1}}\right].$$

As it will be useful below, note that in the steady state, the equation becomes

$$1 = \beta(1+i),$$

which implies $\beta = (1+i)^{-1}$. Next, I use the template found in equation (15.24) from Proposition 15.9 to log-linearize. I get

$$1 = \beta(1+i)\left(\frac{Y}{Y}\right)^{-\eta}\frac{P}{P}\left[1+\frac{1}{1+i}\widetilde{i}_t - \eta\,\mathbb{E}_t\widehat{Y}_{t+1} + \eta\widehat{Y}_t + \widehat{P}_t - \mathbb{E}_t\widehat{P}_{t+1}\right].$$

Canceling terms, the equation simplifies to

$$0 = \frac{1}{1+i}\widetilde{i}_t - \eta\,\mathbb{E}_t\widehat{Y}_{t+1} + \eta\widehat{Y}_t + \widehat{P}_t - \mathbb{E}_t\widehat{P}_{t+1}.$$

I now solve for $\widehat{Y}_t$; using that $\beta = (1+i)^{-1}$, the equation reads

$$\begin{aligned}\eta\widehat{Y}_t &= \eta\,\mathbb{E}_t\widehat{Y}_{t+1} + \mathbb{E}_t\widehat{P}_{t+1} - \widehat{P}_t - \beta\widetilde{i}_t\\ &= \eta\,\mathbb{E}_t\widehat{Y}_{t+1} + (\mathbb{E}_t\widehat{P}_{t+1} - \widehat{P}_t) - \beta\widetilde{i}_t\\ &= \eta\,\mathbb{E}_t\widehat{Y}_{t+1} + \mathbb{E}_t\pi_{t+1} - \beta\widetilde{i}_t,\end{aligned}$$

where the last equality follows the definition of inflation per Remark 15.1. Rearrange one last time to get

$$\widehat{Y}_t = \mathbb{E}_t\widehat{Y}_{t+1} - \frac{1}{\eta}(\beta\widetilde{i}_t - \mathbb{E}_t\pi_{t+1}), \tag{15.25}$$

which is the **New Keynesian IS curve** (aggregate-output version). This expression says that output today (strictly speaking, the deviation of output from its steady-state value) depends on expected output tomorrow and the real interest rate – this follows as the real interest rate equals the nominal rate minus expected inflation. Since the equation describes a negative relationship between output and the interest rate – just like a textbook IS curve – the name seems appropriate.

15.2 Log-Linearization, Part II

Here, I log-linearize the rest of the equilibrium conditions. Note that some of the steps below are not trivial; moreover, some others are required to derive the "standard" version of the NK Phillips and IS curves, which depend on the output gap (instead of real marginal cost and aggregate output, respectively).

15.2.1 Intratemporal Condition

Take equation (15.1); applying Uhlig's rules yields

$$\widehat{W}_t - \widehat{P}_t = \eta \widehat{Y}_t + \chi \widehat{N}_t. \tag{15.26}$$

15.2.2 Final Goods Production Function

Log-linearizing equation (15.4) seems daunting but it is actually a fairly straightforward task. Before doing so, however, I present a result that I will use below.

Lemma 15.10 *If $\pi_{ss} = 0$, then all firms charge identical prices and produce the same amount in the steady state; this means that*

$$Y_{ss} = Y_{ss}(i).$$

Note $\pi_{ss} = 0$ holds by assumption since I'm assuming a zero-inflation steady state, and Lemma 15.2 shows how $P = P^*$ under this assumption. In this sense, Lemma 15.10 closes this loop and guarantees a symmetric equilibrium in the steady state.

Back to the log-linearization procedure. First I apply the log function to the equation; using the rules of logarithms to get rid of the exponent, I get

$$\log Y_t = \frac{\omega}{\omega - 1} \log \left(\int_0^1 Y_t(i)^{\frac{\omega-1}{\omega}} \mathrm{d}i \right).$$

This is a good time to use Uhlig's rule for log-linearizing logarithmic functions. Following Proposition (7.5), the production technology becomes

$$\begin{aligned}
\log Y_{ss} + \widehat{Y}_t &= \frac{\omega}{\omega - 1} \left[\log \left(\int_0^1 Y_{ss}(i)^{\frac{\omega-1}{\omega}} \mathrm{d}i \right) + \left(\frac{\omega - 1}{\omega} \right) \int_0^1 \widehat{Y}_t(i)\, \mathrm{d}i \right] \\
&= \frac{\omega}{\omega - 1} \log \left(Y_{ss}(i)^{\frac{\omega-1}{\omega}} \int_0^1 \mathrm{d}i \right) + \int_0^1 \widehat{Y}_t(i)\, \mathrm{d}i
\end{aligned}$$

$$= \frac{\omega}{\omega - 1}\left[\left(\frac{\omega - 1}{\omega}\right)\log Y_{ss}(i) + \log(1)\right] + \int_0^1 \widehat{Y}_t(i)\,\mathrm{d}i$$

$$= \log Y_{ss}(i) + \int_0^1 \widehat{Y}_t(i)\,\mathrm{d}i,$$

where the second and third equalities follow the laws of logarithms. Then, given Lemma 15.10, it follows that

$$\widehat{Y}_t = \int_0^1 \widehat{Y}_t(i)\,\mathrm{d}i. \tag{15.27}$$

15.2.3 Intermediate Goods Production Function

After log-linearizing, equation (15.6) becomes

$$\widehat{Y}_t(i) = \widehat{A}_t + \widehat{N}_t(i).$$

I can plug this expression in (15.27) to get

$$\widehat{Y}_t = \int_0^1 \left[\widehat{A}_t + \widehat{N}_t(i)\right]\mathrm{d}i = \widehat{A}_t + \int_0^1 \widehat{N}_t(i)\,\mathrm{d}i. \tag{15.28}$$

15.2.4 Labor Market Clearing Condition

Take equation (15.10). In the steady state, the equation reads $N_{ss} = \int N_{ss}(i)\,\mathrm{d}i$, which implies $N_{ss} = N_{ss}(i)$. Repeating the process for the final goods firm production function, the labor market clearing condition can be logged first:

$$\log N_t = \log\left(\int_0^1 N_t(i)\,\mathrm{d}i\right)$$

and then, after log-linearizing:

$$\log N_{ss} + \widehat{N}_t = \log\left(\int_0^1 N_{ss}(i)\,\mathrm{d}i\right) + \int_0^1 \widehat{N}_t(i)\,\mathrm{d}i$$

or simply

$$\widehat{N}_t = \int_0^1 \widehat{N}_t(i)\,\mathrm{d}i. \tag{15.29}$$

15.2.5 Aggregate Output

Even though this is not one of the equilibrium conditions, I can rearrange some of the equations derived above to get a useful expression. If I plug the labor market clearing condition (15.29) into (15.28) to get

$$\widehat{Y}_t = \widehat{A}_t + \widehat{N}_t, \tag{15.30}$$

then the aggregate output is the same as that of each intermediate goods firm output. By inspection, equation (15.30) confirms that price dispersion is *not* an issue when the model is log-linearized.

15.2.6 Marginal-Cost Equation

Equation (15.7) is technically correct, but so far I've used the marginal cost in real terms (mc) and not nominal terms (Λ). To fix this, I divide the equation throughout by P_t:

$$\frac{W_t}{P_t} = \frac{\Lambda_t}{P_t} A_t \implies \frac{W_t}{P_t} = mc_t A_t,$$

then log-linearize to get

$$\frac{W}{P}(1 + \widehat{W}_t - \widehat{P}_t) = mc\, A(1 + \widehat{mc}_t + \widehat{A}_t)$$

so that

$$\widehat{W}_t - \widehat{P}_t = \widehat{mc}_t + \widehat{A}_t. \tag{15.31}$$

15.3 Log-Linearization, Part III

In most applications, the NK Phillips curve (as well as the NK IS curve, see Section 15.3.2 below) is a function of the **output gap** – loosely interpreted as the difference between observed and potential output – instead of a function of real marginal costs as in (15.20). To derive this version of the Phillips curve, I need to find what "potential output" is in the model. As it turns out, this value corresponds to the level of output that would be produced in the absence of nominal rigidities (i.e., under flexible prices).

With these ideas in mind, let's get the NK Phillips curve that takes the output gap as an input.

15.3.1 The NK Phillips Curve, Output-Gap Version

There are two preliminary steps I need to take before arriving at the key expression for the Phillips curve. First, I need to define what potential output is. Then I need to combine this concept with *observed* output to obtain an expression for the model's output gap.

Potential Output

Let's go back to the flexible-price monopolistic competition equilibrium from Section 14.1. From equation (14.14), it is clear that

$$\frac{W_t^F}{P_t} = \frac{\omega - 1}{\omega} A_t,$$

where I use the F superscript to distinguish the flexible-price nominal wage from its sticky-price counterpart. Log-linearizing this expression yields

$$\frac{W^F}{P}\left(1+\widehat{W}_t^F-\widehat{P}_t\right)=\frac{\omega-1}{\omega}A\left(1+\widehat{A}_t\right) \implies \widehat{W}_t^F-\widehat{P}_t=\widehat{A}_t.$$

Now plug this in (15.26) for the flexible-price case

$$\widehat{A}_t=\eta\widehat{Y}_t^F+\chi\widehat{N}_t^F$$

and combine with (15.30):

$$\widehat{A}_t=\eta\left(\widehat{A}_t+\widehat{N}_t^F\right)+\chi\widehat{N}_t^F,$$

which I can rearrange to

$$\widehat{N}_t^F=\frac{1-\eta}{\eta+\chi}\widehat{A}_t.$$

Finally, I plug this expression in (15.30) to obtain the flexible-price level of output,

$$\widehat{Y}_t^F=\widehat{A}_t+\frac{1-\eta}{\eta+\chi}\widehat{A}_t=\frac{1+\chi}{\eta+\chi}\widehat{A}_t. \tag{15.32}$$

From Potential Output to Observed Output

For the second part of the procedure, take equation (15.31) and plug in for $\widehat{W}_t-\widehat{P}_t$ from (15.26) – note this time I don't need to worry about flexible prices:

$$\eta\widehat{Y}_t+\chi\widehat{N}_t=\widehat{mc}_t+\widehat{A}_t.$$

Now use (15.30) to plug in for $\widehat{N}_t$:

$$\eta\widehat{Y}_t+\chi\left(\widehat{Y}_t-\widehat{A}_t\right)=\widehat{mc}_t+\widehat{A}_t$$

and then, solving for $\widehat{mc}_t$, I get

$$\widehat{mc}_t=(\eta+\chi)\widehat{Y}_t-(1+\chi)\widehat{A}_t.$$

Equation (15.32) implies that $\widehat{A}_t=\left[(\eta+\chi)/(1+\chi)\right]\widehat{Y}_t^F$; plugging this expression in the equation above gives

$$\begin{aligned}\widehat{mc}_t&=(\eta+\chi)\widehat{Y}_t-(1+\chi)\left(\frac{\eta+\chi}{1+\chi}\right)\widehat{Y}_t^F\\&=(\eta+\chi)\left(\widehat{Y}_t-\widehat{Y}_t^F\right).\end{aligned} \tag{15.33}$$

The Output-Gap Phillips Curve

Since equation (15.33) gives me an expression for real marginal costs $\widehat{mc}_t$, I can use it in the marginal-cost Phillips curve, equation (15.20):

$$\pi_t=\frac{(1-\theta)(1-\theta\beta)}{\theta}\left[(\eta+\chi)\left(\widehat{Y}_t-\widehat{Y}_t^F\right)\right]+\beta\,\mathbb{E}_t\pi_{t+1}.$$

For the last step, let $\widehat{x}_t\equiv\widehat{Y}_t-\widehat{Y}_t^F$ denote the output gap. Substituting, I get

$$\pi_t=\kappa\widehat{x}_t+\beta\,\mathbb{E}_t\pi_{t+1}, \tag{15.34}$$

where $\kappa \equiv (1-\theta)(1-\theta\beta)(\eta+\chi)/\theta$. Equation (15.34) is the output-gap NK Phillips curve.

15.3.2 The NK IS Curve, Output-Gap Version

This last stage requires me to transform the NK IS curve so that it becomes a function of the output gap $\widehat{x}_t$. To do this, I start from equation (15.25):

$$\widehat{Y}_t = \mathbb{E}_t\widehat{Y}_{t+1} - \frac{1}{\eta}\left(\beta\widetilde{i}_t - \mathbb{E}_t\pi_{t+1}\right)$$

and then add $0 = \widehat{Y}_t^F - \widehat{Y}_t^F = \mathbb{E}_t\widehat{Y}_{t+1}^F - \mathbb{E}_t\widehat{Y}_{t+1}^F$ to both sides of the equation:

$$\widehat{Y}_t + \left(\widehat{Y}_t^F - \widehat{Y}_t^F\right) = \mathbb{E}_t\widehat{Y}_{t+1} + \left(\mathbb{E}_t\widehat{Y}_{t+1}^F - \mathbb{E}_t\widehat{Y}_{t+1}^F\right) - \frac{1}{\eta}\left(\beta\widetilde{i}_t - \mathbb{E}_t\pi_{t+1}\right).$$

Rearrange a bit to get everything in terms of the output gap – and some extra terms:

$$\widehat{x}_t = \mathbb{E}_t\widehat{x}_{t+1} - \frac{1}{\eta}\left(\beta\widetilde{i}_t - \mathbb{E}_t\pi_{t+1}\right) + \left(\mathbb{E}_t\widehat{Y}_{t+1}^F - \widehat{Y}_t^F\right).$$

This looks good, though I still need to figure out what to do with the last term on the right-hand side. For this matter, I use (15.32) to substitute for Y_t^F:

$$\begin{aligned}
\widehat{x}_t &= \mathbb{E}_t\widehat{x}_{t+1} - \frac{1}{\eta}\left(\beta\widetilde{i}_t - \mathbb{E}_t\pi_{t+1}\right) + \frac{1+\chi}{\eta+\chi}\mathbb{E}_t\left(\widehat{A}_{t+1} - \widehat{A}_t\right) \\
&= \mathbb{E}_t\widehat{x}_{t+1} - \frac{1}{\eta}\left(\beta\widetilde{i}_t - \mathbb{E}_t\pi_{t+1}\right) + \frac{1+\chi}{\eta+\chi}\mathbb{E}_t\left(\rho_A\widehat{A}_t + \varepsilon_{At} - \widehat{A}_t\right) \\
&= \mathbb{E}_t\widehat{x}_{t+1} - \frac{1}{\eta}\left(\beta\widetilde{i}_t - \mathbb{E}_t\pi_{t+1}\right) - \frac{(1+\chi)(1-\rho_A)}{\eta+\chi}\widehat{A}_t,
\end{aligned} \tag{15.35}$$

where the second equality follows the log-linearized TFP process, $\widehat{A}_t = \rho_A\widehat{A}_{t-1} + \sigma_A\varepsilon_{At}$. Finally, rewrite equation (15.35) as

$$\widehat{x}_t = \mathbb{E}_t\widehat{x}_{t+1} - r_t$$

where $r_t \equiv (1/\eta)\left(\beta\widetilde{i}_t - \mathbb{E}_t\pi_{t+1}\right) + \left[(1+\chi)(1-\rho_A)/(\eta+\chi)\right]\widehat{A}_t$; the last term in this expression is the **natural rate of interest** (sometimes called r-star). Loosely speaking, this is the interest rate that is consistent with a flexible price level.

15.4 The Full Canonical New Keynesian Model

At this point, it's convenient to summarize the (log-linearized) equilibrium conditions of the model:

$$\pi_t = \kappa\widehat{x}_t + \beta\,\mathbb{E}_t\pi_{t+1}, \tag{15.36}$$

$$\widehat{x}_t = \mathbb{E}_t\widehat{x}_{t+1} - r_t, \tag{15.37}$$

$$\widehat{x}_t = \widehat{Y}_t - \widehat{Y}_t^F, \tag{15.38}$$

$$\widehat{Y}_t^F = \left[(1+\chi)/(\eta+\chi)\right]\widehat{A}_t, \tag{15.39}$$

$$r_t = (1/\eta)\left(\beta\widetilde{i}_t - \mathbb{E}_t\pi_{t+1}\right) + \left[(1+\chi)(1-\rho_A)/(\eta+\chi)\right]\widehat{A}_t, \tag{15.40}$$

$$\widehat{Y}_t = \widehat{A}_t + \widehat{N}_t, \tag{15.41}$$

$$\widehat{W}_t - \widehat{P}_t = \widehat{mc}_t + \widehat{A}_t, \tag{15.42}$$

$$\widehat{W}_t - \widehat{P}_t = \eta\widehat{Y}_t + \chi\widehat{N}_t, \tag{15.43}$$

$$\widehat{mc}_t = (\eta+\chi)\left(\widehat{Y}_t - \widehat{Y}_t^F\right), \tag{15.44}$$

$$\widehat{A}_t = \rho_A\widehat{A}_{t-1} + \sigma_A\varepsilon_{At}. \tag{15.45}$$

Equations (15.36)–(15.45) form a system of 10 equations in 11 variables, namely,

$$\left\{\pi_t, \widehat{x}_t, r_t, \widehat{Y}_t, \widehat{Y}_t^F, \widehat{A}_t, \widetilde{i}_t, \widehat{N}_t, \widehat{W}_t, \widehat{P}_t, \widehat{mc}_t\right\}.$$

As it is, the system is indeterminate – there are more variables than equations. What's missing is the central bank's policy rule that shows how the risk-free interest rate $\widetilde{i}_t$ is determined. For this purpose, I assume that the central bank follows a Taylor (1993) rule of the form

$$\widetilde{i}_t = \gamma\widetilde{i}_{t-1} + (1-\gamma)\nu_\pi\pi_t + (1-\gamma)\nu_x\widehat{x}_t + \sigma_R\varepsilon_{Rt}, \tag{15.46}$$

where $\gamma \in [0,1)$ and $\nu_\pi, \nu_x \geq 0$ are policy parameters that determine the responsiveness of the interest rate to inflation and the output gap, and ε_{Rt} is interpreted as a monetary policy shock. Under the policy rule described by (15.46), the system is determinate and (given parameter values) I am able to solve the equilibrium and find policy functions for all of the model's variables, as I show in the section below.

Remark 15.11 At this point, note equations (15.42) and (15.43) both determine the real wage (since $\widehat{w}_t = \widehat{W}_t - \widehat{P}_t$). However, the real wage does not determine any other value in the system; given values for $\widehat{mc}_t$ and $\widehat{A}_t$ or $\widehat{Y}_t$ and $\widehat{N}_t$, obtaining $\widehat{w}_t$ is straightforward. Thus, in what follows, I swap both (15.26) and (15.31) for $\widehat{w}_t = \widehat{mc}_t + \widehat{A}_t$ in order to work directly with the real wage – as opposed to the nominal wage and the price level.

15.4.1 The Revised System

The system of equations that characterizes equilibrium in the canonical NK model (and will be coded in Dynare) is given by

$$\pi_t = \kappa\widehat{x}_t + \beta\,\mathbb{E}_t\pi_{t+1},$$

$$\widehat{x}_t = \mathbb{E}_t\widehat{x}_{t+1} - r_t,$$

$$\widehat{x}_t = \widehat{Y}_t - \widehat{Y}_t^F,$$

$$\widehat{Y}_t^F = \left[(1+\chi)/(\eta+\chi)\right]\widehat{A}_t,$$

$$r_t = (1/\eta)\left(\beta\widetilde{i}_t - \mathbb{E}_t\pi_{t+1}\right) + \left[(1+\chi)(1-\rho_A)/(\eta+\chi)\right]\widehat{A}_t,$$

$$\widehat{Y}_t = \widehat{A}_t + \widehat{N}_t,$$

$$\widehat{w}_t = \widehat{mc}_t + \widehat{A}_t,$$

$$\widehat{mc}_t = (\eta+\chi)\left(\widehat{Y}_t - \widehat{Y}_t^F\right),$$

$$\widetilde{i}_t = \gamma \widetilde{i}_{t-1} + (1-\gamma)\nu_\pi \pi_t + (1-\gamma)\nu_x \widehat{x}_t + \sigma_R \varepsilon_{Rt},$$
$$\widehat{A}_t = \rho_A \widehat{A}_{t-1} + \varepsilon_{At}.$$

This is a system of 10 equations in $\{\pi_t, \widehat{x}_t, r_t, \widehat{Y}_t, \widehat{Y}_t^F, \widehat{A}_t, \widehat{N}_t, \widehat{w}_t, \widehat{mc}_t, \widetilde{i}_t\}$.

15.4.2 Model Simulations

In what follows, let the model parameters take values

$$\begin{bmatrix} \chi \\ \eta \\ \gamma \\ \nu_\pi \\ \nu_x \\ \theta \\ \beta \\ \rho_A \\ \sigma_A \\ \sigma_R \end{bmatrix} = \begin{bmatrix} 2 \\ 1.25 \\ 0.85 \\ 1.5 \\ 0.125 \\ 0.75 \\ 0.99 \\ 0.9 \\ 0.01 \\ 0.01 \end{bmatrix}.$$

I now show the baseline impulse-response functions, first for a TFP shock (ε_{At}) and then for a monetary policy shock (ε_{Rt}). Section 15.5 presents the corresponding Dynare `mod` file.

A Total Factor Productivity Shock

Figure 15.1 shows the evolution of the percent variables (namely, $\pi_t, \widetilde{i}_t, r_t^*$) after a one-standard-deviation shock to ε_{At}. On impact, inflation decreases slightly (about 20 basis points) and this is immediately countered by a fall in the central bank's target interest rate – a bit less than 10 basis points. Note the path for $\widetilde{i}$ is hump-shaped and has more persistence than inflation. That said, the natural rate of interest increases by about 10 basis points as a result of the improvement in TFP, as implied by the last term in equation (15.40).

Figure 15.2 shows the evolution of all the level variables in the model. Given the parametrization offered in Section 15.4.2, I find that, on impact, output increases by about 0.6%, compared to a larger increase in potential output on the order of 0.9%. Overall, this makes the output gap fall by roughly 0.3%. According to the model, both labor and marginal costs fall on impact, which is a standard result in New Keynesian models.

A Monetary Policy Shock

Figure 15.3 presents the path of the model's percent variables as a result of a monetary policy shock (a one-standard-deviation increase in ε_{Rt}). On impact – and as expected – inflation decreases about 80 basis points, caused by the increase in the nominal interest rate (about 60 basis points). Following equation (15.40), the natural rate r_t^* stays constant.

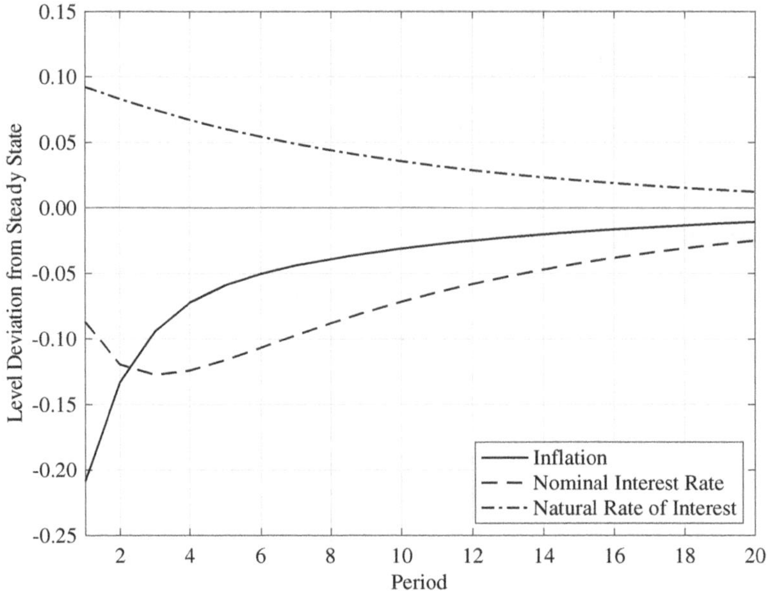

Figure 15.1 Impulse-response functions for $\{\pi_t, \widetilde{R}_t, r_t^*\}$ given a one-standard-deviation shock to ε_{At}.

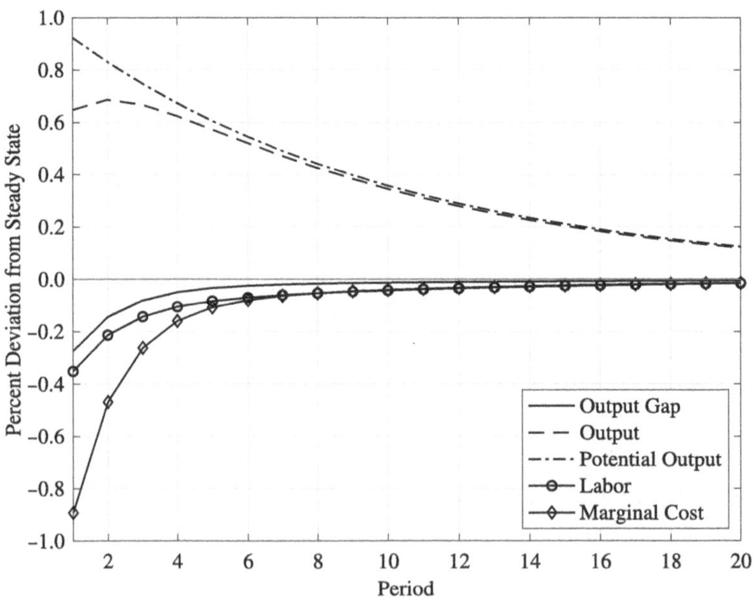

Figure 15.2 Impulse-response functions for $\{\widehat{x}_t, \widehat{Y}_t, \widehat{Y}_t^F, \widehat{N}_t, \widehat{mc}_t\}$ given a one-standard-deviation shock to ε_{At}.

Unlike the dynamics shown in Figure 15.1, here the persistence of all variables is roughly the same.

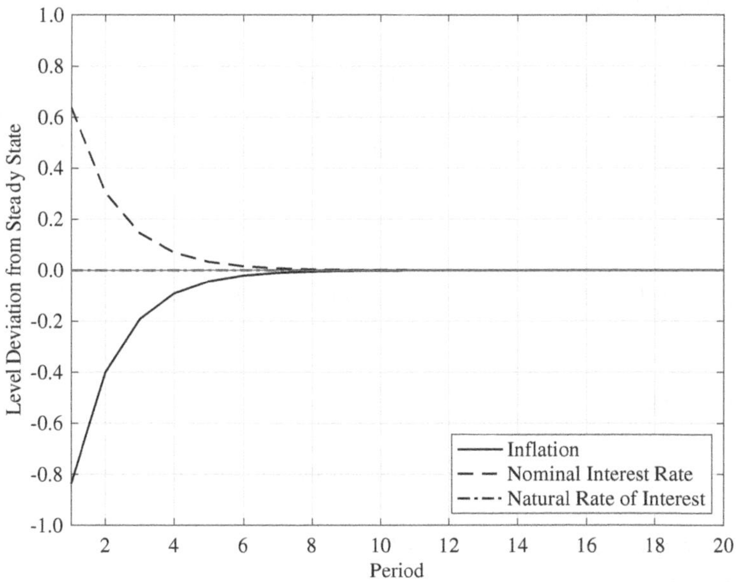

Figure 15.3 Impulse-response functions for $\{\pi_t, \widetilde{R}_t, r_t^*\}$ given a one-standard-deviation shock to ε_{Mt}.

Finally, Figure 15.4 makes it seem like several variables are missing, but they just happen to overlap with one another. Potential output remains at zero, as this variable does not respond to monetary policy shocks – only to real shocks. That said, both output, the output gap, and labor decrease on impact by roughly 1.5%, while marginal costs fall by nearly 5%. This shows that in a New Keynesian world, monetary policy has real effects.

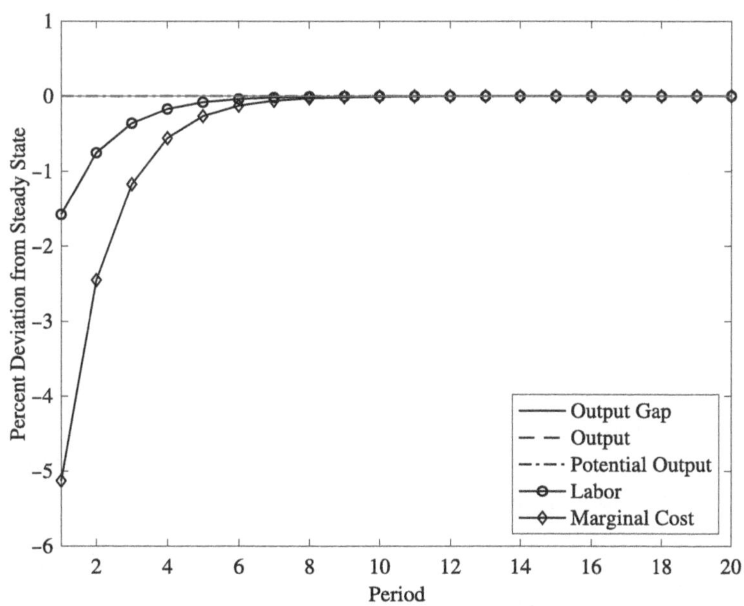

Figure 15.4 Impulse-response functions for $\{\widehat{x}_t, \widehat{Y}_t, \widehat{Y}_t^F, \widehat{N}_t, \widehat{mc}_t\}$ given a one-standard-deviation shock to ε_{Mt}.

15.5 Dynare Code

Below you can find the Dynare implementation of the canonical New Keynesian model from Section 15.4. The online materials for the book also offer a short Matlab script that generates the impulse-response graphs found in Figures 15.1–15.4.

```
/*
nk_canon.mod
Implementation of the canonical New Keynesian model
*/

close all

// PREAMBLE: VARIABLE AND PARAMETER DEFINITIONS

// Endogenous variables (11)
var gap Y YF A N mc w i pi r rstar ;

// Exogenous variables (2)
varexo epsilon_A epsilon_R ;

// Parameters (10)
parameters chi eta gamma nu_pi nu_gap theta beta rho_A sigma_A sigma_R ;

    chi = 2 ;
    eta = 1.25 ;
    gamma = 0.75 ;
    nu_pi = 1.5 ;
    nu_gap = 0.125 ;
    theta = 0.75 ;
    beta = 0.99 ;
    rho_A = 0.9 ;
    sigma_A = 0.01 ;
    sigma_R = 0.01 ;

// MODEL BLOCK

model(linear) ;
    # kappa = (1-theta)*(1-theta*beta)*(eta+chi)/theta ;
    pi = kappa*gap + beta*pi(+1) ;
    gap = gap(+1) - r ;
    gap = Y - YF ;  r = (1/eta)*(beta*i - pi(+1)) + rstar ;
    YF = (1+chi)/(eta+chi)*A ;
    rstar = (1+chi)*(1-rho_A)/
```

```
            (chi+eta)*A;
    Y = A + N ;
    w = eta*Y + chi*N ;
    mc = (eta+chi)*(Y - YF) ;
    i = gamma*i(-1) + (1-gamma)*nu_pi*pi + (1-gamma)*nu_gap*gap
            + sigma_R*epsilon_R ;
    A = rho_A*A(-1) + sigma_A*epsilon_A ;
end ;

// STEADY STATE BLOCK

steady_state_model ;
    gap = 0 ;
    Y = 0 ;
    YF = 0 ;
    w = 0 ;
    A = 0 ;
    N = 0 ;
    mc = 0 ;
    i = 0 ;
    pi = 0 ;
    rstar = 0 ; r = 0 ;
end ;

steady ;
check ;

// SHOCKS BLOCK

shocks ;
    var epsilon_A = 1 ;
    var epsilon_R = 1 ;
end ;

// SIMULATION BLOCK

stoch_simul(irf=20, order=1) ;
```

(Code 15.1)

15.6 Up Next?

It has been quite a bit of material, but we've covered the canonical New Keynesian model. Are we done? Well, sort of. While the canonical model is considered the entry point to the literature, there are several additions that can come in handy. First, the canonical model exhibits sticky *prices*, yet a sizable number of papers also impose sticky *wages* – this being one of the key ideas in Keynes (1936) – which introduce additional dynamics in the model. In addition, incorporating capital into the model (and consequently, investment) is also a handy tool to have around.

Another modification involves adding heterogeneity into an NK model. More precisely, adding *hand-to-mouth* consumers, who are unable to save or borrow and fully consume their disposable income every period. These consumers, of course, benefit from changes in tax policy, which gets amplified via monetary policy.

All of these modifications lead to what the literature calls "medium-scale DSGE models," the kind which are used in central banks around the world. This kind of model has many components – much larger than the ones we've covered so far. However, they can help us understand how policy changes the economic environment in a more precise way.

Alas, we won't be covering any of these extensions. If there is a silver lining, though, it is that your current knowledge should allow you to work on these papers and understand and apply them as you see fit.

What we will do instead is to return to the topic of parametrization. Chapter 9 introduced the concept of calibration, which, while fairly useful, is hard to apply as models become more complicated. Bayesian econometrics have become an important part of the macroeconomics toolkit, and Dynare has had a large role in popularizing the approach. The following chapter concludes the material in the book.

15.7 Bibliographic Notes

The canonical NK model has been built over time, starting perhaps with the contribution of Yun (1996). More extensive discussions of the model can be found in the survey papers by Clarida et al. (1999) and Galí (2018), as well as the textbook-length treatises by Woodford (2003), Galí (2015), and Walsh (2017).

As mentioned in Section 15.1, the New Keynesian literature often linearizes the model's equilibrium conditions around a zero-inflation steady state. This is convenient as it eases the complexity of the operations that follow. However, in the real world, inflation is rarely equal to zero; rather, it takes on a low but positive value. Ascari (2004) points out that this seemingly innocuous assumption can create a lot of problems and that a model linearized around a nonzero inflation steady state behaves very differently from one that assumes $\pi_{ss} = 0$. Ascari and Rossi (2012) compare the effects of trend inflation in models with Calvo and Rotemberg pricing mechanisms. The survey paper by Ascari and Sbordone (2014) provides a solid overview of the issues surrounding this linearization choice.

Walsh (2017, Chapter 8) has a concise but thorough discussion about price dispersion and the mechanism that explains why Δ_t acts like a TFP shock. For a normative view on monetary policy under price distortions, see Yun (2005).

What is a "medium-scale DSGE model"? In a nutshell, a New Keynesian model with sticky prices, sticky wages, and a sizable number of real frictions. The standard references include Christiano et al. (2005) and Smets and Wouters (2007); the textbook by Galí (2015) is a useful starting point to dive into the extensions that this book does not cover.

15.8 Problems

15.8.1 Interpreting the NK Phillips Curve, Part I

Provide an interpretation of the NK Phillips curve (marginal cost version), equation (15.20).

15.8.2 Interpreting the NK Equations

1. Provide an interpretation of the NK IS curve (output version), equation (15.25).
2. Provide an interpretation of the NK Phillips curve (output-gap version), equation (15.34).

15.8.3 Working with the Model, Part I

Use the code in Section 15.5 to perform the following policy experiments:

1. Change the output-gap response parameter ν_x from 0.75 to 1.5.
2. Change the output-gap response parameter ν_x from 0.75 to 0.
3. How do your graphs inform you about the performance of a central bank that only looks at inflation vis-à-vis one that has a dual mandate (i.e., looks at inflation and the output gap)? Explain.

15.8.4 Working with the Model, Part II

Use the code in Section 15.5 to perform the following policy experiments:

1. Change the inflation response parameter ν_π from 1.5 to 3.
2. Change the inflation response parameter ν_π from 1.5 to 0.
3. Why do you get the result you find in part 2? *Hint*: Google "Taylor principle."

Part V

Macroeconometrics

16 Parametrization II: Bayesian Estimation

Why **macroeconometrics**? Perhaps a better question is: *why not?* By now we know that pretty much everything we do depends on parameters. Calibration tools aside (see Chapter 9), "how should we set their values?" is a question worth asking.

Of course, sometimes the model will give us some insights; for example, for $Y_t = K_t^{\alpha} N_t^{1-\alpha}$ it must be that $\alpha \in (0,1)$, but most of the time we're on our own (e.g., is $\alpha \to 0$ or $\alpha \to 1$?). Also, we don't want to be "cherry-picking" parameter values to get the results we want. There must be some systematic (and transparent) procedure to set parameter values, which also makes sense to us as economists. I now share some examples to help us understand the goal of this chapter.

Example 16.1 Consider the household's discount factor β. This parameter is relevant as it is the basis of the household's lifetime utility:

$$U = \sum_{t=0}^{\infty} \beta^t u(C_t, \ell_t).$$

We assume $\beta < 1$ on the basis of impatience: other things the same, a given bundle consumed tomorrow yields less utility than consuming the same bundle today. But would choosing $\beta = 1.035$ pass the smell test? (No.)

Example 16.2 Once again, consider the household's lifetime utility function

$$U = \sum_{t=0}^{\infty} \beta^t u(C_t, \ell_t).$$

What's an appropriate value for β? Suppose the household has access to a one-period government risk-free bond as in Chapter 13, so that its Lagrangian function is

$$\begin{aligned}\mathscr{L} = \mathbb{E}_0 \sum_{t=0}^{\infty} \beta^t \big\{ u(C_t, \ell_t) + \lambda_t \big[r_{kt} K_t + w_t (1-\ell_t) + (1 + r_{t-1}) S_{t-1} \\ - C_t - X_t - S_t \big] + \zeta_t \big[(1-\delta) K_t + X_t - K_{t+1} \big] \big\}.\end{aligned}$$

The first-order condition with respect to savings S_t is

$$\lambda_t = \beta (1 + r_t) \mathbb{E}_t \lambda_{t+1}$$

which, in the steady state, becomes

$$1 = \beta(1 + r).$$

So what? Well, the model's stationary equilibrium imposes a restriction on the value of β – it is tightly connected to the real risk-free interest rate. Let's bring out the **Fisher relation**, namely,

$$1 + r = \frac{1 + i}{1 + \pi},$$

where i denotes the nominal interest rate. If I assume annual inflation stands at 3% while the nominal return on government bonds equals 3.75%, then

$$1 + r = \frac{1 + 0.0375}{1 + 0.0300} = 1.0072$$

and so $\beta = 1/(1 + r) = 0.9928$.

Example 16.3 Suppose our model takes a Cobb–Douglas aggregate production function of the form

$$Y_t = K_t^{\alpha} N_t^{1-\alpha},$$

for which we want to find an appropriate value for α. If we think about a simple utility maximization problem, namely,

$$\max_{\{x,y\}} \; x^{\alpha} y^{1-\alpha}$$
$$\text{subject to } \; p_x x + p_y y = \mathit{income},$$

then we know that the solution is

$$x = \alpha \left(\frac{\mathit{income}}{p_x} \right) \quad \text{and} \quad y = (1 - \alpha) \left(\frac{\mathit{income}}{p_y} \right).$$

Setting $p_x = p_y = 1$, we get that the optimal demand for each good is such that the expenditure shares are constant and equal to the Cobb–Douglas exponents:

$$x = \alpha \cdot \mathit{income} \quad \text{and} \quad y = (1 - \alpha) \cdot \mathit{income}.$$

So what? Suppose I rename the variable *income* as "GDP" and set $x = K$ and $y = N$. Then

$$K = \alpha \,\text{GDP} \quad \text{and} \quad N = (1 - \alpha)\,\text{GDP}$$

and this implies

$$\alpha = \frac{\text{GDP}}{K} \quad \text{or} \quad 1 - \alpha = \frac{\text{GDP}}{N}.$$

If we review our national accounts, Gollin (2002) argues for $(1-\alpha) \in (0.65, 0.80)$. This means $\alpha \in (0.20, 0.35)$ and explains why the focal point value for α has been $\alpha = 1/3$.

These examples (which involve calibration) provide transparent procedures to set parameter values – and make sense to us as economists. But are these procedures systematic? No: it seems as if each parameter is a special case. Moreover, sometimes we won't be as lucky, as the next example shows.

Example 16.4 As discussed in Chapter 11, models with habit persistence in consumption are popular in the macro-finance world. In this case, the household's lifetime utility takes the form

$$U = \sum_{t=0}^{\infty} \beta^t u\big(C_t, C_{t-1}\big).$$

Assuming logarithmic utility, we get

$$u\big(C_t, C_{t-1}\big) = \log C_t - \varkappa \log C_{t-1}.$$

How should we pin down the value of $\varkappa$?

Examples like the one above show why we need a clear way to parametrize a model – and why macroeconometrics matters for us.

What comes next? Section 16.1 puts Bayesian estimation within the context of the most important parametrization approaches used in the literature. Section 16.2 then offers a crash course in Bayesian econometrics – good enough to understand what Dynare is doing in the background, but probably not good enough to have a conversation with a Bayesian statistician. Finally, Section 16.3 presents two examples that show how Dynare handles Bayesian estimation.

16.1 A Non-Exhaustive List of (Different) Approaches

When dealing with parametrization, macroeconomists often look at two broad camps:

1. **Limited-information** methods, such as calibration, generalized method of moments (GMM) or simulated method of moments (SMM), and impulse-response function matching.
2. **Full-information** tools, like maximum likelihood (ML) or Bayesian econometrics.

Let's take a brief look at each of these approaches.

16.1.1 Calibration

This is the same toolkit found in Chapter 9, and the same strategy I followed when dealing with α and β in the examples at the beginning of this chapter. As a refresher, the calibration exercise looks for a long-run average, steady-state condition, or another piece of micro- or aggregate-level data that helps to pin down a parameter's value. Assuming I have solid data regarding a parameter, it's better to calibrate it. What else does calibration offer? Here are some pros:

- Calibration is very easy to implement.
- It allows me to check whether a model "looks right" without the need for a (potentially time-consuming) econometric exercise.

Of course, nothing is perfect:

- (Half-joking) Some people don't like the word "calibration." It's much safer to use "parametrization exercise" instead.
- By definition, there is no standard error on the parameter – and that makes (classic) econometricians suspicious. (In other words, a calibration exercise imposes a degenerate prior on the parameter value.)

16.1.2 GMM/SMM

This approach was received enthusiastically in the 1980s as an answer to calibration woes. The idea is fairly straightforward: the researcher picks some moments (averages, standard deviations, correlations, etc.) from the data and sets parameter values so the model can generate (match) them.

What are the pros of GMM/SMM? The technique is easy to implement and not controversial – it's firmly grounded in econometric theory. However, there are some cons attached to it. First, since I'm only targeting a *finite* set of moments, a lot of data are left unused (hence the "limited information" qualification). Second, as Bayesian methods are now nearly foolproof to use (see Dynare), the number of researchers using this method has gone down considerably.

16.1.3 Impulse-Response Function Matching

Put simply, if I want my DSGE model to match VAR or SVAR evidence, this is the way to go. In a nutshell, impulse-response function matching selects the model's parameters so that the impulse-response functions generated by the DSGE model match that of an estimated time-series model.

A pro of this method is that as the goal is to match what time-series methods generate, I will have the econometricians on my side. However, there are some serious cons. First, it is well known that the results arising from VARs and SVARs depend heavily on the identification strategy I use. Do I really want to import these issues to my DSGE model? Second (and just like for GMM/SMM), as Bayesian methods are now nearly foolproof to use (Dynare), pretty much no one uses this method anymore.

16.1.4 Maximum Likelihood

This approach was received enthusiastically in the 1990s as an answer to limited-information issues. More precisely, all DSGE models have an associated **likelihood function**, and in the 1990s computers became capable of handling likelihood evaluation (of linear models) via the **Kalman filter**. All I need to implement maximum likelihood estimation is a numerical hill-climber to handle the optimization part.

Remark 16.1 Since I'm going to use this concept later, I might as well introduce it right now:

- Loosely speaking, the likelihood function $p(Y_T|\Theta)$ measures "how likely" (in a probabilistic sense) it is to observe the data Y_T given a parameter vector Θ.
- For now, think of Y_T as some real-world data (relevant to the model's variables) that I have around.

What are the pros of maximum likelihood estimation?

- Logits and probits are estimated using ML, so no econometrician will say anything about your parametrization choice.
- If you're fairly fluent in Matlab, Python, or Fortran/C++, then it's fairly easy to implement an ML estimation routine.

The cons, however:

- The maximum likelihood procedure sometimes yields unreasonable estimates (e.g., $\beta > 1$). While it is possible to restrict parameters, once one does so the maximum likelihood starts looking a lot like Bayesian analysis.
- As Bayesian methods are now nearly foolproof to use (Dynare), pretty much no one uses ML anymore.

16.1.5 Bayesian Estimation

This approach was received enthusiastically in the 2000s as an answer to the issues with ML. While it is similar to maximum likelihood in that it uses all available data (a full-information approach), Bayesian estimation takes this concept for a spin as it relies on **Bayes's rule** (more on this topic later in the chapter).

Here are the pros:

- Bayesian estimation fits nicely in the language of macroeconomics. We macroeconomists have "priors" about parameter values and want to see what the data has to say.
- Dynare makes Bayesian econometrics extremely easy to implement.

What about the cons?

- (Half-joking) My econometrician friends will beg me to go back to calibration after hearing I'm a Bayesian.
- (Definitely not joking) If I don't know what's going on, I can end up running the Bayesian equivalent of an OLS regression of GDP on consumption, investment, government expenditure, and net exports – and feel great about it.

16.1.6 Modern Parametrization Tools: Calibration + Bayesian

Given the discussion above, what's the way to go as of the 2020s? The answer is to calibrate a subset of the parameters, then (Bayesian) estimate the rest.

I've spent some time with calibration (again, see Chapter 9), but Bayesian econometrics is a completely different animal. To set ideas, here's a final example that relies on calibration, somewhat inspired by Prescott (2004). There is a very important punchline that follows, so read on.

Example 16.5 Suppose consumer preferences are such that the intratemporal condition is given by

$$-\phi C_t + w_t(1 - N_t) = 0,$$

where $\phi \geq 0$ is the weight of leisure in the utility function. In equilibrium, the real wage satisfies $w_t = (1 - \alpha)Y_t N_t^{-1}$. If I combine both expressions and impose steady-state conditions, I get

$$-\phi C + \frac{(1-\alpha)Y}{N}(1 - N) = 0.$$

Now solve for ϕ:

$$\phi = \frac{(1-\alpha)(1-N)/N}{C/Y}.$$

Next, I use real-world data to uncover the value ϕ. Suppose I

1. Assume a closed economy and use US data from 1984–2007,
2. Follow Gollin (2002) and set $\alpha = 1/3$,
3. Set the average fraction of worked hours to $N = 0.2381$ (i.e., 40 hours worked per week out of $24 \times 7 = 168$ available hours), and
4. Take the long-run consumption-to-output ratio as 0.5531 (i.e., the average ratio of nominal consumption to nominal GDP for $t = 1984, \ldots, 2007$).

Given these assumptions, the leisure weight parameter ϕ equals, after plugging values,

$$\phi = \frac{(1-1/3)(1-0.2381)/0.2381}{0.5531},$$

or $\phi = 3.8569$.

Remark 16.2 What follows is so important that I've already shared it in Remark 9.3, and I'll repeat it here: real-world values need to agree with model values. Why is this relevant?

To start, assumption 1 in Example 16.5 (a closed economy) is not harmless: if I'm assuming a closed economy, then the model's definition of GDP is

$$Y = C + X + G$$

and not $Y = C + X + G + NX$. If I'm (carelessly) getting GDP from national accounts and not adjusting for net exports, then I'm doing it wrong.

Assumption 4 is also critical. What is consumption in the model? Goods I consume today. But what is consumption *in national accounts*? Nondurable consumption, durable consumption, and services. Should durables go in model consumption? No. Instead, I should add a flow of services (from durables) to the model definition. Thus, for determining the C/Y ratio, I use

$$\frac{C}{Y} = \frac{C(\text{nondurables}) + C(\text{services}) + 0.04C(\text{durables})}{C + X + G}.$$

Of course, if I'm just getting consumption (and GDP) from national accounts and not adjusting for durables, I'm still doing it wrong. (McGrattan and Prescott 2005 provide a great exposition of this idea – highly recommended!)

16.2 A Crash Course in Bayesian Econometrics

It's time for a cookie-cutter crash course in Bayesian statistics; I provide enough material to understand the output Dynare shares with us, but not enough to start writing (or, for that matter, reading) papers in Bayesian theory. Before getting into the details, I make a disclaimer: the material in this section offers little original content, as most of it is borrowed from Robert and Casella (2004) and DeJong and Dave (2011).

16.2.1 Bayes's Rule

Moving along – in principle, getting Bayesian estimation to work is straightforward (at least in theory), as everything revolves around **Bayes's rule**:

Proposition 16.3 (Bayes's Rule) *For two events A and B, the probability of observing event A conditional on having observed event B is given by*

$$\mathrm{p}(A|B) = \frac{\mathrm{p}(B|A)\mathrm{p}(A)}{\mathrm{p}(B)}.$$

Proof. By definition

$$\mathrm{p}(A|B) = \frac{\mathrm{p}(A,B)}{\mathrm{p}(B)}$$

and by symmetry

$$\mathrm{p}(B|A) = \frac{\mathrm{p}(A,B)}{\mathrm{p}(A)}.$$

Rewrite this last expression as

$$\mathrm{p}(A,B) = \mathrm{p}(B|A)\mathrm{p}(A)$$

and combine it with the first expression to get Bayes's rule.

As it turns out, I need three key components in order to get Bayesian estimation to work:

1. The likelihood function of the DSGE model, $p(Y_T|\Theta)$,
2. A density function $p(\Theta)$ describing the **priors** the econometrician (i.e., you) has over the parameters, and
3. A computational routine that can handle all the Bayesian procedures described below.

Why do I need these components? Because my goal is to find the probability $p(\Theta|Y_T)$, the **posterior** estimate of the parameter vector Θ, which can be derived from the likelihood function. Indeed, from basic probability,

$$p(\Theta|Y_T) = \frac{p(Y_T, \Theta)}{p(Y_T)} \quad \text{and} \quad p(Y_T|\Theta) = \frac{p(Y_T, \Theta)}{p(\Theta)}.$$

Combining the two gives

$$p(\Theta|Y_T) = \frac{p(Y_T|\Theta)p(\Theta)}{p(Y_T)}.$$

(Yes, it's all about Bayes's rule.) Now, since $p(Y_T)$ is just a constant, the expression above can be set as

$$p(\Theta|Y_T) \propto p(Y_T|\Theta)p(\Theta) \equiv \mathcal{K}(\Theta|Y_T),$$

where $\mathcal{K}(\Theta|Y_T)$ is known as the **posterior kernel**. The kernel depends on the DSGE likelihood $p(Y_T|\Theta)$ and the prior density $p(\Theta)$.

Is that it? No. Getting the likelihood of parameters given data is conceptually easy, yet problems arrive too soon:

- We rarely have any insight about the distribution of $\mathcal{K}(\Theta|Y_T)$.
- Moreover, if I can't find out what $\mathcal{K}(\Theta|Y_T)$ is, how can I move forward?

That's why we rely on Dynare, but I need to add more details to the Bayesian toolkit.

16.2.2 Intermezzo VII: Observable vs. Unobservable Variables

Let's start with the notion of an **observable variable**. These are variables that the econometrician (i.e., you) can observe and that can be measured accurately – up to some measurement error like, say, GDP.

Let y_t be an $n \times 1$ vector with observable variables and let the sequence $\{y_j\}_{j=1}^T$ be denoted by Y_T. Now let s_t denote an $m \times 1$ vector with state variables, which we assume are **unobservable**. I use S_T to denote the sequence $\{s_j\}_{j=1}^T$.

(What's an example of an unobservable variable? Think of the capital stock. We can approximate it with national accounts data but we'll never be able to observe it directly.)

16.2.3 The Three Key Densities

There are three probability distribution functions (densities) that play a key role in what comes next.

The State-Transition Density

First, consider the **state-transition density**, which keeps track of how the state vector evolves as a function of the previous values of the state vector and the observables:

$$p(s_t|s_{t-1}, Y_{t-1}, \Theta).$$

The state-transition density has an associated **state-transition equation** that is nothing more than a law of motion:

$$s_t = f(s_{t-1}, Y_{t-1}, e_t, \Theta),$$

where e_t is a vector of innovations, often denoted **structural shocks**.

Example 16.6 What does a state-transition density (and equation) look like in the DSGE models I've covered so far? Let's consider two individual elements in s_t, say, A_t and K_t. First think of TFP, which is an *exogenous* state variable. The state-transition density is

$$p(A_t|s_{t-1}, Y_{t-1}, \Theta) = p(A_t|A_{t-1}, \rho_A, \sigma_A),$$

where A_t doesn't depend on Y_{t-1} since TFP is a Markov process. Next, the state-transition equation is

$$A_t = f(s_{t-1}, Y_{t-1}, e_t, \Theta) = f(A_{t-1}, \varepsilon_{At}, \rho_A, \sigma_A)$$

or, more precisely,

$$A_t = f(A_{t-1}, \varepsilon_{At}, \rho_A, \sigma_A) \implies \log A_t = (1 - \rho_A)\log A_{ss} + \rho_A \log A_{t-1} + \sigma_A \varepsilon_{At}.$$

Now consider K_t, which is an *endogenous* state variable. The state-transition density is

$$p(K_t|s_{t-1}, Y_{t-1}, \Theta) = p(K_t|K_{t-1}, A_t, \Theta).$$

In this case, K_t doesn't depend on Y_{t-1} because I look at its policy function. The state-transition equation is

$$K_t = f(s_{t-1}, Y_{t-1}, e_t, \Theta) = f(K_{t-1}, A_t, \Theta),$$

where the state-transition equation doesn't depend on e_t directly – only indirectly via A_t. More precisely,

$$K_t = f(K_{t-1}, A_t, \Theta) \implies K_t = \varphi_{kk}(\Theta)K_{t-1} + \varphi_{ka}(\Theta)A_t,$$

where the $\varphi_{ki}(\Theta)$ terms ($i = k, a$) are the policy function coefficients.

The Observation Density

Next, consider the **observation density**, which keeps track of how observable variables evolve as a function of the current state and previous values of the observables:

$$p(y_t|s_t, Y_{t-1}, \Theta).$$

As expected, the observation density has a corresponding **observation equation**

$$y_t = g\left(s_t, Y_{t-1}, u_t, \Theta\right),$$

where u_t is a vector of innovations, often denoted **measurement errors**.

Example 16.7 What does an observation density (and equation) look like in a DSGE model? Let's consider an individual element in y_t, say, investment $\left(X_t\right)$. The observation density for investment is

$$\mathrm{p}\left(X_t|s_t, Y_{t-1}, \Theta\right) = \mathrm{p}\left(X_t|K_t, A_t, \Theta\right),$$

where, again, X_t doesn't depend on Y_{t-1} since I'm dealing with its policy function. Moving along, the observation equation is

$$X_t = g\left(s_t, Y_{t-1}, u_t, \Theta\right) = g\left(K_t, A_t, \Theta\right)$$

or, more precisely,

$$X_t = g\left(K_t, z_t, \Theta\right) \implies X_t = \varphi_{xk}\left(\Theta\right)K_t + \varphi_{xa}\left(\Theta\right)A_t.$$

The Initial Distribution of the State

The third (and final) density is the **initial distribution of the state**,

$$\mathrm{p}\left(s_0|Y_0, \Theta\right).$$

Loosely speaking, this is our "K_0, A_0 given" condition. Most of the time, the steady state of the model is the natural place to set the initial distribution.

16.2.4 State-Space Representations

In Appendix E I show how to map a (log-linearized) system of equilibrium conditions to a matrix system of equations of the form

$$0 = \mathbb{E}_t\left[\mathbf{F}\mathbf{x}_{t+1} + \mathbf{G}\mathbf{x}_t + \mathbf{H}\mathbf{x}_{t-1} + \mathbf{L}\mathbf{z}_{t+1} + \mathbf{M}\mathbf{z}_t\right], \tag{16.1}$$

$$\mathbf{z}_{t+1} = \mathbf{N}\mathbf{z}_t + \mathbf{e}_{t+1}, \tag{16.2}$$

where $\mathbf{x}_t$ is a vector of endogenous variables and $\mathbf{z}_t$ is a vector of exogenous variables. From (16.1) and (16.2), I am able to derive a set of policy functions of the form

$$\mathbf{x}_t = \mathbf{P}\mathbf{x}_{t-1} + \mathbf{Q}\mathbf{z}_t. \tag{16.3}$$

Note equation (16.3) doesn't include measurement errors – this will matter in a bit.

I want to set the system above in a **state-space representation** (SSR) of the form

$$\mathbf{s}_t = \mathbf{A}(\Theta)\mathbf{s}_{t-1} + \mathbf{e}_t, \tag{16.4}$$

$$\mathbf{y}_t = \mathbf{B}(\Theta)^{\mathrm{T}}\mathbf{s}_t + \mathbf{u}_t, \tag{16.5}$$

where $\{s_t, y_t, e_t, u_t\}$ are as described before (the bold versions indicate the matrices that collect all terms), **A** and **B** are matrices that depend on model parameters, and

$$\mathbb{E}\,\mathbf{e}_t\mathbf{e}_t^{\mathrm{T}} = \mathbf{Q}, \quad \mathbb{E}\,\mathbf{u}_t\mathbf{u}_t^{\mathrm{T}} = \boldsymbol{\Sigma}_u.$$

Fortunately, mapping the policy functions (16.2) and (16.3) into an SSR form (16.4) and (16.5) is easy and an example can clear things up.

Example 16.8 I can solve the indivisible labor model of Hansen (1985) using a matrix system of equations. In particular, I arrange the (log-linearized) model variables as

$$\mathbf{x}_t = \begin{bmatrix} K_{t-1} & C_t & N_t & X_t & Y_t \end{bmatrix}^{\mathrm{T}}, \ \mathbf{z}_t = \begin{bmatrix} A_t \end{bmatrix}.$$

(To keep notation light, I'm ignoring the hats on top of variables.) The procedure yields policy functions for $\{K_t, C_t, N_t, X_t, Y_t\}$ as a function of the states $\{K_{t-1}, A_t\}$:

$$\begin{aligned} K_t &= \varphi_{kk}K_{t-1} + \varphi_{ka}A_t, \\ C_t &= \varphi_{ck}K_{t-1} + \varphi_{ca}A_t, \\ N_t &= \varphi_{nk}K_{t-1} + \varphi_{na}A_t, \\ X_t &= \varphi_{xk}K_{t-1} + \varphi_{xa}A_t, \\ Y_t &= \varphi_{yk}K_{t-1} + \varphi_{ya}A_t. \end{aligned}$$

Armed with these policy functions, I build the state-transition equation (16.4) as

$$\underbrace{\begin{bmatrix} K_t \\ A_t \end{bmatrix}}_{\mathbf{s}_t} = \underbrace{\begin{bmatrix} \varphi_{kk} & \varphi_{ka} \\ 0 & \rho_A \end{bmatrix}}_{\mathbf{A}(\Theta)} \underbrace{\begin{bmatrix} K_{t-1} \\ A_{t-1} \end{bmatrix}}_{\mathbf{s}_{t-1}} + \underbrace{\begin{bmatrix} 0 \\ \varepsilon_{At} \end{bmatrix}}_{\mathbf{e}_t}.$$

If the econometrician (i.e., you) can measure consumption, hours, investment, and GDP, then the observable equation (16.5) is

$$\underbrace{\begin{bmatrix} C_t \\ N_t \\ X_t \\ Y_t \end{bmatrix}}_{\mathbf{y}_t} = \underbrace{\begin{bmatrix} \varphi_{ck} & \varphi_{nk} & \varphi_{xk} & \varphi_{yk} \\ \varphi_{ca} & \varphi_{na} & \varphi_{xa} & \varphi_{ya} \end{bmatrix}^{\mathrm{T}}}_{\mathbf{B}(\Theta)^{\mathrm{T}}} \underbrace{\begin{bmatrix} K_t \\ A_t \end{bmatrix}}_{\mathbf{s}_t} + \underbrace{\begin{bmatrix} u_t^c \\ u_t^n \\ u_t^x \\ u_t^y \end{bmatrix}}_{\mathbf{u}_t}.$$

Remark 16.4 Do I need to add the measurement error components (the u_t^i terms)? The answer is "not really," since this choice is just an assumption about how the econometrician (i.e., you) gets to observe the data and how it is related to model variables. However, if I don't add them, then the entire stochastic behavior of the model observables depends on the structural shock e.

Is that all? Not exactly. The only hard requirement for the estimation procedure to work is

$$\#e_t + \#u_t \geq \#y_t, \tag{16.6}$$

that is, the sum of structural shocks and measurement errors needs to be *at least the same* as that of observable variables y. What happens if this condition is not met? Then the model will have **stochastic singularity**. Put differently, if $\#e_t + \#u_t < \#y_t$, there exist linear combinations of observables that will be predicted as deterministic, making the likelihood analysis fail.

16.2.5 Likelihood Analysis and the Kalman Filter

Let Θ denote all parameters contained in the SSR. The likelihood function is

$$\mathrm{p}(Y_T|\Theta)$$

which, as mentioned above, is (loosely) the probability of observing the sequence Y_T given the parameter vector Θ. As it turns out, the likelihood function has a recursive nature and can be constructed as

$$\mathrm{p}(Y_T|\Theta) = \prod_{t=1}^{T} \mathrm{p}(y_t|Y_{t-1}, \Theta).$$

In the expression above, $\mathrm{p}(y_t|Y_{t-1}, \Theta)$ is the **period-t likelihood function**, initialized as

$$\mathrm{p}(y_1|Y_0, \Theta) = \mathrm{p}(y_1|\Theta).$$

The task at hand is to derive the model's likelihood function $\mathrm{p}(Y_T|\Theta)$. I'll work on this one step at a time.

The Period-t Likelihood Function

Remember the measurement density $\mathrm{p}(y_t|s_t, Y_{t-1}, \Theta)$? It looks very similar to the period-t likelihood $\mathrm{p}(y_t|Y_{t-1}, \Theta)$, right? I eliminate the conditionality over s_t by *marginalizing* over s_t:

$$\mathrm{p}(y_t|Y_{t-1}, \Theta) = \int \mathrm{p}(y_t|s_t, Y_{t-1}, \Theta)\, \mathrm{p}(s_t|Y_{t-1}, \Theta)\, \mathrm{d}s_t.$$

Here, $\mathrm{p}(s_t|Y_{t-1}, \Theta)$ is the density of s_t conditional on the sequence Y_{t-1}; this is also known as the **prediction density**.

The Prediction Density

Remember the state-transition density $\mathrm{p}(s_t|s_{t-1}, Y_{t-1}, \Theta)$? It looks very similar to the prediction density $\mathrm{p}(s_t|Y_{t-1}, \Theta)$, right? As above, I go from one expression to the other by marginalizing over s_{t-1}:

$$\mathrm{p}(s_t|Y_{t-1}, \Theta) = \int \mathrm{p}(s_t|s_{t-1}, Y_{t-1}, \Theta)\, \mathrm{p}(s_{t-1}|Y_{t-1}, \Theta)\, \mathrm{d}s_{t-1}.$$

Here, $\mathrm{p}(s_{t-1}|Y_{t-1}, \Theta)$ is known as the $t-1$ **filtering density**.

The Filtering Density

The filtering density is key to the analysis, since $p(s_t|Y_t)$ describes the probabilities of particular state-vector realizations given the sequence Y_t. From Bayes's rule:

$$p(s_t|Y_t,\Theta) = \frac{p(y_t, s_t|Y_{t-1},\Theta)}{p(y_t|Y_{t-1},\Theta)} = \frac{p(y_t|s_t, Y_{t-1},\Theta)p(s_t|Y_{t-1},\Theta)}{p(y_t|Y_{t-1},\Theta)}, \tag{16.7}$$

or, in words,

$$\text{filtering density} = \frac{\text{observation density} \times \text{prediction density}}{\text{period-}t\text{ likelihood}}.$$

Connecting the Pieces

Believe it or not, this entire process is recursive, as I show below. Here are the three key steps:

Step 1 I start at $t = 0$ from the initial distribution of the state, namely,

$$p(s_0|Y_0,\Theta).$$

The state-transition density for $t = 1$ equals

$$p(s_1|s_0, Y_0,\Theta).$$

Next, combine this expression with the initial distribution of the state to get

$$\int p(s_1|s_0, Y_0,\Theta)\, p(s_0|Y_0,\Theta)\, ds_0 = p(s_1|Y_0,\Theta),$$

which is the prediction density for $t = 1$.

Step 2 Take the prediction density for $t = 1$ I just calculated in Step 1,

$$p(s_1|Y_0,\Theta),$$

and remember the observation density for $t = 1$, which is

$$p(y_1|s_1, Y_0,\Theta).$$

Combine both expressions to get

$$\int p(y_1|s_1, Y_0,\Theta)\, p(s_1|Y_0,\Theta)\, ds_1 = p(y_1|Y_1,\Theta),$$

which is the period-t likelihood function for $t = 1$.

Step 3 For the last iteration step, use equation (16.7), reproduced below in words:

$$\text{filtering density} = \frac{\text{observation density} \times \text{prediction density}}{\text{period-}t\text{ likelihood}}.$$

Here it is again, but now in equations:

$$p(s_1|Y_1,\Theta) = \frac{p(y_1|s_1, Y_0,\Theta)\, p(s_1|Y_0,\Theta)}{p(y_1|Y_0,\Theta)},$$

which is the filtering density for $t = 1$.

I repeat these steps until $t = T$, and I'm done.

The Kalman Filter

If the state-transition equations and observable equations are *linear* and the structural innovations and measurement errors are Gaussian, then the likelihood and filtering densities are easily handled by the Kalman filter. The filter automates the steps described above and is a part of the likelihood-based routines found in the usual places (e.g., Dynare).

Remark 16.5 What if the assumptions for the Kalman filter are not satisfied? It is still possible to obtain the desired likelihood, but the procedure is not as clean cut anymore. The right tool to use is called the *particle filter*, but alas, this filter is way above the level of this book. See Fernández-Villaverde et al. (2016) for details.

So, are we there yet? No. As of now, I know how to derive the likelihood function $\mathrm{p}\left(Y_T|\Theta\right)$ and have a good idea of what the prior density function $\mathrm{p}\left(\Theta\right)$ looks like. However, I still need to figure out how to *sample* from the posterior kernel $\mathcal{K}\left(\Theta|Y_T\right) \equiv \mathrm{p}\left(Y_T|\Theta\right)\mathrm{p}\left(\Theta\right)$. This last fact means that I must open another can of worms: **random variable generation**.

16.2.6 The Fundamental Theorem of Simulation

As first things go first, I need to lay out these words of wisdom from John von Neumann:

> Anyone who considers arithmetical methods of reproducing random digits is, of course, in a state of sin.

Why is this quote relevant? It may seem as if the tools below generate random numbers, but the computer just generates sequences of numbers that *look* random, but aren't. I'll keep these words around as I work with these random-variable-generation methods.

In what follows, I consider a typical probability space

$$\left(\Omega, \mathscr{F}, \mathbb{P}\right) = \left(\left[0, 1\right], \mathcal{B}, \mathcal{U}_{[0,1]}\right)$$

where

1. $\mathcal{B}$ represents the Borel sets in $[0, 1]$ and
2. $\mathcal{U}_{[0,1]}$ is a uniform distribution in $[0, 1]$.

Armed with the notion of a probability space, I provide the following definition:

Definition 16.6 For a nondecreasing function $F : \mathbb{R} \to \mathbb{R}$, the *generalized inverse* of F, denoted F^{-}, is given by

$$F^{-}(u) = \inf\{x : F(x) \geq u\}.$$

What does the definition say? Here's an example to make sense of it.

Example 16.9 Let's borrow an example from Robert and Casella (2004). Here I calculate the generalized inverse for an exponential distribution $\mathcal{E}xp(\lambda)$. Let $X \sim \mathcal{E}xp(\lambda)$ and $\lambda = 1$, so that $F(x) = 1 - e^{-x}$. Solving for x in $u = 1 - e^{-x}$ yields

$$e^{-x} = 1 - u \iff x = -\log(1 - u).$$

Random Variable Generation in Practice

Definition 16.6 is important because it allows me to make sense of the following result:

Lemma 16.7 *If* $U \sim \mathcal{U}_{[0,1]}$, *then the random variable* $F^{-}(U)$ *has the distribution* F.

Proof. See Robert and Casella (2004, p. 39). □

In plain English, Lemma 16.7 tells me that in order to get a random draw from an arbitrary distribution F, I should

1. Generate a draw $u \sim \mathcal{U}_{[0,1]}$.
2. Calculate $x = F^{-}\left(u\right)$.

I now share an example to show what Lemma 16.7 can do for me.

Example 16.10 Let's continue working on Example 16.2.6. Suppose I want to get a random draw from the $\mathcal{E}xp(1)$ distribution. From Example 16.2.6, I know that for $X \sim \mathcal{E}xp(1)$,

$$1 - e^{-x} \iff x = -\log\left(1 - u\right).$$

Hence, if $U \sim \mathcal{U}_{[0,1]}$, then the random variable $X = -\log U$ has an exponential distribution.

While it's hard to conceptualize how to do this procedure with pen and paper, doing it with a computer is very easy. To set ideas, here's what I would type in Matlab:

```
% First I draw random numbers from U[0,1]
Ndraws   = 1000 ;
u        = rand(Ndraws, 1) ;

% Now I calculate the draws from the generalized inverse
x   = -log(u) ;
```

Figure 16.1 compares the true distribution and the one generated from the artificial draws, as seen through the distribution and density functions.

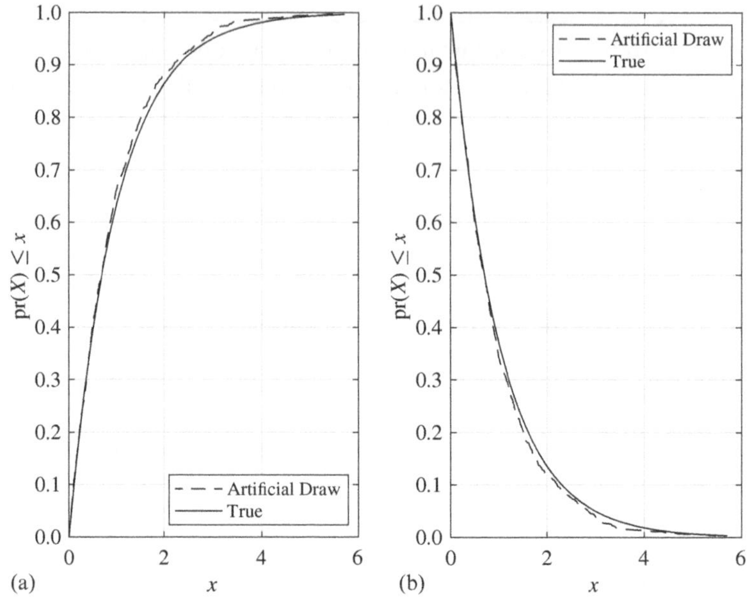

Figure 16.1 (a) Distribution function, true and implied from draws. (b) Density function, true and implied from draws.

The Fundamental Theorem of Simulation

The usefulness of Lemma 16.7 ends when I cannot calculate the generalized inverse function F^{-}. However, there is a way forward. Suppose f is a target density that I want to simulate from. Then, by definition,

$$f(x) = \int_0^{f(x)} \mathrm{d}u.$$

Hence, f is the marginal density of the joint distribution

$$(X, U) \sim \mathcal{U}\{(x, u) : 0 < u < f(x)\}. \tag{16.8}$$

In somewhat convoluted English: since (16.8) is the joint distribution of X and U, I can get random draws by generating *uniform* random variables in the constraint set $\{(x, u) : 0 < u < f(x)\}$. However, as the marginal distribution of X is $f(x)$, by generating a uniform random variable in $\{(x, u) : 0 < u < f(x)\}$ I have just generated a random variable from f. And this random variable was produced without using the original density f – other than through the calculation of $f(x)$.

The long paragraph above describes

Theorem 16.8 (Fundamental Theorem of Simulation) *Simulating $X \sim f(x)$ is equivalent to simulating*

$$(X, U) \sim \mathcal{U}\{(x, u) : 0 < u < f(x)\}.$$

Am I done? Not so fast. The theorem is still half-baked, in the sense that while I can simulate $X \sim f(x)$ and then $U|X \sim \mathcal{U}_{[0,f(x)]}$, these steps are not that useful. What I do in practice is simulate the pair (X, U) directly – and then check whether the constraints are satisfied.

For example, suppose that

$$\int_a^b f(x)\,\mathrm{d}x = 1$$

and that f is bounded above by some constant $m \in \mathbb{R}$. I can simulate the pair $(Y, U) \sim \mathcal{U}_{[0,m]}$ by first drawing $Y \sim \mathcal{U}_{[a,b]}$ and then $U|Y = y \sim \mathcal{U}_{[0,m]}$. I keep the pair of values only if $0 < u < f(y)$ is satisfied. This idea is relatively easy to generalize:

Corollary 16.9 *Let $X \sim f(x)$ and let $g(x)$ be a density function that satisfies $f(x) \leq Mg(x)$ for some $M \geq 1$. Then, to simulate $X \sim f$, it is sufficient to generate*

$$Y \sim g \;\; and \;\; U|Y = y \sim \mathcal{U}_{[0,Mg(y)]}.$$

The most important implication of Corollary 16.9 is that I can simulate from *any* density f that is known up to a multiplicative factor. Moreover, I don't need to know the normalizing constant of f – I only need the ratio f/M. This last fact is very useful, since the posterior distribution looks like

$$\mathrm{p}(\Theta|Y_T) \propto \mathrm{p}(Y_T|\Theta)\,\mathrm{p}(\Theta).$$

All this discussion leads to the fundamental idea underlying how Dynare calculates Bayesian estimates, the *accept–reject algorithm*. Let f be the target density and let g be the proposal density. Then, at iteration i,

1. Generate $X \sim g(x)$ and $U \sim \mathcal{U}_{[0,1]}$.
2. Accept X if $U \leq f(X)/Mg(X)$.
3. Otherwise, reject and return to step 1.

16.2.7 Simulating the Likelihood Function

The Kalman filter (or the particle filter, for that matter) provides an efficient way of obtaining the likelihood function $\mathrm{p}(Y_T|\Theta)$ of the DSGE model. At the same time, I also know the prior density $\mathrm{p}(\Theta)$, as it is set by the econometrician (in this case, me). That said, I still have a final obstacle to go through, which is to figure out how to actually get the parameter estimates.

As it turns out, I need a sampling method to simulate the posterior kernel $\mathcal{K}(\Theta|Y_T)$. To do this, I first apply the log function to the posterior kernel:

$$\log \mathcal{K}(\Theta|Y_T) = \mathrm{p}(Y_T|\Theta) + \mathrm{p}(\Theta).$$

I already know both terms on the right-hand side of the equation. Hence, I can maximize $\log \mathcal{K}(\Theta|Y_T)$ with respect to Θ; doing so yields the mode of the posterior distribution of Θ.

Next, I simulate the posterior distribution using the **Metropolis–Hastings Markov chain** (also known as Markov-chain Monte Carlo, MCMC). The underlying idea is fairly simple: start from a guess Θ°, build a proposal distribution Θ^{*}, and accept Θ^{*} with some probability. I keep on with this iteration until the distribution converges to the target density. Without getting into fairly dense details (but see Robert and Casella 2004 or Fernández-Villaverde et al. 2016 if you want to see them), I should arrive at the posterior distribution after a long chain of iterations.

This process can be summarized in four steps:

Step 1 Start from the posterior mode Θ°.

Step 2 Obtain a proposal Θ^{*} from the jumping distribution J, given by

$$J\left(\Theta^{*}|\Theta^{t-1}\right) = \mathcal{N}\left(\Theta^{t-1}, c\Sigma_m\right),$$

where c is a scale factor and Σ_m is the inverse of the Hessian at Θ°.

Step 3 Calculate the acceptance ratio:

$$r = \frac{\mathrm{p}\left(\Theta^{*}|Y_T\right)}{\mathrm{p}\left(\Theta^{t-1}|Y_T\right)} = \frac{\mathcal{K}\left(\Theta^{*}|Y_T\right)}{\mathcal{K}\left(\Theta^{t-1}|Y_T\right)}.$$

Step 4 Accept or reject Θ^{*} following

$$\Theta^{t} = \begin{cases} \Theta^{*} & \text{with probability } \min\{r, 1\}, \\ \Theta^{t-1} & \text{otherwise.} \end{cases}$$

(Yes, Dynare takes care of all this in the background.)

I need to go to all of this trouble because, while simulating the posterior kernel, I want to ensure that I visit the entire domain of the posterior distribution. The key item in this procedure is the scale factor c, which directly affects the acceptance ratio r.

In applications (e.g., Dynare) I want r to be approximately 25%. The literature says $r \in [0.2, 0.4]$ is good enough. Why do I want to avoid other values of r? If the value is too high, I'll never visit the tails of the distribution. If it's too low, I might get stuck in a subspace of Θ.

16.2.8 Up Next

This section has been dense, but not as dense as it could be. For now, let's pack what we've learned and share an example.

16.3 Example: An RBC-Style Model

Why do I choose an RBC-flavored model? I can think of two reasons:

1. As it has fewer moving parts than its New Keynesian counterparts, everything becomes more transparent. (Though, to be fair, Bayesian estimation is far more useful in NK models.)
2. It's much easier to see how Dynare implements the estimation process.

To make things clearer, I start with a *Monte Carlo experiment*, but not one related to the MHMC routine. What do I mean? I first simulate the model and save the simulated data; in this way I know the values that the underlying parameters take. In a second step, I ask Dynare to estimate the parameters given the simulated data. This process tells me how accurate Dynare is in a controlled environment.

Hence, let's bring back Hansen's (1985) indivisible labor model.

16.3.1 A Monte Carlo Indivisible Labor Model

Dynare Code

The code below is fairly standard and follows what's included in the online materials for the book. That said, I include an additional variable, called `Y_obs`, which will be the *observable variable* used in the Bayesian estimation procedure.

```
// PREAMBLE: VARIABLE AND PARAMETER DEFINITIONS

// Endogenous variables (8)
var Y K N C X w A Y_obs ;

// Exogenous variables (1)
varexo epsilon_A ;

// Parameters (9)
parameters beta phi alpha delta rho_A sigma_A A_ss N0 varphi ;

    beta = 0.99 ;
    phi = 2 ;
    delta = 0.025 ;
    alpha = 0.36 ;
    rho_A = 0.95 ;
    sigma_A = 0.00712 ;
    A_ss = 1 ;
    N0 = 0.53 ;
    varphi = -phi*log(1-N0)/N0 ;

// MODEL BLOCK

model ;
    Y = A*K(-1)^alpha*N^(1-alpha) ;
    varphi*C*N = (1-alpha)*Y ;
    1/C = alpha*beta*Y(+1)/K/C(+1) + beta*(1-delta)/C(+1) ;
    Y = C + X ;
```

```
    K = (1-delta)*K(-1) + X ;
    w = (1-alpha)*Y/N ;
    log(A) = (1-rho_A)*log(A_ss) + rho_A*log(A(-1))
              + sigma_A*epsilon_A ;
    Y_obs = Y ;
end ;

// STEADY STATE BLOCK

steady_state_model ;
    A = A_ss ;
    ome_y = (1-beta*(1-delta))/alpha/beta ;
    ome_c = ome_y - delta ;
    N = (1-alpha)*ome_y/varphi/ome_c ;
    K = N / ome_y^(1/(1-alpha)) ;
    Y = ome_y*K ;
    X = delta*K ;
    C = ome_c*K ;
    w = (1-alpha)*Y/N ;
    Y_obs = Y ;
end ;

steady ;
check ;

// SHOCKS BLOCK

shocks ;
    var epsilon_A = 1 ;
end ;

// SIMULATION BLOCK

stoch_simul(periods=115, order=1, replic=100) ;
datatomfile('simdata') ;
```

(Code 16.1)

What does the last line in the simulation block do? It stores the simulation results in the Matlab file `simdata.m`.

The Estimation Block

After running the `mod` file to get the simulated data, it's time to go into Dynare's estimation block. Just as with previous commands, most things in the estimation block are self-explanatory (though you may need to look at the manual from time to time).

In short, I need to tell Dynare:

1. The model variables that I consider observables;
2. The set of parameters to be estimated, alongside details on the prior density $p(\Theta)$;
3. A file with the data to be used for estimation; and
4. All the estimation options (more on this below).

At this point, it's useful to show what the estimation block looks like inside a `mod` file. At the very bottom of the file, I add the following lines of code:

```
// ESTIMATION BLOCK
varobs Y_obs ;

estimated_params ;
    varphi, gamma_pdf, 3, 0.3 ;                // true value: 2.8491
    delta, beta_pdf, 0.03, 0.0025 ;            // true value: 0.025
    rho_A, beta_pdf, 0.9, 0.025 ;              // true value: 0.85
    sigma_A, inv_gamma_pdf, 0.01, inf ;        // true value: 0.007
end ;

estimation(order=1, datafile='simdata', mh_replic=250000,
    mh_nblocks=2, mh_drop=0.5, mh_jscale=1.35, mode_compute=5) ;
```

(Code 16.2)

Once this is done, I run the `mod` file once more, taking care of commenting the simulation block. I now show the bulk of Dynare's output – with comments.

Prior Densities Plot

First, Dynare shows me the prior densities I've picked. This is useful to verify I am using the prior densities I want – not ones that arise from a typo when capturing the parameters of each prior distribution. Figure 16.2 shows the output produced by Dynare.

Posterior Mode

Dynare then calculates the mode of the posterior kernel $\mathcal{K}(\Theta|Y_T)$ (i.e., the **posterior mode**). After a long string of text that reports the outcome of the hill-climbing optimizer, you should see the following output:

```
RESULTS FROM POSTERIOR ESTIMATION
parameters
        prior mean     mode    s.d.  prior pstdev

varphi       3.0000  2.6502  0.0812   gamm 0.3000
delta        0.0300  0.0291  0.0024   beta 0.0025
rho_A        0.9000  0.9151  0.0182   beta 0.0250
```

```
sigma_A      0.0100   0.0074  0.0005   invg    Inf

Log data density [Laplace approximation] is 294.769195.
```

(Code 16.3)

Once the posterior mode has been calculated, Dynare runs the Metropolis–Hastings Markov-chain algorithm. A separate prompt will indicate the progress and the acceptance ratio.

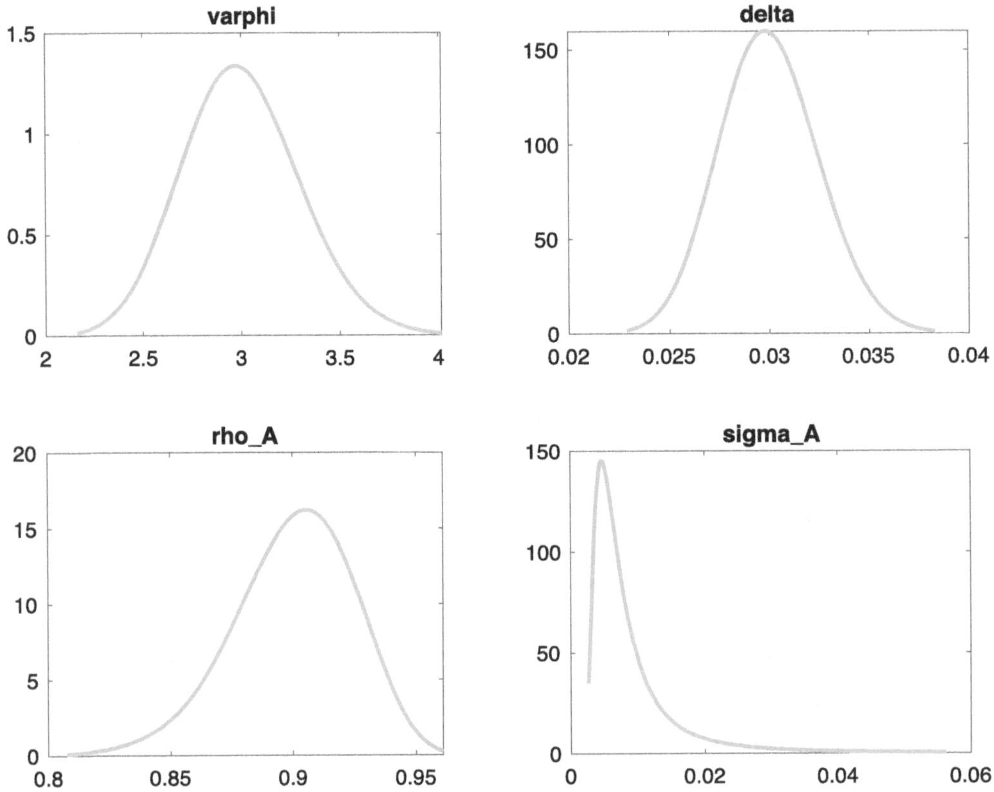

Figure 16.2 A graphical description of the prior density for each estimated parameter.

Estimation Results

After a while, Dynare will print the estimated values:

```
ESTIMATION RESULTS

Log data density (Modified Harmonic Mean) is 294.801767.
parameters
          prior mean   post. mean        90% HPD interval     prior    pstdev

varphi         3.000       2.6533      2.5219      2.7963      gamm    0.3000
delta          0.030       0.0292      0.0252      0.0330      beta    0.0025
rho_A          0.900       0.9166      0.8873      0.9462      beta    0.0250
sigma_A        0.010       0.0076      0.0067      0.0085      invg       Inf
```

(Code 16.4)

At this point it's useful to remember that I'm running a Monte Carlo experiment: I generated artificial data from an indivisible labor model with parameters $\varphi = 2.84$, $\delta = 0.025$, $\rho_A = 0.85$, and $\sigma_A = 0.007$. Given that I know the true parameter values, is the estimation "good"? (Yes, I think so.)

Convergence Diagnostics

After this step, I get a lot more graphical output that's meant to help me diagnose whether the posterior distribution converged or not. Dynare gives me two different kinds of diagnostics: a first batch that describes the convergence over each parameter, and a second one that looks at the overall (model) convergence.

Figures 16.3 and 16.4 give an example of each of these diagnostics. Within each graph, each line represents a Markov chain; ideally, both of these should move together and be fairly constant as the number of observations grows.

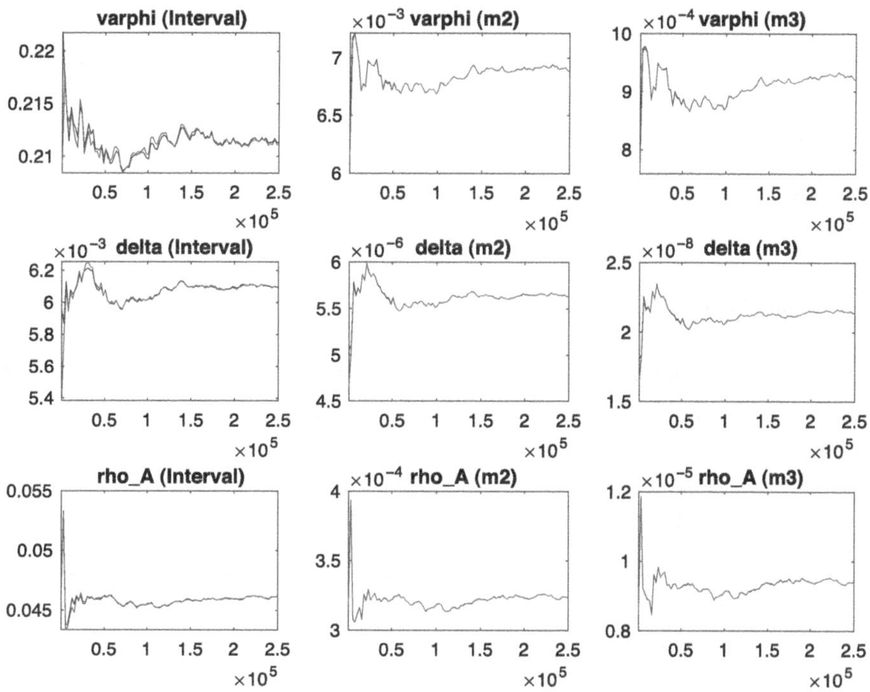

Figure 16.3 (Subset of) MCMC univariate diagnostics: both lines should be constant and converge.

Posterior Densities Plot

The last piece of the graphical diagnostic tools compares the prior I offered with the posterior that Dynare obtained, as shown in Figure 16.5. Ideally, the posterior distribution should be unimodal and the posterior mode should align with the posterior mean.

Taking Stock

While instructive, the exercise I just presented relies on simulated data; moreover, since I happen to know the true parameter values, I can assess whether Dynare does a good job

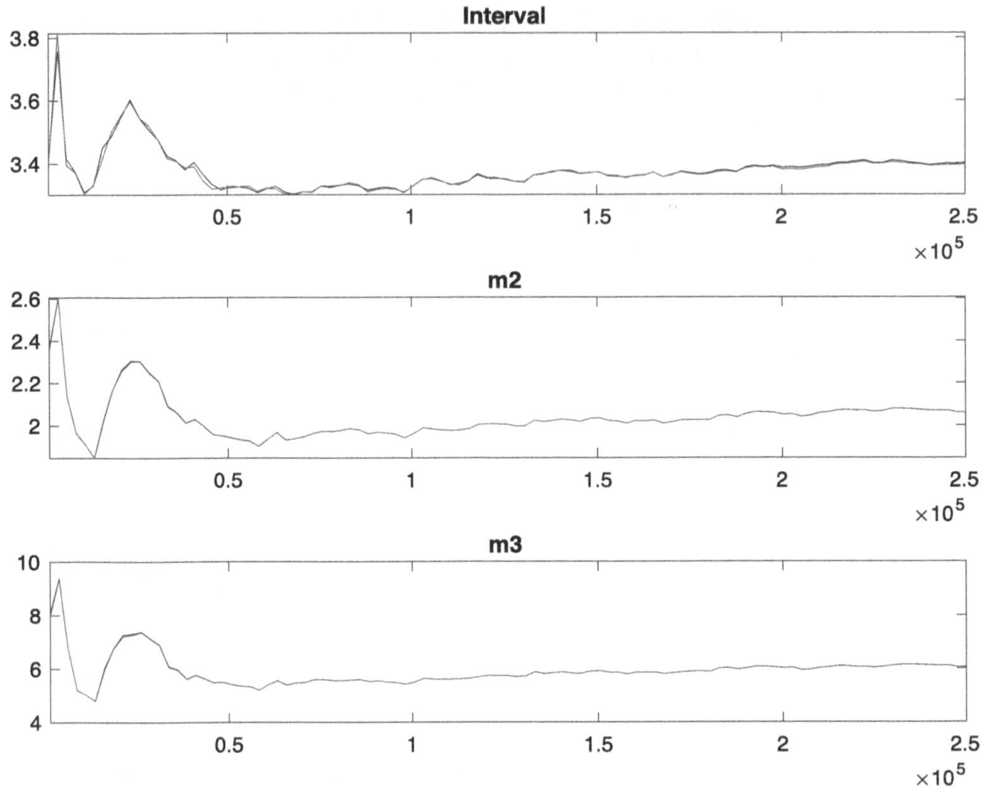

Figure 16.4 MCMC multivariate diagnostics: both lines should be constant and converge.

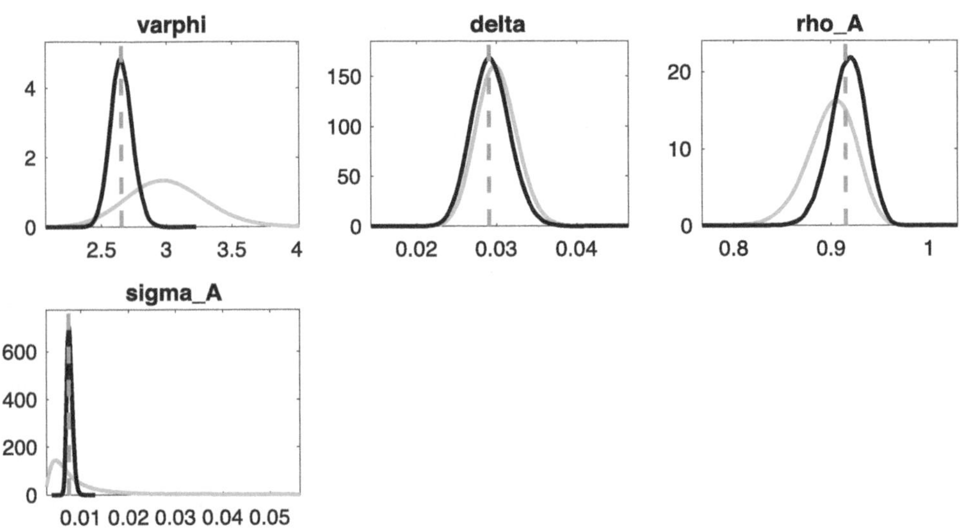

Figure 16.5 Prior and posterior means; the posterior distribution should be unimodal and the mode should align with the mean.

in the Bayesian estimation routine. But what if I were to use real-world data? That's the next step. But before that, I make a small tweak to the model.

16.3.2 An Indivisible Labor Model with Preference Shocks

Consider a modification of the indivisible labor model, which is now subject to preference shocks (see Problem 11.5.2). The associated SPP reads

$$\begin{aligned} \max_{\{C_t, X_t, N_t\}} \quad & \mathbb{E}_t \sum_{t=0}^{\infty} \beta^t z_t \left[\log C_t + \varphi(1 - N_t) \right] \\ \text{subject to} \quad & C_t + X_t = A_t K_t^{\alpha} N_t^{1-\alpha}, \\ & K_{t+1} = (1 - \delta) K_t + X_t, \end{aligned}$$

where, as usual, I need to include the exogenous processes

$$\begin{aligned} \log A_t &= (1 - \rho_A) \log A_{ss} + \rho_A \log A_{t-1} + \sigma_A \varepsilon_{At}, \\ \log z_t &= (1 - \rho_z) \log z_{ss} + \rho_z \log z_{t-1} + \sigma_z \varepsilon_{zt}. \end{aligned}$$

Relative to the indivisible labor model from Chapter 10, the equilibrium conditions change to

$$\begin{aligned} Y_t &= A_t K_t^{\alpha} N_t^{1-\alpha}, \\ \varphi C_t N_t &= (1 - \alpha) Y_t, \\ z_t C_t^{-1} &= \alpha\beta\, \mathbb{E}_t z_{t+1} Y_{t+1} (C_{t+1} K_{t+1})^{-1} + \beta(1 - \delta) \mathbb{E}_t z_{t+1} C_{t+1}^{-1}, \\ Y_t &= C_t + X_t, \\ K_{t+1} &= (1 - \delta) K_t + X_t, \end{aligned}$$

together with the laws of motion for the TFP and preference shocks.

As mentioned in Remark 16.2, I need to be careful how I define my observable variables. Why? Because real-world values need to agree with model values. In the model, GDP is set in levels, but this does not trend upwards like real-world GDP. Since I don't want to go through the hassle of detrending real GDP, I use the (gross) growth rate of GDP as an observable variable. Moreover, as I now have two shocks, I can add another observable per equation (16.6). I include the fraction of hours worked per capita.

Observation Equations

I now take care of the model's **observation equations**. First, let's look at GDP. In the model, GDP:

- Is defined as the sum of consumption and investment, so it's not consistent with GDP as found in national accounts;
- Is expressed in real terms; and
- Is set in per-capita terms (since the model assumes a representative household).

Here's how I build a consistent measure of GDP:

1. I take nominal aggregate consumption and investment from NIPA Table 1.1.5; I add them to generate model GDP in nominal terms.
2. I divide the result from part 1 by the GDP deflator, found in NIPA Table 1.1.4. This value now equals model GDP in real terms.
3. I divide the result from part 2 by the population series found in NIPA Table 2.1. I end up with a model-adjusted measure of real GDP per capita, which I call Y_t^{obs}.
4. Finally, I generate the ratio

$$gy_t^{\text{obs}} = \frac{Y_t^{\text{obs}}}{Y_{t-1}^{\text{obs}}} - 1.$$

Variable gy_t^{obs} is the value that goes into the data file for estimation purposes.

Moving on: in the model, hours worked are defined as the fraction of total available time spent working in market activities. As was the case for GDP, this value is set in per-capita terms. To get the right measure of hours worked:

1. I obtain (i) average hours worked per year and (ii) annual number of people engaged from the Penn World Table (PWT) dataset. I multiply them to get total hours worked per year.
2. I divide the result from part 1 by the population series found in NIPA Table 2.1. I now have total hours worked per capita per year.
3. To get the fraction of time spent working, I assume a person can work at most 5,200 hours – equivalent to 100 hours per week – every year.
4. I then multiply 5,200 times the annual number of people engaged from the PWT dataset; then, I divide by population to get the maximum amount of hours worked per year.
5. Finally, I divide the result from part 2 by that from part 4 in order to get the fraction of total available time spent working in market activities. Denote this by N_t^{obs}.

Variable N_t^{obs} is the value that goes into the data file for estimation.

Dynare Code

For completeness, I now share the Dynare code for the revised model.

```
/*
indivisible_estimation_real.mod
Solution and Bayesian estimation of an indivisible labor supply
model (see Hansen 1985).
*/

close all

// PREAMBLE: VARIABLE AND PARAMETER DEFINITIONS

// Endogenous variables (9)
```

```
var K C N X Y A z gY_obs N_obs ;

// Exogenous variables (2)
varexo epsilon_A epsilon_z ;

// Parameters (9)
parameters beta delta alpha phi N0 varphi ;
parameters rho_A rho_z sigma_A sigma_z A_ss z_ss ;

    beta = 0.99 ;
    delta = 0.025 ;
    alpha = 0.36 ;
    phi = 2 ;
    N0 = 0.53 ;
    varphi = -phi*log(1-N0)/N0 ;
    rho_A = 0.95 ;
    rho_z = 0.5 ;
    sigma_A = 0.007 ;
    sigma_z = 0.01 ;
    A_ss = 1 ;
    z_ss = 1 ;

// MODEL BLOCK

model ;
    Y = A*K(-1)^alpha*N^(1-alpha) ;
    varphi*C*N = (1-alpha)*Y ;
    z/C = beta*(z(+1)/C(+1))*(alpha*Y(+1)/K + 1 - delta) ;
    Y = C + X ;
    K = (1-delta)*K(-1) + X ;
    log(A) = (1 - rho_A)*log(A_ss) + rho_A*log(A(-1))
             + sigma_A*epsilon_A ;
    log(z) = (1 - rho_z)*log(z_ss) + rho_z*log(z(-1))
             + sigma_z*epsilon_z ;
    gY_obs = Y/Y(-1) ;
    N_obs = N ;
end ;

// STEADY STATE BLOCK

steady_state_model ;
    A = A_ss ;
    z = z_ss ;
    omega_y = (1-beta*(1-delta))/alpha/beta ;
```

```
    omega_c = omega_y - delta ;
    N = (1-alpha)*omega_y/varphi/omega_c ;
    K = N / omega_y^(1/(1-alpha)) ;
    Y = omega_y*K ;
    X = delta*K ;
    C = omega_c*K ;
    w = (1-alpha)*Y/N ;
    gY_obs = 1 ;
    N_obs = N ;
end ;

steady ;
check ;

// SHOCKS BLOCK

shocks ;
    var epsilon_A = 1 ;
    var epsilon_z = 1 ;
end ;

// ESTIMATION BLOCK
varobs gY_obs N_obs ;

estimated_params ;
    delta, beta_pdf, 0.1, 0.03 ;
    varphi, gamma_pdf, 3, 0.3 ;
    rho_A, beta_pdf, 0.8, 0.05 ;
    rho_z, beta_pdf, 0.5, 0.1 ;
    sigma_A, inv_gamma_pdf, 0.01, inf ;
    sigma_z, inv_gamma_pdf, 0.01, inf ;
end ;

estimation(order=1, datafile='realdata', mh_replic=250000,
    mh_nblocks=2, mh_drop=0.5, mh_jscale=0.95, mode_compute=5) ;
```

(Code 16.5)

(Yes, I'm getting 250,000 draws from the posterior kernel.) Here are the estimation results:

```
ESTIMATION RESULTS

Log data density (Modified Harmonic Mean) is 165.967664.
parameters
          prior mean   post. mean       90% HPD interval     prior    pstdev

delta          0.100       0.2175     0.1550      0.2771      beta    0.0300
varphi         3.000       2.8919     2.8665      2.9168      gamm    0.3000
rho_A          0.800       0.9631     0.9469      0.9806      beta    0.0500
rho_z          0.500       0.6088     0.4821      0.7384      beta    0.1000
sigma_A        0.010       0.0306     0.0241      0.0371      invg       Inf
sigma_z        0.010       0.0115     0.0081      0.0149      invg       Inf
```

(Code 16.6)

For this set of estimators, the value for δ seems too high relative to what theory would imply. (Remember, I'm using annual-frequency data, which is consistent with a value of roughly 10%.) In addition, the volatility of the TFP process is almost four times as large as what the calibrated model of Chapter 9 suggests. Does this mean that the estimation is "bad"? (No.)

16.4 Bibliographic Notes

There are a few sources that dig deeper into Bayesian econometrics, but most of them are at a level that's much more advanced than what I present in this book. The works by Canova (2007), DeJong and Dave (2011), and Herbst and Schorfheide (2016) can prove useful for advanced readers. In addition, quite a bit of the contents found in Fernández-Villaverde et al. (2016) relate to estimation topics, especially when the Kalman filter no longer applies.

Finally, the Monte Carlo exercise found in Section 16.3 is inspired by McGrattan (2004).

16.5 Problems

16.5.1 Replication 101

Choose one paper among the following: Erceg, Henderson, and Levin (2000); Christiano et al. (2005); Justiniano et al. (2010); Leeper et al. (2010); McGrattan (2012); Schmitt-Grohé and Uribe (2012). (Or better yet, pick a paper of your preference that involves a DSGE model.) Replicate it. Go ahead, you are ready for it. Just have fun!

APPENDIX A
Linear Algebra Basics

This appendix presents the basics of linear algebra. It offers a "cookbook" approach, since my goal is to get working with the main material as soon as possible. While linear algebra is not a prerequisite for this book, it doesn't hurt having a bit of background knowledge. At any rate, all of the concepts used in the book are introduced within this appendix. Finally, I should add that there is little original content here, as I mostly follow Simon and Blume (1994) and Heer and Maussner (2024).

A.1 Vectors

Any point on the real line can be identified by a number $x \in \mathbb{R}$ and any point on the Cartesian plane can be matched to a pair of numbers $(x_1, x_2) \in \mathbb{R}^2$. Similarly, a point in $\mathbb{R}^3$ can be described by a triple of numbers (x_1, x_2, x_3). Now let's generalize this idea: given some arbitrary space $\mathbb{R}^N$, any point in such space can be associated with an N-dimensional **vector**, which is an N-tuple of numbers $x_i \in \mathbb{R}$, $i = 1, \ldots, N$:

$$\mathbf{x} = \begin{bmatrix} x_1 \\ \vdots \\ x_N \end{bmatrix}.$$

Notation A.1 A vector is identified with a bold lowercase letter (e.g., $\mathbf{x}$), while its components use a standard font (x_i). Similarly, a matrix (see Section A.2) is identified with a bold uppercase letter $\mathbf{A}$, while its components a_{ij} use a standard font.

A.1.1 Vector Addition

As the name suggests, vector addition requires adding pairs of vectors component by component. More precisely, if $\mathbf{x}, \mathbf{y} \in \mathbb{R}^N$ are arbitrary vectors, then their sum $\mathbf{z} = \mathbf{x} + \mathbf{y}$ is given by

$$\mathbf{z} = \begin{bmatrix} x_1 \\ \vdots \\ x_N \end{bmatrix} + \begin{bmatrix} y_1 \\ \vdots \\ y_N \end{bmatrix} = \begin{bmatrix} x_1 + y_1 \\ \vdots \\ x_N + y_N \end{bmatrix}.$$

Vector addition requires both vectors to have the same dimension: given two arbitrary vectors $\mathbf{p} \in \mathbb{R}^N$ and $\mathbf{q} \in \mathbb{R}^M$, $\mathbf{p} + \mathbf{q}$ is not defined unless $N = M$.

Example A.1 Let $\mathbf{x}, \mathbf{y} \in \mathbb{R}^3$ be the vectors

$$\mathbf{x} = \begin{bmatrix} 3 \\ -2 \\ 0 \end{bmatrix}, \mathbf{y} = \begin{bmatrix} 1 \\ 7 \\ -8 \end{bmatrix}.$$

To find $\mathbf{z} = \mathbf{x} + \mathbf{y}$, just add the vectors row by row:

$$\mathbf{z} = \begin{bmatrix} 3 \\ -2 \\ 0 \end{bmatrix} + \begin{bmatrix} 1 \\ 7 \\ -8 \end{bmatrix} = \begin{bmatrix} 4 \\ 5 \\ -8 \end{bmatrix}.$$

A.1.2 Scalar Multiplication

Scalar multiplication is self-explanatory. For any scalar $\alpha \in \mathbb{R}$ and any vector $\mathbf{x} \in \mathbb{R}^N$, multiply α by each component of the vector. Thus, $\mathbf{v} = \alpha\mathbf{x}$ is given by

$$\mathbf{v} = \alpha \begin{bmatrix} x_1 \\ \vdots \\ x_N \end{bmatrix} = \begin{bmatrix} \alpha x_1 \\ \vdots \\ \alpha x_N \end{bmatrix}.$$

In addition, combining scalar multiplication and vector addition allows us to create a linear combination of any given set of vectors.

Example A.2 Let $\mathbf{x} \in \mathbb{R}^3$ be defined as in Example A.1 and let $\alpha = -2$. To find $\mathbf{v} = \alpha\mathbf{x}$, multiply each vector component by α:

$$\mathbf{v} = (-2) \begin{bmatrix} 3 \\ -2 \\ 0 \end{bmatrix} = \begin{bmatrix} (-2)(3) \\ (-2)(-2) \\ (-2)(0) \end{bmatrix} = \begin{bmatrix} -6 \\ 4 \\ 0 \end{bmatrix}.$$

Example A.3 Let $\mathbf{x}, \mathbf{y} \in \mathbb{R}^3$ be defined as in Example A.1. Then $\mathbf{w} = 5\mathbf{x} + (-3)\mathbf{y}$ equals

$$\mathbf{w} = \begin{bmatrix} (5)(3) \\ (5)(-2) \\ (5)(0) \end{bmatrix} + \begin{bmatrix} (-3)(1) \\ (-3)(7) \\ (-3)(-8) \end{bmatrix} = \begin{bmatrix} 15 \\ -10 \\ 0 \end{bmatrix} + \begin{bmatrix} -3 \\ -21 \\ 24 \end{bmatrix} = \begin{bmatrix} 12 \\ -31 \\ 24 \end{bmatrix}.$$

Example A.3 also provides an indirect result: we can specify vector subtraction as a two-step process where first we do a scalar multiplication (with $\alpha = -1$) and then a vector addition. For example, $\mathbf{x} + (-1)\mathbf{y} \equiv \mathbf{x} - \mathbf{y}$.

A.2 Matrices

Loosely speaking, a **matrix** is a collection of numbers. In particular, a matrix **A** (with typical element $a_{ij} \in \mathbb{R}$) is the $M \times N$ array of numbers

$$\mathbf{A} = \begin{bmatrix} a_{11} & a_{12} & \cdots & a_{1N} \\ a_{21} & a_{22} & \cdots & a_{2N} \\ \vdots & \vdots & \ddots & \vdots \\ a_{M1} & a_{M2} & \cdots & a_{MN} \end{bmatrix}.$$

Here M represents the number of rows and N represents the number of columns of matrix **A**; we say matrix **A** has **dimension** $M \times N$. If $M = N$ then **A** is a **square matrix** (with dimension N).

For square matrices, we often talk about **diagonal matrices**, such as

$$\begin{bmatrix} a_{11} & 0 & \cdots & 0 \\ 0 & a_{22} & \cdots & 0 \\ \vdots & \vdots & \ddots & \vdots \\ 0 & 0 & \cdots & a_{NN} \end{bmatrix};$$

and **upper-triangular matrices**, of the form

$$\begin{bmatrix} a_{11} & a_{12} & \cdots & a_{1N} \\ 0 & a_{22} & \cdots & a_{2N} \\ \vdots & \vdots & \ddots & \vdots \\ 0 & 0 & \cdots & a_{NN} \end{bmatrix}.$$

(**Lower-triangular matrices** are similar to upper-triangular matrices, with the key difference being that in the former matrices, the elements below the diagonal are nonzero.)

Finally, we introduce the **identity matrix**, which is a special case of a diagonal matrix and is often denoted by **I**:

$$\mathbf{I} = \begin{bmatrix} 1 & 0 & \cdots & 0 \\ 0 & 1 & \cdots & 0 \\ \vdots & \vdots & \ddots & \vdots \\ 0 & 0 & \cdots & 1 \end{bmatrix}.$$

Sometimes it's convenient to append a subscript to the identity matrix **I** in order to denote its dimension. Thus, a 3×3 identity matrix can be identified as $\mathbf{I}_3$.

A.2.1 Matrix Addition

Suppose **A** and **B** are both $M \times N$ matrices. Matrix addition requires component-by-component addition; if $\mathbf{C} = \mathbf{A} + \mathbf{B}$, then

$$\mathbf{C} = \begin{bmatrix} a_{11} & \cdots & a_{1N} \\ \vdots & \ddots & \vdots \\ a_{M1} & \cdots & a_{MN} \end{bmatrix} + \begin{bmatrix} b_{11} & \cdots & b_{1N} \\ \vdots & \ddots & \vdots \\ b_{M1} & \cdots & b_{MN} \end{bmatrix}$$
$$= \begin{bmatrix} a_{11}+b_{11} & \cdots & a_{1N}+b_{1N} \\ \vdots & \ddots & \vdots \\ a_{M1}+b_{M1} & \cdots & a_{MN}+b_{MN} \end{bmatrix}.$$

As with vector addition, the sum $\mathbf{A} + \mathbf{B}$ is not defined unless both matrices have the same dimension $M \times N$.

A.2.2 Scalar Multiplication

As in the vector case, scalar multiplication is also done component-wise; if $\alpha \in \mathbb{R}$ and **B** is an $M \times N$ matrix, then $\mathbf{D} = \alpha\mathbf{B}$ is given by

$$\mathbf{D} = \alpha \begin{bmatrix} b_{11} & \cdots & b_{1N} \\ \vdots & \ddots & \vdots \\ b_{M1} & \cdots & b_{MN} \end{bmatrix} = \begin{bmatrix} \alpha b_{11} & \cdots & \alpha b_{1N} \\ \vdots & \ddots & \vdots \\ \alpha b_{M1} & \cdots & \alpha b_{MN} \end{bmatrix}.$$

A.2.3 Matrix Multiplication

Suppose **A** has dimension $M \times N$ while **B** has dimension $N \times L$. In this case, we say matrices **A** and **B** are **conformable** and we can multiply **A** and **B** to get a new matrix **C** with dimension $M \times L$.

To set ideas, suppose (without loss of generality) that **A** is a 3×3 matrix and **B** is a 3×2 matrix. If $\mathbf{C} = \mathbf{AB}$, then the dimension of **C** is 3×2. (Following the notation above, $M = 3$, $N = 3$, and $L = 2$. It follows that $M \times L = 3 \times 2$.) The operations to obtain **C** are

$$\mathbf{C} = \begin{bmatrix} a_{11} & a_{12} & a_{13} \\ a_{21} & a_{22} & a_{23} \\ a_{31} & a_{32} & a_{33} \end{bmatrix} \begin{bmatrix} b_{11} & b_{12} \\ b_{21} & b_{22} \\ b_{31} & b_{32} \end{bmatrix}$$
$$= \begin{bmatrix} a_{11}b_{11} + a_{12}b_{21} + a_{13}b_{31} & a_{11}b_{12} + a_{12}b_{22} + a_{13}b_{32} \\ a_{21}b_{11} + a_{22}b_{21} + a_{23}b_{31} & a_{21}b_{12} + a_{22}b_{22} + a_{23}b_{32} \\ a_{31}b_{11} + a_{32}b_{21} + a_{33}b_{31} & a_{31}b_{12} + a_{32}b_{22} + a_{33}b_{32} \end{bmatrix}.$$

If **A** and **B** are not conformable, it is not possible to perform the matrix multiplication operation. Moreover, matrix multiplication is not commutative: assuming **A** and **B** are conformable, it is generally not the case that **AB** = **BA**.

Example A.4 Let $\mathbf{A}$ and $\mathbf{B}$ be square matrices of dimension 2 given by

$$\mathbf{A} = \begin{bmatrix} 1 & 2 \\ 3 & 4 \end{bmatrix}, \quad \mathbf{B} = \begin{bmatrix} 6 & 9 \\ 5 & 2 \end{bmatrix}.$$

A bit of work (or computer software) shows that the product $\mathbf{AB}$ equals

$$\mathbf{AB} = \begin{bmatrix} 16 & 13 \\ 38 & 35 \end{bmatrix},$$

yet the product $\mathbf{BA}$ is

$$\mathbf{BA} = \begin{bmatrix} 33 & 48 \\ 11 & 18 \end{bmatrix}.$$

Then $\mathbf{AB} \neq \mathbf{BA}$, which shows that matrix multiplication is not commutative.

A.2.4 Transpose of a Matrix

Let $\mathbf{A}$ be a matrix of dimension $M \times N$ given by

$$\mathbf{A} = \begin{bmatrix} a_{11} & a_{12} & \cdots & a_{1N} \\ a_{21} & a_{22} & \cdots & a_{2N} \\ \vdots & \vdots & \ddots & \vdots \\ a_{M1} & a_{M2} & \cdots & a_{MN} \end{bmatrix}.$$

The **transpose** of matrix $\mathbf{A}$, denoted $\mathbf{A}^{\mathrm{T}}$, is the $N \times M$ matrix obtained by interchanging the rows and columns of $\mathbf{A}$:

$$\mathbf{A}^{\mathrm{T}} = \begin{bmatrix} a_{11} & a_{21} & \cdots & a_{M1} \\ a_{12} & a_{22} & \cdots & a_{M2} \\ \vdots & \vdots & \ddots & \vdots \\ a_{1N} & a_{2N} & \cdots & a_{NM} \end{bmatrix}.$$

Example A.5 Let $\mathbf{A}$ be given by

$$\mathbf{A} = \begin{bmatrix} 2 & 3 & 4 \\ 1 & 5 & 9 \end{bmatrix}.$$

Interchanging the rows and columns results in $\mathbf{A}^{\mathrm{T}}$, namely,

$$\mathbf{A}^{\mathrm{T}} = \begin{bmatrix} 2 & 1 \\ 3 & 5 \\ 4 & 9 \end{bmatrix}.$$

Transposition also applies to vectors; in particular, the transpose of a column vector is a row vector (and vice versa):

$$\mathbf{x} = \begin{bmatrix} x_1 \\ x_2 \\ \vdots \\ x_N \end{bmatrix} \iff \mathbf{x}^{\mathrm{T}} = \begin{bmatrix} x_1 \; x_2 \; \cdots \; x_N \end{bmatrix}.$$

I use this notation when I want to display a column vector within a paragraph; the same vector $\mathbf{x}$ from above can be conveniently expressed as $\mathbf{x} = [\, x_1 \; x_2 \; \cdots \; x_N \,]^{\mathrm{T}}$.

A.2.5 Systems of (Linear) Equations in Matrix Form

Consider the linear system of N equations in N variables given by

$$\begin{aligned} a_{11}x_1 + a_{12}x_2 + \cdots + a_{1N}x_N &= b_1, \\ a_{21}x_1 + a_{22}x_2 + \cdots + a_{2N}x_N &= b_2, \\ &\vdots \\ a_{N1}x_1 + a_{N2}x_2 + \cdots + a_{NN}x_N &= b_N. \end{aligned}$$

I can rewrite the system above using matrices: first, let $\mathbf{A}$ be the $N \times N$ matrix

$$\mathbf{A} = \begin{bmatrix} a_{11} & a_{12} & \cdots & a_{1N} \\ a_{21} & a_{22} & \cdots & a_{2N} \\ \vdots & \vdots & \ddots & \vdots \\ a_{N1} & a_{N2} & \cdots & a_{NN} \end{bmatrix}$$

and let the vectors $\mathbf{x}, \mathbf{b} \in \mathbb{R}^N$ be given by

$$\mathbf{x} = \begin{bmatrix} x_1 \\ x_2 \\ \vdots \\ x_N \end{bmatrix}, \; \mathbf{b} = \begin{bmatrix} b_1 \\ b_2 \\ \vdots \\ b_N \end{bmatrix}.$$

Then, the system of equations can be written as

$$\begin{bmatrix} a_{11} & a_{12} & \cdots & a_{1N} \\ a_{21} & a_{22} & \cdots & a_{2N} \\ \vdots & \vdots & \ddots & \vdots \\ a_{N1} & a_{N2} & \cdots & a_{NN} \end{bmatrix} \begin{bmatrix} x_1 \\ x_2 \\ \vdots \\ x_N \end{bmatrix} = \begin{bmatrix} b_1 \\ b_2 \\ \vdots \\ b_N \end{bmatrix},$$

or simply $\mathbf{Ax} = \mathbf{b}$.

Example A.6 Consider the demand-and-supply system

$$Q^d = 10 - 2P,$$

$$Q^s = 1 + P,$$
$$Q^d = Q^s.$$

(This example is easy on purpose. First, you may remember how to do this from the principles of economics – the solution is $P^* = 3$ and $Q^* = 4$. This will be important in Example A.8.) To cast this system in $\mathbf{Ax} = \mathbf{b}$ form, use the third equation (market clearing) in the other two and rearrange to get

$$Q + 2P = 10,$$
$$Q - P = 1.$$

It follows that $\mathbf{A}$ and $\mathbf{b}$ are given by

$$\mathbf{A} = \begin{bmatrix} 1 & 2 \\ 1 & -1 \end{bmatrix}, \quad \mathbf{b} = \begin{bmatrix} 10 \\ 1 \end{bmatrix},$$

where $\mathbf{x} = [\, Q\, P\,]^{\mathrm{T}}$.

A.2.6 Rank of a Matrix

Let $\mathbf{A}$ be a square matrix of dimension N given by

$$\mathbf{A} = \begin{bmatrix} a_{11} & a_{12} & \cdots & a_{1N} \\ a_{21} & a_{22} & \cdots & a_{2N} \\ \vdots & \vdots & \ddots & \vdots \\ a_{N1} & a_{N2} & \cdots & a_{NN} \end{bmatrix}.$$

I can rearrange $\mathbf{A}$ to be the (row) vector formed by

$$\mathbf{A} = \begin{bmatrix} \mathbf{a}_1 & \mathbf{a}_2 & \cdots & \mathbf{a}_N \end{bmatrix}$$

where $\mathbf{a}_i = [\, a_{i1}\, a_{i2}\, \cdots\, a_{iN}\,]'$, $i = 1, 2, \ldots, N$. Each $\mathbf{a}_i$ represents a column of matrix $\mathbf{A}$. I also need the following:

Definition A.2 The vectors $\mathbf{x}_1, \mathbf{x}_2, \ldots, \mathbf{x}_N \in \mathbb{R}^N$ are **linearly dependent** if there exist scalars $\alpha_1, \alpha_2, \ldots, \alpha_N$, not all zero, such that

$$\alpha_1 \mathbf{x}_1 + \alpha_2 \mathbf{x}_2 + \cdots + \alpha_N \mathbf{x}_N = 0.$$

Conversely, the vectors are **linearly independent** if

$$\alpha_1 \mathbf{x}_1 + \alpha_2 \mathbf{x}_2 + \cdots + \alpha_N \mathbf{x}_N = 0 \iff \alpha_1 = \alpha_2 = \cdots = \alpha_N = 0.$$

The **rank** of an arbitrary square matrix of dimension N is the maximal number of linearly independent columns of $\mathbf{A}$. If the rank of $\mathbf{A}$ equals N, we say matrix $\mathbf{A}$ has **full rank**.

Example A.7 Let **A**, **B**, and **I** be square matrices of dimension 3 given by

$$\mathbf{A} = \begin{bmatrix} 1 & 2 & 3 \\ 2 & 4 & 6 \\ 3 & 6 & 9 \end{bmatrix}, \mathbf{B} = \begin{bmatrix} 1 & 6 & 5 \\ 2 & 8 & 6 \\ 2 & -4 & -6 \end{bmatrix}, \mathbf{I}_3 = \begin{bmatrix} 1 & 0 & 0 \\ 0 & 1 & 0 \\ 0 & 0 & 1 \end{bmatrix}.$$

The rank of matrix **A** equals 1, as there is only one linearly independent column – note that $\mathbf{a}_2 = 2\mathbf{a}_1$ and $\mathbf{a}_3 = 3\mathbf{a}_1$. Similarly, the rank of matrix **B** equals 2, since $\mathbf{b}_3 = \mathbf{b}_2 - \mathbf{b}_1$. Finally, the identity matrix $\mathbf{I}_3$ has full rank (rank 3).

A.2.7 Inverse of a Matrix

The inverse of a matrix is one of the most important operations in linear algebra. To make sense of matrix inversion, we need a couple of definitions. First, let's polish the notion of rank a little bit:

Definition A.3 A square matrix **A** is **nonsingular** if the rank of the matrix equals the number of its columns (or rows). Alternatively, the matrix is nonsingular if it has full rank.

Second, let's formally define what an inverse is – though I still fall short of explaining how to calculate this object:

Definition A.4 Let **A** be a square matrix of dimension N. The $N \times N$ square matrix **B** is an **inverse** for **A** if $\mathbf{AB} = \mathbf{BA} = \mathbf{I}$. If this matrix **B** exists, we say matrix **A** is *invertible*.

Why are inverse matrices so important? Consider a system of equations in the form $\mathbf{Ax} = \mathbf{b}$. It then seems natural to "solve" for the vector **x** by doing an operation similar to division by **A**: intuitively, I'm thinking of the operation $\mathbf{x} = \mathbf{b}/\mathbf{A}$.

Sadly, there is no such thing as division in linear algebra. However, the notion of a matrix inverse allows me to perform this operation. Provided the inverse matrix $\mathbf{A}^{-1}$ exists – which is not always the case – I can pre-multiply both sides of $\mathbf{Ax} = \mathbf{b}$ by the inverse matrix $\mathbf{A}^{-1}$, so that

$$\mathbf{A}^{-1}\mathbf{Ax} = \mathbf{A}^{-1}\mathbf{b} \implies \mathbf{x} = \mathbf{A}^{-1}\mathbf{b},$$

where I've used the fact that $\mathbf{A}^{-1}\mathbf{A} = \mathbf{I}$ per Definition A.4.

Remark A.5 There's a related operation, *post-multiplication*, which yields $\mathbf{AxA}^{-1} = \mathbf{bA}^{-1}$ instead. Of course, these operations need not work out, and if they do, most likely they will return nonsense. But you get the idea.

Example A.8 Recall the demand-and-supply system from Example A.6, which can be set in $\mathbf{Ax} = \mathbf{b}$ form as

$$\begin{bmatrix} 1 & 2 \\ 1 & -1 \end{bmatrix} \begin{bmatrix} Q \\ P \end{bmatrix} = \begin{bmatrix} 10 \\ 1 \end{bmatrix}.$$

The inverse of matrix $\mathbf{A}$ is given by

$$\mathbf{A}^{-1} = \begin{bmatrix} 1/3 & 2/3 \\ 1/3 & -1/3 \end{bmatrix}.$$

(No, I haven't told you how to calculate $\mathbf{A}^{-1}$, but you can easily verify that $\mathbf{AA}^{-1} = \mathbf{I}_2$, right?) It follows that $\mathbf{x} = \mathbf{A}^{-1}\mathbf{b}$ can be calculated as

$$\begin{bmatrix} Q \\ P \end{bmatrix} = \begin{bmatrix} 1/3 & 2/3 \\ 1/3 & -1/3 \end{bmatrix} \begin{bmatrix} 10 \\ 1 \end{bmatrix} = \begin{bmatrix} 10/3 + 2/3 \\ 10/3 - 1/3 \end{bmatrix} = \begin{bmatrix} 12/3 \\ 9/3 \end{bmatrix},$$

or $Q = 4$, $P = 3$, which is the same answer we obtained in Example A.6.

I now state some important facts about inverse matrices.

Proposition A.6 *Any square matrix can have at most one inverse.*

Proof. For a contradiction, suppose $\mathbf{B}$ and $\mathbf{C}$ are both inverses of $\mathbf{A}$. Repeated use of Definition A.4 and properties of matrix multiplication gives

$$\mathbf{C} = \mathbf{CI} = \mathbf{C}(\mathbf{AB}) = (\mathbf{CA})\mathbf{B} = \mathbf{IB} = \mathbf{B}.$$

Hence, $\mathbf{C} = \mathbf{B}$ and thus matrix $\mathbf{A}$ has at most one inverse. □

Proposition A.6 proves that a matrix $\mathbf{A}$ can have *at most* one inverse; however, it doesn't guarantee that $\mathbf{A}^{-1}$ exists. The following proposition – which I state without proof – adds more detail to the concept of an inverse.

Proposition A.7 *Let* $\mathbf{A}$ *be a square matrix. The following statements are equivalent:*

1. $\mathbf{A}$ *is invertible.*
2. *Every system* $\mathbf{Ax} = \mathbf{b}$ *has at least one solution for every* $\mathbf{b}$.
3. *Every system* $\mathbf{Ax} = \mathbf{b}$ *has at most one solution for every* $\mathbf{b}$.
4. $\mathbf{A}$ *is nonsingular.*
5. $\mathbf{A}$ *has full rank.*

Proposition A.7 shows that a matrix $\mathbf{A}$ is invertible if and only if it has full rank. Putting parts 1 and 4 together, we can deduce the following:

Corollary A.8 *Singular matrices do not have an inverse.*

This result is a very useful check to determine whether a matrix can be inverted or not. That said, we still don't know how to calculate the inverse of a matrix, but we know some properties about it. The next sections take care of this calculation.

A.2.8 Determinants and Inverses

Let $\mathbf{A}$ be a square matrix of dimension 2. The **determinant** of $\mathbf{A}$, denoted $\det[\mathbf{A}]$, is given by

$$\det[\mathbf{A}] = a_{11}a_{22} - a_{12}a_{21}.$$

While the notion of a determinant may seem abstract (and it is), its usefulness will be apparent soon. For now, some examples follow.

Example A.9 Let $\mathbf{A}$ and $\mathbf{B}$ be the same matrices as those in Example A.4. Then,

$$\det[\mathbf{A}] = (1)(4) - (2)(3) = -2, \quad \det[\mathbf{B}] = (6)(2) - (9)(5) = -33.$$

Note the determinant is a real number.

Clearly, the procedure above only works for matrices of dimension 2. For bigger matrices, we need more firepower.

Definition A.9 Let $\mathbf{A}$ be a square matrix of dimension N and let $\mathbf{A}_{ij}$ be the $(n-1) \times (n-1)$ **submatrix** obtained by eliminating row i and column j from $\mathbf{A}$. The scalar $M_{ij} = \det[\mathbf{A}_{ij}]$ is called the (i,j)th **minor** of $\mathbf{A}$ and the scalar $C_{ij} = (-1)^{i+j}M_{ij}$ is called the (i,j)th **cofactor** of $\mathbf{A}$. Then, the determinant of $\mathbf{A}$ is given by

$$\begin{aligned}\det[\mathbf{A}] &= a_{11}C_{11} + a_{12}C_{12} + \cdots + a_{1n}C_{1n} \\ &= a_{11}(-1)^{1+1}M_{11} + a_{12}(-1)^{1+2}M_{12} + \cdots + a_{1n}(-1)^{1+n}M_{1n}.\end{aligned}$$

(Yuck.) Of course, an example can help here, and that's what I do next.

Example A.10 Let's calculate the determinant of the 3×3 matrix

$$\mathbf{A} = \begin{bmatrix} 1 & 5 & 2 \\ 0 & 2 & 1 \\ 4 & 4 & 7 \end{bmatrix}.$$

From Definition A.9,

$$M_{11} = \det\begin{bmatrix} 2 & 1 \\ 4 & 7 \end{bmatrix}, \; M_{12} = \det\begin{bmatrix} 0 & 1 \\ 4 & 7 \end{bmatrix}, \; M_{13} = \det\begin{bmatrix} 0 & 2 \\ 4 & 4 \end{bmatrix}.$$

We can easily verify that $M_{11} = 10$, $M_{12} = -4$, and $M_{13} = -8$. (Just in case: $M_{11} = 2 \times 7 - 1 \times 4 = 10$, $M_{12} = 0 \times 7 - 1 \times 4 = -4$, and $M_{13} = 0 \times 4 - 2 \times 4 = -8$.) Then,

$$\det[\mathbf{A}] = (1)(10) - (5)(-4) + (2)(-8),$$

or $\det[\mathbf{A}] = 14$.

The following proposition, stated without proof, is a very useful shortcut to determine whether a matrix has an inverse or not:

Proposition A.10 *The square matrix* $\mathbf{A}$ *is nonsingular if and only if* $\det[\mathbf{A}] \neq 0$.

With this at hand, we're very close to finding a procedure for calculating the inverse of a matrix. Here's the last item we need:

Definition A.11 Let $\mathbf{A}$ be a square matrix of dimension N. The $N \times N$ matrix whose (i, j)th entry is the (j, i)th cofactor C_{ji} of $\mathbf{A}$ is called the **adjoint** of $\mathbf{A}$ and is denoted by $\text{adj}[\mathbf{A}]$.

Now I can calculate a matrix inverse using the following result (I omit the proof):

Proposition A.12 *Let* $\mathbf{A}$ *be a square matrix. Then the inverse of* $\mathbf{A}$ *can be calculated as*

$$\mathbf{A}^{-1} = \frac{1}{\det[\mathbf{A}]} \text{adj}[\mathbf{A}].$$

Calculating determinants and inverses is hard for humans, but trivial for computers. Since a computer can calculate an inverse faster than you can type up the matrix, I'll put a pin on this topic and revisit it later.

Example A.11 Consider the system of equations from Example 3.1. This system determines the optimal choice of a household whose utility is given by

$$u(C_0, \ell_0) + \beta u(C_1, \ell_1) = \log C_0 + \log \ell_0 + \beta\big(\log C_1 + \log \ell_1\big)$$

and faces prices and parameter values $w_0 = 5$, $w_1 = 8$, $r_{k0} = r_{k1} = 0.05$, $\beta = 0.95$, $K_0 = 100$, $h = 16$, and $\delta = 0$. I showed that the 5×5 system that characterizes the household's optimal choice is

$$\begin{aligned} C_0 &= 5\ell_0, \\ C_1 &= 8\ell_1, \\ C_1 &= 0.9975 C_0, \\ C_0 + K_1 &= 185 - 5\ell_0, \\ C_1 &= 128 - 8\ell_1 + 1.05 K_1. \end{aligned}$$

I also showed how to solve this system using brute force. However, I can also solve it using the tools of linear algebra; first note I can rewrite the equations above as

$$\begin{aligned} C_0 - 5\ell_0 &= 0, \\ C_1 - 8\ell_1 &= 0, \\ C_1 - 0.9975C_0 &= 0, \\ C_0 + K_1 + 5\ell_0 &= 185, \\ C_1 + 8\ell_1 - 1.05K_1 &= 128, \end{aligned}$$

which is equivalent to the matrix equation $\mathbf{Ax} = \mathbf{b}$, where

$$\begin{aligned} \mathbf{A} &= \begin{bmatrix} 1 & -5 & 0 & 0 & 0 \\ 0 & 0 & 1 & -8 & 0 \\ -0.9975 & 0 & 1 & 0 & 0 \\ 1 & 5 & 0 & 0 & 1 \\ 0 & 0 & 1 & 8 & -1.05 \end{bmatrix}, \\ \mathbf{x} &= \begin{bmatrix} C_0 & \ell_0 & C_1 & \ell_1 & K_1 \end{bmatrix}^{\mathrm{T}}, \\ \mathbf{b} &= \begin{bmatrix} 0 & 0 & 0 & 185 & 128 \end{bmatrix}^{\mathrm{T}}. \end{aligned}$$

The solution is obtained by calculating $\mathbf{x} = \mathbf{A}^{-1}\mathbf{b}$, which equals

$$\mathbf{x} = \begin{bmatrix} 78.6935 & 15.7387 & 78.4968 & 9.8121 & 27.6129 \end{bmatrix}^{\mathrm{T}},$$

just as in Example 3.1.

A.3 Norms

If you took physics in high school, maybe you remember the idea that a vector gives you both a magnitude and a direction in space. Sometimes, we want to determine a measure of distance from any point (represented by a vector) to the origin. More formally,

Definition A.13 The **norm** of a vector $\|\cdot\| : \mathbb{R}^N \to \mathbb{R}$ is a function that satisfies

1. $\|\mathbf{x}\| \geq 0$ for all $\mathbf{x} \in \mathbb{R}^N$.
2. $\|\mathbf{x}\| = 0$ if and only if $\mathbf{x} = 0 \in \mathbb{R}^N$.
3. $\|\alpha\mathbf{x}\| = |\alpha| \cdot \|\mathbf{x}\|$ for all $\mathbf{x} \in \mathbb{R}^N$ and all $\alpha \in \mathbb{R}$.
4. $\|\mathbf{x}+\mathbf{y}\| \leq \|\mathbf{x}\| + \|\mathbf{y}\|$ for all $\mathbf{x}, \mathbf{y} \in \mathbb{R}^N$.

Two norms will be very useful for our purposes. The first one is the **uniform norm** $\|\cdot\|_\infty$ (also called the **sup norm**), defined as

$$\|\mathbf{x}\|_\infty \equiv \max_{1\leq i\leq n} |x_i|.$$

The second one is the **Euclidean norm** $\|\cdot\|_2$, defined as

$$\|\mathbf{x}\|_2 \equiv \left(\sum_{i=1}^{n} x_i^2\right)^{1/2}.$$

Example A.12 Let $\mathbf{x} \in \mathbb{R}^3$ be defined by

$$\mathbf{x} = \begin{bmatrix} 1 \\ 3 \\ -8 \end{bmatrix}.$$

The sup norm is given by

$$\|\mathbf{x}\|_\infty = \max\{|1|, |3|, |-8|\} = 8$$

and the Euclidean norm is

$$\|\mathbf{x}\|_2 = (1 + 9 + 64)^{1/2} = 74^{1/2} = 8.0623.$$

While not identical, both measures are fairly similar.

A.4 Problems

A.4.1 Matrix Addition

Let **A**, **B**, and **C** be square matrices of dimension 2. Show by example that matrix addition satisfies the following properties:

1. $\mathbf{A} + \mathbf{B} = \mathbf{B} + \mathbf{A}$.
2. $\mathbf{A} + (\mathbf{B} + \mathbf{C}) = (\mathbf{A} + \mathbf{B}) + \mathbf{C}$.

A.4.2 Matrix Multiplication, Part I

Assume **A** and **B** are square matrices of dimension 2. Find appropriate values for **A** and **B** such that $\mathbf{AB} = \mathbf{BA}$. Can you generalize this result?

A.4.3 Matrix Multiplication, Part II

Let **A**, **B**, **C**, and **D** be square matrices of dimension 2. Show by example that matrix multiplication satisfies the following properties:

1. $\mathbf{A}(\mathbf{B} + \mathbf{C}) = \mathbf{AB} + \mathbf{AC}$.
2. $\mathbf{A}(\mathbf{BC}) = (\mathbf{AB})\mathbf{C}$.
3. $\mathbf{A}(\mathbf{B} + \mathbf{C})\mathbf{D} = \mathbf{ABD} + \mathbf{ACD}$.

A.4.4 The Identity Matrix

Let $\mathbf{A}$ be a square matrix of dimension N. Show that $\mathbf{A}\mathbf{I}_N = \mathbf{I}_N\mathbf{A} = \mathbf{A}$.

A.4.5 Properties of Matrix Transposition

Let $\mathbf{A}$ and $\mathbf{B}$ be square matrices of dimension 2 and $\alpha \in \mathbb{R}$. Show by example that the following properties hold:

1. $\left(\mathbf{A}^{\mathrm{T}}\right)^{\mathrm{T}} = \mathbf{A}$.
2. $(\mathbf{A}+\mathbf{B})^{\mathrm{T}} = \mathbf{A}^{\mathrm{T}} + \mathbf{B}^{\mathrm{T}}$.
3. $(\mathbf{A}\mathbf{B})^{\mathrm{T}} = \mathbf{B}^{\mathrm{T}}\mathbf{A}^{\mathrm{T}}$.
4. $(\alpha\mathbf{B})^{\mathrm{T}} = \alpha\mathbf{B}^{\mathrm{T}}$.

A.4.6 Systems of Linear Equations

Rewrite the following system of equations in $\mathbf{A}\mathbf{x} = \mathbf{b}$ form:

$$\begin{aligned} 5x + y - 3z &= 0, \\ x + 2y + 3z &= 2, \\ -x - y + z &= 1. \end{aligned}$$

Then solve the system using matrix algebra.

A.4.7 Matrix Inversion

Use Proposition A.12 to verify that the inverse of

$$\mathbf{A} = \begin{bmatrix} 2 & 1 & 5 \\ 0 & 2 & 0 \\ 1 & 0 & 1 \end{bmatrix}$$

is given by

$$\mathbf{A}^{-1} = \begin{bmatrix} -1/3 & 1/6 & 5/3 \\ 0 & 1/2 & 0 \\ 1/3 & -1/6 & -2/3 \end{bmatrix}.$$

Note the question is *not* asking you to verify that $\mathbf{A}\mathbf{A}^{-1} = \mathbf{I}_3$.

A.4.8 Competitive Equilibrium

Redo Example A.11 but now assume that the household's endowments of capital and labor decline; in particular, let $K_0 = 85$ and $h = 14$. How do the equilibrium values change? Discuss.

A.4.9 Norms, Part I

1. Let $\mathbf{x}$ be as in Example A.12 and set $\alpha = 5$. Show by example that items 1 and 3 in Definition A.13 hold.
2. Let $\mathbf{x}$ and $\mathbf{y}$ be as in Example A.1. Show by example that item 4 in Definition A.13 holds.

A.4.10 Norms, Part II

Consider the following vectors in $\mathbb{R}^2$:

1. $\mathbf{x} = \begin{bmatrix} -2 & 4 \end{bmatrix}^{\mathrm{T}}$.
2. $\mathbf{y} = \begin{bmatrix} 1 & 1 \end{bmatrix}^{\mathrm{T}}$.
3. $\mathbf{z} = \begin{bmatrix} -5 & 5 \end{bmatrix}^{\mathrm{T}}$.

Plot each of these vectors on graph paper; use a ruler so you're able to get a very precise diagram. Once you've done this, find both the sup and Euclidean norms for these vectors. Do the norms offer similar or contradicting results?

APPENDIX B
Models with Trend Growth

All the models covered in the book are, by construction, **stationary**: model variables fluctuate around the steady state but do not exhibit an upward or downward trend over time.

The real world, however, is different. Real GDP trends upward, and so do consumption, investment, and government expenditure. The price of investment goods (e.g., computing equipment) has been on a downward trajectory since the 1980s. As it turns out, our solution methods are not suitable for dealing with trends – and that explains why I've only dealt with stationary models.

Thus, we arrive at this question: how can we include trend growth in our environments? The answer is that we must assume that either (i) all model variables grow at some deterministic rate $\gamma > 0$ or (ii) all model variables grow at some stochastic rate along the balanced growth path.

These notes present the blueprint to deal with both cases. Fortunately, both cases are sufficiently similar that you don't need to learn a different skill if you want to make the jump from the deterministic to the stochastic case. (There's only a bit more algebra to deal with.)

To set ideas, I work with an RBC model that is subject to a *nonstationary* labor productivity shock, which is the origin of the trend growth in this environment. I derive the optimality conditions of the model, show how to handle this trend, and present a way in which this model can be implemented in Dynare.

B.1 Deterministic Growth

I first look at the case in which the economy grows because we assume it. If it helps, think about the Solow model from Online Appendix 3: TFP grows without bound and this translates into output growing without bound as well, though the model doesn't explain why TFP grows in the first place.

To avoid unnecessary complications, I assume that the model economy only has two kinds of agents: a representative household and a representative firm. Since there are no distortions, I will directly set up the SPP.

Notation B.1 In what follows, lowercase letters will denote stationary variables while uppercase letters will denote nonstationary (i.e., trending) variables.

B.1.1 The Social Planner Problem

The social planner chooses sequences of consumption C_t, hours worked n_t, and investment X_t in order to solve

$$\max \quad \mathbb{E}_0 \sum_{t=0}^{\infty} \beta^t \left[\log C_t + \phi \log \left(1 - n_t\right)\right]$$

$$\text{subject to} \quad Y_t = A_t K_t^{\alpha} \left(\Gamma_t n_t\right)^{1-\alpha}, \tag{B.1}$$

$$Y_t = C_t + X_t, \tag{B.2}$$

$$K_{t+1} = \left(1 - \delta\right) K_t + X_t, \tag{B.3}$$

given the process for TFP

$$\log A_t = \left(1 - \rho_A\right) \log A_{ss} + \rho_A \log A_{t-1} + \sigma_A \varepsilon_{At} \tag{B.4}$$

and the trend growth process

$$\log \Gamma_t = \log \Gamma_{t-1} + \log \gamma_{ss}. \tag{B.5}$$

The problem above is standard: equation (B.1) denotes the production technology, (B.2) represents the aggregate feasibility constraint, and (B.3) is the law of motion for capital. The main difference is the presence of a trend growth component, given by variable Γ_t: even though hours worked are stationary – by definition, $n_t \in \left[0, 1\right]$ – the value of hours that goes into the production function is multiplied by Γ_t. In turn, Γ_t grows over time at the (gross) steady-state growth rate γ_{ss}. As is clear from (B.5),

$$\log \Gamma_t = \log \Gamma_{t-1} + \log \gamma_{ss} \implies \frac{\Gamma_t}{\Gamma_{t-1}} = \gamma_{ss}.$$

B.1.2 Solving the SPP

The associated Lagrangian is

$$\mathscr{L} = \mathbb{E}_0 \sum_{t=0}^{\infty} \beta^t \Big\{ \log C_t + \phi \log \left(1 - n_t\right) + \lambda_t \left[A_t K_t^{\alpha} \left(\Gamma_t n_t\right)^{1-\alpha} - Y_t\right]$$
$$+ \zeta_t \left[Y_t - C_t - X_t\right] + \iota_t \left[\left(1 - \delta\right) K_t + X_t - K_{t+1}\right] \Big\}.$$

Note there's no problem in setting up the Lagrangian function with several multipliers – nor do I get a problem when combining all restrictions: it's easy to show that the three constraints can be merged into the single expression $C_t + K_{t+1} - \left(1 - \delta\right) K_t = A_t K_t^{\alpha} \left(\Gamma_t n_t\right)^{1-\alpha}$. First-order conditions are

$$C_t: \quad C_t^{-1} - \lambda_t = 0,$$

$$n_t: \quad -\phi(1 - n_t)^{-1} + (1 - \alpha)\lambda_t A_t K_t^{\alpha} \Gamma_t^{1-\alpha} n_t^{-\alpha} = 0,$$

$$X_t: \quad -\zeta_t + \iota_t = 0,$$

$$Y_t: \quad -\lambda_t + \zeta_t = 0,$$

$$K_{t+1}: \quad -\iota_t + \beta\, \mathbb{E}_t \left[\alpha \lambda_{t+1} A_{t+1} K_{t+1}^{\alpha-1} \left(\Gamma_{t+1} n_{t+1}\right)^{1-\alpha} + \left(1 - \delta\right) \iota_{t+1}\right] = 0,$$

$$\begin{aligned} \lambda_t: &\quad A_t K_t^{\alpha} (\Gamma_t n_t)^{1-\alpha} - Y_t = 0, \\ \zeta_t: &\quad Y_t - C_t - X_t = 0, \\ \iota_t: &\quad (1-\delta) K_t + X_t - K_{t+1} = 0. \end{aligned}$$

The first-order conditions for X_t and Y_t imply $\zeta_t = \iota_t = \lambda_t$; substituting $\zeta_t = \iota_t = \lambda_t = C_t^{-1}$ as needed, I get

$$\phi C_t n_t = (1-\alpha) Y_t (1-n_t), \tag{B.6}$$

$$C_t^{-1} = \beta \mathbb{E}_t C_{t+1}^{-1} (\alpha Y_{t+1} K_{t+1}^{-1} + 1 - \delta), \tag{B.7}$$

$$Y_t = A_t K_t^{\alpha} (\Gamma_t n_t)^{1-\alpha}, \tag{B.8}$$

$$Y_t = C_t + X_t, \tag{B.9}$$

$$K_{t+1} = (1-\delta) K_t + X_t, \tag{B.10}$$

where I also need to add the TFP and trend growth processes, equations (B.4) and (B.5).

B.1.3 Balanced Growth

Next, I calculate the growth rates of the model variables along the **balanced growth path**. (Useful fact: just as in a steady state, all stochastic disturbances are zero along a balanced growth path.) From equation (B.9), it is clear that C, X, and Y are all growing at the same rate, which for the time being I denote by g. Equation (B.10) implies that K also grows at rate g. Using this conjecture in equation (B.8), it must be that

$$\underbrace{Y_t = A_t K_t^{\alpha} (\Gamma_t n_t)^{1-\alpha}}_{\text{in levels}} \implies \underbrace{g = 1 \cdot g^{\alpha} (\gamma_{ss} \cdot 1)^{1-\alpha}}_{\text{in growth rates}},$$

where the second equation uses that the gross growth rates of TFP and hours worked equal 1 (because the variables are stationary to begin with). Hence,

$$g = \gamma_{ss}$$

and we conclude that all variables grow at rate γ_{ss} and that the **trend** for C, X, K, and Y is given by Γ_t. Thus, I can **detrend** model variables via the transformations

$$c_t = \frac{C_t}{\Gamma_t}, \; y_t = \frac{Y_t}{\Gamma_t}, \; k_{t+1} = \frac{K_{t+1}}{\Gamma_t}, \; x_t = \frac{X_t}{\Gamma_t}. \tag{B.11}$$

B.1.4 Detrending

I now use the transformations defined in (B.11) to set the model in stationary form. First, equation (B.6) becomes

$$\phi c_t \Gamma_t n_t = (1-\alpha) y_t \Gamma_t (1-n_t)$$

or, dividing across by Γ_t,

$$\phi c_t n_t = (1-\alpha) y_t (1-n_t), \tag{B.12}$$

so that all variables in the intratemporal condition are now stationary.

Moving on to (B.7), the intertemporal condition, I first put everything in terms of fractions to get

$$\frac{1}{c_t\Gamma_t} = \beta\,\mathbb{E}_t \frac{1}{c_{t+1}\Gamma_{t+1}} \left(\frac{\alpha y_{t+1}\Gamma_{t+1}}{k_{t+1}\Gamma_t} + 1 - \delta \right).$$

Now I multiply across by Γ_t,

$$\frac{1}{c_t} = \beta\,\mathbb{E}_t \frac{\Gamma_t}{c_{t+1}\Gamma_{t+1}} \left(\frac{\alpha y_{t+1}\Gamma_{t+1}}{k_{t+1}\Gamma_t} + 1 - \delta \right),$$

and, given $\Gamma_{t+1}/\Gamma_t = \gamma_{ss}$, the equation becomes

$$\frac{1}{c_t} = \beta\,\mathbb{E}_t \frac{1}{\gamma_{ss} c_{t+1}} \left(\frac{\alpha \gamma_{ss} y_{t+1}}{k_{t+1}} + 1 - \delta \right)$$

or, rearranging one last time,

$$c_t^{-1} = \alpha\beta\,\mathbb{E}_t y_{t+1} \left(c_{t+1}k_{t+1}\right)^{-1} + \beta\gamma_{ss}^{-1}(1-\delta)\mathbb{E}_t c_{t+1}^{-1}. \tag{B.13}$$

Equation (B.8) is

$$y_t\Gamma_t = A_t \left(k_t\Gamma_{t-1}\right)^{\alpha} \left(\Gamma_t n_t\right)^{1-\alpha}.$$

This doesn't look like progress, but dividing across by Γ_t and using that $\Gamma_t \equiv \Gamma_t^{\alpha}\Gamma_t^{1-\alpha}$, I get

$$y_t = A_t \left(\frac{k_t\Gamma_{t-1}}{\Gamma_t}\right)^{\alpha} \left(\frac{\Gamma_t n_t}{\Gamma_t}\right)^{1-\alpha}$$

and thus, I rewrite the expression as

$$y_t = \gamma_{ss}^{-\alpha} A_t k_t^{\alpha} n_t^{1-\alpha}. \tag{B.14}$$

Equation (B.9) is very easy: detrending results in

$$y_t\Gamma_t = c_t\Gamma_t + x_t\Gamma_t$$

and so, dividing across by Γ_t, I get

$$y_t = c_t + x_t. \tag{B.15}$$

Finally, equation (B.10) equals

$$k_{t+1}\Gamma_t = (1-\delta)k_t\Gamma_{t-1} + x_t\Gamma_t$$

and dividing across by Γ_t gives

$$k_{t+1} = \gamma_{ss}^{-1}(1-\delta)k_t + x_t. \tag{B.16}$$

B.1.5 The Steady State in the Stationary Model

Noting that in the steady state $A_{ss} = 1$, equations (B.12)–(B.16) become

$$\phi cn = (1-\alpha)y(1-n), \tag{B.17}$$
$$1 = \alpha\beta y k^{-1} + \beta\gamma_{ss}^{-1}(1-\delta), \tag{B.18}$$
$$y = \gamma_{ss}^{-\alpha}k^{\alpha}n^{1-\alpha}, \tag{B.19}$$
$$y = c + x, \tag{B.20}$$
$$k = \gamma_{ss}^{-1}(1-\delta)k + x. \tag{B.21}$$

I now solve the system (B.17)–(B.21). From (B.18), solve for y as a function of k. I get

$$y = \left[\frac{1-\beta\gamma_{ss}^{-1}(1-\delta)}{\alpha\beta}\right]k \equiv \omega_y k.$$

Using the result above, take (B.21) and solve for x as a function of k. A bit of algebra shows that

$$x = \left[1-\gamma_{ss}^{-1}(1-\delta)\right]k \equiv \omega_x k.$$

I can do the same for (B.20) and obtain c as a function of k:

$$c = y - x = (\omega_y - \omega_x)k \equiv \omega_c k.$$

Now put these expressions in (B.17) to solve for n:

$$\phi\omega_c kn = (1-\alpha)\omega_y k(1-n),$$

which results in

$$n = \frac{(1-\alpha)\omega_y}{\phi\omega_c + (1-\alpha)\omega_c}.$$

Finally, use this expression in (B.19) to solve for k:

$$\omega_y k = \gamma_{ss}^{-\alpha}k^{\alpha}n^{1-\alpha},$$

so that

$$k = \left(\frac{1}{\gamma_{ss}^{\alpha}\omega_y}\right)^{1/(1-\alpha)} n.$$

Working backwards, I use this value to obtain y, c, and x.

B.2 Stochastic Growth

The analysis in the previous section assumes a constant growth rate. How can I think about shocks to the trend growth of the economy? Fortunately, this question is fairly easy to answer. I can reuse most of the work that's already been done. The updated SPP is

$$\max \quad \mathbb{E}_0 \sum_{t=0}^{\infty} \beta^t \left[\log C_t + \phi \log \left(1 - n_t\right) \right] \tag{B.22}$$

$$\text{subject to} \quad Y_t = A_t K_t^{\alpha} \left(\Gamma_t n_t\right)^{1-\alpha}, \tag{B.23}$$

$$Y_t = C_t + X_t, \tag{B.24}$$

$$K_{t+1} = \left(1 - \delta\right) K_t + X_t \tag{B.25}$$

$$\log A_t = \left(1 - \rho_A\right) \log A_{ss} + \rho_A \log A_{t-1} + \sigma_A \varepsilon_{At}, \tag{B.26}$$

$$\log \Gamma_t = \log \Gamma_{t-1} + \log \gamma_t, \tag{B.27}$$

$$\log \gamma_t = \left(1 - \rho_\gamma\right) \log \gamma_{ss} + \rho_\gamma \log \gamma_{t-1} + \sigma_\gamma \varepsilon_{\gamma t}. \tag{B.28}$$

The problem above is virtually identical to the one in Section B.1.1: the planner's objective function is (B.22), while (B.23)–(B.26) correspond to (B.1)–(B.4). However, as is evident from equations (B.27) and (B.28), the trend variable Γ_t exhibits stochastic growth; to see this, note (B.27) implies

$$\frac{\Gamma_t}{\Gamma_{t-1}} = \gamma_t \neq \gamma_{ss}.$$

Other than this minor difference, the rest of the model's solution is identical to what I've done throughout Section B.1.

B.3 Problems

B.3.1 Simulating an Economy under Deterministic Growth

Let $\beta = 1/1.05$, $\phi = 1.5$, $\alpha = 0.36$, $\delta = 0.1$, $\rho_A = 0.9$, $\sigma_A = 0.007$, and $\gamma_{ss} = 1.0326$. Use Dynare and the equations from Section B.1 to simulate time series for consumption, output, hours worked, and investment over a horizon of 100 periods. You should have two graphs: one for stationary (detrended) series, and another one for trending ones.

B.3.2 The First-Order Conditions under Stochastic Growth

Consider the stochastic growth model from Section B.2. Verify that the first-order conditions are given by

$$\begin{aligned}
\phi c_t n_t &= \left(1 - \alpha\right) y_t \left(1 - n_t\right), \\
c_t^{-1} &= \alpha \beta \, \mathbb{E}_t y_{t+1} \left(c_{t+1} k_{t+1}\right)^{-1} + \beta \left(1 - \delta\right) \mathbb{E}_t \left(\gamma_{t+1} c_{t+1}\right)^{-1}, \\
y_t &= A_t \gamma_t^{-\alpha} k_t^{\alpha} n_t^{1-\alpha}, \\
y_t &= c_t + x_t, \\
k_{t+1} &= \left(1 - \delta\right) \gamma_t^{-1} k_t + x_t.
\end{aligned}$$

B.3.3 Simulating an Economy under Stochastic Growth

Let $\beta = 1/1.05$, $\phi = 1.5$, $\alpha = 0.36$, $\delta = 0.1$, $\rho_A = 0.9$, $\sigma_A = 0.007$, $\rho_\gamma = 0.5$, $\sigma_\gamma = 0.033$, and $\gamma_{ss} = 1.0326$. Use Dynare and the equations from Section B.1 and Problem B.3.2 to simulate time series for consumption, output, hours worked, and investment over a horizon of 100 periods. You should have two graphs: one for stationary (detrended) series, and another one for trending ones. How do your results differ from those in Problem B.3.1?

APPENDIX C
Taylor Expansions

If you believe $\log\left(1+\gamma_t\right) \approx \gamma_t$ for γ_t small, that's okay. Otherwise, read on. First I need the following result from mathematical analysis:

Proposition C.1 *Let f be a continuous and $\mathscr{C}^2$ function defined over an interval $\left[a,b\right]$. Suppose $\left\{x, x_0\right\}$ are contained in $\left[a,b\right]$. Then*

$$f(x) \approx f(x_0) + (x - x_0)f'(x_0). \tag{C.1}$$

Proposition C.1 describes the (first-order) **Taylor expansion** of f around x_0, and it works best when x and x_0 are very close.

Now let's see why "$\log\left(1+\gamma_t\right) \approx \gamma_t$ for γ_t small" holds true: let $f(x) = \log\left(1+x\right)$ and suppose I expand around $x_0 = 0$. (Here x is a growth rate: think 0.02 for 2%, so that x and $x_0 = 0$ are close.) Substituting these values, equation (C.1) becomes

$$\log\left(1+x\right) \approx \log\left(1+0\right) + (x-0)\left(\frac{1}{1+0}\right).$$

Working out the algebra, I get

$$\log\left(1+x\right) \approx \log 1 + x = x,$$

as needed.

APPENDIX D
Constant Returns to Scale and Profits

The constant returns to scale (CRS) concept is a direct application of the following mathematical idea (see, e.g., Mas-Colell, Whinston & Green 1995, Appendix M.B):

Definition D.1 A real-valued function $f: \mathbb{R}^N_+ \to \mathbb{R}$ is homogeneous of degree $k \in \mathbb{Z}$ if, for every $\upsilon > 0$, I have $f(\upsilon \mathbf{x}) = \upsilon^k f(\mathbf{x})$.

Mathematically, CRS implies that the production function is homogeneous of degree one. Given CRS and the way I've set up the firm's problem, profits are zero in any equilibrium. To show this fact I need the following lemma, which I state without proof:

Lemma D.2 (Euler's theorem) *Let $f: \mathbb{R}^N_+ \to \mathbb{R}$ be a differentiable homogeneous function of degree $k \in \mathbb{Z}$. Then, for any $\mathbf{x}^\star \in \mathbb{R}^N_+$,*

$$x_1^\star \frac{\partial f}{\partial x_1}(\mathbf{x}^\star) + x_2^\star \frac{\partial f}{\partial x_2}(\mathbf{x}^\star) + \cdots + x_N^\star \frac{\partial f}{\partial x_N}(\mathbf{x}^\star) = kf(\mathbf{x}^\star).$$

The lemma may look complicated but its application is straightforward, as Proposition 2.3 (reproduced below for convenience) shows.

Proposition D.3 *Let $F(K_F, N_F)$ be a CRS production function. Then equilibrium profits are zero.*

Proof. Let $f(\mathbf{x})$ be the function $F(K_F, N_F)$, for which $k = 1$. It follows that the partial derivatives $\partial f/\partial x_j, j = 1, 2$, are equal to the marginal products, so that

$$K_F \text{MP}_K(K_F, N_F) + N_F \text{MP}_N(K_F, N_F) = F(K_F, N_F).$$

Since this relation holds for all pairs $\{K_F, N_F\}$, it also holds for the profit-maximizing pair $\{K_F^*, N_F^*\}$:

$$K_F^* \text{MP}_K(K_F^*, N_F^*) + N_F^* \text{MP}_N(K_F^*, N_F^*) = F(K_F^*, N_F^*).$$

Use (2.8) and (2.9) to get

$$K_F^* r + N_F^* w = F(K_F^*, N_F^*). \tag{D.1}$$

Finally, rearranging (D.1) and using the definition of profits from (2.7) yields

$$F(K_F^*, N_F^*) - r_k^* K_F^* - wN_F^* = 0$$

so optimal profits are zero, as claimed. □

APPENDIX E
Solving via Matrix Equation Systems

So far, I've obtained the model's policy functions by solving quadratic and linear equations. As it turns out, there is a way to automate the procedure – and stop using pencil and paper – by relying on the tools of linear algebra (see Appendix A). While computer packages will perform all the calculations in the background, it is still useful to know what's going on. This section will solve the system of log-linearized equations (7.27)–(7.30) as a matrix equation.

E.1 Setting Up the Matrix Equation System

Take the set of log-linearized equations (7.27)–(7.29) and set them equal to zero. (The TFP equation? I'll return to it in a second.) I get

$$0 = -\widehat{C}_t + \mathbb{E}_t\widehat{C}_{t+1} - \mathbb{E}_t\widehat{Q}_{k,t+1}, \tag{E.1}$$

$$0 = K^{\alpha}\widehat{A}_t + Q_k K\widehat{K}_t - C\widehat{C}_t - K\widehat{K}_{t+1}, \tag{E.2}$$

$$0 = Q_k\widehat{Q}_{kt} - \alpha K^{\alpha-1}\widehat{A}_t - \alpha(\alpha-1)K^{\alpha-1}\widehat{K}_t. \tag{E.3}$$

By inspection, the model includes three endogenous variables ($\widehat{C}_t$, $\widehat{Q}_{kt}$, and $\widehat{K}_{t+1}$) and one exogenous variable ($\widehat{A}_t$).

Let $\mathbf{x}_t$ be an $m \times 1$ vector of endogenous variables and $\mathbf{z}_t$ be a $k \times 1$ vector of exogenous variables. For this model, these vectors are

$$\mathbf{x}_t = \begin{bmatrix} \widehat{C}_t \\ \widehat{Q}_{kt} \\ \widehat{K}_{t+1} \end{bmatrix}, \quad \mathbf{z}_t = \begin{bmatrix} \widehat{A}_t \end{bmatrix}.$$

The goal is to map the system (E.1)–(E.3) into a matrix equation of the form

$$0 = \mathbb{E}_t\left[\mathbf{F}\mathbf{x}_{t+1} + \mathbf{G}\mathbf{x}_t + \mathbf{H}\mathbf{x}_{t-1} + \mathbf{L}\mathbf{z}_{t+1} + \mathbf{M}\mathbf{z}_t\right]. \tag{E.4}$$

I need to figure out what the matrices $\mathbf{F}$, $\mathbf{G}$, $\mathbf{H}$, $\mathbf{L}$, and $\mathbf{M}$ are in (E.4). Let's do this one step at a time. To find matrix $\mathbf{F}$, I need to find out the coefficients for the elements in $\mathbf{x}_{t+1} = \begin{bmatrix} \widehat{C}_{t+1} & \widehat{Q}_{k,t+1} & \widehat{K}_{t+2} \end{bmatrix}^{\mathrm{T}}$. I conclude that

$$\mathbf{F} = \begin{bmatrix} 1 & -1 & 0 \\ 0 & 0 & 0 \\ 0 & 0 & 0 \end{bmatrix}$$

since $\widehat{C}_{t+1}$ and $\widehat{Q}_{k,t+1}$ are only included in (E.1). (There is no $\widehat{K}_{t+2}$ anywhere in the system.) Now let's go for matrix **G**: since $\mathbf{x}_t = \left[\begin{array}{ccc} \widehat{C}_t & \widehat{Q}_{kt} & \widehat{K}_{t+1} \end{array}\right]^{\mathrm{T}}$, I get

$$\mathbf{G} = \begin{bmatrix} -1 & 0 & 0 \\ -C & 0 & -K \\ 0 & Q_k & 0 \end{bmatrix}.$$

By now this process should be making sense; matrices **H**, **L**, and **M** are given by

$$\mathbf{H} = \begin{bmatrix} 0 & 0 & 0 \\ 0 & 0 & Q_k K \\ 0 & 0 & -\alpha(\alpha - 1)K^{\alpha-1} \end{bmatrix},$$

$$\mathbf{L} = \begin{bmatrix} 0 \\ 0 \\ 0 \end{bmatrix},$$

$$\mathbf{M} = \begin{bmatrix} 0 \\ K^{\alpha} \\ -\alpha K^{\alpha-1} \end{bmatrix}.$$

In addition, I map the TFP process (7.30) into the matrix equation

$$\mathbf{z}_{t+1} = \mathbf{N}\mathbf{z}_t + \mathbf{e}_{t+1}, \tag{E.5}$$

where

$$\mathbf{N} = \left[\begin{array}{c} \rho_A \end{array}\right].$$

At the end of this process, I'm looking for a matrix policy function of the form

$$\mathbf{x}_t = \mathbf{P}\mathbf{x}_{t-1} + \mathbf{Q}\mathbf{z}_t, \tag{E.6}$$

which tells me that the current-period endogenous variables are a linear combination of yesterday's endogenous variables and today's exogenous ones, where the latter are generated by equation (E.5). In order to derive the values for matrices **P** and **Q**, I need some additional concepts and results that I share below.

E.2 Matrix Vectorization

The key ingredient is the concept of **matrix vectorization**, which is a matrix operator that takes an $m \times n$ matrix and produces a vector of length mn. This is better explained with an example.

Example E.1 Let **A** be the 2×3 matrix

$$\mathbf{A} = \begin{bmatrix} a_{11} & a_{12} & a_{13} \\ a_{21} & a_{22} & a_{23} \end{bmatrix}.$$

The matrix vectorization of $\mathbf{A}$, denoted $\text{vec}\left[\mathbf{A}\right]$, is the 6×1 vector

$$\text{vec}\left[\mathbf{A}\right] = \begin{bmatrix} a_{11} \\ a_{21} \\ a_{12} \\ a_{22} \\ a_{13} \\ a_{23} \end{bmatrix}.$$

Note how the vectorization operator just "stacks" the columns of the matrix, working from left to right.

E.3 Solving the System

I now present the following result; for a proof, see Uhlig (1999) or McCandless (2008).

Proposition E.1 *The policy function* $\mathbf{x}_t = \mathbf{P}\mathbf{x}_{t-1} + \mathbf{Q}\mathbf{z}_t$ *is obtained by solving the matrix quadratic equation*

$$\mathbf{0} = \mathbf{F}\mathbf{P}^2 + \mathbf{G}\mathbf{P} + \mathbf{H} \tag{E.7}$$

for $\mathbf{P}$*, and the matrix equation*

$$\mathbf{V}\text{vec}\left[\mathbf{Q}\right] = -\text{vec}\left[\mathbf{L}\mathbf{N} + \mathbf{M}\right] \tag{E.8}$$

for $\mathbf{Q}$*, where*

$$\mathbf{V} \equiv \mathbf{I}_k \otimes \left(\mathbf{F}\mathbf{P} + \mathbf{G}\right) + \mathbf{N}^T \otimes \mathbf{F} \tag{E.9}$$

and $\otimes$ *denotes the Kronecker product.*

Remark E.2 Equation (E.7) tells me that the key matrix coefficient, $\mathbf{P}$, is the solution of a quadratic (matrix) equation – just like in Sections 7.2.2 and 7.3.5. The complicated part, of course, is that solving a quadratic matrix equation is, well, hard. That's why I need a computer to do the heavy lifting for me.

E.4 Model Solution

It is possible to code the solution system (E.7)–(E.9) described above and derive matrices $\mathbf{P}$ and $\mathbf{Q}$. If I do so, I get

$$\mathbf{P} = \begin{bmatrix} 0 & 0 & 0.5966 \\ 0 & 0 & -0.0200 \\ 0 & 0 & 0.9676 \end{bmatrix}, \quad \mathbf{Q} = \begin{bmatrix} 0.2044 \\ 0.0298 \\ 0.0767 \end{bmatrix}.$$

What does this mean? Since the matrix policy function takes the form $\mathbf{x}_t = \mathbf{P}\mathbf{x}_{t-1} + \mathbf{Q}\mathbf{z}_t$ per equation (E.6) and $\mathbf{x}_t = \left[\, \widehat{C}_t \, \widehat{Q}_{kt} \, \widehat{K}_{t+1} \,\right]^{\mathrm{T}}$, it follows that the individual policy functions are

$$\begin{aligned}
\widehat{C}_t &= 0.5966\widehat{K}_t + 0.2044\widehat{A}_t, \\
\widehat{Q}_{kt} &= -0.0200\widehat{K}_t + 0.0298\widehat{A}_t, \\
\widehat{K}_{t+1} &= 0.9676\widehat{K}_t + 0.0767\widehat{A}_t,
\end{aligned}$$

which are the same results I obtained in Example 7.6.

APPENDIX F
Dynare Codes for Chapter 8

F.1 Nonlinear Model

This code replicates all the results in Section 8.3. The model is captured in levels.

```
/*
nonlinear.mod
Implementation of the stochastic, infinite horizon benchmark SPP.
*/

close all

// PREAMBLE: VARIABLE AND PARAMETER DEFINITIONS

// Endogenous variables (6)
var Y A K Qk C X ;

// Exogenous variables (1)
varexo epsilon_A ;

// Parameters (6)
parameters beta delta alpha rho_A sigma_A A_ss ;

    beta = 0.99 ;
    delta = 0.08 ;
    alpha = 0.33 ;
    rho_A = 0.85 ;
    sigma_A = 0.007 ;
    A_ss = 1 ;

// MODEL BLOCK

model ;
    Y = A*K(-1)^alpha ;
```

```
    Qk = alpha*Y/K(-1) + 1 - delta ;
    1/C = beta*Qk(+1)/C(+1) ;
    Y = C + X ;
    X = K - (1-delta)*K(-1) ;
    log(A) = (1-rho_A)*log(A_ss) + rho_A*log(A(-1))
             + sigma_A*epsilon_A ;
end ;

// STEADY STATE BLOCK

steady_state_model ;
    A = A_ss ;
    Qk = 1/beta ;
    omega_y = (Qk - 1 + delta)/alpha ;
    K = 1/omega_y^(1/(1 - alpha)) ;
    Y = A*K^alpha ;
    X = delta*K ;
    C = Y - X ;
end ;

steady ;
check ;

// SHOCKS BLOCK

shocks ;
    var epsilon_A = 1 ;
end ;

// SIMULATION BLOCK

stoch_simul(irf=40, order=1) A K Qk Y C X ;
```

(Code F.1)

F.2 Log-Linear Model

This code replicates all the results in Section 8.5. The model is captured after log-linearizing by hand.

```
/*
loglinear.mod
Implementation of the loglinear stochastic, infinite horizon
benchmark SPP.
```

```
*/

close all

// PREAMBLE: VARIABLE AND PARAMETER DEFINITIONS

// Endogenous variables (6)
var Y A K Qk C X ;

// Exogenous variables (1)
varexo epsilon_A ;

// Parameters (6)
parameters beta delta alpha rho_A sigma_A A_ss ;

    beta = 0.99 ;
    delta = 0.08 ;
    alpha = 0.33 ;
    rho_A = 0.85 ;
    sigma_A = 0.007 ;
    A_ss = 1 ;

// MODEL BLOCK

model(linear) ;
    # Qk_SS = 1/beta ;
    # ome_y = (Qk_SS - 1 + delta)/alpha ;
    # K_SS = 1/ome_y^(1/(1 - alpha)) ;
    # Y_SS = A_ss*K_SS^alpha ;
    # X_SS = delta*K_SS ;
    # C_SS = Y_SS - X_SS ;

    Y = A + alpha*K(-1) ;
    Qk_SS*Qk = alpha*K_SS^(alpha - 1)*A
                + alpha*(alpha - 1)*K_SS^(alpha - 1)*K(-1) ;
    C = C(+1) - Qk(+1) ;
    Y_SS*Y = C_SS*C + X_SS*X ;
    delta*X = K - (1 - delta)*K(-1) ;
    A = rho_A*A(-1) + sigma_A*epsilon_A ;
end ;

// STEADY STATE BLOCK

steady_state_model ;
```

```
    Y = 0 ;
    A = 0 ;
    K = 0 ;
    Qk = 0 ;
    C = 0 ;
    X = 0 ;
end ;

steady ;
check ;

// SHOCKS BLOCK

shocks ;
    var epsilon_A = 1 ;
end ;

// SIMULATION BLOCK

stoch_simul(irf=40, order=1) A K Qk Y C X ;
```

(Code F.2)

APPENDIX G
Dynare Code for Section 13.2

The code below implements the three-tax economy from Section 13.2. Since I find these objects useful, I include four variables that deal with tax revenue: total revenue (taxrev) and that coming from capital (taxrev_k), labor (taxrev_n), and consumption (taxrev_c) taxes.

```
/*
three_taxes.mod
Canonical RBC model with capital and labor income taxes,
consumption taxes, and stochastic government expenditure.
*/

close all

// PREAMBLE: VARIABLE AND PARAMETER DEFINITIONS

// Endogenous variables (20)
var G g Y A K N rk w lambda C zeta X tau_k tau_n tau_c T ;
var taxrev taxrev_k taxrev_n taxrev_c ;

// Exogenous variables (5)
varexo epsilon_A epsilon_g epsilon_k epsilon_n epsilon_c ;

// Parameters (19)
parameters alpha phi beta delta ;
parameters rho_A A_ss sigma_A ;
parameters rho_g g_ss sigma_g ;
parameters rho_k tau_kss sigma_k ;
parameters rho_n tau_nss sigma_n ;
parameters rho_c tau_css sigma_c ;

    alpha = 0.33 ;
    phi = 2 ;
```

```
    beta = 0.99 ;
    delta = 0.025 ;
    rho_A = 0.9 ;
    A_ss = 1 ;
    sigma_A = 0.01 ;
    rho_g = 0.8 ;
    g_ss = 0.2 ;
    sigma_g = 0.01 ;
    rho_k = 0.95 ;
    tau_kss = 0.28 ;
    sigma_k = 0.03 ;
    rho_n = 0.7 ;
    tau_nss = 0.18 ;
    sigma_n = 0.05 ;
    rho_c = 0.99 ;
    tau_css = 0.07 ;
    sigma_c = 0.005 ;

// MODEL BLOCK

model ;
    Y = A*K(-1)^alpha*N^(1-alpha) ;
    rk*K(-1) = alpha*Y ;
    w*N = (1 - alpha)*Y ;
    lambda*(1 + tau_c) = 1/C ;
    phi = lambda*(1 - tau_n)*w*(1 - N) ;
    lambda = zeta ;
    zeta = beta*lambda(+1)*(1 - tau_k(+1))*rk(+1)
           + beta*(1 - delta)*zeta(+1) ;
    K = (1 - delta)*K(-1) + X ;
    (1 - g)*Y = C + X ;
    G = g*Y ;
    log(A) = (1 - rho_A)*log(A_ss) + rho_A*log(A(-1))
             + sigma_A*epsilon_A ;
    g = (1 - rho_g)*g_ss + rho_g*g(-1) + sigma_g*epsilon_g ;
    tau_k = (1 - rho_k)*tau_kss + rho_k*tau_k(-1)
             + sigma_k*epsilon_k ;
    tau_n = (1 - rho_n)*tau_nss + rho_n*tau_n(-1)
            + sigma_n*epsilon_n ;
    tau_c = (1 - rho_c)*tau_css + rho_c*tau_c(-1)
            + sigma_c*epsilon_c ;
    T = G - (tau_k*rk*K(-1) + tau_n*w*N + tau_c*C) ;
    taxrev = tau_k*rk*K(-1) + tau_n*w*N + tau_c*C ;
    taxrev_k = tau_k*rk*K(-1) ;
```

```
    taxrev_n = tau_n*w*N ;
    taxrev_c = tau_c*C ;
end ;

// STEADY STATE BLOCK

steady_state_model ;
    A = A_ss ;
    g = g_ss ;
    tau_k = tau_kss ;
    tau_n = tau_nss ;
    tau_c = tau_css ;
    rk = (1 - beta*(1 - delta))/(beta*(1 - tau_k)) ;
    omega_y = rk/alpha ;
    omega_c = (1 - g)*omega_y - delta ;
    N = (1 - alpha)*omega_y*(1 - tau_n)/
            (phi*(1 + tau_c)*omega_c
            + (1 - alpha)*omega_y*(1 - tau_n)) ;
    K = N/omega_y^(1/(1 - alpha)) ;
    Y = omega_y*K ;
    X = delta*K ;
    C = omega_c*K ;
    w = (1 - alpha)*Y/N ;
    lambda = 1/((1 + tau_c)*C) ;
    zeta = lambda ;
    G = g*Y ;
    T = G - (tau_k*rk*K + tau_n*w*N + tau_c*C) ;
    taxrev = tau_k*rk*K + tau_n*w*N + tau_c*C ;
    taxrev_k = tau_k*rk*K ;
    taxrev_n = tau_n*w*N ;
    taxrev_c = tau_c*C ;
end ;

steady ;
check ;

// SHOCKS BLOCK

shocks ;
    var epsilon_A = 1 ;
    var epsilon_g = 1 ;
    var epsilon_k = 1 ;
    var epsilon_n = 1 ;
    var epsilon_c = 1 ;
```

```
end ;

// SIMULATION BLOCK

stoch_simul(irf=40, order=1) ;
```

(Code G.1)

APPENDIX H
The Role of the Lagrange Multiplier

Consider a simple constrained maximization problem: we want to solve

$$\begin{aligned} \max \quad & f(x,y) \\ \text{subject to} \quad & h(x,y) = a, \end{aligned} \tag{H.1}$$

where $f : \mathbb{R}^2 \to \mathbb{R}$, $h : \mathbb{R}^2 \to \mathbb{R}$, and $a \in \mathbb{R}$ is a parameter. Let the associated Lagrangian function be given by

$$\mathscr{L} = f(x,y) + \lambda[a - h(x,y)].$$

Assume that the problem has a well-defined solution; note further that the solution of the problem depends directly on the value of a.

Theorem H.1 *Let f and h be C^1 functions of two variables. For any fixed value of the parameter a, let $(x^*(a), y^*(a))$ be the solution of problem* (H.1) *with corresponding multiplier $\lambda^*(a)$. Suppose that x^*, y^*, and λ^* are C^1 functions of a. Then*

$$\lambda^*(a) = \frac{d}{da} f(x^*(a), y^*(a)). \tag{H.2}$$

Proof. See Simon and Blume (1994, thm. 19.1). □

In (not-so-plain) English: equation (H.2) shows that $\lambda^*(a)$ measures the effect of a unit increase in a over the optimal value $f(x^*(a), y^*(a))$. (This increase is exactly equal when the change is infinitesimal, since we're talking about derivatives.)

Example H.1 (Follows Simon & Blume 1994.) We want to maximize $f(x,y) = x^2y$ given the constraint $h(x,y) = 2x^2 + y^2$, with $a = 3$. Hence, the problem we have is

$$\begin{aligned} \max \quad & x^2y \\ \text{subject to} \quad & 2x^2 + y^2 = 3. \end{aligned}$$

Standard methods yield $x^*(a = 3) = y^*(a = 3) = 1$ and $\lambda^*(a = 3) = 0.5$. Also note that

$$f(x^*(a = 3), y^*(a = 3)) = (1)^2(1) = 1.$$

Suppose we need to redo the problem for $a' = 3.3$. More algebra shows that the solution is $x^*(a' = 3.3) = y^*(a' = 3.3) = \sqrt{1.1}$ and that $f(x^*(a' = 3.3), y^*(a' = 3.3)) = 1.1537$. Clearly,

$$f(x^*(a' = 3.3), y^*(a' = 3.3)) - f(x^*(a = 3), y^*(a = 3)) = 0.1537.$$

Using Theorem H.1, the value of the objective function after increasing a by 0.3 should be

$$0.3 \times \lambda^* = 0.3 \times 0.5 = 0.15,$$

which is very close to the actual value of 0.1537.

References

Abel, A. (1990), 'Asset prices under habit formation and catching up with the Joneses', *American Economic Review* **80**(2), 38–42.

Acemoglu, D. (2009), *Introduction to Modern Economic Growth*, Princeton University Press, Princeton, NJ.

Adjemian, S., Juillard, M., Karamé, F., Mutschler, W., Pfeifer, J., Ratto, M., Rion, N. and Villemot, S. (2024), Dynare: Reference Manual, Version 6, Dynare Working Papers 80, CEPREMAP.

Andolfatto, D. (1996), 'Business cycles and labor-market search', *American Economic Review* **86**(1), 112–32.

Arias, A., Hansen, G. and Ohanian, L. (2007), 'Why have business cycle fluctuations become less volatile?', *Economic Theory* **32**(1), 43–58.

Ascari, G. (2004), 'Staggered prices and trend inflation: some nuisances', *Review of Economic Dynamics* **7**(3), 642–67.

Ascari, G., Castelnuovo, E. and Rossi, L. (2011), 'Calvo vs. Rotemberg in a trend inflation world: an empirical investigation', *Journal of Economic Dynamics and Control* **35**(11), 1852–67.

Ascari, G. and Rossi, L. (2012), 'Trend inflation and firms price-setting: Rotemberg versus Calvo', *Economic Journal* **122**(563), 1115–41.

Ascari, G. and Sbordone, A. (2014), 'The macroeconomics of trend inflation', *Journal of Economic Literature* **52**(3), 679–739.

Athreya, K. (2013), *Big Ideas in Macroeconomics: A Nontechnical View*, MIT Press, Cambridge, MA.

Barro, R. (1997), *Macroeconomics*, MIT Press, Cambridge, MA.

Baxter, M. and King, R. (1993), 'Fiscal policy in general equilibrium', *American Economic Review* **83**(3), 315–34.

Baxter, M. and King, R. (1999), 'Measuring business cycles: approximate band-pass filters for economic time series', *Review of Economics and Statistics* **81**(4), 575–93.

Bellman, R. (1957), *Dynamic Programming*, Princeton University Press, Princeton, NJ.

Blades, D. (2015), 'A short-cut method of estimating capital stocks: when can it be used and how well does it work?', *Review of Income and Wealth* **61**(2), 373–93.

Blanchard, O. and Kahn, C. (1980), 'The solution of linear difference models under rational expectations', *Econometrica* **48**(5), 1305–11.

Boldrin, M., Christiano, L. and Fisher, J. (2001), 'Habit persistence, asset returns, and the business cycle', *American Economic Review* **91**(1), 149–66.

Braun, A. (1994), 'Tax disturbances and real economic activity in the postwar United States', *Journal of Monetary Economics* **33**(3), 441–62.

Burnside, C. and Eichenbaum, M. (1996), 'Factor-hoarding and the propagation of business-cycle shocks', *American Economic Review* **86**(5), 1154–74.

Calvo, G. (1983), 'Staggered prices in a utility-maximizing framework', *Journal of Monetary Economics* **12**(3), 383–98.

Campbell, J. (1994), 'Inspecting the mechanism: an analytical approach to the stochastic growth model', *Journal of Monetary Economics* **33**(3), 463–506.

Canova, F. (2007), *Methods for Applied Macroeconomic Research*, Princeton University Press, Princeton, NJ.

Chari, V. V. & Kehoe, P. (1999), 'Optimal fiscal and monetary policy', in J. Taylor & M. Woodford (eds.), *Handbook of Macroeconomics*, Vol. 1C, North Holland, Amsterdam, pp. 1671–45.

Christiano, L. (2002), 'Solving dynamic equilibrium models by a method of undetermined coefficients', *Computational Economics* **20**(1–2), 21–55.

Christiano, L. and Eichenbaum, M. (1992), 'Current Real-Business-Cycle theories and aggregate labor-market fluctuations', *American Economic Review* **82**(3), 430–50.

Christiano, L., Eichenbaum, M. and Evans, C. (2005), 'Nominal rigidities and the dynamic effects of a shock to monetary policy', *Journal of Political Economy* **113**(1), 1–45.

Christiano, L., Eichenbaum, M. and Trabandt, M. (2018), 'On DSGE models', *Journal of Economic Perspectives* **32**(3), 113–40.

Clarida, R., Galí, J. and Gertler, M. (1999), 'The science of monetary policy: a New Keynesian perspective', *Journal of Economic Literature* **37**(4), 1661–707.

Clark, T. (2009), 'Is the Great Moderation over? An empirical analysis', *Federal Reserve Bank of Kansas City Economic Review* **94**(Q IV), 5–42.

De Araujo, P., O'Sullivan, R. and Simpson, N. (2013), 'What should be taught in intermediate macroeconomics?', *Journal of Economic Education* **44**(1), 74–90.

DeJong, D. and Dave, C. (2011), *Structural Macroeconometrics*, 2nd ed., Princeton University Press, Princeton, NJ.

Del Negro, M., Eusepi, S., Giannoni, M., Sbordone, A., Tambalotti, A., Cocci, M., Hasegawa, R. and Linder, H. (2013), The FRBNY DSGE model, Staff Report 647, Federal Reserve Bank of New York.

Del Negro, M. & Schorfheide, F. (2013), 'DSGE model-based forecasting', in G. Elliot & A. Timmermann (eds.), *Handbook of Economic Forecasting*, Vol. 2A, Elsevier, Amsterdam, pp. 57–140.

Erceg, C., Henderson, D. and Levin, A. (2000), 'Optimal monetary policy with staggered wage and price contracts', *Journal of Monetary Economics* **46**(2), 281–313.

Fernández de Córdoba, G. and Kehoe, T. (2000), 'Capital flows and real exchange rate fluctuations following Spain's entry into the European Community', *Journal of International Economics* **51**(1), 49.

Fernáandez-Villaverde, J., Rubio-Ramírez, J. & Schorfheide, F. (2016), 'Solution and estimation methods for DSGE models', in J. Taylor & H. Uhlig (eds.), *Handbook of Macroeconomics*, Vol. 2A, Elsevier, Amsterdam, pp. 527–724.

Furlanetto, F., Natvik, G. and Seneca, M. (2013), 'Investment shocks and macroeconomic co-movement', *Journal of Macroeconomics* **37**, 208–16.

Galí, J. (2015), *Monetary Policy, Inflation, and the Business Cycle: An Introduction to the New Keynesian Framework and its Applications*, 2nd ed., Princeton University Press, Princeton, NJ.

Galí, J. (2018), 'The state of New Keynesian economics: a partial assessment', *Journal of Economic Perspectives* **32**(3), 87–112.

Galí, J. and Gambetti, L. (2009), 'On the sources of the Great Moderation', *American Economic Journal: Macroeconomics* **1**(1), 26–57.

Galí, J. and Rabanal, P. (2004), 'Technology shocks and aggregate fluctuations: how well does the Real Business Cycle model fit postwar U.S. data?', *NBER Macroeconomics Annual* **19**, 225–88.

Gollin, D. (2002), 'Getting income shares right', *Journal of Political Economy* **110**(2), 458–74.

Greenwood, J., Hercowitz, Z. and Huffman, G. (1988), 'Investment, capacity utilization, and the real business cycle', *American Economic Review* **78**(3), 402–17.

Greenwood, J., Hercowitz, Z. and Krusell, P. (1997), 'Long-run implications of investment-specific technological change',

American Economic Review **87**(3), 342–62.

Hamilton, J. (2018), 'Why you should never use the Hodrick-Prescott filter', *Review of Economics and Statistics* **100**(5), 831–43.

Hansen, G. (1985), 'Indivisible labor and the business cycle', *Journal of Monetary Economics* **16**(3), 309–28.

Hansen, L. P. and Heckman, J. (1996), 'The empirical foundations of calibration', *Journal of Economic Perspectives* **10**(1), 87–104.

Heer, B. and Maussner, A. (2024), *Dynamic General Equilibrium Modeling: Computational Methods and Applications*, 3rd ed., Springer, Berlin.

Herbst, E. and Schorfheide, F. (2016), *Bayesian Estimation of DSGE Models*, Princeton University Press, Princeton, NJ.

Hodrick, R. and Prescott, E. (1997), 'Postwar U.S. business cycles: an empirical investigation', *Journal of Money, Credit and Banking* **29**(1), 1–16.

Inada, K.-I. (1963), 'On a two-sector model of economic growth: comments and a generalization', *Review of Economic Studies* **30**(2), 119–27.

Judd, K. (1997), 'Computational economics and economic theory: substitutes or complements?', *Journal of Economic Dynamics and Control* **21**(6), 907–42.

Justiniano, A., Primiceri, G. and Tambalotti, A. (2010), 'Investment shocks and business cycles', *Journal of Monetary Economics* **57**(2), 132–45.

Justiniano, A., Primiceri, G. and Tambalotti, A. (2011), 'Investment shocks and the relative price of investment', *Review of Economic Dynamics* **14**(1), 102–21.

Kaldor, N. (1961), 'Capital accumulation and economic growth', in D. Hague (ed.), *The Theory of Capital*, Palgrave Macmillan, London, pp. 177–222.

Kehoe, T. (2003), 'What can we learn from the current crisis in Argentina?', *Scottish Journal of Political Economy* **50**(5), 609–33.

Keynes, J. M. (1936), *The General Theory of Employment, Interest and Money*, Palgrave Macmillan, London.

King, R., Plosser, C. and Rebelo, S. (1988), 'Production, growth and business cycles I: the basic Neoclassical model', *Journal of Monetary Economics* **21**(2–3), 195–232.

King, R., Plosser, C. and Rebelo, S. (2002), 'Production, growth and business cycles: technical appendix', *Computational Economics* **20**(1–2), 87–116.

King, R. & Rebelo, S. (1999), 'Resuscitating Real Business Cycles', in J. Taylor & M. Woodford (eds.), *Handbook of Macroeconomics*, Vol. 1B, North Holland, Amsterdam, pp. 927–1007.

Klein, P. (2000), 'Using the generalized Schur form to solve a multivariate linear rational expectations model', *Journal of Economic Dynamics and Control* **24**(10), 1405–23.

Kocherlakota, N. (1996), 'The equity premium: it's still a puzzle', *Journal of Economic Literature* **34**(1), 42–71.

Kydland, F. and Prescott, E. (1982), 'Time to build and aggregate fluctuations', *Econometrica* **50**(6), 1345–70.

Kydland, F. and Prescott, E. (1991), 'The econometrics of the general equilibrium approach to business cycles', *Scandinavian Journal of Economics* **93**(2), 161–78.

Leeper, E. (2010), 'Monetary science, fiscal alchemy', *Proceedings – Economic Policy Symposium – Jackson Hole*, pp. 361–434.

Leeper, E., Plante, M. and Traum, N. (2010), 'Dynamics of fiscal financing in the United States', *Journal of Econometrics* **156**(2), 304–21.

Leeper, E., Traum, N. and Walker, T. (2017), 'Clearing up the fiscal multiplier morass', *American Economic Review* **107**(8), 2409–54.

Leeper, E., Walker, T. and Yang, S.-C. S. (2013), 'Fiscal foresight and information flows', *Econometrica* **81**(3), 1115–45.

Leeper, E. and Yang, S.-C. S. (2008), 'Dynamic scoring: alternative financing

schemes', *Journal of Public Economics* **92**(1–2), 159–82.
Lucas, R. (1976), 'Econometric policy evaluation: a critique', *Carnegie-Rochester Conference Series on Public Policy* **1**(1), 19–46.
Lucas, R. (1977), 'Understanding business cycles', *Carnegie-Rochester Conference Series on Public Policy* **5**(1), 7–29.
Lucas, R. (1980), 'Methods and problems in business cycle theory', *Journal of Money, Credit and Banking* **12**(4), 696–715.
Lucas, R. (1993), 'Making a miracle', *Econometrica* **61**(2), 251–72.
Lucas, R. and Prescott, E. (1971), 'Investment under uncertainty', *Econometrica* **39**(5), 659–81.
Mas-Colell, A., Whinston, M. and Green, J. (1995), *Microeconomic Theory*, Oxford University Press, Oxford.
McCandless, G. (2008), *The ABCs of RBCs*, Harvard University Press, Cambridge, MA.
McGrattan, E. (1994), 'The macroeconomic effects of distortionary taxation', *Journal of Monetary Economics* **33**(3), 573–601.
McGrattan, E. (2004), 'Comment: Technology shocks and aggregate fluctuations: how well does the Real Business Cycle model fit postwar U.S. data?', *NBER Macroeconomics Annual* **19**, 289–308.
McGrattan, E. (2012), 'Capital taxation during the U.S. Great Depression', *Quarterly Journal of Economics* **127**(3), 1515–50.
McGrattan, E. (2023), 'Taxes, regulations, and the value of U.S. corporations: a reassessment', *Review of Economic Dynamics* **50**, 131–45.
McGrattan, E. and Ohanian, L. (2010), 'Does Neoclassical theory account for the effects of big fiscal shocks? Evidence from World War II', *International Economic Review* **51**(2), 509–32.
McGrattan, E. and Prescott, E. (2005), 'Taxes, regulations, and the value of U.S. and U.K. corporations', *Review of Economic Studies* **72**(3), 767–96.
Mehra, R. and Prescott, E. (1985), 'The equity premium: a puzzle', *Journal of Monetary Economics* **15**(2), 145–61.
Merz, M. (1995), 'Search in the labor market and the real business cycle', *Journal of Monetary Economics* **36**(2), 269–300.
Prescott, E. (2004), 'Why do Americans work so much more than Europeans?', *Federal Reserve Bank of Minneapolis Quarterly Review* **28**(1), 2–13.
Ravn, M., Schmitt-Grohé, S. and Uribe, M. (2006), 'Deep habits', *Review of Economic Studies* **73**(1), 195–218.
Ravn, M. and Uhlig, H. (2002), 'On adjusting the Hodrick-Prescott filter for the frequency of observations', *Review of Economics and Statistics* **84**(2), 371–80.
Robert, C. and Casella, G. (2004), *Monte Carlo Statistical Methods*, 2nd ed., Springer, New York.
Rogerson, R. (1988), 'Indivisible labor, lotteries and equilibrium', *Journal of Monetary Economics* **21**(1), 3–16.
Rotemberg, J. (1982), 'Monopolistic price adjustment and aggregate output', *Review of Economic Studies* **49**(4), 517–31.
Sargent, T. (1987), *Macroeconomic Theory*, 2nd ed., Emerald Group Publishing, Bingley.
Sargent, T. and Ljungqvist, L. (2018), *Recursive Macroeconomic Theory*, 4th ed., MIT Press, Cambridge, MA.
Schmitt-Grohé, S. and Uribe, M. (2012), 'What's news in business cycles', *Econometrica* **80**(6), 2733–64.
Simon, C. and Blume, L. (1994), *Mathematics for Economists*, W. W. Norton & Company, New York.
Sims, C. (2002), 'Solving linear rational expectation models', *Computational Economics* **20**(1–2), 1–20.
Smets, F. and Wouters, R. (2007), 'Shocks and frictions in U.S. business cycles: a Bayesian DSGE approach', *American Economic Review* **97**(3), 586–606.
Solis-Garcia, M. (2021), 'A (pedagogical) note on the log-linearization of functions of several variables', *International Review*

of Economics Education **37**, Article Number 100210.

Stock, J. and Watson, M. (2002), 'Has the business cycle changed and why?', *NBER Macroeconomics Annual* **17**, 159–218.

Stokey, N., Lucas, R. and Prescott, E. (1989), *Recursive Methods in Macroeconomic Dynamics*, Harvard University Press, Cambridge, MA.

Taylor, J. (1980), 'Aggregate dynamics and staggered contracts', *Journal of Political Economy* **88**(1), 1–23.

Taylor, J. (1993), 'Discretion versus policy rules in practice', *Carnegie-Rochester Conference Series on Public Policy* **39**, 195–214.

Uhlig, H. (1999), 'A toolkit for analyzing nonlinear dynamic stochastic models easily', in R. Marimon & A. Scott (eds.), *Computational Methods for the Study of Dynamic Economies*, Oxford University Press, Oxford, pp. 30–61.

Walsh, C. (2017), *Monetary Theory and Policy*, 4th ed., MIT Press, Cambridge, MA.

Williamson, S. (2017), *Macroeconomics*, 6th ed., Pearson, Boston, MA.

Woodford, M. (2003), *Interest and Prices*, Princeton University Press, Princeton, NJ.

Yun, T. (1996), 'Nominal price rigidity, money supply endogeneity, and business cycles', *Journal of Monetary Economics* **37**(2), 345–70.

Yun, T. (2005), 'Optimal monetary policy with relative price distortions', *American Economic Review* **95**(1), 89–109.

Index

Printed in the United Kingdom by TJ Clays Ltd.